OECD Journal on Development

Volume 9 – Issue 2

D1310349

Measuring Human Rights and Democratic Governance

EXPERIENCES AND LESSONS FROM METAGORA

Edited by
Claire Naval, Sylvie Walter and Raul Suarez de Miguel

Development Assistance Committee

OECD

ORGANISATION FOR ECONOMIC CO-OPERATION AND DEVELOPMENT

The OECD is a unique forum where the governments of 30 democracies work together to address the economic, social and environmental challenges of globalisation. The OECD is also at the forefront of efforts to understand and to help governments respond to new developments and concerns, such as corporate governance, the information economy and the challenges of an ageing population. The Organisation provides a setting where governments can compare policy experiences, seek answers to common problems, identify good practice and work to co-ordinate domestic and international policies.

The OECD member countries are: Australia, Austria, Belgium, Canada, the Czech Republic, Denmark, Finland, France, Germany, Greece, Hungary, Iceland, Ireland, Italy, Japan, Korea, Luxembourg, Mexico, the Netherlands, New Zealand, Norway, Poland, Portugal, the Slovak Republic, Spain, Sweden, Switzerland, Turkey, the United Kingdom and the United States. The Commission of the European Communities takes part in the work of the OECD.

OECD Publishing disseminates widely the results of the Organisation's statistics gathering and research on economic, social and environmental issues, as well as the conventions, guidelines and standards agreed by its members.

This work is published on the responsibility of the Secretary-General of the OECD. The opinions expressed and arguments employed herein do not necessarily reflect the official views of the Organisation or of the governments of its member countries.

Also available in French under the title:

Revue de l'OCDE sur le développement, volume 9, n° 2
Mesurer les droits de l'homme et la gouvernance démocratique
EXPÉRIENCES ET ENSEIGNEMENTS DE MÉTAGORA

© Photo by: Shabtai Gold

Corrigenda to OECD publications may be found on line at: *www.oecd.org/publishing/corrigenda*.

© OECD 2008

Executive Summary

This issue of the *OECD Journal on Development* focuses on the assessment of human rights and democratic governance. How can these key dimensions of development be measured? By whom? Under which conditions? And for which purposes? Metagora, an innovative international project, has been formulating a response to these questions.

A decentralised laboratory

Metagora was launched in February 2004, under the auspices of the OECD/PARIS21, and will conclude its operations in August 2008. It is a concrete follow-up to the *Conclusions* of the 2000 Montreux Conference on *Statistics, Development and Human Rights*. It emerged from a multidisciplinary North/South network of institutions, including national Human Rights Institutions, Research Centres, National Statistical Offices, and Civil Society Organisations. Seven organisations committed, under Partnership Agreements with the OECD, to take the lead in implementing global, regional and national operations in Africa, Asia, the Middle East and Latin America.

Metagora's original strategic goal is to enhance evidence-based assessment and monitoring of human rights and democratic governance. The main objective of the project has been to develop robust methods and tools to obtain data and create indicators upon which national policies can be formulated and evaluated. To reach this goal, Metagora was designed as a decentralised laboratory: through its Partners, it has been undertaking pilot experiences in different regions of the world in an interactive fashion. On the basis of this field work, all Partners involved in the project have been formulating together significant lessons and recommendations.

An innovative bottom-up approach

Since its inception Metagora has systematically been following a bottom-up approach aimed at strengthening national capacities and leadership in assessing human rights and democratic governance. In each pilot participating country, this approach consisted of:

- the identification, by domestic stakeholders and experts, of key human rights and democratic governance issues for which evidence-based assessment would be highly relevant;
- the measurement and analysis of the selected issues with statistical methods that, combined with qualitative approaches, are adapted to the particular national context;
- the assessment of these methods for their capacity to provide reliable and policy-relevant information;
- the formulation, on the basis of the indicators and analysis produced, of shared knowledge on the policy issues at stake;
- the broad dissemination and policy use of this newly acquired knowledge;
- the drawing of global lessons from the pilot experiences and the formulation of recommendations for further application of the tested methods elsewhere.

In line with the principles of ownership and participation formulated in the *Paris Declaration on Aid Effectiveness*, the specific objectives of each national pilot experience were therefore defined by domestic stakeholders. The activities were designed – with a sound technical basis and a strong policy orientation – to address sensitive issues, such as abuses and ill-treatment by police forces, corruption within public administration, obstacles to and weaknesses in democratic participation, political exclusion of the poor or infringement of indigenous peoples' rights. These pilots were conducted in complex environments, difficult circumstances and diverse political, social and cultural contexts. Through this purposely selected variety of experiences, the project has proved both the technical feasibility and the political relevance of measuring human rights and democratic governance.

Significant lessons from pilot national experiences

This publication presents the processes and achievements of the national experiences undertaken by the Metagora community, highlighting their policy relevance and methodological implications. These experiences illustrate how quantitative methods, properly combined with qualitative approaches, can be applied for assessing key national issues and enhancing evidence-based reporting and monitoring mechanisms.

The present publication therefore provides decision makers, policy actors, analysts and civil society actors with significant examples of how sensitive data on human rights and governance issues can be collected and analysed. It highlights how qualitative and quantitative data can interrelate to provide reliable information. It shows how, on the basis of this information, it is possible to produce national indicators which are relevant and useful for political decision and action. It also illustrates that statistical analysis and quantitative indicators bring significant value-added to the work of national Human Rights Institutions, as well as to the research and advocacy of Civil Society Organisations. And, last but not least, it highlights how – and under which conditions – National Statistical Offices can be involved in the measurement of human rights and democratic governance.

A strong impact in the field

In the various specific national contexts in which the project has been operating, it has clearly depicted the nature, magnitude and characteristics of crucial human rights, democratic and governance issues. The assessment tools generated by Metagora therefore shed light on the kind of actions and measures that have to be taken to improve domestic policies and legislation on the issues at stake – and these have become influential in the hands of human rights champions, committed stakeholders and policy actors.

Metagora has also had an important impact in interlinking and empowering domestic actors of change. In a number of countries where activities were implemented, key institutions and leading people who had not interacted before, are now working together to inform policy-making with evidence-based assessments and putting the issues at stake on the national political agendas. The policy-oriented reports and the materials generated by the project are creating common ground among national stakeholders and policy makers on the conditions and opportunities for developing robust monitoring tools. Moreover, in some countries, household surveys on democratic participation and governance issues – conducted by National Statistical Offices – are now becoming institutional routine tools and are therefore starting to generate time series that can serve as a sound basis for monitoring progress.

A rich legacy to the international community

As this publication shows, after four and a half years of intensive activity, the Metagora community can be proud of providing an innovative contribution to a work that, as revealed by a worldwide survey, is widespread and growing across the globe. Indeed, at this concluding step, the project is able to deliver six main types of outcomes:

- documented multidisciplinary and participatory working methods for integrating well-established quantitative methods and proper qualitative approaches;
- measurement tools and methodologies, including data collection techniques, survey-based assessments, and dynamic databases;
- selected examples of good practices of evidence-based assessment of human rights and democratic governance;
- examples of relevant information and indicators on key national issues and policies, which empower the analysis and concrete action of policy makers, parliamentarians, civil society, human rights defenders and other actors of change;
- national policy-oriented reports that, based on the information collected and analysed, highlight the relevance of the assessments' findings and have been instrumental for enhancing democratic dialogue and evidence-based policy-making;
- online resources, including a substantive set of *Training Materials* and a worldwide *Inventory of Initiatives Aimed at Enhancing Evidence-based Assessment of Human Rights and Democratic Governance* (both available at: www.metagora.org).

Emerging and ambitious initiatives and programmes: perspectives for future work

Finally, this publication puts the Metagora achievements both in context and in perspective as it includes, in a second part, contributions from other key international initiatives on their current and planned efforts to further enhance the measurement and assessments of human rights and democratic governance. It includes substantive chapters on the on-going development of indicators on human rights, contributed by the Office of the UN High Commissioner for Human Rights, Prof. Audrey Chapman and the Centre for Economic and Social Rights.

Moreover, this second part introduces the UNDP *Global Programme on Capacity Development for Democratic Governance Assessments and Measurements*, which is based on the bottom-up approach and on the principles of ownership, inclusivity, policy focus, professional rigour and enhancement of national capacities, as promoted by Metagora. As pointed out in the *Conclusion*, this publication marks strong ties of continuity between the conclusion of Metagora and the emergence of this global project, to which the resources, tools, documentation and network of expertise developed by Metagora are being passed on.

Preface

Democracy, human rights and good governance may appear today as quasi utopian goals in many countries. Nevertheless, as the 2000 and 2002 editions of the *Human Development Report* noted, significant changes in various regions of the globe point to the emergence of a promising – but also very challenging – trend.

In the course of the last 20 years or so, an increasing number of countries in the developing world and in Europe have moved away from dictatorship and authoritarian eras. In most cases, the transition towards democratic systems has been much more complex, difficult and slow than originally expected. Very often, the initial enthusiasm for political change was followed by deep popular frustration as democratic rule appeared ineffective to address major national concerns such as increasing poverty, weak labour markets, poor social security, inefficient delivery of public services, or widespread corruption. Moreover, newly established democracies have been confronted with numerous unsolved human rights problems and governance issues inherited from past regimes – as well as with related cultural patterns that still imbue the social, economic and political behaviour today. Enhancement of national monitoring of human rights and democratic governance is therefore considered in many of these countries as a key precondition for the consolidation of democracy and further implementation of fair, participatory and sustainable development.

Since the mid-1990s, the Development Assistance Committee of the OECD (DAC) has set out – with High Level Meeting endorsement – key principles and priorities for action in the promotion of human rights and democratic governance as an inherent part of development co-operation. On 15 February 2007, the DAC approved an *Action-Oriented Policy Paper on Human Rights and Development* that updates its position on human rights and complements other policy guidelines on governance and participatory democracy in the context of development co-operation.

The DAC Policy Paper outlines three priority action areas – one of which is the strengthening of human rights assessments and indicators. Such a priority area is closely linked with a major concern in the international community: the enhancement of national statistical and analytical capacities, which constitutes a precondition for implementing proper evidence-based assessment of public policies. In other words, there is a direct link between, on the one side, DAC commitment to reinforce assessments and indicators of human rights and democratic governance, and, on the other side, the support provided by the Partnership in Statistics for Development in the 21st Century (PARIS21) to the enhancement of national capacities to produce and use robust statistics and indicators for assessing key development issues, evaluating impact of policies and properly monitoring progress.

The Metagora project emerged and has been operating at the intersection of the above-mentioned priorities. Implemented since February 2004 under the auspices of PARIS21 and conducted on a North/South partnership basis, Metagora has developed working methods and measurement tools aimed at enhancing national capacities and leadership in assessing human rights and democratic governance. Its scope is therefore fully consistent with OECD/DAC policy guidelines and its work usefully complements key initiatives undertaken by the DAC Network on Governance (GOVNET).

In the course of the last four years, Metagora successfully implemented all planned field operations and policy-oriented analysis, broadly disseminated their results, drew a set of significant lessons and guidelines for future action, and delivered all expected products. These include in particular two important resources: a first substantive set of *Metagora Training Materials* and an *Inventory of Initiatives Aimed at Enhancing Evidence-based Assessment of Human Rights and Democratic Governance* (both available at: www.metagora.org).

We are therefore glad to present to the public this issue of the *OECD Journal on Development* that focuses on the main results and lessons of Metagora. This publication shows, through the outcomes of the various Metagora pilot experiences, that measuring human rights and democratic governance is technically feasible and politically relevant. It also attests to the centrality of the Metagora bottom-up approach in complementing the top-down approaches followed by leading international organisations. Indeed, in line with the *Paris Declaration*, assessments of human rights and democratic governance should be based on national ownership of measurement tools, inclusive and consultative local processes, and a strong enhancement of national capacities and institutional mechanisms.

This publication not only reflects the achievements reached by Metagora in a very short time, but also the real enthusiasm and commitment of the numerous Metagora Partners that have permitted such progress. We hope that, in the near future, the steps undertaken and the progress reached by Metagora will inspire and serve as a basis for new national and international initiatives, projects and programmes aimed at enhancing evidence-based assessments of human rights and democratic governance.

It is crucial that, following the example of Metagora, these initiatives and programmes further strengthen the multidisciplinary approach and the synergies among official and academic statisticians, human rights practitioners, social and political scientists and other stakeholders.

Dr. Mark Orkin

Chairman of the
Metagora Partners Group

Eckhard Deutscher

Chairman of
DAC–OECD and PARIS21

Foreword

This publication is the result of a collective effort by the various institutions and numerous persons who form the North/South Metagora community. The synthesis of the Metagora results and findings was initiated and nourished by a task team led by Jan Robert Suesser and comprising Jana Asher, Claire Naval, Mireille Razafindrakoto, Michael Aliber, Mark Orkin and Raul Suarez de Miguel. The team produced a series of substantive documents based on the reports of national pilot activities, background documents, as well as methodological and thematic contributions from several project partners. C. Naval, M. Orkin and J.R. Suesser drafted a framework document on substantive questions and methodological issues emerging from the Metagora work. On this basis, a first draft of this publication was produced by the staff of the Metagora Co-ordination Team based in the OECD Secretariat (Brigitte Julé-Demarne, Claire Naval, Sylvie Walter, Paul Clare, Thomas Heimgartner and Raul Suarez de Miguel). The text was then reviewed, taking into account numerous remarks and suggestions by the OECD Editorial Board and the Metagora Steering Committee. Finally, Fiona Hall kindly improved the quality and editing of the original English text of this publication, which was then also translated and published in French and Spanish.

The Metagora project was successfully implemented thanks to generous voluntary contributions from Canada (CIDA), France (Ministry of Foreign Affairs), Sweden (SIDA), Switzerland (SDC) the European Free Trade Association (EFTA) and the European Union (under the budget of the European Initiative for Democracy and Human Rights). Beyond this financial support, the project also benefited from seconded experts and other in-kind substantial contributions from the Swiss Federal Department of Foreign Affairs, the Swiss Federal Statistical Office, Statistics Sweden, the National Statistical Institute of Italy (ISTAT), the Co-operation Agency of the French Ministry of Finance (ADETEF) and the Danish Institute for Human Rights.

This synthesis of the results and lessons from Metagora is published under the sole responsibility of the project's Co-ordination Team. The views expressed in it do not necessarily reflect the views or policies of the OECD or donor institutions.

Metagora's terms of reference are largely based on the operational *Conclusions* of the Montreux 2000 Conference on *Statistics, Development and Human Rights* (see *Chapter 1*). The design and preparation of the project was initiated in 2001 by a post-Montreux Task Force formed by Carol Mottet, Mireille Razafindrakoto, Rosa María Rubalcava, Hasan Abu-Libdeh, Mark Orkin, François Roubaud, Matthew Sudders, Jan Robert Suesser and Raul Suarez de Miguel. Its work was vigorously supported by committed senior officials from Eurostat (Yves Franchet, Daniel Byk and Gilles Rambaud-Chanoz), the European Commission EuropeAid (Timothy Clarke and Mario-Rui Queiro), the Swiss Development and Co-operation Agency (Walter Fust and Serge Chapatte), the Swiss Federal Statistical Office (Carlo Malaguerra, Adelheid Bürgi-Schmelz and Gabriel Gamez), the Swiss State Secretary for Education and Research (Charles Kleiber), the Swiss Federal Department of Foreign Affairs (Peter Maurer and Rudolf Metzler) and the Swedish International Development Co-operation Agency (Lehnard Nordström).

The integration of the project within the Partnership in Statistics for Development in the 21st Century (PARIS21) was strongly supported by Jean-Claude Faure, Richard Manning and Pali Lehohla (co-Chairmen), as well as by Antoine Simonpietri, Manager, and several members of the PARIS21 Steering Committee in 2002 and 2003 — namely Hasan Abu-Libdeh (Arab States), Oladejo O. Ajayi and Guest Charumbira (Anglophone Africa), Lamine Diop (Francophone Africa), Zarylbek Kudabaev (Commonwealth of Independent States), José Luis Carvajal (Central and South America), Philippe Pommier (France) and Romulo A. Virola (East Asia). In December 2003, the OECD Council decided to host Metagora within the Secretariat of the Organisation and under the auspices of PARIS21.

The success of Metagora was largely due to the commitment and authoritative leadership of the heads of seven organisations that signed partnership agreements with the OECD for implementing the project's national, regional and global actions: Audrey Chapman and Mona Younis (AAAS, Washington), Purificacion Valera Quisumbing (Commission on Human Rights of the Philippines, CHR, Manila), Jean-Pierre Cling and Jacky Fayolle (DIAL, Paris), Sergio Aguayo and Helena Hofbauer (Fundar, Mexico), Allan Wagner Tizón (General Secretariat of the Andean Community, SG-CAN, Lima), Mark Orkin and Olive Shisana (Human Sciences Research Council of South Africa, HSRC, Pretoria), as well as Hasan Abu-Libdeh and Loai Shabana (Palestinian Central Bureau of Statistics, PCBS, Ramallah).

The heads of the Metagora Partner Organisations not only played a key role in ensuring the relevance and policy impact of the pilot experiences, but also efficiently networked and convinced other leading personalities to join, support and enrich the project's policy work. Some of these personalities deeply influenced the course of the project in their countries as well as at the global level. This was the case in particular of Emilio Álvarez-Icaza, Ombudsman of Mexico City; Reuben Lingating, Chairman of the National Commission on Indigenous Peoples of the Philippines; Romulo A. Virola, Secretary General of the National Statistical Coordination Board of the Philippines; Michel Tubiana, President of the French League for Human Rights and former Vice-President of the International Federation for Human Rights; Narandram Kollapen, Chairman of the South African Human Rights Commission; Miloon Kothari, UN Special Rapporteur on adequate housing; and Jan Robert Suesser, Director of ADETEF.

Throughout this publication, the many national organisations and people who were involved in implementing the various pilot exercises are mentioned at the beginning of each chapter. Particular acknowledgement should be expressed here to those who were in charge of organising and implementing these exercises in each Partner Organisation: Jana Asher in AAAS; Anita Chauhan and Jacqueline Veloria-Mejia in the CHR; François Roubaud, Mireille Razafindrakoto and Javier Herrera in DIAL; Claire Naval, Gloria Labastida and Juan Salgado in Fundar; Guillermo Lecaros in the SG-CAN; Maxine Reitzes, Michael Aliber and Udesh Pillay in the HSRC; and Mustafa Khawaja in the PCBS.

The Metagora community benefited from substantive contributions, sound advice and various forms of support from numerous outstanding experts, namely Roberta D'Arcangelo and Michelle Jouvenal (ISTAT, Italy); Rosa María Rubalcava (Mexico); Hans-Otto Sano (Danish Institute for Human Rights); Christopher Scott (London School of Economics and Political Science); Nicolas Meunier and René Padieu (France); Miron Straf (National Academy of Sciences, USA); Stephen Fienberg (Carnegie Mellon, USA); Romesh Silva and Miguel Cruz (Human Rights Data Analysis Group, USA); Richard Öhrvall (Statistics Sweden); and Marlene Roefs (HSRC). A particularly warm acknowledgement goes to Jana Asher (USA), who authoritatively conducted the design and preparation of the online *Metagora Training Materials* and reviewed or authored many substantive elements of these Materials.

In the course of its implementation, Metagora received guidance, encouragement and strong support from its Steering Committee, which gathers together representatives of all the donor institutions: Timothy Clark, Dominique Dellicour, Joanna Athlin, Marie-Claire Lefèvre and Mario-Rui Queiro (European Commission); Adair Heuchan, Amy Baker and Noah Schiff (Canada); Séverine Bellina, Thomas Buffin, Hervé Magro and Jean-François Divay (France); Lehnard Nordström, Mikael Boestrom and Ewa Westman (Sweden); Catherine Graf and Paul Obrist (Switzerland); as well as Jean Eric Aubert (World Bank), Antoine Simonpietri (PARIS21) and Brian Hammond (OECD).

A panel of six outstanding senior experts was in charge of assessing the implementation of Metagora. This Independent Panel of Experts comprises Jean-Louis Bodin, former President of the International Statistical Institute (Chairman); Milva Ekonomi (Albania); Haishan Fu (ESCAP); Kwaku Twum-Baah (Ghana); Carlo Malaguerra (Switzerland); and William Seltzer (USA). Their findings, conclusions and recommendations - largely based on an intermediate in-depth technical review of the survey-based pilot experiences, conducted by Prof. Herbert Spirer and William Seltzer (2006) and a Consolidated Review Report by William Seltzer (2007) - were invaluable for guiding and improving the work of the Metagora community and formulating lessons for future work in this field.

Many of the project's achievements were made possible due to close dialogue and fruitful co-operation between the Metagora community and other international networks and projects. Metagora's institutional location - in PARIS21 and within the OECD Development Co-operation Directorate - allowed for progress reports to be presented to highly qualified groups such as the OECD Development Assistance Committee (DAC) and the PARIS21 Steering Committee. Thanks to Bathylle Missika and Sebastian Bartsch, Metagora developed synergies and joint initiatives with the DAC Network on Governance (GOVNET). It also benefited from substantive exchanges with the OECD Development Centre during the elaboration of the study on *Uses and Abuses of Governance Indicators* (Arndt and Oman, 2006). Moreover, thanks to Enrico Giovannini, OECD Chief Statistician, Metagora was fully integrated within the OECD global project on *Measuring the Progress of Societies*; numerous Metagora Partners helped organise special sessions on measuring human rights and democratic governance within large regional conferences held in Cartagena de Indias, Seoul, and Sanaa, as well as at the World Forum on Progress of Societies held in Istanbul on 27-30 June 2007.

Metagora benefited from close working relations with Rajeev Malhotra and Nicolas Fasel from the Research and Development Branch of the Office of the UN High Commissioner for Human Rights (OHCHR). Metagora Partners actively contributed to the work of the expert group that provided guidance to the OHCHR on the establishment of a conceptual framework for the development of indicators of national compliance with international human rights standards. Close relations were also established with Bjoern Foerde, Alexandra Wilde, Noha El-Mikawy and Joachim Nahem of the UNDP Oslo Governance Centre, with which Metagora shares a common approach to nationally-based indicators of democratic governance. Metagora also had fruitful exchanges with the UNDP/Mongolia project on national assessment of democratic governance, implemented as a follow-up to the fifth *International Conference on New or Restored Democracies*. Informal meetings and videoconferences were also held with Robin Hodess and Marie Wolkers from Transparency International, as well as with Daniel Kaufmann from the Governance Group of the World Bank Institute, who made a substantive contribution to the Metagora Forum in May 2005.

The Metagora Co-ordination Team and several project partners collaborated closely with José Gregori and Célia Cristina (Sao Paulo Municipal Commission for Human Rights) as well as with Neide Patarra and Paulo de Martino Jannuzzi (National School of Sciences and Statistics, Brazil) in co-organising a large Latin American Workshop on Human Rights Indicators in Sao Paulo in June 2007. Fruitful working ties were also established with Prof. Hilal Al-Bayyati and staff of the Arab Institute for Training and Research in Statistics (AITRS) in co-organising a seminar on *Democratic Governance Statistics*, held in Amman in October 2007 and attended by heads of National Statistical Offices of fourteen Arab States.

The Metagora Co-ordination Team also benefited from stimulating exchanges with Marike Radstaake and Jan de Vries from Aim for Human Rights, formerly named "HOM-Netherlands" (in the context of annual workshops on *Human Rights Impact Assessment*); with Eitan Felner and Ignacio Saiz from the Centre for Economic and Social Rights, CESR (in the context of the design of a project to assess, with quantitative methods, the implementation of economic and social rights); with Dave Gordon and Peter Townsend from Bristol University and the London School of Economics and Political Science (in the context of the global project on *Poverty and the Rights of the Child*); as well as with Michael Ignatieff, Fernande Raine, Kate Desormeau, Eleanor Benko, Rory Stewart and Andrea Rossi from the Carr Center for Human Rights Policy of the John F. Kennedy School of Governance, Harvard University. Metagora and the Carr Center exchanged invitations to attend the important *Harvard Conference on Measuring Human Rights* and the Metagora Paris Forum, both held in May 2005. Last but not least, the Metagora co-ordinator was kindly invited by Robert Greenhill, President of CIDA-Canada, to attend two international *Round Tables on Human Rights Measurement* in Ottawa in January 2006 and May 2007. These events marked significant steps in the process of dialogue and mutual support among the institutions and experts committed to promoting evidence-based assessment and monitoring of human rights worldwide.

Table of Contents

List of Tables

List of Figures

Acronyms and Abbreviations

AAAS	American Association for the Advancement of Science
ADETEF	Co-operation Agency of the French Ministry of Finance
AFRISTAT	Economic and Statistical Observatory of Sub-Saharan Africa
AGEB	*Area Geo Estadística Básica* (Basic Geo-Statistical Areas, Mexico)
AIDS	Acquired Immune Deficiency Syndrome
AITRS	Arab Institute for Training and Research in Statistics
ANC	African National Congress
APRM	African Peer Review Mechanism
ASA	American Statistical Association
CADT	Certificate of Ancestral Domain Title (Philippines)
CAT	Convention Against Torture
CDH-DF	Commission for Human Rights of the Federal District (Mexico)
CEDAW	Convention on the Elimination of All Forms of Discrimination against Women
CERD	Convention on the Elimination of All Forms of Racial Discrimination
CESCR	Committee on Economic, Social and Cultural Rights
CESR	Centre for Economic and Social Rights
CHA	Consortium of Humanitarian Agencies (Sri Lanka)
CHR	National Commission on Human Rights (Philippines)
CIDA	Canadian International Development Agency
CMI	Chr. Michelsen Institute
CODI-ECA	Committee on Development Information of the UN Economic Commission for Africa
CRC	Convention on the Rights of the Child
CRDP	Convention on the Rights of Persons Disabilities
CTAR	*Consejos Transitorios de Administración Regional* (Transitory Regional Governments, Peru)
DAC	OECD Development Assistance Committee
DANE	*Departamento Administrativo Nacional de Estadística* (National Statistical Office of Colombia)

DANIDA	Danish International Development Agency
DFID	Department for International Development (United Kingdom)
DGSCN	*Direction Générale de la Statistique et de la Comptabilité Nationale* (National Statistical Office of Togo)
DGG	Democratic Governance Group (UNDP)
DIAL	*Développement, Institutions et Analyses de Long terme* (Centre of the Institute for Development Research, IRD, France)
DNSI	*Direction Nationale de la Statistique et de l'Informatique* (National Statistical Office of Mali)
DPS	*Direction de la Prévision et de la Statistique* (National Statistical Office of Senegal)
DRA	Development Research Africa (South Africa)
EAs	Enumerator Areas
EC	European Commission
ENAHO	*Encuesta Nacional de Hogares sobre Condiciones de Vida y Pobreza* (National Household Survey on Poverty and Living Conditions, Peru)
ENCE	*Escola Nacional de Ciências Estatísticas* (National School of Statistical Science, Brazil)
ENIGHU	*Encuesta Nacional de Ingresos y Gastos* (National Income and Expenditure Survey, Ecuador)
ESCR	Economic, Social and Cultural Rights
ESSALUD	*Seguro Social de Salud* (Social Security Insurance, Peru)
EU	European Union
EUROSTAT	Statistical Office of the European Communities
FGD	Focus Group Discussion
FHD	Forum for Human Dignity (Sri Lanka)
FONCODES	*Fondo de Cooperación para el Desarrollo Social* (Co-operation Fund for Social Development, Peru)
GCRT	Georgian Centre for Psychosocial and Medical Rehabilitation of Torture Victims
GID	Gender, Institutions and Development Database (OECD, Development Centre)
GOVNET	DAC Network on Governance
HDI	Human Development Index
HDR	Human Development Report
HHR	Home for Human Rights (Sri Lanka)
HIV	Human Immunodeficiency Virus
HOM	*Humanistisch Overleg Mensenrechten* (Netherlands Humanist Committee on Human Rights)
HRAC	Human Rights Accountability Coalition (Sri Lanka)

HRC	Human Rights Committee
HRI	Human Rights Institutions
HSRC	Human Sciences Research Council (South Africa)
IAOS	International Association for Official Statistics
IBGE	*Instituto Brasileño de Geografía y Estadística* (Brazilian Institute of Geography and Statistics)
ICCPR	International Covenant on Civil and Political Rights
ICESCR	International Covenant on Economic, Social and Cultural Rights
ICNRD	International Conference on New or Restored Democracies
ICRC	International Committee of the Red Cross
IHR	Institute of Human Rights (Sri Lanka)
ILO	International Labour Organisation
INDEC	*Instituto Nacional de Estadística y Censos* (National Statistical Office of Argentina)
INE	*Instituto Nacional de Estadística* (National Statistical Offices of Bolivia and Venezuela)
INEC	*Instituto Nacional de Estadística y Censos* (National Statistical Office of Ecuador)
INEGI	*Instituto Nacional de Estadística, Geografía e Informática* (National Statistical Office of Mexico)
INEI	*Instituto Nacional de Estadística e Informática* (National Statistical Office of Peru)
INS	*Institut National de la Statistique* (National Statistical Offices of Niger and Côte d'Ivoire)
INSAE	*Institut National de la Statistique et de l'Analyse Économique* (National Statistical Office of Benin)
INSD	*Institut National de la Statistique et de la Démographie* (National Statistical Office of Burkina Faso)
INSTAT	*Institut National de la Statistique* (National Statistical Office of Madagascar)
IPE	Independent Panel of Experts
IPRA	Indigenous Peoples Rights Act of 1997 (Philippines)
IRD	*Institut de Recherche pour le Développement* (Institute for Development Research, France)
IRR	Inter-Rater Reliability
ISI	International Statistical Institute
ISTAT	*Instituto Nazionale di Statistica* (National Statistical Office of Italy)
LPM	Landless People's Movement (South Africa)
LRA	Land Registration Authority (Philippines)
LRAD	Land Redistribution for Agricultural Development (South Africa)
MADIO	MAdagascar-Dial-Instat-Orstom

MDG	Millennium Development Goals
MECOVI	*Mejoramiento de las Encuestas de Hogares y la Medición de Condiciones de Vida* (Improving Household Surveys and Measurement of Living Conditions, Bolivia)
NCIP	National Commission on Indigenous Peoples (Philippines)
NEPAD	New Partnership for Africa's Development
NGO	Non-Governmental Organisation
NSCB	National Statistical Coordination Board (Philippines)
NSDS	National Strategies for the Development of Statistics
NSO	National Statistical Office
ODI	Overseas Development Institute (United Kingdom)
OECD	Organisation for Economic Co-operation and Development
OHCHR	United Nations Office of the High Commissioner for Human Rights
OSCE-ODIHR	Organisation for Security and Co-operation in Europe - Office for Democratic Institutions and Human Rights
PARIS21	Partnership in Statistics for Development in the 21st Century
PCBS	Palestinian Central Bureau of Statistics
PRSP	Poverty Reduction Strategy Papers
PSU	Primary Sampling Units
RBM	Rights-based monitoring
RDP	Reconstruction and Development Program (South Africa)
RENIEC	*Registro Nacional de Identificación y Estado Civil* (National Register of Identification and Civil Status, Peru)
SADC	Southern African Development Community
SCINCE	*Sistema para la Consulta de Información Censal* (Consultation System for Census Information, Mexico)
SDC	Swiss Agency for Development and Cooperation
SG-CAN	*Secretaría General de la Comunidad Andina* (General Secretariat of the Andean Community)
SIDA	Swedish International Development Co-operation Agency
SIEH	*Sistema Integrado de Encuestas a Hogares* (Integrated System of Household Surveys, Ecuador)
SRTC	Statistical Research and Training Centre (Philippines)
UN	United Nations
UNDP	United Nations Development Programme
UN-ECOSOC	United Nations Economic and Social Council
UNESCO	United Nations Educational, Scientific and Cultural Organisation

OECD JOURNAL ON DEVELOPMENT – VOLUME 9, ISSUE 2 – ISBN 978-92-64-04943-7 – © OECD 2008

UNFPA	United Nations Population Fund
UN-HRI	United Nations – International Human Rights Instruments
UNICEF	United Nations Children's Fund
UNO	United Nations Organisation
UNVFTV	United Nations Voluntary Fund of Torture Victims
USAID	United States Agency for International Development
WBI	World Bank Institute
WGA	World Governance Assessment
WHO	World Health Organization

Introduction

More than one decade ago, the Development Assistance Committee of the Organisation for Economic Co-operation and Development (OECD/DAC) adopted a visionary report entitled *Shaping the 21st Century: The Contribution of Development Co-operation*. This report proposed a set of international development objectives which, in the course of subsequent years, evolved into what are now known as the Millennium Development Goals.

Shaping the 21st Century stated that "*essential to the attainment of these measurable goals are qualitative factors in the evolution of more stable, safe, participatory and just societies. These include capacity development for effective, democratic and accountable governance, the protection of human rights and respect for the rule of law.*" In this context, OECD/DAC member countries firmly committed to "*continue to address these less easily quantified factors of development progress*" (OECD, 1996, p.2).

The international community at large progressively adopted these views, and democracy and human rights are now considered as fully-fledged dimensions of good governance and participatory development. The need for conducting regular and more rigorous assessments of these dimensions has been highlighted not only in several OECD/DAC guidelines and EU key policy statements, but also by major international initiatives such as the New Partnership for Africa's Development or the International Conference on New or Restored Democracies (see OECD, 1996, 2007a; European Commission, 2003, 2005, 2006; NEPAD, 2002, 2003; and ICNRD, 2003).

In the same line of thought, the UNDP Oslo Governance Centre recently developed conceptual frameworks and guides for the production and use of "indicators for human rights based approaches to development" and "democratic governance indicators". The latter refer to a measurement tool aimed at capturing the interrelated dimensions of human rights, democracy, participation, rule of law and accountability of public authorities (UNDP, 2005a, 2005b, 2005c, 2006a, 2006b, 2007).

Some may see in this growing interest for robust assessments of human rights and democratic governance one of those seasonal rhetoric fashions that so often mark major events and solemn statements within the international arena. However, such an impression does not stand up to the evidence of unprecedented widespread efforts to enhance methods and tools for measuring the implementation of rights, progress of democracy or improvement of governance. Indeed, a Metagora worldwide survey, carried out in 2005 and 2006, revealed the existence of many on-going assessment attempts undertaken in various regions of the globe at the initiative of national and local organisations.

From Auckland to Baku, from Sao Paulo to Moscow, from Kigali to Ulaanbaatar, domestic stakeholders are currently joining forces to assess particular human rights problems and policy issues which matter to the people in their specific cultural, national and local contexts. Often modest in scope, implemented with few resources, based on rudimentary methods, but conducted with strong commitment and determination, these numerous initiatives attest, from the bottom, of a true universal need for enhancing the capacities and tools for measuring human rights and democratic governance.

More and more national stakeholders – such as policy makers, Human Rights Institutions, and civil society groups – are discovering the huge potential that applied statistics and quantitative methods can offer in the fields of monitoring, advocacy and policy design. As this publication will highlight, a number of these actors are already experiencing the powerful leverage that reliable figures and robust analysis can have on their everyday work. Also, multilateral organisations and development agencies are increasingly seeking relevant human rights statistics and governance indicators to inform policy dialogue, evaluate progress and better target development aid. In other words, when it comes to consider human rights issues, democracy gaps or governance weaknesses, domestic and international actors tend to apply the motto: "*if you can measure it, you can address it.*"

Such a global measurement trend attests to an increased awareness of the need for enhancing, with proper and robust tools, the rigour, reliability and efficiency of existing reporting and monitoring mechanisms. This publication will show how this growing awareness is leading to new and promising forms of collaboration between human rights practitioners, institutional actors, statisticians and social scientists – a collaboration that marks a significant difference with the reluctance and lack of communication that prevailed in the past.

The **First Part** of this publication presents the background, processes, results and lessons of the work implemented by the Metagora project from 2004 to 2008.

Chapter 1 - based on materials contributed by Jana Asher, Audrey Chapman, Mark Orkin, Jan Robert Suesser and Raul Suarez de Miguel - depicts the long processes that led the international statistical and human rights families to overcome widespread reluctances to engage in measuring human rights and democratic governance issues. It recalls the pioneering work of American and European leading experts in this area and points out the reasons for which the growing measurement trend in the field of governance during the last decade has been both opening promising perspectives and raising very serious methodological issues.

An important section of this chapter highlights the boost of the operational *Conclusions* of the 2000 Montreux Conference on *Statistics, Development and Human Rights*. It shows how, in the aftermath of this major event, work was organised and substantive initiatives taken to design an ambitious international project aimed at enhancing the use of well-established statistical methods for assessing human rights and democratic governance. It describes how this work contributed to define the approach, objectives and concrete action plan of what became the Metagora project.

Chapter 2 - based on materials contributed by Claire Naval, Sylvie Walter, Paul Clare, Thomas Heimgartner and Raul Suarez de Miguel - highlights the goals, rationale, original bottom-up approach and general *modus operandi* of the project. It describes the participatory approach and cross-fertilisation dynamics that characterise both the pilot experiences and the project's global working structures. It draws attention to the multidisciplinary constituency of the Metagora community of Partners and its working methods. Subsequent chapters (3 to 8) provide an overview of the various Metagora pilot experiences.

Chapters 3, 4 and 5 - based on materials contributed, respectively, by Gloria Labastida, Claire Naval and Juan Salgado; Anita Chauhan, Fe Dyliacco, Estrella Domingo, Reuben Lingating and Romulo Virola; and Maxine Reitzes, Marlene Roefs and Michael Aliber - present the specific processes, results and impact of the pilot experiences conducted in **Mexico City** (Federal District), the **Philippines** and **South**

Box I.1. **On-going initiatives aimed at enhancing assessments of human rights and democratic governance over the world**

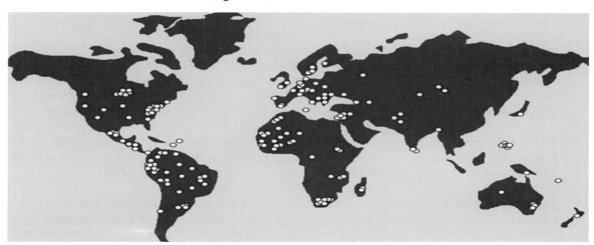

Source: Inventory of Initiatives, www.metagora.org

Africa, consisting of sample survey-based studies on issues of major public concern: abuses and ill-treatment by police forces, indigenous peoples' rights and land reform issues. These pilot experiences were conducted by authoritative research centres and Human Rights Institutions, with the strong support of professional, academic and official statistical organisations.

Mexico, the Philippines and South Africa have quite different cultural, historical, economic and social backgrounds, but they present an important common characteristic: while these countries have embarked on vigorous democratisation processes, all three are still tackling serious human rights problems and democratic governance related issues, as well as social and cultural patterns inherited from past regimes. In these countries, reinforcing democratic governance and enhancing human rights monitoring mechanisms are generally considered as important elements for the consolidation of democracy. Thus the pilot experiences had a common goal: to enhance assessments and monitoring through the use of well-established statistical tools – such as sampling methods and survey questionnaire design – for the collection and analysis of sensitive data. These chapters show how significant the results, and how strong the policy impact, of such measurement methods have been.

Chapter 6 - based on materials contributed by Mireille Razafindrakoto, Javier Herrera and François Roubaud - focuses on two large regional experiences conducted by National Statistical Offices in eight countries of Francophone Africa (**Benin, Burkina Faso, Côte d'Ivoire, Madagascar, Mali, Niger, Senegal and Togo**) and in three Andean countries (**Bolivia, Ecuador and Peru**). Activities were undertaken under the operational co-ordination of AFRISTAT and the General Secretariat of the Andean Community, and with the technical support and further analysis of DIAL, a centre of the French Institute for Development Research. These experiences consist in using regular official household surveys to collect relevant data on poverty, democracy and governance issues. Their multi-country scope aimed both at testing, at a significant scale, a measurement method and at responding to crucial information needs of the countries involved.

Indeed, African target countries face similar development problems which tend to converge in extreme poverty, problematic access to basic services, widespread corruption and many other rampant governance issues. The experience therefore aimed at anchoring, in this difficult development context, a light but powerful method for measuring democracy and governance issues. Through the use of regular household surveys, it allowed to better grasp the multidimensional phenomena of poverty as well as different dimensions of participatory and democratic governance.

In the case of the countries of the Andean region, the experience also focused on "hearing the voice of the poor" on democracy, social integration and governance. While Bolivia, Ecuador and Peru have moved from military and authoritative regimes to democratic rule, this process has taken time and has not been as smooth as initially expected. Democracy is still fragile and its consolidation is increasingly being endangered by the unresolved problems of poverty, weak labour markets and inefficient delivery of public services. In this context, the chapter shows that the measurement method adopted has been instrumental in providing relevant data which allow to identify problematic areas and issues of institutional accountability at national and sub-national levels, as well as to address policy gaps and weaknesses.

This chapter also includes a section on an innovative *Mirror Survey* aimed to compare, on the one hand, aggregated data based on an open panel of experts with, on the other hand, statistically robust results from sample household surveys, both focusing on the same questions and on the same countries. While for a number of technical reasons this exercise should be considered with some caution, impressive gaps between these two sources tend to question the reliability of measurement tools and indicators based on expert pools. This points towards possible future research on tools for assessing robustness, consistency and relevance of existing governance and democracy indicators.

Chapter 7 - based on materials contributed by Mustafa Khawaja, Jamil Helal, Hadeel Qazzaz, Jana Asher and Audrey Chapman - presents an original attempt undertaken in **Palestine** to develop indicators and a public information tool on a key human right: the right to education. This pilot experiment presents several interesting facets. First of all, while launched and technically conducted by a National Statistical Office, it involved – and was ultimately steered – by a national community of academic centres, policy actors and leading NGOs. It consisted in the identification and collection of existing official and non-official data that could be relevant for measuring the right to education. The information collected was either quantitative or narrative, and was gathered together in a prototype database intended to become, in a later stage, an online public information tool.

This chapter makes evident that measuring human rights and democratic governance is not a mere technical operation: it is a complex process of high political and social significance, which changes the relations among the various stakeholders and experts involved. Thus the Palestinian pilot experience clearly confirms a motto endorsed by the UN Statistical Commission: "*identifying statistical indicators for monitoring purposes is neither a pure policy nor a pure statistical issue*", but a process conducted "*by joint determination*" of statisticians and policy actors (see Box 1.4).

Chapter 8 - based on materials contributed by Lakmali Dasanayake, Dinesha de Silva Wikramanayake, Kohilanath Rajanayagam and Romesh Silva - reports on work conducted in **Sri Lanka** by a group of local NGOs, the Human Rights Accountability Coalition, with the support of The Asia Foundation Office in Colombo. The work carried out in Sri Lanka aims to harmonise the collection of data by NGOs on massive human rights violations, as well as to encode narrative information in order to enable statistical analysis and therefore improve estimates of the magnitude and trends of violations. Thus, this chapter shows the kind of statistical approaches, methods and tools that can be used to improve systematic documentation and processing of information on human rights violations, of various nature and from different sources.

Unfortunately, Sri Lanka has still not moved away from what has become an endless tragic period of its post-independence history. Political and ethnical violence is still rampant and, at the closing of this publication, media news continue to report atrocities, blind suicide bombings and recurrent use of civil populations as shields by armed parties. The work conducted in this dark environment by the Human Rights Accountability Coalition is exemplary not only in terms of commitment, courage and determination, but also in terms of effective organisation, quality control and technical rigour. This chapter therefore shows that, even in very difficult circumstances, proper statistical approaches and tools can considerably empower the documentation, analysis, reporting and advocacy work of civil society actors.

Chapter 9 elaborates on the synthesis of results and lessons from the entire Metagora experience, as formulated by the community of project Partners. This chapter not only shows that Metagora has given a solid empirical response to several controversial questions on the feasibility and relevance of measuring human rights and democratic governance, but also that it has shed light on a number of implications that these responses have both at the policy and at the methodological levels.

This chapter highlights the powerful effect of the bottom-up approach followed by Metagora and, in particular, of the participatory assessment processes that involved a wide range of stakeholders and experts. It summarises the many promising perspectives opened by the project for developing further co-operational work of national Human Rights Institutions, research centres, NGOs and National Statistical Offices. It also presents two online resources and reference tools generated by the project: the *Metagora Training Materials* and an *Inventory of Initiatives* aimed to inform actors interested – or already involved – in measuring human rights and democratic governance about existing work, key issues and relevant methods in this area.

The **Second Part** of this publication contains four contributions that usefully complement the lessons from the work carried out by Metagora.

Chapter 10, contributed by the Office of the UN High Commissioner for Human Rights (OHCHR), provides the outline of a conceptual and methodological framework for developing indicators aimed at monitoring national compliance with international human rights treaties. This text is the result of substantive discussions within an international group of senior experts who were requested by the High Commissioner to make recommendations towards a uniform approach to human rights indicators within the UN system.

This group of senior experts – in which some Metagora Partners and the general co-ordinator of the project took an active part – reached for the first time wide consensus on the main conceptual basis for building indicators. A synthesis of the conclusions of the group was established by Rajeev Malhotra and Nicolas Fasel and served as a basis for two subsequent background papers submitted by OHCHR to the Inter-committee meetings of the UN Treaty Bodies in 2006 and 2008.

This chapter therefore authoritatively reflects the current state of the evolving consensus on indicators of compliance with international human rights standards. It is supplemented by two appendices that detail indicators for 12 selected human rights and present examples of meta-data sheets on human rights indicators.

Chapter 11, contributed by Audrey Chapman, addresses the need for developing indicators as a central instrument for effectively monitoring economic, social and cultural rights and evaluating the performance of the countries in the "progressive implementation" of these rights. It presents a structured proposal for a series of indicators for monitoring the right to education, matured in the aftermath of earlier proposals by Paul Hunt concerning indicators on economic and social rights, and taking into account the general conceptual framework described in *Chapter 10*.

This chapter therefore provides a concrete illustration of the way in which a specific right can be translated from the abstract legal norms in which it is framed into operational standards. Thus it stands at the intersection of the Metagora efforts - and in particular of the pilot experience in Palestine - and the growing international consensus on the conceptual framework for building structural, process and outcome indicators on human rights.

Chapter 12, contributed by Eitan Felner, of the Centre for Economic and Social Rights (CESR), focuses on measuring economic and social rights in order to hold governments accountable for avoidable deprivations. It argues that a toolbox of quantitative methods is needed to properly use existing indicators to assess government compliance with specific human rights obligations.

This chapter elaborates on how to use simple quantitative tools to measure various dimensions of state obligations with respect to economic and social rights, in particular the obligations to progressively realise rights in accordance with available resources, to provide a minimum core set of rights, and to not discriminate in terms of rights and services. It also discusses some of the conceptual and normative issues surrounding these internationally-recognised obligations, which need to be further elucidated to properly monitor the compliance of states. Finally, it presents a summary of a CESR case study on India, an example of the Centre's current activities aimed at informing the work of UN Treaty Bodies and NGOs with evidence-based visualisation of current issues and the status of individual state compliance with the *International Covenant on Economic, Social and Cultural Rights*.

Chapter 13, contributed by the UNDP Oslo Governance Centre, presents the rationale and main components of the *Global Programme on Capacity Development for Democratic Governance Assessments and Measurements* that is about to be launched by the UNDP. This programme is based on the conviction shared by UNDP and its Partner Countries that governance assessments can be catalysts for nationally-driven reforms, especially if these assessments are configured and undertaken through inclusive consultative processes. The *Global Programme*'s approach to democratic governance assessments and indicators emphasises national ownership, capacity development and harmonisation with national development planning instruments.

Thus the various sections of this chapter show that there is much more than a mere chronological sequence between the conclusion of the Metagora project and the launching of the UNDP *Global Programme*. Since 2004, the UNDP Oslo Governance Centre has worked closely with Metagora and several of its Partners. Thus it is natural that the *Global Programme* presents several elements of continuity with the efforts and working methods of Metagora. This chapter describes the assumptions, objectives and main lines of action of this promising *Programme* on democratic governance assessments and indicators, which, in line with the *Conclusions* of the 2000 Montreux Conference, will be conducted "*under an institutional umbrella that is universal, solid and respected*".

The **Conclusion** summarises the main results, products and impact of the project, highlighting how these respond to the expectations raised and the perspectives opened by the 2000 Montreux Conference. It articulates the successful conclusion of Metagora with the emergence of international projects – in particular the UNDP *Global Programme* – that are based on the bottom-up approach and on the principles of ownership, inclusivity, policy focus, professional rigour and enhancement of national capacities, as promoted by Metagora.

In conformity with the original Terms of Reference of the project, this *Conclusion* comments on the steps that have been taken to ensure an efficient handing over of the results, lessons, documentation and resources generated by Metagora to relevant organisations and to the international community at large. In the spirit of such a handing over, this *Conclusion* retrospectively identifies some characteristics of the project that were determinant for its success, and prospectively briefly suggests how these could be internalised by emerging initiatives.

This publication also includes **six useful appendices:**

Appendix 1 contains a series of *Methodological and technical outlines of the Metagora pilot experiences*. As the various chapters of this publication are addressed to a broad public who is not necessarily interested, nor able to digest, all the technicalities sustaining the Metagora pilot experiences, it was important to provide readers who are more familiar with statistical methods, or who have more scientifically-oriented interests, with a closer insight on the techniques applied in these pilots.

Appendices 2 and 3 complement the information provided in *Chapter 9* on the Metagora worldwide survey that was conducted to identify and document initiatives aimed to enhance evidence-based assessment of human rights and democratic governance. Appendix 2 contains the questionnaire used in that survey and Appendix 3 presents three examples of the many initiatives that were identified, documented and integrated in the online *Inventory* available at www.metagora.org.

Appendices 4 and 5, contributed by the OHCHR, complement *Chapter 10* with a detailed description of indicators for selected human rights and illustrative examples of meta-data sheets that are being developed to duly document these indicators.

Appendix 6 contains an *Independent assessment report on the implementation and results of Metagora*. In line with one of the main *Conclusions* of Montreux concerning the principle of scientific transparency and the need for external supervision, since early 2005, an independent panel of senior experts has been scrutinising the scientific, technical and operational facets of the project. Its assessment report highlights the strengths and weaknesses of the project and formulates recommendations that are of the highest importance for whoever intends to conduct, organise or support initiatives aimed at measuring human rights and democratic governance in the future.

Last but not least, an abundant **Bibliography** closes this publication. As part of the handing over of the project's findings, the Co-ordination Team, with the support of Jana Asher, tried to include in this bibliography all relevant literature and materials it or its project Partners identified in the course of the last four years. By publishing the *Bibliography* in a simple alphabetical order, a rough stock of information is being transmitted to those who, in the future, could be in a position not only to update it, but also to edit it in a more analytically structured form.

Part I

Chapter 1

On the Road to Montreux and Beyond

The feasibility and relevance of measuring human rights, democracy and governance have long been controversial both in the human rights community and in the international statistical family. Within the human rights community, the term "indicator" has had two distinct - and somewhat contrasting - meanings: while for some it designated, in the strict statistical sense, quantitative synthetic information based on robust data (Türk, 1990; Alston, 1998), for many others it designated a qualitative synthetic overview based on extensive sets of questions or "checklists" related to key human rights dimensions (Green, 2001). The latter meaning has deeply marked the approach to human rights assessments that has prevailed within the UN system and among most human rights leading experts during the last decades.

Overcoming reluctance of human rights practitioners...

Until recent years, many human rights practitioners were unwilling to mix their qualitative assessments (based on sound expertise and extensive field experience) with statistically-based facts and figures. They considered that numbers could not reflect the multi-dimensional complexity of human rights issues and many were allergic to the idea of "quantifying human suffering". Statistical methods appeared obscure to them and, in fact, they were - and still are - technically unqualified to properly evaluate the quality and reliability of those methods.

As a matter of fact, to date, little relevant quantitative data have been used by human rights practitioners or national Human Rights Institutions - and very few aggregate tools have been developed to measure progress in the implementation of human rights. This is not only due to a number of stereotypes and misconceptions related to the use of statistical indicators in this field, but also – and perhaps mainly – to widespread ignorance about existing datasets and potential data sources that could be very useful for assessment and monitoring purposes. Also, in spite of an increased awareness of the importance of statistical information for measuring, in particular, economic and social rights, only in very few countries have human rights practitioners already started to work together with the producers of official statistics (Chapman, 2005a; Metagora, 2007).

This chapter was drafted on the basis of substantive contributions and working documents authored by:

Jana Asher, Audrey Chapman, Mark Orkin, Jan Robert Suesser and *Raul Suarez de Miguel*

In the international scene, and during the last fifteen years, UN Treaty Bodies have increasingly been requesting statistical data and indicators to inform their work in monitoring national compliance with international standards. *General Comments* of the UN Committee on Economic, Social and Cultural Rights on the scope of obligations related to specific rights – including its comments on the rights to education, health and water – called for the development of statistically-based indicators. So have many of the UN Special Rapporteurs – such as Paul Hunt in the field of the right to health or Miloon Kothari in the field of the right to adequate housing.

The UN human rights system has been slow in responding to these demands, but recent developments have marked real progress. In 2003 the Office of the High Commissioner for Human Rights (OHCHR) established a small unit to support Treaty Bodies in using data and indicators, and to conduct conceptual work on indicators of compliance with international standards. In 2005 it also established an international group of senior experts to make recommendations towards a uniform approach to human rights indicators within the UN system. In 2006 this group reached, for the first time, fair consensus on the main conceptual and methodological basis for building indicators. Its approach and conclusions were welcomed by the Inter-Committee Meeting of the UN Treaty Bodies (see OHCHR, 2005; UN-HRI, 2006b, 2008a; and *Chapter 10* of this publication).

These developments were generally welcomed by the international human rights community; nevertheless, authoritative experts and practitioners have identified a potential dark shadow behind statistical data and indicators. In particular, they have been warning against the temptation some international actors may have to further develop international aggregate indices of human rights or even to make a "global human rights report" which, following the example of the *Human Development Report*, would include country rankings.

Such a strong reluctance to build aggregate indices or rank countries was confirmed during a Conference convened in May 2005 by the Carr Center for Human Rights Policy of Harvard University. On that occasion, "*attendants strongly cautioned against such an approach to human rights measurement, noting that any broad reporting mechanism aspiring to systematic objectivity was premature at best. Such an endeavour would not only be politically explosive (...) and practically unfeasible (...), but also methodologically problematic and potentially counterproductive. (...) The reasons many participants cited for their resistance centred around five general objections: redundancy, inappropriateness, imprecision, over-simplification, and uncertain political usefulness*" (Carr Center for Human Rights, 2005, p. 26).

While understandable and well-argued, such an opposition to hypothetical "global human rights indices" must not be over-interpreted. The few existing relevant human rights data and indicators – such as those on the rights of the child developed, on the basis of the *Multiple Indicator Cluster Surveys*, under the aegis of UNICEF – have proved to be relevant, appropriate, comprehensive and politically useful (see Childwatch, 1996, 1999; UNICEF, 1998, 2002, 2004, 2007, 2008; Delamonica, Komarecki and Minujin, 2006; Hancioglu and Vadnais, 2008). The international human rights community has extensively used these indicators for advocacy purposes – as it will certainly use the emerging indicators on economic and social rights and the indicators of national compliance with international human rights standards promoted by the OHCHR. The issue of real concern to the human rights community is not that human rights be measured and indicators developed, but the risk that aggregate figures be misused.

... and resistances by statisticians

For their part, statisticians – and in particular those working in the field of official statistics – have long been more than reluctant to engage in the measurement of "sensitive political issues". Many of

---

Box 1.1. **Gauging the scope and magnitude of a human rights problem**

"Before a human rights organization begins working on any sort of human rights issue, it needs an understanding of the baseline – the scope and magnitude of the problem we are setting out to solve. How big is the problem? Is it getting bigger? Does it disproportionately affect certain areas or segments of the population? Answering these questions is crucial to ensuring that intervention strategies are appropriate to the problem at hand.

"Indeed, human rights practitioners often justify their concern with a particular human rights problem by noting that it is "widespread and systematic". Too often, however, we make these claims with nothing but impressionistic options to back them up. Before claiming that a violation is "widespread", we must ascertain that the violation affects a statistically significant segment of the population. Before claiming that the violation is "systematic", we must demonstrate that there is some concerted policy behind the violation, or that there is some attribute that the victims of this violation share. (…) Literature about human trafficking typically opens with the dire claim that the phenomenon is a "large and growing" problem. In truth, how large it is, and how quickly it is growing, are difficult to say. But once we have made this assertion – even if erroneously – it becomes even harder to back down from it without appearing to diminish the seriousness of the problem or the need for intervention.

"Misusing these terms will not only erode the credibility of the human rights movement, but it may also lead activists to mistake the nature and the causes of a problem and to undertake misdirect efforts to combat it. An empirically-based understanding of the magnitude and scope of a human rights violation, therefore, is critical to calibrating appropriate intervention strategies and targeting them at the right segments of the population."

Michael Ignatieff and Kate Desormeau
Carr Center for Human Rights Policy
John F. Kennedy School of Governance, Harvard University
(Carr Center for Human Rights, 2005, p. 6)

---

them actually considered that involving statistics in human rights or democratic governance assessments would endanger the "scientific neutrality" of their profession. Others objected that, assuming surveys on such sensitive issues would be technically, operationally and institutionally feasible, individuals would never accept to respond to a questionnaire about how their fundamental rights are respected – or not – or about how the government is performing its tasks.

The reluctance of statisticians to deal with human rights or democratic governance issues has also been linked to the quite rudimentary basis – in strict statistical terms – of the methods applied to produce indicators and indices in these fields. The approaches and pools of purposely selected respondents sustaining these indices appeared for long to many professional statisticians as a sort of technical quicksand, and therefore prevented them from approaching or supporting such measurement attempts.

The first significant impulse towards involving the statistical profession in human rights issues was given by the American Statistical Association (ASA) with the creation, in the late 1970s, of a Standing Committee on Scientific Freedom and Human Rights. This was done – not without opposition – as a reaction to the disappearance, under the Argentinean military regime, of Carlos Noriega and Graciela Mellibovsky Saidler. Noriega was the Director of the National Statistical Office of Argentina (INDEC) and a former researcher of the OECD Development Centre. Mellibovsky was a young social scientist. The first actions of the Committee aimed at making the case for these two victims of the "dirty war" and at putting pressure on Argentina's government to obtain information on what had happened to them.

Most of the founding members of the ASA Committee expected that this would enlarge the scope of its action so as to explore possible applications of statistics to monitor the status of human rights; nevertheless, during some years, they were refrained from engaging the Committee in this path. It was only in 1985 that the ASA allowed the Committee to work on "*statistical questions relating to data on human rights*" and to "*assist scientific societies and other responsible organizations, upon request, in statistical questions relating to the measurement, evaluation and analysis of data on human rights*" (Jabine and Samuelson, 2008, p.189).

In parallel to this crucial move, the American Association for the Advancement of Science (AAAS) took the lead, in 1985 and under the direction of Eric Stover and the chair of Thomas B. Jabine, of a collective research project aimed at evaluating the role of statistics in the documentation of human rights violations. The results of this pioneering project were two publications that remained, for long, the main bibliographical reference on measuring human rights: a special issue of *Human Rights Quarterly* and the book *Human Rights and Statistics: Getting the Record Straight*, gathering together substantive contributions by renown statisticians like David Banks, Herbert Spirer or Douglas Samuelson (Claude and Jabine, 1986, 1992).

These publications were complemented by other important contributions evidencing the potential of statistical analysis for enhancing rigour and reliability of reporting on human rights violations (in particular those of Frank, 1988; Jabine, 1989; Presser, 1989; Spirer, 1990). Such a substantive scientific impulse had a considerable impact within the American statistical community and stimulated several young graduates to deepen further the research and to embark on innovative human rights measurement projects. Workshops on statistics and human rights within the ASA and other academic circles became a natural part of the American scientific landscape, and to date there is a good record of fruitful research implemented in this field (see for instance: Ball, 1996a; Jennings *et al.*, 1998, 2000a; Ball *et al.*, 1994, 1999, 2002, 2003; Jennings and Swiss, 2000, 2001; Asher and Ball, 2001; Amowitz *et al.*, 2004; Asher, Banks and Scheuren, 2008).

At the initiative of Ann Mitchell and Jean-Louis Bodin, a European Working Group on Statisticians and Human Rights was established in 1982. Its action mostly focused on taking the defence of statisticians in peril; however it did not evolve, as in the USA, towards substantive methodological work. Of course, there have been significant European contributions to the development of methods for measuring human rights and democratic governance, such as those of the demographers Helge Brunborg, Henrik Urdal and Ewa Tabeau, the comparative studies of Todd Landman, the long-lasting work undertaken by Mireille Razafindrakoto and François Roubaud since 1995, or, more recently, the project on child poverty conducted by David Gordon and Peter Townsend – to mention just a few (see Foweraker and Landman, 1997; Landman, 2004, 2006a; Brunborg, 2000, 2002; Brunborg, Lyngstad and Urdal, 2003; Brunborg and Lacina, 2004; Brunborg and Tabeau, 2005; Brunborg and Urdal, 2005; Roubaud, 2003a, 2003c; Gordon and Townsend, 2002; Gordon *et al.*, 2003). Nevertheless, these contributions remained somewhat fragmented, and scientific exchanges on measuring human rights and democratic governance were almost incidental due to the lack of an *ad hoc* well-established European forum.

At the global level – and similarly to what happened in the early 1980s within the ASA –, the International Statistical Institute (ISI) opposed strong resistance to attempts by some of its members to involve it more in human rights matters. While a contributed paper meeting on Statistics, Statisticians and Human Rights was initially accepted and scheduled for the 1985 Amsterdam session of the ISI, the Bureau of the Institute later decided to remove it from the programme – instead it was held as an informal gathering. Until very recent years, this reluctance to mix scientific statistical work with "sensitive political issues" was broadly shared within the ISI. It was only in 1999 that – at the initiative of Jean-Louis Bodin, Yves Franchet and Carlo Malaguerra – the International Association for Official Statistics (IAOS) accepted that the 2000 edition of its bi-annual Conference be devoted to the use of statistics to assess human rights and some aspects of democratic governance, in particular in the context of development processes.

Pioneering work of the American Association for the Advancement of Science

If the last twenty years have been characterised by a progressive change in the attitude of many statisticians and human rights practitioners towards possibilities for properly measuring human rights and democratic governance, it is largely due to pioneer initiatives undertaken by the Science and Human Rights Program of the American Association for the Advancement of Science (AAAS), the world's largest federation of scientific and engineering societies.

Beyond the project on human rights mentioned in the previous section, the Science and Human Rights Program pioneered, in the 1990s and under the direction of Audrey Chapman, applications of a wide range of scientific methods to human rights research and investigations: the forensic sciences, genetics, a large variety of social science methodologies and, last but not least, information technology and statistical methods. The latter work included specialised research, survey design, interviewing techniques, and development of databases.

A Human Rights Data Analysis Group was created within the Program under the leadership of Patrick Ball. It benefited from the wise guidance of outstanding statisticians – in particular from Herbert and Louise Spirer, Fritz J. Sheuren and William Seltzer. In the mid-1990s, it established technical and scientific methodologies for documenting and measuring large-scale human rights violations. Since then, it has been conducting successful projects and providing technical assistance and training to several Truth Commissions, Tribunals, Ombudsmen and NGOs in Guatemala, South Africa, Haiti, Honduras, Cambodia, East Timor, Kosovo, Ghana and Sierra Leone. In 2002 the group left the AAAS and joined Benetech, a non-profit organisation (see Ball, 1999, 2000b, 2001a; Ball, Kobrak and Spirer, 1999; Ball and Chapman, 2001; Ball et al., 1994, 2002a; Ball, Spirer and Spirer, 2000).

The Program also made major contributions to developing methodologies and resources for monitoring economic, social and cultural rights based on a "violations approach". It thereby played an important bridging role between social scientists, statisticians, and the human rights community. In 1996, the Program, together with the Human Rights Information and Documentation Systems International (HURIDOCS), initiated a project that led to the online and print publications of the *Thesaurus of Economic, Social and Cultural Rights*. This reference resource organises and classifies the rights – as defined in the *International Covenant on Economic, Social and Cultural Rights* – and provides a standardised and uniform vocabulary to identify and document violations. It therefore constitutes a first step in the development of a coherent monitoring system (see AAAS and HURIDOCS, 2002; Chapman and Russell, 2002; Chapman, 2005b).

A growing measurement trend

Though the reluctance of human rights practitioners and statisticians to involve quantitative methods in assessing human rights and democratic governance has not totally disappeared yet, it started to decline in concomitance with a growing demand for a more rigorous benchmarking and monitoring of public policies and programmes.

In the international scene, the launching of the *Human Development Report* within the UNDP gave impetus, in the 1990s, to a worldwide debate on how to conduct systematic evidence-based assessment of the human dimensions of development. This debate showed that the main interest of measuring human development is to inform democratic dialogue and enhance the accountability of governmental authorities. It is not a case of fortuity if the 2000 and 2002 editions of the Report focused on *Human Rights and Human Development* and *Deepening Democracy in a Fragmented World* (UNDP, 2000, 2002).

Following the path opened by the *Human Development Report*, the measurement trend has shaped the design of major UN initiatives and policies – and is now being articulated around the monitoring of progress towards the Millennium Development Goals, defined in terms of quantified targets. In this context, national and international policy makers progressively discovered the centrality of assessing governance and participatory democracy as key factors for the success of development policies and, in particular, for an effective and efficient implementation of programmes aimed at eradicating poverty.

Whilst since the mid-1990s there has been little progress in the development of human rights indicators as such, over the same period, a plethora of indicators have emerged, aimed to measure, from an international perspective, issues like governance performance or corruption. These new measurement tools respond to a demand from more and more diversified actors. Indeed, information on the quality of governance has become a critical issue not only in the field of development policy and international aid but also in the areas of foreign investment and country risk analysis. Thus many indicators, mostly based on expert pools or "well informed persons", have progressively been developed to address this need for information. The World Bank Institute, Transparency International, the ODI project on *World Governance Assessments*, as well as many other international initiatives have engaged in this way (see for instance Kaufmann, Kraay and Zoido-Lobaton, 1999a, 1999b, 2000, 2001, 2002; Kaufmann, Kraay and Mastruzzi, 2004, 2005, 2006a, 2007a; Transparency International, 2007a, 2008a; Hyden *et al.*, 2007; Court, Hyden and Mease, 2002a, 2002b, 2003a).

A debate has emerged around the use and limits of such indicators. Aimed to provide data at a country level on the quality of governance, they are essentially being produced and used by external actors such as international agencies, bilateral donors, investors, or academic researchers from the global North. More and more, these indicators tend to feed discussions related, not to the improvement or deterioration of quality of governance and its causes, but rather to comparisons and ranking between countries. Thus, their scope and usefulness, especially for the countries being monitored, has been questioned.

A number of methodological critiques have been raised regarding, in particular, the aggregate governance indicators produced by the World Bank Institute under the direction of Daniel Kaufmann. Concerns relate to the robustness and validity of such indicators due, among other factors, to potential construction biases and errors, lack of methodological transparency or problematic comparisons overtime. Kaufmann and fellows have duly responded to these critiques, but the debate remains open (see Arndt and Oman, 2006; Knack, 2006; Kurtz and Shrank, 2007; Thomas, 2007; and the response by Kaufmann, Kraay and Mastruzzi, 2007).

As a matter of fact, the quality and reliability of existing governance indicators have rarely been subject to systematic external assessments. The methodologies sustaining their construction and in particular the sampling or purposive selection of their panels of respondents are often opaque. In spite of all this, many of these indicators are becoming authoritative sources both for the media and for international policy makers. Whether statisticians or social scientists like it or not, these indicators are *de facto* filling an information gap, which is due to the absence of reliable data and robust technical methods for measuring the quality of governance, including its democracy and human rights dimensions.

This is one of the main challenges that, by the end of the 1990s, motivated a number of senior official statisticians, analysts and policy actors to organise an international conference aimed at promoting the involvement of sound statistical expertise in the development and improvement of indicators on governance, democracy and human rights. They considered that such a conference had to relate to national development issues rather than to reporting needs of international or supranational agencies. They shared the conviction that measurement tools should not primarily serve purposes of international comparison, but rather focus on national policy concerns and further measure effective national progress towards the realisation of rights, better governance and a participatory democracy.

The boost of Montreux

The International Conference on *Statistics, Development and Human Rights* – held in Montreux, Switzerland, on 4-8 September 2000 – was organised under the aegis of the International Association for Official Statistics, a specialised branch of the International Statistical Institute, the largest and most authoritative scientific organisation worldwide in the field of statistics. The Conference was jointly convened and supported by two Swiss federal agencies: the Development and Co-operation Agency and the Federal Statistical Office.

The Montreux Conference was attended by more than 700 people from 123 countries, 37 international organisations and many non-governmental organisations. The universal scope and centrality of its theme was attested by vigorous political messages delivered by the UN High Commissioner for Human Rights, several heads of UN agencies, European Commissioners, national ministers and keynote speakers such as Awa Quedraogo, Thomas Hammarberg, Michael Ward and Carlos Jarque. The shared North/South interest in the substantive programme was reflected by an unexpected number of technical and scientific contributions – more than 300 invited or contributed papers, half of them submitted by experts from developing countries.

The Conference consisted of 5 intensive working days including 9 plenary sessions, 20 parallel invited paper sessions, and 25 parallel contributed paper sessions (see IAOS 2000). Its programme covered seven main substantive areas:

- fundamental issues and challenges, and emerging measurement methods;
- measuring and assessing civil and political rights;
- statistics, human rights and population issues, including consequences of war;
- human development and economic and social rights, including the policy impact of indicators and the monitoring of public programmes;
- measuring and monitoring the rights of the child;
- official statistics within the democratic process, including uses and misuses of statistical data;
- human rights and official statistical policies, including challenges of political, economic and social reforms; the promotion of human rights within programmes of international statistical co-operation; and the role, capacities and duties of the international statistical system in relation with the monitoring of human rights.

For the first time, the Conference allowed qualified representatives of three international communities – human rights practitioners, statisticians and development experts – to gather together and share expectations, experiences and views on why and how to develop evidence-based assessment and monitoring. The debates showed that human rights defenders are best positioned to know that, when faced with widespread human rights issues or massive violations, a proper estimation of the scope and magnitude of the problem is of greater value than any other kind of consideration. The problem – in particular in the case of violations – is that in most countries measuring human rights is discouraged by a dramatic lack of reliable information.

Several speakers highlighted that the information provided by human rights monitoring mechanisms mostly focuses on individual cases of violations. While an individual case – or series of individual cases – can be emblematic of a situation of general infringement of human rights, it does not allow to grasp the true dimension of the problem, how it emerges and expands, or whether the situation is deteriorating, stable or improving. In other words, information captured through existing monitoring mechanisms often fails to help formulate policy proposals in terms of corrective plans and redressing measures.

The Conference allowed statisticians, human rights practitioners and development experts to establish common grounds on possible contributions of well-established statistical methods and tools – such as sampling survey approaches or use of administrative statistical data – for improving estimates on the dimension and impact of human rights issues. Through the many case studies and conceptual approaches discussed during the Conference, it became clear that proper measurement of human rights and democracy issues, complemented by equally proper qualitative work, can effectively empower the work of human rights practitioners and development experts.

The Conference, convened under the umbrella of a non-governmental organisation, the IAOS, had neither the mandate nor the appropriate procedures for adopting official conclusions. Nevertheless, during the Conference, the Chairpersons of the various sessions hold several meetings to identify the main issues and trends emerging from the debates. Their general impression was that the Conference confirmed the enormous potential of statistical information and methods for reinforcing the monitoring of human development, human rights and related governance issues. They observed that the exchanges among statisticians, development experts, and human rights practitioners opened many perspectives and raised high expectations for future co-operational work. They therefore requested that the results of the Conference be formulated "*in the perspective of future action*".

A synthesis of the Chairpersons' views was therefore drawn by the co-directors of the Conference project, Carol Mottet and Raul Suarez de Miguel. This synthesis was presented and commented by Carlo Malaguerra at the closing session. It highlighted **ten operational *Conclusions*** based on "*the major lines of action, which, at the end of the Conference, seem to be the subject of a general consensus between the experts in the fields of statistics, development and human rights*":

(1) **Multidisciplinary approach:** attendants were unanimous in considering that this peculiar characteristic of the Conference had to be further enriched and deepened. "*A wide variety of scientific and professional skills are needed to address the complexity of the problems that we have to examine, and to produce the information needed for enhancing development policies and the promotion of human rights.*" Debates showed that the diverse professional communities had many shared reasons and common expectations for measuring human rights and democratic governance – but it was noticed that, to be effective, multidisciplinary work requires "*a basic conceptual framework agreed by the experts in the various fields*".

(2) **Professionalism:** the Conference demonstrated the need for increased use of well-established professional techniques in the assessment and analysis of human rights and development issues. "*There is considerable need for more effective quantitative methods and analytical tools. Special attention has to be paid to the enhancement of scientific rigour and impartiality of observation and measuring instruments.*"

Box 1.2. **A founding event: the IAOS international Conference on**
Statistics, Development and Human Rights
(Montreux, Switzerland, 4-8 September 2000)

"The subject of your work here (…) is nothing less than a quest for a science of human dignity. This is a vital endeavour. When the target is human suffering, and the cause human rights, mere rhetoric is not adequate to the task at hand. What are needed are solid methodologies, careful techniques, and effective mechanisms to get the job done."

Mrs. Mary Robinson
Then UN High Commissioner for Human Rights
(Opening address; see IAOS, 2000)

---

(3) **Partnership between experts in the fields of statistics, development and human rights:** the Conference revealed a unanimous will to build "*a genuine partnership*" for designing and implementing future action. "*We should work together to identify and select existing information, as well as to assess it for its pertinence and quality. We should work together for a better definition of the appropriate expertise in the context of tangible projects (…) We should work together for the development of indicators, methods and analysis tools.*"

(4) **Role of National Statistical Offices (NSOs):** the Conference marked a historical step within the international statistical community, as attendants strongly called for an effective "*integration of the human rights dimension (…) in the conception and implementation of the information policies of NSOs. Certainly, NSOs do not have to produce all relevant information and analysis on human rights issues. They can, nevertheless, on the one hand better orient the existing sectoral statistics (…) to inform policies related to human rights and, on the other hand, they can provide expertise and technical support to scientific institutions and NGOs*" (see Box 1.4).

(5) **Proper use of statistical information and methods** by governmental organisations, independent institutions and NGOs in charge of development policies and human rights: this was emphasised not only by attendants from NGOs, but also by the representatives of national Human Rights Institutions and by members of parliaments. "*Statisticians should commit themselves with determination to the development of support services and the provision of statistical expertise to NGOs and national Human Rights Institutions.*"

(6) **Building an operational network:** attendants considered that, in the aftermath of the fruitful exchanges during the Conference, further action should aim to develop operationally-oriented ties of co-operation between statisticians, development experts, human rights practitioners and policy actors. "*An international network has just been born in Montreux: it must now be nourished and allowed to grow. (…) Exchanges of knowledge, experience and professional expertise must be pursued.*"

(7) **Conceptual basis and frameworks for building indicators:** the *Conclusions* stressed the need for further substantive work on "*the improvement of the definitions and methods enabling relevant measurement of human rights and governance*" as well as for "*a review of the basic statistics, definitions and methods on which development indicators are built.*" In this regard, it was noticed "*with insistence*" that "*ranking countries according to progress measured by development indicators, carries risks of abusive extrapolation and misinterpretation. (…) International comparison of development achievements must deal with situations that are genuinely comparable. (…) Comparative approaches at the regional level should be preferred, focusing on groups of countries that are experiencing similar situations, cultural contexts and development problems.*"

(8) **Enhancement of national statistical capacities:** "*the reinforcement of statistical capacities of developing countries constitutes a prior and unavoidable condition for more rigorous observation of progress in terms of development and human rights. There are therefore grounds for building responsible partnerships with the most underprivileged countries. (…) International co-operation (…) should aim not only at supporting the transfer of professional know-how (…) but also at promoting the institutional development of public statistics that are impartial and at the service of society as a whole.*"

(9) **Integrity and quality of statistical work:** while these are fundamental principles that apply to any statistical professional work, they are of most critical importance when this work aims to enhance assessments of development processes, human rights issues or progress in democratic governance. "*This statistical work should be supervised by independent bodies (…) What is important here is (…) the respect for the principle of scientific transparency.*"

(10) **International co-ordination of initiatives and projects** aimed at establishing indicators and measurement tools in the fields of development, human rights and governance: attendants were unanimous in considering this as an urgent need. Effective co-ordination "*should be built on a light mechanism (…) under an institutional umbrella that is universal, solid and respected. (…) The international institutions in charge of development policies and the promotion of human rights should consult more together on the orientation and priorities of their work.*" In this context, it was stressed that "*it is the duty of the specialists, and the statisticians in particular, to assume the leadership and full responsibility for the organization and implementation of the tasks relating to the development of definitions, methods and information bases, as well as for the co-ordination and consolidation of indicators and measurement instruments.*"

Setting the basis for concrete action

The *Conclusions* noted "*the general voice of the participants calling for a serious follow-up and for the implementation of tangible actions*", as well as the interest of most relevant international institutions in "*setting up a common consultation framework for ensuring such a follow-up*". Thus the Conference organisers committed to inform the relevant UN bodies and the International Statistical Institute on the perspectives opened in Montreux, and to convene a consultative meeting, gathering international organisations active in the fields of statistics, development and human rights, as well as leading national institutions willing to engage in the follow-up to the work initiated in Montreux.

Box 1.3. **Opening the window of official statistics**

"There were three noteworthy respects in which this Conference has, I believe, changed the terrain of how official statistics relates to other kinds of statistics produced by other kinds of agencies. This has advanced both our understanding and our prospects for contributing to informed and constructive action."

"Firstly, it has constituted a bridge across what was previously a divide. It has become clear that in our statistical work we may be placed along a spectrum *of institutions*, rather than in a series of discrete boxes: a spectrum that extends from the official data productions of the government agencies to the inventive databases of the NGOs, with the policy institutes providing further analyses of the data coming to hand from each side."

"Secondly, we are all alike in moving back and forth as the purpose requires to move along a spectrum of *method and methodology*, from participative to qualitative to quantitative. In the design of a census questionnaire, no less than in that of a questionnaire for human rights infractions, we now know to begin not in the mind of the enquirer but in that of the respondent. Thereafter, we must apply the best techniques we have at hand, whatever the context, in order to move the data through analysis to what it can reveal to the users, and preferably also to the respondents."

"Thirdly, there is the continuity in the span of the *subject matter*, so well captured in the title of the Conference: *Statistics, Development and Human Rights*. Through appropriate institutions and methods we must expect to collaborate along a spectrum, from the capturing of human rights violations in all their diversity and combination - against women, or ethnic groups, or indigenous populations, or forced migrants, or religions, or children - to measuring progress regarding democratization and human rights, to selecting indicators of socio-economic development, and (hopefully) finally to assessing evidence of progress towards a clean environment and a peaceful world. If official statistics, in its service to the public and their representatives, cannot itself span the range, then it has the obligation to make and seek to improve the necessary partnerships; and this Conference has helped to open the possibilities and the prospects."

Dr. Mark Orkin
(then CEO of the Human Sciences Research Council of South Africa
and former Director General of Statistics South Africa)
Concluding address to the Montreux 2000 Conference on *Statistics, Development and Human Rights*
(see Orkin, 2000)

The results of the Conference were presented by Switzerland to the UN Statistical Commission at its 32nd session (2001). They were further examined by the "Friends of the Chair" of this Commission in the framework of a general assessment of the existing and new statistical work needed to produce the statistical indicators requested by several UN Summit Meetings. A report of this high level group considered that the perspectives opened by Montreux merited being explored further. It recommended that an informal mechanism be created, involving statisticians and policy actors, to establish the basis for and give impetus to the development of statistical indicators of human rights and governance. This recommendation was endorsed by the UN Statistical Commission (see Box 1.4).

Also, in March 2001, Switzerland convened an open-ended consultation meeting in the UNO headquarters in New York. It was attended by representatives of numerous international organisations and the European Commission, members of the UN Statistical Commission and several key national actors of Montreux. This meeting confirmed a shared strong interest for a tangible follow-up to the Conference, and provided guidance on the steps to be taken. It was recommended that an international project be designed and launched outside the UN institutional framework, in an appropriate environment allowing for voluntary-based commitment, effective North/South partnership, free multidisciplinary research and flexibility in the organisation of field, analytical and reporting work.

The momentum generated by the Conference was echoed by initiatives of highly motivated institutions and personalities around the world – for instance, several surveys on poverty and democratic governance issues, carried out by National Statistical Offices in Francophone Africa, with the scientific and technical assistance of DIAL, or a publication of the UN Economic Commission for Europe on *Measuring Human Rights* (Garonna ed., 2001). These initiatives contributed to convince the European Commission and Switzerland to support the organisation of a series of workshops and consultations aimed at deepening the *Conclusions* of the Conference and formulating objectives and plans for the post-Montreux project.

An EU workshop on *Measuring Governance*, organised by InWent, was held in Munich in January 2002. The Mexican National Commission for Human Rights convened an international seminar on *Indicators and Diagnosis on Human Rights*, with particular focus on the case of torture, held in Merida in April 2002. And a second EU workshop, focusing on *Measuring Human Rights*, was then held in Brussels in November 2002.

Box 1.4. **UN report echoes the *Conclusions* of Montreux …**

At the request of the UN Economic and Social Council (ECOSOC), in 2001 a group of "Friends of the Chair" of the UN Statistical Commission, under the leadership of Tim Holt, drafted and submitted for worldwide consultation a comprehensive report on **An Assessment of the Statistical Indicators derived from United Nations Summit Meetings.** This report was endorsed by the Commission at its 33rd session (5-8 March 2002). It stated and recommended the following:

"Identifying statistical indicators for monitoring purposes is neither a pure policy nor a pure statistical issue. The basic expression of the policy goal must drive the monitoring requirement, but turning that expression into a statistical indicator that will be relevant, reliable and acceptable to the various stakeholders is a statistical function. The tension between the policy view of what is needed and the statistical view of what is feasible and technically sound should be resolved by joint determination (…).

"Relevance is a dominating requirement of statistical information. If statistics are not relevant to the policy need, they will not command the attention, nor have the impact that they should. In particular, failure to meet national needs will undermine the requirement to develop sustainable statistical capacity (…) It will also undermine evidence-based policy as a basis for good governance and public administration within countries. From the United Nations perspective, that would as a result undermine the provision of statistical indicators for international monitoring purposes (…).

"The development of statistical indicators for human rights and good governance will not be easy and will take time. We recommend that the [UN Statistical] Commission establish a mechanism (…) involving statisticians and others, including policy officials, to develop statistical indicators of human rights and good governance. Whatever is established needs to take account of existing initiatives in the field, in particular of follow-up activities to the IAOS Conference held in Montreux, Switzerland (…). Although we recognize the importance of this area, we take the view that it would be better to "get it right" rather than "get it quick", if widespread ownership of the indicators is to be established around the world." (UN-ECOSOC, 2002, pp. 8 and 16, paras. 17, 20 and 65).

> **Box 1.5. ... the World Bank Institute highlights the importance of nationally-based indicators...**
>
> The 2005 report of the World Bank Institute on "Governance matters" stressed that: "while... aggregate governance indicators have been useful in providing a general snapshot of the countries of the world for various broad components of governance, now for 8 years, and while the margins of error have declined over time, they remain a rather blunt instrument for specific policy advice at the country level. As we have argued in the past, these aggregate indicators need to be complemented with in-depth in-country governance diagnosis, based on micro-surveys of households, firms and public officials within the country. The lessons being drawn from these combined aggregate and micro-data sets do point to the importance of moving concretely to the next stage of governance reforms, in Africa and elsewhere. These, among others, are to stress reforms in transparency (such as natural resource revenue transparency mechanisms, disclosure of assets to politicians, voting records of parliamentarians, political campaign contributions, and fiscal accounts), in altering incentives in institutions so to increasingly focus on prevention and deterrence (rather than overly relying on prosecutions), and in working more closely with other actors outside the public sector as well, such as the therefore neglected private sector" (Kaufmann, Kraay and Mastruzzi, 2005, p. 41).

This process allowed to gather expertise and mature proposals. It led to the creation of a post-Montreux Task Force, which was requested to draft an outline and a tentative budget for a project to be submitted for grant to various donor institutions. The European Commission and the members of the Task Force requested the Swiss Federal Statistical Office to act as a facilitator of this work. The Task Force held several meetings and exchanged many notes and working documents to give form and content to an ambitious project. An important part of its work consisted in establishing an agreed framework and defining a project approach that truly encompassed the concerns, lines of action and expectations highlighted in the Conference *Conclusions*.

First mapping of relevant initiatives

As part of the Montreux follow-up process, Eurostat, the Statistical Office of the European Community, took two determinant steps: first, it gave mandate to the Human Rights Centre of the University of Essex to conduct a broad map-making and analysis of the main international initiatives aimed to develop indicators on democracy and good governance; and, second, it conducted jointly with the UNDP Oslo Governance Centre a first review of existing sources for governance indicators.

The map-making of Essex, conducted by Todd Landman and Julia Häussermann, revealed the existence of *"over 170 initiatives having served as seminal efforts to measure democracy, human rights, and good governance. Of all of the reviewed initiatives, 45 have developed methodologies or indicators that have stood the test of time, are used frequently in empirical studies and policy documents, are updated regularly or are cited as examples of best practices."* The Essex report concentrated its analysis on 12 "key initiatives" which have wide geographical and temporal coverage, and highlighted their methodological strengths and weaknesses in terms of validity, reliability, measurement bias, lack of transparency, representativeness, variance truncation, information bias and aggregation problems (see Landman and Häusermann, 2003).

The Eurostat/UNDP *Users' Guide on Governance Indicators*, established by Matthew Sudders and Joachim Nahem, aimed to *"equip users with the wherewithal to make sensible use of sources of governance indicators"*. As Pieter Everaers and Georges Nzongola-Ntalaja stressed in the Foreword, this publication reflects the strong commitment of the European Commission and the UNDP *"to place Governance at the heart of our programmes"* and to respond to the *"increasing demand to measure various aspects of democracy, human rights and governance (…). There are other overviews on governance indicators, but this is the first publication that brings together 'how to use' and 'where to find' material on these sources."*

This first edition of the *Users' Guide* provided detailed information on 33 sources of governance indicators. Just as the map-making of Essex, it concentrates on indicators with a wide geographical scope that *"enable cross-national coverage"*. For each source, it describes the main characteristics, type of data used, geographical and time coverage, methodology and format of results. It also explains potential valid and invalid uses of these indicators, describes their underlying assumptions and, when it applies, their structural or technical weaknesses (see Eurostat and UNDP, 2004; UNDP, 2007).

Box 1.6. … and a key NGO engages in measuring economic and social rights.

"Developing rigorous monitoring tools has been a persistent challenge for human rights NGOs working on economic and social rights. Since most of these rights depend in varying degrees on the availability of resources, a monitoring methodology must take into account notions of resource availability and "progressive realization" (State's continuous obligation to move as expeditiously as possible towards the full realization of these rights). Such a monitoring mechanism requires quantitative research tools – typically not part of the research toolkit of human rights organizations, which were originally developed to monitor civil and political rights. (…)

"The Centre for Economic and Social Rights (CESR) will monitor the multiple dimensions of governments' obligations pertaining to economic and social rights, focusing in particular on economic and social rights violations that can be identified and critically assessed only using socio-economic tools and quantitative methods. The most obvious cases for which such tools are required are those related to the availability of resources. (…) These tools are also necessary in order to analyze discriminatory policies related to resource allocations (as opposed to discriminatory laws, or lack of enforcement of laws). For example, CESR will conduct budget analyses and use indicators disaggregated by race, ethnicity or gender in order to gauge the extent to which large disparities among groups within a country, in education and health outcomes (child mortality, enrolment in primary education, etc.), may be the result of (or exacerbated by) discriminatory policies in public social spending.

"The unique power of this strategy will be in the combination of methods and strategies. While an economic analysis of quantitative data can provide objective validity to claims that often the problem is not resource availability but rather resource distribution, the rich, normative categories of a human rights framework – of individual dignity and government accountability – can provide a powerful ethical, legal and political tool to criticize these policies. And while statistics show the scope of a human rights problem, CESR will use the testimonies of individuals show the real impact of those problems on people's lives.

"CESR will undertake several projects that will serve both as pilot projects for testing the potential of CESR's new methodology and as a platform for engaging in concrete advocacy work. A crucial element of the overall strategy will be to work whenever possible in collaborative projects with local NGOs. "

Centre for Economic and Social Rights
A New Approach to Measure and Advocate for Economic and Social Rights
December 2005

Dealing with a variety of dimensions and approaches

The findings of the map-making of Essex and the *Users' Guide*, together with the information gathered through the communications submitted to the Montreux Conference, showed that "measuring democracy, human rights and governance" embodies a variety of dimensions and approaches, and is being implemented by a wide range of national and international institutions and NGOs. Thus the post-Montreux Task Force tried to explore if and how such diverse dimensions and approaches could be integrated within a coherent framework.

In this context, a first basic question arose: what do indicators and assessments of human rights and democratic governance intend to measure? Democracy, human rights and governance issues can be considered as three overlapping themes, each containing its own various sub-themes. Human rights range from civil and political to economic, social, cultural and environmental rights. As for defining concepts of governance and democracy, a large number of criteria need to be taken into consideration, such as participation, transparency, responsibility, the rule of law, effectiveness and equity – to mention just a few. "Democratic governance" itself is a broad, inclusive, multi-dimensional concept, which *per se* suggests that evidence-based assessment can neither be conducted with a single approach, nor with a unique tool.

Substantive analysis and discussions led the Task Force to consider that the work of "measuring democracy, human rights and governance" should be considered and tackled with a multi-level approach.

Indeed measurement attempts vary depending on the *nature* of the human rights, democracy or governance issues that are being focused upon – such as economic or political rights or the extent of corruption; the *geographical level* at which these are being considered – ranging from local through national to global; and the *type of data* employed, with their respective characteristic methodologies.

For purposes of comparing and discussing the features of different attempts to develop evidence-based assessment of human rights and democratic, it may be useful to conceive a three-dimensional graph using axes related to (see Figure 1.1):

Figure 1.1. **A variety of measurement approaches depending on the nature, scope and method**

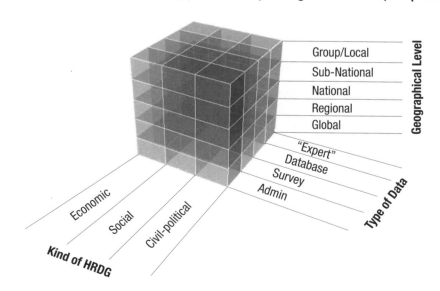

- the nature of the human rights or democratic governance issues that are being focused upon – thus a conceptual axis;
- the scope of the assessments – thus a geographical axis; and
- the type of data employed – thus a technical/methodological axis.

The graph – known as "Mark's Cube" – illustrates how particular measurement initiatives or projects may be approximated to occupying a specific cell – or more – of the cube. The spectrum along each side of the cube may be amenable to more than one interpretation. The spectrum of *data types* basically extends from what may be termed "objective" and usually "quantitative data" at one end to "subjective" and usually "qualitative data" at the other. The spectrum of *geographic levels* tends to coincide, on the local end, with potentially contextual conceptions of rights of various social groups; and, on the global end, with universal rights which can be regarded, in given contexts, as too abstract by local actors. As for the spectrum of *rights*, first generation rights covering civil and political issues tend to be located at one end, whereas second and third generation rights, which cover economic and social aspects of human rights and democratic governance, are situated at the other end.

Of course, the graph should not be over-interpreted. First, a particular measurement exercise may span much of one side of the cube. Second, the conceptions mentioned, and their arrangement along the sides of the cube, may be defined differently by users. Third, other dimensions, or additional interpretations of the three existing dimensions, could be introduced. For instance, cultural and environmental rights could be added to the axis "kind of HRDG". Also, the *kind of organisation* involved in a given project could be contemplated: National Statistical Offices, academic or research institutes, NGOs or even private firms. Similarly, other criteria could be included, such as the origin of the data – depending, for instance, on whether it derives from statistical surveys or administrative registers. However, provided one bears these reservations in mind, Mark's Cube may be of assistance in considering along which dimension it may be relevant to expand a monitoring project; or in identifying what additional studies should be identified or carried out to fill gaps.

The post-Montreux Task Force agreed that the diverse categories of information described above require distinct sets of tools and methodological approaches. Thus, whilst taking into account the limits or weaknesses of given approaches and tools – for instance, the top-down approach of international indicators –it considered important to highlight the principle of complementarity between the various approaches, as well as their potential to be combined. Moreover, the Task Force realised that to deal correctly and properly with such a large variety of dimensions and approaches to measuring human rights and democratic governance, long-lasting work should aim to constitute a well-filled **measurement toolbox** including a variety of proper, reliable and efficient methods and instruments, adapted to the diversity of themes, situations and dynamics under study.

A determinant factor: who conducts the assessments?

With such a framework and development perspective in mind, the Task Force had to define the specific approach that a post-Montreux project could take to effectively contribute to further the progress of evidence-based assessment methods in the fields of human rights and democratic governance. It was obvious that this specific approach should be based on one of the main novelties emerging from the Montreux Conference: the discovery that many measurement initiatives, conducted by domestic actors and focusing on domestic policy issues, are rising at the local and national levels.

The Task Force noted that the nature and specific situation of the actors who conduct human rights and democratic governance assessments are determinant with regard to the approaches, scopes and purposes of these assessments. The nature and main characteristics of the assessment process itself will largely depend on who is in the driving seat. Obviously, the methods, focus and policy targets of the assessments will differ based on whether they are conducted by international agencies and external experts, or by domestic experts, stakeholders, NGOs and research centres.

In this respect, it is worth noting that overviews of human rights and governance assessment approaches generally concentrate on work undertaken by international organisations and American or European research programmes, independent foundations, foreign ministries or development agencies – and not on local or national actors. Even in very recent overviews, initiatives conducted at the national and local levels by domestic actors – including those presented in this publication – are referred to as work conducted by international organisations (see for instance the overview of ODI, 2007; and Hyden *et al.*, 2008). This reveals a somewhat preoccupying commonplace: in general, it is taken for granted that assessments conducted by national actors in the Southern hemisphere can be serious and significant only if guided by international organisations or by tutors from the global North.

Unfortunately, such a commonplace still prevails in on-going discussions on so-called "donor approaches to governance assessment" – that is to say, assessments conducted by foreign ministries and development agencies of industrialised countries such as, for instance, the USAID *Democracy and Governance Assessment Framework*, the *Strategic Governance and Corruption Assessments* of the Ministry of Foreign Affairs of the Netherlands and the DFID *Country Governance Assessments* (United Kingdom). This kind of assessment is essentially intended to inform the allocation of funds (conditionality of aid), identify needs and priorities for action and, in some cases, evaluate the impact of development aid.

A recent survey documented not less than 38 different donor-driven governance assessments (see OECD, 2008). While based on different methods, these assessments have fundamental common characteristics: they are carried out by international experts and are intended to respond to internal programming needs of development agencies, as well as to accountability obligations of the latter in relation to their political authorities, parliaments and taxpayers. In other words, these assessments primarily respond to donor institutions' own needs, rather than to national priorities or issues of concern to the people in the countries being assessed. Sometimes opaque or inaccessible, such assessments are not generally shared nor trusted by the experts, authorities or citizens of the countries being assessed. Thus they have little or no influence in national policy-making processes.

Having said that, multilateral and bilateral donor institutions have pushed for further involvement of domestic NGOs, research centres and other civil society actors in a particular form of assessment: they have been pressuring civil society actors to measure and evaluate the impact of their own work in the field. In many cases, this has actually become an explicit or implicit precondition for obtaining further financial support. Thus, NGOs receiving grants – as well as NGOs aspiring to be granted – have gradually internalised impact assessment into their project cycles in order to show how well their work is running and how much effective impact it has had on foreseen targets (see Raine, 2006).

The scope and effects of these externally requested assessments are quite limited. While considerable efforts have been invested in the development of conceptual frameworks and methods for assessing "human rights impact" and the effect on governance of projects supported by international aid – for instance by Aim for Human Rights, formerly named HOM-Netherlands – there are many political and methodological issues relating to the whole impact assessment approach (see NORAD, 2001; Radstaake, 2001, 2002; Andreasen and Sano, 2004; Hunt and MacNaughton, 2006; HRIRC, 2008).

In the last years, several domestic Human Rights Institutions, NGOs and academic research centres have decided, by themselves, to engage in assessments of human rights and democratic governance issues relating to specific situations, institutions, policies or population groups. For instance, a mapping of national and local initiatives aimed at measuring corruption and governance in Latin America revealed the existence of close to 100 tools in 17 countries (see Transparency International and UNDP, 2006). The increase in efforts, at the local and national levels, to collect data to produce more robust human rights and governance assessments have been confirmed by a Metagora worldwide survey (see *Chapter 9*).

The main reasons domestic stakeholders and experts have undertaken democratic governance assessments are: the need to empower their policy or advocacy work; their will to effectively influence the policy-making process; and, ultimately, their commitment to improve the present state of affairs. This is the kind of assessment process that has been at the centre of the discussions held in 2002 and 2003 in the post-Montreux workshops and Task Force meetings. In line with the *Conclusions* of Montreux, and anticipating the principles that were later formulated by the *Paris Declaration on Aid Effectiveness* (see OECD, 2005), the Task Force concluded that the post-Montreux project had to focus on these local and national efforts and commitment. It therefore adopted a bottom-up approach aimed to further develop:

- **true ownership** of measurement and analysis processes and tools by domestic stakeholders and experts;
- **genuine domestic leadership** of the field and policy work which sustain the measurement and assessment processes;
- **broad participation** of a wide range of national actors in the identification of issues to be measured and policy targets to be reached;
- **effective policy-orientation** of the measurement and analysis processes; and,
- **strong commitment** by domestic actors to use evidence-based assessments to impact on policies, influence decision-making processes and contribute to improve the human rights and democratic governance issues at stake.

Building on nationally-based pilot experiences

The Task Force therefore opted for a project outline with two main elements: first, the development and production of resources aimed at increasing knowledge and exchanges of experiences on nationally-based assessments; and, second, a set of national pilot experiences aimed at testing applications of well-established statistical tools to the measurement of human rights and democratic governance. It was decided that the main contribution of this post-Montreux project should consist in verifying and deepening the Conference *Conclusions* and on formulating general lessons based on the processes and results of these empirical pilot experiences.

Several organisations from different regions of the world – including independent research centres, Human Rights Institutions and National Statistical Offices – offered to take the lead of specific pilot experiences in their respective countries and regions. They presented detailed descriptions of planned activities, foreseen domestic partners and experts, and related provisional budgets. A general project outline was then agreed by the Task Force and submitted for grant to several donor institutions. At the request of the European Commission, this outline was reviewed at a Strategic Workshop, held in Paris in May 2003, which gathered together all foreseen project partners. Thanks to positive and generous reactions of a few donors, the post-Montreux project – Metagora – was launched in February 2004.

Chapter 2

Metagora: a Decentralised Laboratory

Metagora is an international project focusing on methods, tools and frameworks for measuring human rights and democratic governance. It was launched in February 2004, under the auspices of the OECD/PARIS21, and will conclude its operations in August 2008. Its name results from the association of two Greek words: *meta* and *agora*.

In ancient Greece, the *agora* (αγορα) was an open space, at the core of the city, which served as a meeting ground for various of the citizens' activities: it was the market place, the main social arena and the gathering point of the assembly of the people. For the classical Greeks of the 5th Century BC the *agora* was therefore the centre and the scene of all public affairs – and it became, in the modern political philosophy, a symbol of the participatory grounds of democratic life.

The Greek preposition and prefix *meta-* (μετα) means "after" and "beside" (such as in "metaphysics" or "metanomic") and can have a connotation of "transformation" or "change" (such as in "metamorphosis" or "metabolism"). It can also mean "among" or "with", thus suggesting common action, community or joint participation. In modern languages the prefix *meta-* is also used to mean "about its own category" (such as "metadata", meaning "data about data" in statistics and information sciences; or "metaknowledge" and "metatheory" in epistemology).

The polysemic scope of *meta-agora* intends to highlight the various dimensions of increased critical knowledge, robust analysis and transformational collective action that are today required all over the world to meet – and further build on – the fundamentals of our modern *agora*: the rule of law, the respect for human dignity, effective progressive implementation of social, economic and cultural rights, as well as increased democratic participation and fair, transparent and accountable governance mechanisms.

A strong North/South commitment to an ambitious goal

Metagora's original strategic goal was **to enhance evidence-based assessment and monitoring** of human rights and democratic governance. Its main objective has been to develop robust methods and tools to obtain data and create indicators upon which national policies can be formulated and evaluated.

This chapter was drafted on the basis of substantive contributions and working documents authored by:

Claire Naval, Sylvie Walter, Paul Clare, Thomas Heimgartner and *Raul Suarez de Miguel*

Metagora emerged from a multidisciplinary North/South network of institutions. The project gathered together the expertness of leading organisations and individuals from different continents, including human rights practitioners, political analysts, statisticians and academics. It has been a catalyst of expertise: it identified and documented national and local initiatives aimed at enhancing evidence-based assessment of human rights and democratic governance, and facilitated exchanges and networking among experts involved in these initiatives.

A variety of pilot experiences

To reach its goal, Metagora was designed and implemented as a decentralised laboratory: it was the first international project on measuring human rights and democratic governance to undertake several pilot experiences in different regions of the world in an interactive fashion. These experiences included:

- three pilot surveys on human rights and related governance issues carried out in Mexico City (on abuse and ill-treatment by police forces), in the Philippines (on indigenous peoples' rights) and in South Africa (on the implementation of land reform);
- two multi-country surveys on poverty, democracy and governance issues, progressively implemented by National Statistical Offices in eight capital cities of Francophone Africa (since 2001) and in three countries of the Andean Community (since 2002);
- the development of indicators and a database on the right to education in Palestine;
- the establishment of a *Controlled Vocabulary* allowing NGOs to collect and analyse harmonised data on human rights violations in Sri Lanka (since 2001);
- a worldwide survey on initiatives aimed at enhancing evidence-based assessments of human rights and democratic governance;
- the production of a substantive set of online *Training Materials*, largely based on the various pilots.

These experiences were designed to address sensitive issues and were conducted in complex environments, difficult circumstances and diverse political, social and cultural contexts. Through this purposely selected variety of experiences, Metagora has been proving both the technical feasibility and the political relevance of measuring human rights and democratic governance. These experiences have also allowed Metagora to address crucial monitoring issues, such as proper matching of quantitative and qualitative information.

On the basis of this field work, all Partners involved in the project have been formulating together **significant lessons and recommendations** for further application of the tested methods elsewhere. The Metagora pilot experiences are therefore parts of **a coherent whole**; their implementation has led to common achievements, thus converging in a common attainment of the project's global objectives.

An empirical response to controversial questions

All pilot experiences produced valuable information and had significant policy implications; however, their main interest is actually beyond their specific findings: it relies on the answers that were given to a series of questions – still controversial among statisticians and human rights practitioners – on the **feasibility, relevance and usefulness of measuring human rights and democratic governance with statistical methods and tools.**

Box 2.1. **Metagora: piloting experiences in an interactive fashion**

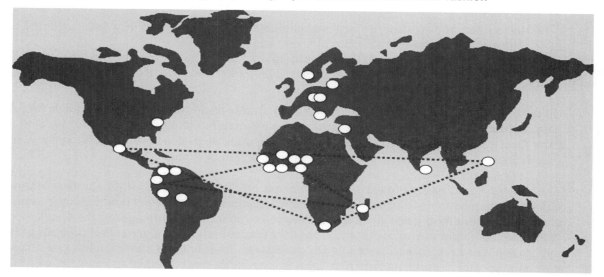

The pilot experiences were intended to address, within a short time frame and with few resources, specific sets of questions. For instance, the three policy-oriented surveys on human rights and democracy issues implemented in Mexico, the Philippines and South Africa (see *Chapters 3, 4* and *5*), specifically addressed the following:

- Can a survey questionnaire target and reflect the multi-dimensional complexity of phenomena like human rights violations, abuses by public authorities or failure of key policies to reach their goals?
- Will sample randomly selected people (who are not necessarily motivated or committed to the issue at stake) accept being interviewed, and respond to sensitive questions?
- Can data collected through a survey questionnaire provide significant information allowing the assessment of human rights and democratic governance issues in terms of accountability of public institutions and political authorities, policy weaknesses and policy needs?
- How can qualitative approaches inform and enrich survey plans and questionnaire design, and how can they interrelate with quantitative approaches for empowering the analysis and interpretation of survey results?

An innovative bottom-up approach

Since its inception Metagora has systematically followed an innovative bottom-up approach aimed at **strengthening national capacities and leadership** in assessing human rights and democratic governance. The originality of Metagora in comparison to other existing international initiatives and projects resides in this particular approach. In each pilot experience, it consisted of:

- the identification, by local stakeholders and experts, of key human rights and democratic governance issues for which evidence-based assessment is highly relevant;
- the measurement and analysis of the selected issues with statistical methods that, combined with qualitative approaches, are adapted to the particular national context;

- the assessment of these methods for their capacity to provide reliable and policy-relevant information;
- the impulse and steering, by local stakeholders, of advocacy and policy dialogue based on the acquired knowledge on the issues at stake; and
- the identification – through the assessment of the processes, results and outcomes of each "local" pilot experience – of methodological lessons that can be of a "global" scope.

On the basis of this bottom-up approach, Metagora has been **addressing national needs for reliable data and indicators**. In line with the principles of ownership and participation formulated in the Paris Declaration, the specific objectives of each pilot experience were defined by domestic stakeholders and the experiences themselves were driven by domestic actors.

The project has broadly proved that such a nationally-owned and nationally-based approach efficiently complements the traditional "top-down approach" of indicators produced by international governmental and non-governmental organisations. Indeed, as pointed out in the *Chapter* 1, while these indicators are useful for international comparison and global overview, they have limited application when it comes to assessing key national issues related to human rights and democratic governance – and in particular when the goal is to enhance monitoring of national policies.

A partnership of leading organisations

Metagora has been managed by a central Co-ordination Team hosted by the OECD/PARIS21 Secretariat based in Paris. Nevertheless its effective implementation relies on a broad and inclusive community of organisations and individuals. The core of this community is formed by representatives and experts of seven organisations that signed Partnership Agreements with the OECD for the implementation of the global, multi-country and national project operations:

- the **American Association for the Advancement of Science**, **AAAS** (Washington);
- **DIAL Centre of the Institute for Development Research** (Paris);
- **Fundar, Centre for Analysis and Research** (Mexico City);
- the **Human Sciences Research Council of South Africa**, **HSRC** (Pretoria);
- the **Palestinian Central Bureau of Statistics**, **PCBS** (Ramallah);
- the **National Commission on Human Rights of the Philippines**, **CHR** (Manila); and
- the **General Secretariat of the Andean Community**, **SG-CAN** (Lima).

The link of Metagora with **The Asia Foundation** project in Sri Lanka was not based on a formal partnership agreement with the OECD; however, The Asia Foundation project team (based in Colombo) and the member organisations of the **Human Rights Accountability Coalition of Sri Lanka** have been considered and treated *de facto* by the Metagora community as fully-fledged key project partners.

All these Partner Organisations are internationally known as authoritative institutions in their respective field of work. They have different skills, organisational profiles, specific missions and particular agendas. Such diversity constituted in itself a major asset for the Metagora community. The Partner Organisations played different roles within the project: four conducted pilot operations and policy-oriented studies in their countries (CHR, Fundar, HSRC and PCBS), two co-ordinated regional multi-country actions (DIAL and SG-CAN), and two provided technical assistance and intellectual services (AAAS and DIAL). All contributed to the project's cross-cutting activities.

Partner Organisations were responsible for the organisation and management of their planned activities. On the basis of the resources provided to them through the project's budget, they recruited

Figure 2.1. **Metagora working structure**

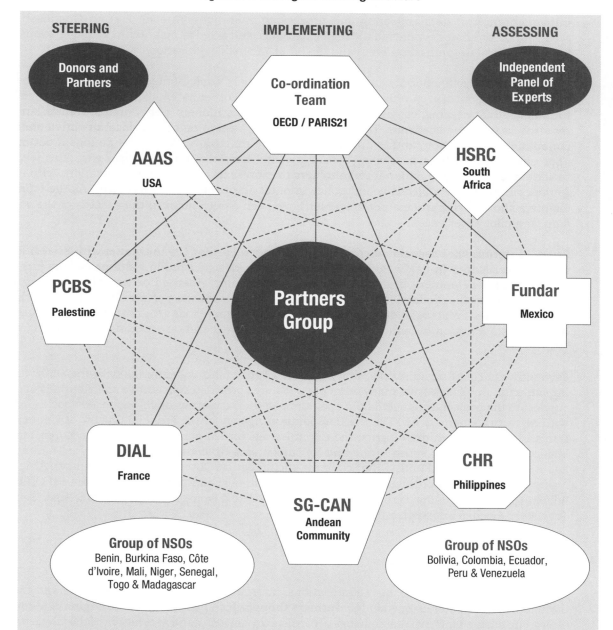

- A light central Co-ordination Team has been in charge of the overall management of the project.
- Seven organisations based in different regions of the world conducted policy-oriented pilot experiences and co-ordinated the work of other national organisations involved in the project.
- The Partners Group gathers together representatives of partner organisations, the Co-ordination Team, and all associated consultants involved in the implementation of the project. It fosters substantive cohesion of the whole project, common orientation of the various activities towards the Metagora goals, as well as cross-fertilisation and interaction among the Partners.
- A Steering Committee gathers together representatives of donor institutions, partner organisations and key international stakeholders.
- An Independent Panel of Experts has been in charge of assessing the implementation of Metagora.

staff and local consultants. They also contracted firms for provision of services – namely for the implementation of data collecting and processing operations. In each Partner Organisation, a Metagora Co-ordinator conducted the pilot experience and acted as an antenna in the relations with both the central Co-ordination Team and the other Partner Organisations.

Partner Organisations not only ensured proper and timely implementation of field operations and analytical work, but also co-ordinated the interventions of other national organisations and led **local multidisciplinary teams,** consisting of human rights practitioners, policy actors, statisticians and researchers from the academia. They mobilised an impressive number of **local qualified staff and consultants.** In addition, and to ensure the genuine materialisation of the Metagora bottom-up approach, they have been developing consultative mechanisms and participatory working methods to allow **a wide range of national stakeholders** to express their views and expectations with regard to the content, scope, objectives and policy orientation of the pilot experiences. As the following chapters show, such participatory processes have been determinant in the success of the various Metagora pilot experiences.

Several **international associated consultants** provided Partner Organisations with scientific and technical assistance in fields like survey questionnaire design, sampling, statistical analysis, data encoding, or development of databases. Some experts implemented or supported cross-cutting activities such as the production of *Training Materials* and the *Inventory of Initiatives*. Others conducted training courses for stakeholders and staff of Partner Organisations, in particular on the use and misuse of statistics on human rights, on building databases and on encoding and using narrative information.

Beyond the circle of organisations that concluded Partnership Agreements with the OECD for the implementation of Metagora, many other organisations provided substantive contributions or *ad hoc* support to the project, conducted field operations in their countries or co-organised specific actions with Metagora – namely ADETEF the Co-operation Agency of the French Ministry of Finance; the Danish Institute for Human Rights; the Commissions for Human Rights of Kenya, Korea, Malawi, Mexico City, Sao Paulo, South Africa and Sri Lanka; as well as the Arab Institute for Training and Research in Statistics, AFRISTAT the Economic and Statistical Observatory of Sub-Saharan Africa, the National Statistical Coordination Board of the Philippines, and the National Statistical Offices of Bolivia, Colombia, Ecuador, Peru, Benin, Burkina Faso, Côte d'Ivoire, Madagascar, Mali, Niger, Senegal, Togo, Italy, Sweden and Switzerland.

A global working structure

Heads and experts of all Partner Organisations, international associated consultants and the Co-ordination Team gathered together in a **Partners Group,** which has been **the true engine of Metagora.** This group ensured internal methodological consistency and substantive cohesion of the whole project. It fostered interaction and mutual support between the various pilot experiences and checked the adequacy of each with overall project objectives. It has drawn global lessons from the pilot experiences and examined and endorsed the materials, tools and products elaborated by the project. Frequent meetings of the Partners Group, in plenary or in *ad hoc* task teams, were devoted to review work in progress and to identify Partners' needs for scientific and technical support. In other words, the structure and dynamics of the Group truly reflected a strong commitment of each Partner Organisation and expert to both the specific objectives of each pilot experience and Metagora global goals.

The two multi-country pilot experiences supported by DIAL in Francophone Africa and in the Andean region were based on existing **institutional mechanisms for regional co-operation: AFRISTAT**, the

Statistical Institute for Francophone Africa, and **the Andean Community**. The Statistical Committees of these institutions, formed by Directors-General of National Statistical Offices, set up specific working frameworks for developing exchanges and collaboration in the field of measuring democratic participation and governance issues.

A **Steering Committee** – first formed by representatives of donor institutions and then extended so as to include representatives of Partner Organisations and selected international stakeholders – closely followed the advancement and results of the project and provided guidance and support to the Co-ordination Team. It examined progress reports, discussed strategic issues and approved proposals for changes in the working programme, as well as re-allocation of funds within the project budget. As a clear mark of its commitment, this Committee will have had no less than nine meetings and two videoconferences from the inception until the conclusion of the project.

An **Independent Panel of Experts** has been in charge of assessing the scientific and technical rigour of project operations and in particular of identifying the strengths and weaknesses of the project. This Panel worked with total independence with regard to both the Metagora implementing structures and the Steering Committee. It delivered in 2005 and 2006 two interim reports, largely based on an in-depth review of the implementation and outcomes of the survey-based pilots. The intermediate findings, conclusions and recommendations of the Independent Panel of Experts were discussed together by the members of the Panel and the entire Partners Group during a Methodological Workshop held in Paris on 29-31 January 2007. In August 2007, the Independent Panel of Experts adopted a general *Assessment report* covering the period February 2004-July 2007 that is enclosed to the present publication as *Appendix 6*.

A common working framework

While Metagora has been operating with largely decentralised working structures, it was implemented within a common working framework. To ensure that all pilot experiences be brought together into a coherent whole and that results be shared and delivered within the planned deadlines, it was crucial that the Metagora community adopt and follow **a common synchronised schedule.** This represented the major operational challenge of the project – and also the most constraining burden for the Partner Organisations and experts involved in the pilot experiences.

Metagora inherited from substantive work carried out prior to the launching of the project, namely in Francophone Africa, Peru and Sri Lanka. In all other pilot experiences, Partner Implementing Organisations succeeded within fourteen months to design, organise and implement all planned field operations. They then produced, reviewed and released results and, finally, drafted and broadly disseminated policy-oriented reports based on these results. The various pilot experiences progressed through **six main phases**:

- **The preparatory work** for each pilot experience included in particular the organisation of local teams; preliminary consultations of relevant institutions, stakeholders and experts; defining the scope and specific objectives of the pilot; and, most importantly, designing surveys, questionnaires and databases.
- **The implementation of field operations** consisted of data collection, processing and statistical analysis, as well as the development of databases.
- **The analysis of results and technical reporting** included a systematic documentation of problems encountered; sharing and analysing of preliminary results with stakeholders; complementing quantitative data with qualitative information; and drawing pilot indicators.

- **The evaluation of the tested methods and the validation and delivery of final results** led to the presentation of the conclusions of the pilot experiences to national stakeholders and to the media, as well as to the production and broad dissemination of policy-oriented reports.
- **The impulse to policy dialogue based on newly acquired knowledge** was given through meetings with governmental authorities and policy actors, recommendations on possible concrete governance improvement and regulatory measures, as well as public advocacy events involving both public authorities and civil society actors.
- **The global synthesis of results and lessons** was drawn by the Metagora Partners Group and is reflected in the present publication (see *Chapter 9*).

A cross-fertilisation process

Throughout the project's above-mentioned phases, Partner Organisations and international associated consultants engaged in sound professional exchanges aimed at ensuring solidity, technical rigour, and policy relevance in each step. They mutually reviewed the design of all survey questionnaires, the sampling plans, the problems encountered in field operations of data collection, the quality of the data gathered, the analytical frames, as well as the consistency and meaningfulness of the results.

Metagora has therefore been a process of cross-fertilisation, mutual learning and mutual support. Cross-fertilisation materialised both at the local level, among domestic experts and practitioners from academic, governmental and non-governmental organisations involved in the pilot experiences and, at the global level, among all Partners and experts contributing to the implementation and assessment of the different phases of the project.

A strong policy impact in the field

The impact of Metagora in the field is tangible. In the various specific national contexts in which the project has been operating, it clearly depicted the nature, magnitude and characteristics of crucial human rights and democratic governance issues. The assessment tools generated by Metagora have therefore shed light on the kind of actions and measures that have to be taken to improve domestic policies and legislation on the issues at stake – and these have become powerful in the hands of human rights champions, committed stakeholders and policy actors.

Metagora has also had an important impact in **interlinking and empowering domestic actors of change.** In a number of countries where pilot experiences were implemented, key institutions and leading people who never met or interacted before, are now working together to inform policy-making with evidence-based assessments and putting the issues at stake on the national political agendas. The policy-oriented reports and the materials generated by the project are creating common ground among national stakeholders and policy makers on the conditions and opportunities for developing robust monitoring tools. Moreover, in some countries, household surveys on poverty, democratic participation and governance issues – conducted by National Statistical Offices – are becoming institutional routine tools and are therefore starting to generate time series that can further serve as a basis for monitoring progress.

A fostering of synergies in the international arena

Over the last four years, Metagora has also been facilitating exchanges among key international actors and playing a role as a catalyst of synergies between on-going and emerging initiatives aimed

Box 2.2. **True ownership and genuine partnership**

"The Montreux 2000 Conference has been remarkable, and unusual, in that the South has assumed its proper place in the share of presentations and participants. (…) Many of us have had the experience of being hastily included at the last minute in international gatherings to provide some geographical spread and legitimacy to what would otherwise have been events at which the North took decisions about what they thought the South really needed. This Conference has been fundamentally different in this regard (…) The consequent range and involvement of participants will ensure that the partnership we shall build in going forward together is a genuine partnership of equal concern and involvement among all the stakeholders".

Dr. Mark Orkin
(then CEO of the Human Sciences Research Council of South Africa)
Concluding address to the Montreux 2000 Conference on *Statistics, Development and Human Rights*
(see IAOS 2000b)

"Donor-driven or international experts-driven governance assessments have well-known limitations and bias. The Metagora community has developed a genuine alternative to the top-down approach that underlies those kinds of assessments. It can be summarised as the BLISS model, consisting of:

B = bottom-up dynamics, canvassing citizens and local stakeholders, who choose the focus;
L = locally-led assessments, based on ownership of tools and participatory processes;
I = inter-institutional working structures, connecting statistical, human rights and research agencies;
S = statistical plus to ensure empirical evidence – while qualitative information is necessary, there is no substitute for the statistical;
S = South-South collaboration, which, as Metagora has proved, constitutes the main way forward.

"True ownership of tools and leadership of projects by domestic stakeholders, and a genuine international partnership in which the South assumes its proper place in the share of responsibilities and efforts: this is what Metagora has been promoting and building – and this is what donors and international organisations can further support, deepen and enhance".

Dr. Mark Orkin
Chairman of the Metagora Partners Group
Contribution to the OECD/DAC/GOVNET Conference on
Governance Assessments and Aid Effectiveness (London, 20-21 February 2008)

at fostering evidence-based assessment of human rights and democratic governance. It developed close ties of collaboration with leading institutions, such as the Office of the UN High Commissioner for Human Rights or the UNDP Oslo Governance Centre.

A Metagora Forum held in Paris in 2005 gathered together most key actors and on-going initiatives. Metagora also organised or co-organised regional workshops in Bamako, La Paz, Sao Paulo and Amman aimed at enhancing participatory dialogue, collaboration and joint action among the national and international actors currently involved – or interested – in measuring democratic governance and human rights in Francophone Africa, Latin America and the Arab region.

Metagora has been fully integrated within the OECD global programme on *Measuring the Progress of Societies* and, in particular, has been in charge of organising special sessions on Measuring Progress in Human Rights and Democratic Governance within the OECD regional conferences held in Cartagena de Indias, Seoul and Saana, as well as in the Istanbul World Forum held in 2007.

Through these actions, Metagora has had **a significant impact in the regional and global arenas**: it contributed to increase awareness on the feasibility and relevance of starting to measure human rights and democratic governance.

Chapter 3

Abuses and Ill-Treatment by Police Forces in Mexico City

In most countries, current human rights monitoring mechanisms are primarily based on reporting of individual cases, by victims or NGOs, to Human Rights Institutions or tribunals, as well as on judicial decisions. As it has been mentioned in Chapter 1, this form of monitoring can certainly be very effective and useful for purposes of advocacy on individual cases, but it cannot provide information on the dimension and trends of specific forms of human rights violations.

Indeed, the mechanism underlying this form of "monitoring" generates a sequence of gaps and filters of information. Even in countries where human rights violations such as ill-treatment and torture constitute a large scale phenomenon, only a limited number of cases are reported to Human Rights Institutions and NGOs. Moreover, for various reasons, among these reported cases, only a few are subject to judicial suit – and only in a marginal number of cases does this effectively lead to conviction and sanctions. Human rights reporting that is based on cases identified through these various steps therefore provides a picture that is far from reflecting the real dimension and mechanisms of the phenomenon.

The Montreux 2000 Conference has shown that, in order to efficiently address such a situation, it is today important to reverse the focus of human rights reporting (based on individual cases) and to

This chapter was drafted on the basis of substantive reports, working documents and publications authored by:

Gloria Labastida, Claire Naval and **Juan Salgado**

The pilot experience was conducted in Mexico by **Fundar, Centre for Analysis and Research**.

Chairman: Dr. Sergio Aguayo
Executive Director: Mrs. Helena Hofbauer
Metagora Co-ordinator: Mr. Juan Salgado, in collaboration with Mrs. Claire Naval
www.fundar.org.mx

The pilot survey was designed with the assistance of Dr. Rosa María Rubalcava, Prof. Ignacio Méndez and Prof. Miguel Cervera. It was implemented by the firm Pearson under the direction of Mrs. Gloria Labastida, Vice-President, assisted by Mrs. Yesenia Gonzalez Pedraza.

Mrs. Jana Asher (USA) and Mr. Jan Robert Suesser (France) provided technical assistance in survey design, planning, and the analysis of results.

develop methods and tools, such as sampling survey approaches and data coding techniques, that allow estimating the dimension and impact of human rights issues. Measuring human rights with such kind of tools should be considered as a specific type of monitoring, different (but complementary) to other forms of human rights activities: its role is not to denounce individual cases of human rights violations, but to produce information on the characteristics and evolution of human rights issues.

This approach therefore aims at developing policy-oriented assessment tools that provide reliable information to the civil society and to the public authorities on how respect for human rights evolves, and in which direction corrective plans and measures can usefully be implemented. This is the approach that has been followed in the Mexican pilot experience, as well as in the Philippines and South Africa.

Background

In the aftermath of the Montreux Conference, the Mexican National Commission for Human Rights convened an international seminar on *Human Rights Diagnosis*, held in Merida in April 2002. This seminar mainly focused on torture and degrading forms of treatment (see Asatashvili, Fix Fierro and Lozano, 2003). However, subsequent exploratory work conducted by the independent research centre Fundar – consisting in meetings and consultations with stakeholders and leading experts – suggested that torture and severe forms of ill-treatment have greatly diminished in Mexico over the past two decades, though cases of torture are still being reported to Human Rights Institutions.

These exploratory consultations highlighted that abusive behaviour by law enforcement authorities is still frequent, and consists of various forms of law infringement and human rights violations ranging from minor but very current abuses to severe violations such as illegal detention and use of force. Experts and stakeholders therefore confirmed a common opinion of the Mexican public: in spite of the country's democratic process and the commitment of local and national authorities to enhance the rule of law, weak governance, inefficiency and corruption are still the natural environment of the daily action of law enforcement agents. Thus, the relations of police forces with the population are often entailed by arbitrary or harsh police behaviour, false accusations, intimidation, extortion of bribes – popularly named *mordidas*, literally meaning "bites" –, as well as police tolerance of – or collusion with – crime, such as drug-dealing.

In the course of these exploratory consultations, the views of experts and stakeholders converged in four main characteristics of the issue at stake:

- Police agents are generally considered to be "poor" in both economic and educational terms. They lack respect and support from society as much as they lack professional training, appropriate equipment and clear guidelines, in particular concerning the use of force.
- People are confused by the complexity and opacity of the police and public security system. There are about 300 police corporations nationwide and 11 in the Federal District, so that most people do not distinguish very well between the various bodies and few people correctly understand their respective roles and powers. Most people only recognise the traffic police, the judicial police (in the case of the latter, perhaps because of fear) and the preventive police.
- The role of the *Ministerio Público* – which acts both as Prosecutor and Attorney – is generally considered as excessive. Processes for the provision of justice are based on a legal framework that empowers police forces without providing redress or victim support, and on an administrative system that is unduly bureaucratic. Agents of the *Ministerio Público* are seen as having inadequate and intimidating installations, denying impartial advice or legal support,

using misleading information or coercive behaviour in interrogations and to secure declarations, presuming guilt, among other elements. These factors were compounded by an overload of cases, backward technology for databases, poor collaboration with other law enforcement authorities and between federal and statal security bodies.

- The real size, trend and distribution of irregularities, abuses of power and ill-treatment by law enforcement authorities are unknown as there is a general lack of reliable official data on this matter, and information from other sources (such as the registers and statistics of complaints addressed to the National and Federal District's Commissions on Human Rights) does not allow proper estimates to be made.

Scope, aim and expected policy impact

The pilot experience therefore focused on irregularities, abuses of power and ill-treatment by law enforcement authorities. It aimed to measure the magnitude of abusive behaviour in Mexico City (Federal District) and to explore to what extent such abuses weaken the relationship which should prevail in a democratic and well-governed context between the population and authorities working in the public security and procurement of justice systems.

The pilot study aimed to have a strong impact on policy and to complement and enrich the human rights diagnosis and monitoring instruments established within the framework of the National Human Rights Programme. In concrete terms, it was intended to provide political authorities, heads of police forces and Human Rights Institutions with specific evidence-based analysis to inform policy measures, manage human resources, design training programmes and formulate clear guidelines on the use of force by police agents. In the words of the Chairman of the Commission for Human Rights of the Federal District, "*Metagora should contribute, through the information and analysis provided by this pilot survey, to enhance policy-making aiming at dignifying the role of the police as an institution and strengthening the professional profile of police agents*".

Budget constraints and other practicalities limited the survey's geographical scope to the area of the Federal District, thus encompassing only part of the urban area of Mexico City (the second largest city in the world, after Tokyo). While in strict statistical terms the survey only measures irregularities, abuses of power and acts of ill-treatment in this restricted target area, study findings are of high political significance for addressing a problem that seems to extend to all of Mexico City and - though this should be measured further - most probably to other cities and areas of the country.

The survey targeted an open population aged 15 or over living in dwellings, and recorded events that occurred in a one-year reference period: between November 2003 and October 2004.

Qualitative exploratory approach and survey design

In order to identify the various situations and circumstances in which abuse by law enforcement officers typically occurs, as well as the general profile of the actors involved (perpetrators and victims), the research team drew both a basic grid of patterns of contact between individuals and law enforcement authorities, and a thematic guide to address the issue at stake. These were tested through in-depth narrative interviews with 23 informants: 6 police officers from 3 different security forces and 17 victims of different forms of abuse. Interviews provided extensive factual and contextual information, popular vocabulary and expressions for the phenomena under study, and other rich material, allowing the team to draft the survey questionnaire on the strongest possible basis.

Though the survey exclusively targets household respondents, qualitative work included detention centres and narrative interviews with prisoners to better grasp the complexity of the issues at stake and the relations between individuals and the authority. Detention centres were reported to be characterised by even harsher and more generalised forms of abuse than are attributed to the police or personnel of the *Ministerio Público*, including inadequate facilities, payment for basic subsistence goods and services, generalised abuse or assault (including sexual), lack of effective social rehabilitation programmes, and tolerance of in-jail crime such as drug-dealing; all exacerbated by severe overcrowding.

Based on this qualitative information, a draft questionnaire was prepared and discussed by different groups of Mexican and international experts, examined in the Metagora Partners Group, substantially reviewed, and pre-tested in the field on 49 households in a poor neighbourhood randomly chosen from one of Mexico City's basic geo-statistical areas (AGEBs). Following feedback meetings with interviewers, further changes were made to the format and content of the questionnaire in order to make it as clear and easy to use as possible.

The questionnaire was then tested in October 2004 on 216 dwellings in 18 AGEBs. The objective was to define the ideal sample size by calculating the variance of the main estimators (*i.e.* percentage of people with contact with public authorities, or percentage of people suffering some form of abuse by law enforcement agents), the design effect, and the estimated non-response rate among different socio-economic levels. The test revealed a higher non-response rate among high-class sectors, indicating the need for special measures in subsequent field work to improve this rate.

The final sample size to be used in the survey was 8,688 dwellings from 362 AGEBs. This figure was determined on the basis of the test findings and estimated response rates; depending on the final response rate, the number of effective interviews was expected to range from 2,567 to 3,726. In the end, 3,666 individual interviews were conducted, representing some 6.4 million teenage and adult inhabitants.

Results

High incidence of abuse

The data produced in this survey are representative of the Federal District. Analysis suggests that, in 2004, about one in four inhabitants of the Federal District aged 15 or more have had at least one contact with law enforcement officers - either police, the *Ministerio Público*, military forces or prison personnel (see Figure 3.1). These individuals had one or several contacts, totalising some 2.3 million separate instances of contact.

Half of the 1.52 million people who had such contacts have been abused in some way. It was broadly estimated that about 7% of these abused persons were victims of physical ill-treatment. Whilst this attests that this problem exists in the Federal District, the reported figure needs to be taken with caution due to limitations of statistical inference.

About 30% of all contacts include asking for money (bribes), making it the most frequent abuse

Bribes (*mordidas*) are so frequent in Mexico that there was no need to make a survey to prove their existence. Nevertheless, what was important to analyse was the real magnitude of this phenomena as well as the related practices of different police bodies.

Figure 3.1. **Measuring irregularities, abuses of power and ill-treatment in Mexico City (Federal District)**

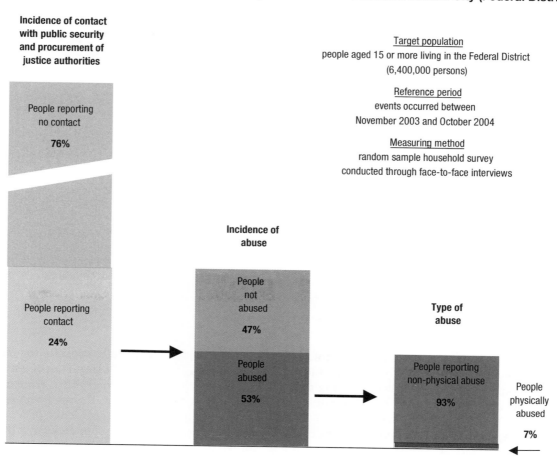

Source: Fundar, Centre for Analysis and Research (Mexico City).

The survey confirmed that the most frequent forms of abuse suffered by the population include being asked for money, having been insulted or humiliated, as well as being threatened to be accused on false grounds, undergoing threats to obtain a confession or some information, or being threatened of getting hurt (see Figure 3.2). Less frequent are: retention of official documents to exert pressure, being compelled to confess, and undergoing threats aimed towards family members. The high number and frequency of some violations justifies tackling their elimination through the design and implementation of a series of specific policies.

Certain situations increase the probability of abuse

The type of abuse varies according to the function of the authority concerned. Traffic police are responsible for regulating traffic and imposing traffic fines; although traffic police accounted for 33% of all contacts, they accounted for 46% of all instances where an individual was unlawfully asked for money. Preventive officers, who patrol the streets to prevent crimes, were linked to 40% of false accusations and 33% of humiliations (and to 29% of instances where an individual was illegally asked for money), although they account for only 24% of contacts. Judicial police agents, who report to the *Ministerio Público* and are involved in crime investigation, disproportionately resorted to threats in order to obtain a confession or information compared with other authorities.

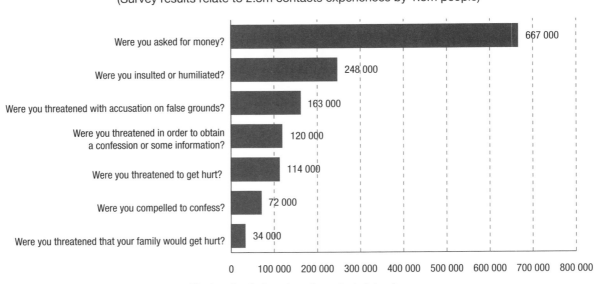

Figure 3.2. **Non-physical abuse in contacts with law enforcement authorities**
(Survey results relate to 2.3m contacts experiences by 1.5m people)

(Number of contacts per type of non-physical abuse)

Source: Fundar, Centre for Analysis and Research (Mexico City).

Transportation of individuals by police forces constitutes a critical situation: it increases the probability of abuse and involves all kinds of police. According to the survey, seven out of ten "transfer contacts" (compared to five out of ten for all contacts) involved some form of abuse. Nine out of ten such contacts involved male victims. Youngsters and people from the lowest socio-economic categories were also heavily over-represented. There is an above-average incidence of requests for money, humiliations, or compulsions to confess during this type of contact. Moreover, whilst most individuals involved in transfer contacts are presumed guilty (in so far as individuals should only be arrested and taken away if caught in flagrancy or if an arrest warrant has been issued), in more than one-third of such contacts the individual is not taken - as should be the case - to the premises of the *Ministerio Público* to face justice, but rather "dropped off" on the way by the authorities.

Contacts with all police forces involve high rates of abuse. However, this dramatically rises up to 67% in contacts with *Ministerio Público* personnel. Having said that, almost none of these cases included physical ill-treatment. They tended to involve, for instance, giving incomplete information, soliciting a bribe, or insults. Among indicted persons in particular, procedural irregularities were frequent: for example, one in eight people reported not being informed of the charges against them, and almost one in two people reported not being informed of their right to make a phone call.

Low levels of confidence in law enforcement authorities

The survey revealed that low levels of confidence in law enforcement authorities are widespread among the population. When asked why, respondents most frequently mentioned corruption, followed by inefficiency and abuse of power or ill-treatment. When asked for the causes of these deficiencies, respondents emphasised contextual factors - the low levels of education and salaries of officers, poor organisation and deficient regulations - over internal corruption, lack of an ethical culture, and impunity *per se*. The latter explanations were dominant in the case of respondents referring to the judicial police and *Ministerio Público* personnel. Moreover, these factors correspond closely to those encountered during the qualitative consultations.

Unreported abuse: a symptom of weak democratic governance

The survey found that in 94% of cases of abuse, the victims did not complain to any relevant body. This issue is severely jeopardising the basic grounds of democratic governance. The main reasons given by victims of abuse for their silence reveal a widespread perception of poor governance in the systems of public security and procurement of justice (see Figure 3.3):

- The inefficiency of the authorities, the general feeling that "*problems never get solved*" and that "*one is not paid attention to*" (this was the response of one-third of victims).
- Lack of evidence: the perception that authorities will remain deaf to complaints that are not based on solid proof (this was the response of one-third of victims).
- Unimportance: one quarter of respondents subject to abuse did not even consider themselves as victims. They considered the irregularities, abuses of power or acts of ill-treatment in which they were involved as not really important and therefore did not see a reason for complaining. In other words, for a significant number of people, irregularities, bribes or abuses of power are part of life and of citizens' day-to-day relations with law enforcement authorities.
- Mistrust of a corrupt procurement of justice system and fear of further trouble echo the survey findings on the low levels of confidence in law enforcement authorities commented upon above.

Does this mean that the targeted population of the Federal District accepts poor governance and weak rule of law? Not at all: when asked to indicate the most important rights a person has with regard to the authorities, 38% of all respondents mentioned "*the right to respect from the authorities*" and 29% referred to "*the right to fair treatment*". These rights were even more important for those who experienced contact with law enforcement authorities (43% and 34% respectively).

Figure 3.3. **In 94% of cases of abuse, victims did not complain to any relevant authority. Why?**
(spontaneous multi-answers)

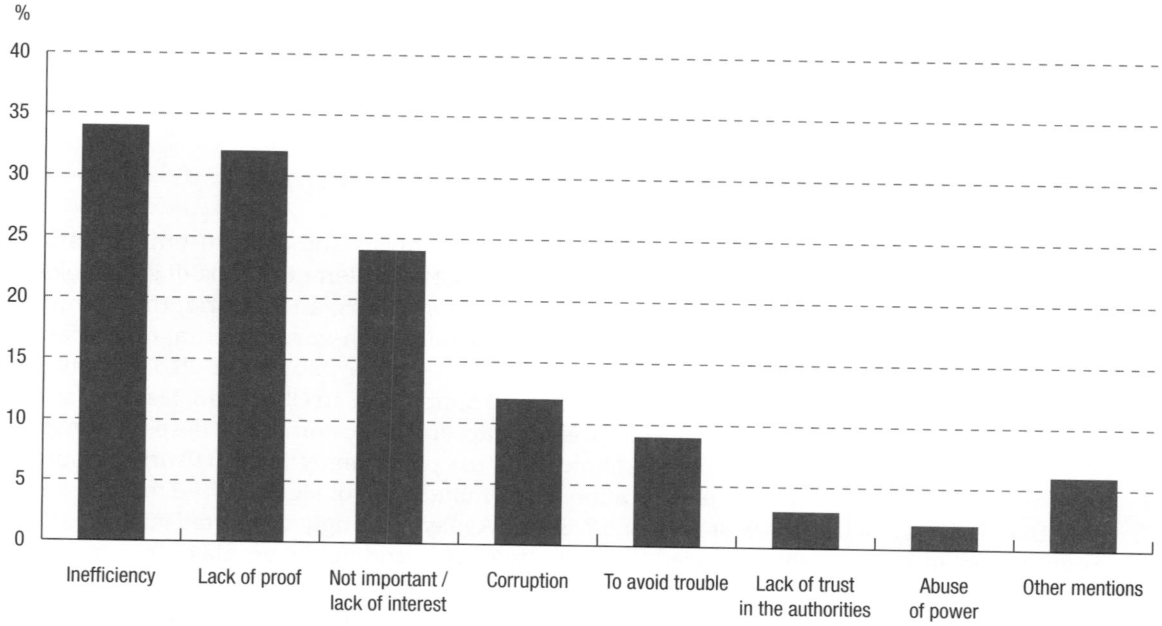

Source: Fundar, Centre for Analysis and Research (Mexico City).

A challenge for public authorities and for the wider society

Corruption has been presented as one of the main issues when dealing with contacts between the population and the authorities. This survey has revealed that the culture of corruption does not only exist among the authorities. Whilst in three out of ten contacts the authorities requested money, further analysis shows that of all respondents who gave money, a quarter reported having offered the bribe themselves.

It thus appears that, as far as corruption is involved, both the authorities and the population are immersed in a culture of disregard for the law, whether intentionally or due to a lack of knowledge of the law: i.e. rights and obligations. This questions society at large with regard to the rule of law and governance issues. Without in any way underestimating neither the responsibility of public agents, nor the gravity of such acts, it is important to stress that changes on behalf of both the authority and the population are necessary for tackling this issue.

Post-survey qualitative research

As a follow-up to this study's quantitative analysis, and in order to overcome some of the limitations inherent to the sample size and response rate, qualitative research was also carried out after the survey to complement and further inform the results obtained. This has been instrumental in particular for refining and illustrating the existence of patterns of abuse on behalf of law enforcement authorities and of particularly vulnerable groups.

The context of the contact can favour acts of extortion (e.g. during the night, with few witnesses present, or on weekends), so can the social characteristics of the people involved (for instance, their socio-economic level, their knowledge and skills in dealing with the authorities). In the case of the judicial police, for example, it appears that when, in the context of an offence or crime, the authority makes abusive use of its competencies and exceeds its mission, it tends to be against people from the middle-low and low socio-economic groups. Moreover, such contacts involve acts of extortion more frequently than is the case with other types of contact. This specific pattern is partly made possible by the lack of information of the population - and, in particular, of the lower socio-economic groups - about the role and limits of the judicial police, which enables police officers to act within a certain framework of impunity.

Disseminating results and enhancing their policy impact

Before being made public, survey results, preliminary analysis and draft recommendations were presented and discussed in various meetings involving two different groups of stakeholders: first, officials of security forces, governmental actors and politicians, and second, the Commission of Human Rights of the Federal District (CDH-DF) and several non-governmental organisations. The overall Metagora project and the main results of the Mexico pilot were also presented at the *International Conference on Public Security* (held on 8-10 March 2006 in Queretaro, Mexico), attended by a broad audience of academics, governmental officials and police officers. These meetings were an excellent way to involve all relevant stakeholders in the policy analysis of the surveys' outcomes as well as in the refinement of their presentation. The Ombudsman of Mexico City, Emilio Álvarez-Icaza, and the Chairman of the Board of Fundar, Dr. Sergio Aguayo, strongly supported such a participatory process and authoritatively enhanced the policy relevance and public profile of the study.

A policy-oriented report, *Irregularities, Abuses of Power and Ill-Treatment in the Federal District: The Relation between Police Officers and Ministerio Público Agents, and the Population,* was published in hard copy and online in Spanish and English (Naval and Salgado, 2006). This report highlights the context in which abusive behaviour by public authorities occurs, the specific forms and patterns of contact and abuse, and the characteristics of the victims. It also makes recommendations for police forces and the personnel of the *Ministerio Público*, as well as for improving relations between the authorities and the

---

Box 3.1. **A strong impact in the field**

Why has an Ombudsman like me been involved in Metagora? My first and spontaneous answer is: because this project is enhancing my work as human rights defender, enlarging the scope of my mission and opening new perspectives to my action.

How has this happened? From the 40,000 cases of human rights violations reported every year to the Commission for Human Rights of Mexico City (Federal District), we have some 8,000 formal complaints – and, out of them, around 1,500 against police forces. I have therefore known for quite some time that, beyond the follow-up I can give to all these individual cases of human rights violations, I should find appropriate tools for fighting against these violations as a major structural problem.

The Metagora survey on abuses and ill-treatment by police forces in the Federal District provided me – and the Mexican society at large – with an evidence-based picture of the magnitude and main characteristics of this phenomenon. For the first time I have in hand a tool for fighting against the widespread culture of impunity and non-respect for human dignity that still prevails today within the behaviour of police forces in my City.

After the release of the results of the Metagora survey implemented by Fundar in Mexico City I got in touch with the government of the Federal District and with the local legislative Congress to discuss how to address, in terms of policy and legislation, the problem of massive abuses by police forces. Discussing this issue on the basis of solid data marked a substantial difference in the kind of dialogue I used to have with public officials and political authorities. Normally officials and civil servants don't like at all to discuss human rights issues related to individual cases of victims of police abuse. The situation is different when you can show with strong evidence the nature and magnitude of the structural problem you would like to address together with them. Confronted with facts and figures, they accept to enter into a more constructive and positive policy dialogue.

At the present stage of this on-going dialogue, we are considering the possibility of drafting a law aimed at controlling abuses of police forces. Moreover, we are trying to set up a five-year human rights program for the Federal District. In this context, we are developing the kind of indicators promoted by Metagora and we are using the Metagora Training Materials as a guide and a common ground to develop solid monitoring tools.

This is what Metagora has really been changing in Mexico and in other countries participating in the project: it is generating the methods and tools that make the difference in fighting against structural human rights violations, and it is providing common ground for policy dialogue on measures and norms that can improve the daily relations between people and public authorities.

It is not a coincidence if, under the impetus of Metagora, several Human Rights Institutions from Latin America, Africa and Asia are now developing plans and a common agenda for enhancing evidence-based assessment of structural human rights issues.

Emilio Álvarez-Icaza
Chairman, Commission of Human Rights of Mexico City (Federal District)

---

population. The report was presented by Fundar - together with the CDH-DF and outstanding specialists on human rights and security issues - to academia, public authorities, civil society organisations and the media at a public event in the prestigious *Colegio de México* in April 2006. This event had front-page coverage in a couple of national newspapers and was followed by several radio interviews with the Fundar team, and by presentations in various events organised by universities, civil society organisations and the CDH-DF.

One of the main challenges for Fundar in the dissemination process was avoiding misuse or manipulation of the data and policy analysis by the media or political parties. This was a particular danger in the context of the extremely polarised political campaign for the Mexican presidency, in which the former Mayor of the Federal District was one of the main candidates. Fundar therefore managed to balance the broad release of press bulletins with a low-profile approach to potentially controversial media channels and events.

Fundar successfully targeted relevant policy actors - including police officials, public authorities, civil society organisations and academic experts - for developing responsible dialogue on accountability and possible policy responses to the problems and questions raised by the study. It had meetings with senior police officers and with the Sub-Secretary of Public Security of the Federal District, in which the implications of the study were frankly discussed. Steps were also taken to ensure continued collaboration between Fundar, the CDH-DF and the *Colectivo por la Seguridad Pública* (association of NGOs and research centres working on public security issues). Finally, as the new government was installed in December 2006, Fundar took a number of steps to ensure a more pro-active politically and institutionally sustainable follow-up to this successful pilot.

In conclusion, two major lessons can be drawn from the Metagora pilot in Mexico: first, it demonstrates that relevant data on sensitive human rights and democratic governance issues can be collected and analysed using well-established statistical tools. Second, it shows that involving public authorities and relevant policy actors in the analysis can create a constructive dialogue that, despite differences in political views and interests, is based on information that is robust and shared. The data gathered through the pilot survey - although restricted to one urban area - provides a first measure of a phenomenon of major concern for Mexican society, and is a first step towards proper monitoring of irregularities, abuses of power and ill-treatment. Regular data collection and the progressive extension of this experience to other major cities - and, ideally, to the entire country - should, in the medium and long term, allow for monitoring and evaluations to support policies and programmes to improve the governance of the security and police forces, enhance accountability and prevent abuses by the authorities.

On the basis of the experience and lessons of the pilot survey conducted in the Federal District, Fundar approached the Commissions for Human Rights in selected States of the Mexican Federation to discuss the relevance of, and potential for, conducting similar surveys elsewhere in the country. Thanks to a generous grant from the Tinker Foundation, Fundar is currently replicating the survey in the City of Queretaro (over 900,000 inhabitants). The results and related policy-oriented report will be available by the end of 2008.

Box 3.2. **Implications of the pilot experience in Mexico City (Federal District)**

Policy implications

- The pilot survey on irregularities, abuses of power and acts of ill-treatment by police forces provided for the first time relevant information on the magnitude and dynamics of a human rights and governance issue that is of major concern for the Mexican society at large.

- This study reveals a dramatic need for improving the professionalism of police officials through better working conditions and salaries, as well as appropriate training, introduction of performance criteria, awards and strict rules prohibiting all forms of abuse.

- Patterns of contact and abuse were evidenced by the study. They relate to the specific activities of each authority: traffic police are most likely to ask for money, preventive police to resort to humiliations and aggressions, judicial police to seek to extract forced confessions and resort to threats, and *Ministerio Público* officials to deny procedural rights. Thus, discussions on police and public security reforms should pay specific attention to the issues specific to each law enforcement body.

- There is a high level of abuses in patrol cars. The use of control mechanisms, such as radios or surveillance cameras in patrol cars, as well as an increase in the actual reporting of detention by officers could inhibit these abuses.

- Within the *Ministerio Público*, better training, performance management, and technology for controls and records should be established to diminish the level of procedural violations. This could be driven by improved legislation and citizen participation. Control mechanisms in detention venues, like those suggested for police cars, are required. Alternative conflict-resolution schemes or a system of restorative justice should also be considered to reduce the overload of the *Ministerio Público*.

- There are great needs for educating the public about their rights and obligations, and creating transparency measures (such as strongly requiring officials to wear identification to combat the widespread culture of impunity of abuses). Information campaigns as well as multi-sector partnerships, especially for vulnerable groups, would also be relevant in this context.

- Debates on the respect for human rights and democratic governance are considerably enhanced when they rely on evidence-based assessments. Effective monitoring should be based on regular robust surveys. Here, rhetoric and slogans are ineffective: national and local political authorities must commit to fund politically independent and scientifically skilled institutions to get the job done.

Major methodological implications

- Relevant data on sensitive issues regarding human rights and democratic governance can be collected and analysed using well-established statistical tools.

- Qualitative methods such as in-depth narrative interviews of victims of abuse and police agents provide solid information on the everyday experiences, perceptions and vocabulary of victims and perpetrators of abuse, as well as on their views and expectations on their rights. Thus they provide invaluable input into the formulation of quantitative instruments (such as survey questionnaires and guides for interviews).

- Violations of rights are sensitive issues that require special measures during the field work to overcome the reluctance of respondents and ensure the safety of field workers.

- The violation of specific rights may be relatively rare, requiring special pilot investigation if the sampling and statistical tools are to capture a relevant number of cases.

- Collaboration with field experts and the Commission of Human Rights of the Federal District enhanced the relevance, policy impact and public profile of the study.

Chapter 4

Indigenous Peoples' Rights in the Philippines

The Metagora pilot survey in the Philippines focused on indigenous peoples' rights. It was designed, prepared and carried out through a vigorous participatory process, leading to one of Metagora's strongest and most inclusive national structures (see box below).

This chapter was drafted on the basis of substantive reports, working documents and publications authored by:

Anita Chauhan, Fe Dyliacco, Estrella Domingo, Reuben Lingating and **Romulo Virola**

The Metagora activity in the Philippines was conducted by the **Commission on Human Rights**.

Chairperson: Atty. Purificacion Valera Quisumbing
Metagora Co-ordinator: Mrs. Anita Chauhan
www.chr.gov.ph

The activity was implemented in close collaboration with the **National Statistical Coordination Board** (NSCB, Secretary General: Dr. Romulo A. Virola) and the **National Commission on Indigenous Peoples** (Chairman: Atty. Reuben Dasay A. Lingating succeeded by Atty. Jannette C. Serrano). See www.nscb.gov.ph and www.ncip.gov.ph.

The survey was designed with the assistance of experts from NSCB (Assistant Secretary General Estrella V. Domingo, Mrs. Lina B. Castro and Mrs. Fe Dyliacco) and implemented with the support of the **National Statistical Office** (Director: Adm. Carmelita N. Ericta; experts involved: Dep. Adm. Paula Monina Collado, Mrs. Janice R. Ybanez) and the **Statistical Research and Training Centre** (Director: Exec. Dir. Gervacio G. Selda, Jr.; expert involved: Mr. Winecito L. Tan). See www.census.gov.ph and www.srtc.gov.ph.

Heads of all these institutions gathered together in a **"Metagora Advisory Council"**, the national policy-making body of the project. Experts of the mentioned institutions, together with representatives of academic circles and the civil society (including indigenous peoples' organisations, NGOs, individual human rights practitioners) formed the **"Implementing Group of Experts"**.

Technical assistance to the survey design and planning was provided by Mrs. Jana Asher (USA).

Background

Indigenous peoples are estimated today at one sixth of the national population of the Philippines. The *Indigenous Peoples Rights Act* (IPRA) came into force in 1997 to address their marginalisation and powerlessness. This act intends to redress historical injustices against indigenous peoples, whose rights, cultural identity and ancestral lands were alienated first through the feudal *jura regalia* by the Spanish Crown, then *de facto*, by their successors: the American colonial government, and thereafter by the Philippine Republic. For the first time, IPRA settles the rights of indigenous peoples and establishes the basis for a proactive public policy, including implementing mechanisms and the allocation of funds. IPRA recognises and promotes in particular: the rights of indigenous peoples to ancestral domains and lands; the right to self-governance; economic and social rights; and cultural integrity - including indigenous culture, traditions and institutions.

These different elements are closely interrelated and all refer to the essential concept of indigenous peoples' ownership of their ancestral domains; including not only agricultural lands, but also all natural resources found therein. These domains are community property, belonging to all generations and therefore cannot be sold, disposed or destroyed. Today, indigenous peoples' claims for ancestral domains total 5.2 million hectares, representing 17.5% of the total land area of the country. In this context, the National Commission on Indigenous Peoples (NCIP), the government agency responsible for implementing IPRA, not only delineates and titles ancestral domains and lands, but also promotes sustainable development plans and enhances indigenous peoples' consultative mechanisms and bodies at the provincial, regional and national level.

The Metagora pilot experience in the Philippines focused on the implementation of the *Indigenous Peoples Rights Act*. It consisted of a relatively small but incisive survey-based study, implemented in three northern regions of the country, where there is a high concentration of indigenous peoples.

Scope, aim and expected policy impact

The objective of this pilot was to develop evidence-based assessment methods and tools which combine quantitative and qualitative approaches. The study aimed to measure four aspects of the rights of indigenous peoples to their ancestral domains and lands:

- indigenous peoples' perceptions and awareness of their rights;
- the exercise or violation of these rights;
- government measures and customary laws for realising these rights; and
- the availability of mechanisms for redressing or fulfilling rights.

Consultative process and qualitative exploratory approach

Following the Metagora bottom-up approach, the process started with consultations and meetings with stakeholders and field experts to select the issues to be tackled by the pilot survey and to define a general conceptual framework. The National Commission on Indigenous Peoples played a key role in facilitating and supporting the consultation of indigenous peoples and in providing substantive advice on the issues to be raised through the survey.

A first large consultation workshop was held in Baguio City in June 2004, gathering some 40 representatives of indigenous peoples' communities from the north of the Philippines. This consultation was followed by bi-lateral meetings with the leaders of the tribes targeted by the survey.

A second large consultation workshop was held in September 2004. These participatory consultations showed:

- the centrality of land issues in any attempt to implement or redress indigenous peoples' rights, and in particular their social, economic and cultural rights;
- the close interrelation between human rights, governance and democracy issues affecting indigenous peoples;
- the need to adapt human rights standards to the specific cultural context of indigenous peoples; and
- the importance of the policy orientation of the study for observing and measuring if and how national norms (IPRA) and international human right standards are being effectively implemented.

The consultations also identified a number of institutional and practical issues, such as the legal obligation to obtain "free prior informed consent" from indigenous peoples' communities to be part of the survey. A simplified procedure called "ancestral domain consultation" was then conducted in the three northern regions of the country.

Survey design

In each of the three northern regions (Regions I, II/III and Cordillera) an ancestral domain was selected according to three main criteria: the domain had to be inhabited by one main tribe (thus guaranteeing common language and culture), of easy access and located in areas where the survey can be conducted safely (thus not in areas suffering from insecurity or endemic political violence). This allowed three **target tribes of indigenous peoples** to be purposely identified: the **Bago,** the **Bugkalot/Ilongot** and the **Kankanaey.**

A draft questionnaire (in English) was reviewed by the national Consultative Experts Group, with several stakeholders and with the Metagora Partners. It was then translated into the local dialects: Ilocano (for the Bago Tribe), Bugkalot/Ilongot and Kankanaey, and pre-tested twice in two different localities to determine the effectiveness and appropriateness of the translation.

Focus group discussions (FGDs) were conducted in January 2005 with three different groups in each tribe: tribal leaders, women and young people. These had two aims: first, prior to the survey, qualitative information helped to enrich and refine the survey questionnaire; and second, following the survey, this information complemented and contextualised the quantitative data drawn from responses to the survey (see Box 4.1).

All persons involved in implementing the survey (and in particular in field operations) were trained in the concepts and definitions used in the survey, as well as in the procedures for conducting interviews, filling in the questionnaires, supervising interviewers, and checking filled forms. An *Interviewers' Manual* was drafted to support the training process and to guide field work. Field operations were conducted immediately after the training sessions for enumerators and supervisors, from 14 to 18 March 2005.

The survey was conducted on a randomly selected sample of 750 households, comprising 250 Kankaney, 150 Bagos and 350 Bugkalots/Ilongots households, and targeted heads of households. In all three tribes, approximately 90% of the heads of household were male, and the average household size was slightly above five people. Approximately one-third of household members were under 15 years of age, and another third were aged between 15 and 45. Two-thirds of household members worked as farmers or other cultivators, and one-fifth had not worked in the last year.

Results

Good awareness of rights

The survey revealed that indigenous peoples are generally aware of their rights to ancestral domains and lands. Awareness was highest among the Bugkalot/Ilongot tribe (71%), followed by the Bago (68%) and Kankanaey (61%). The better awareness amongst the Bugkalot/Ilongot can perhaps be explained by the finding that they were most likely to have relied on the government or tribal council for their information on these rights, and least likely to have relied on family or neighbours. The situation was the reverse for the Kankanaey.

The survey showed a high level of general knowledge and understanding of the specific rights regarding ancestral domains and lands, as stated under the IPRA (*Indigenous Peoples Rights Act*). Some 80-90% of respondents in all three tribes felt that several of these rights were adequately protected. This was in particular the case of the rights to own, to conserve and to develop their ancestral domains and lands; to regulate the entry of migrants and organisations; and to have access to safe and clean water. However, regarding the rights of families in the case of displacement, there was greater variation between the tribes: among the Bugkalot/Ilongots, only 39% considered that government would assure them of basic services and livelihoods, compared to 69% among the Bago and 72% among the Kankanaey.

The survey also tested awareness of specific rights to ancestral domains and lands by describing a number of hypothetical situations (vignettes). For example, would the government be correct in:

- renewing the lease of a portion of ancestral domain to a private corporation, despite the tribe's claim of possession?
- granting a permit for gold mining to a company rather than to the owners of the ancestral domain?
- resettling a community to create a wildlife sanctuary in part of an ancestral domain?

Responses by all tribes were similar, although levels of awareness varied, and almost all responses were correct. In particular, large majorities of all three tribes were aware that customary law is the appropriate means for regulating land disputes among clans within the tribe.

Qualitative focus group discussions confirmed that the rights to own and develop lands and natural resources and to stay in territories were well-understood, as was the purpose of the IPRA. The vignettes provided in the survey actually proved to be a better research tool than the more abstract questions raised in the focus group discussions in distinguishing respondents' understanding of the difference between the more specific right to ancestral lands, and the broader rights to ancestral domains (which includes access to water and ownership of resources). Discussions also revealed aspects in which rights were given indigenous interpretations. Tribal leaders and women had higher awareness of these rights than young people (see Box 4.1). However, there appeared to be low awareness of other human rights listed under the IPRA.

Good entitlement to ancestral domains or land

The survey revealed that a large percentage of the three tribes (71%) was aware that their community had acquired title to their ancestral domains or land. The government was the most mentioned institution having provided assistance (44%), followed by tribal leaders and elders (10%). Respondents generally considered that acquiring these titles has been very beneficial for their tribes in terms of affirmation of their culture, unity and empowerment.

Box 4.1. **Linking quantitative and qualitative approaches to assess rights**

Quantitative approach:

SURVEY FINDINGS

- High perception and awareness of rights to ancestral domain and land (Bago 68%, Bugkalot 71% and Kankanaey 61%).

- Government is in second place as source of information of rights to ancestral domain and land: Bago 29%, Bugkalot 54% and Kankanaey 22%, behind the family or tribal associations and councils.

- Have experienced violations of rights via encroachment (Bago 9%, Bugkalot 31% and Kankanaey 13%); pollution (Bago 7%, Bugkalot 18% and Kankanaey 9%); illegal entry (Bago 8%, Bugkalot 46% and Kankanaey 12%).

- Victims of land grabbing saw their land taken away primarily by private individuals (Bago 50%, Bugkalot 56% and Kankanaey 56%), followed by council of elders and others.

- Substantial awareness and use of governmental programmes and services.

- Exercising land ownership and acquisition of right to ancestral domain.

- Average satisfaction about delivery of government programmes and services (between 68-78% depending on the specific programme/service).

- 90% considered customary laws helpful in solving land issues; 52% of land issues are resolved by customary laws.

- Top five primary needs: adequate food, housing, water system, livelihood and education.

Qualitative approaches:

FOCUS GROUP DISCUSSIONS

- Tribal leaders and women have highest awareness and perception of rights to ancestral domain and land. Young people have the lowest awareness. Right of ownership to develop lands and natural resources and to stay in territories is well-understood. Low or no awareness of other rights listed under IPRA. Apparent confusion of rights due to lack of knowledge about the distinction or difference between rights to ancestral domain and land.

- Positive effect of IPRA on indigenous peoples' rights to ancestral domain and rights.

- Violations occurring by tribesmates, other tribes, private mining companies.

- Recognition of government efforts in fulfilling rights to ancestral domain and land.

- Customary law as primary source of dispute resolution affecting rights to ancestral domain and land.

LOCAL CONSULTATIONS

- Demand for relevant and deeper human rights and IPRA education.

- Need for livelihood and organisation, especially among women.

- Development aggression of private sectors permitted/not controlled by government and co-opted by some tribal leaders.

- Lack of delivery of vital services.

- Discriminatory policies to access rights to education and other social services.

- Pollution of and inadequate water resources.

- Peace and order to ensure personal security.

Source: Commission on Human Rights (CHR) of the Philippines.

87% of all households indicated that they owned land within the ancestral domain. For most of them, this ownership had occurred through inheritance. Of those owning land, just over half had title or evidence of ownership, mainly in the form of certificates or tax receipts. For indigenous peoples, the main benefits of owning land are economic security and security of tenure.

The role of government had clearly been influential. It had provided assistance in securing title to 63% of households among the Bago, 34% among the Bugkalot/Ilongot, and 51% among the Kankanaey. Tribal leaders or elders were the next most-mentioned actor to assist in the process, but in a quarter of instances or less. It is worth noting that among those households who did not have evidence of title, while most desired to obtain it, two-thirds had not taken any action to achieve it.

The focus group discussions confirmed the importance that indigenous peoples attach to having proof of title to their inherited ancestral lands, including a sense of security and empowerment. They also acknowledged the positive role of government and the IPRA in assisting the process. For instance, during the consultations, indigenous peoples' leaders mentioned a memorandum of agreement between the Philippine Land Registration Authority (LRA) and the National Council of Indigenous Peoples to register certificates of ancestral domains (CADTs) for free.

The study indicated that respondents are aware of the duties entailed by rights of ownership. In the focus group discussions, women spoke of the duty to nurture and improve the land. This is consistent with a factual finding of the survey: four-fifths or more of surveyed households had made agricultural improvements. For their part, elders emphasised the importance of controlling immigration.

Evidence of violations of rights

The pilot survey revealed significant differences in the experience of rights violations among the tribes (see Figure 4.1): ranging from 21% among the Bago, through 36% among the Kankanaey, to as

Figure 4.1. **Violation of land rights to ancestral domains in three indigenous tribes**

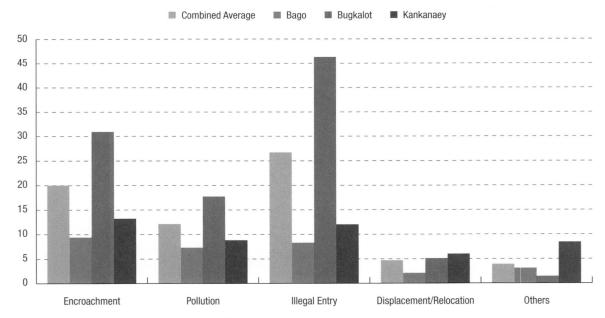

Source: NSCB in collaboration with CHR (Philippines).

Box 4.2. **Interlinking and empowering national actors of change**

In the Philippines, as in several other countries around the world, there is clearly a "before" and an "after" the arrival of Metagora.

Already by the end of 2000 the Philippine attendants to the international Conference on *Statistics, Development and Human Rights* established a "Montreux-Manila Group", gathering together human rights defenders, activists of various civil society organisations, academic researchers and official statisticians. Their common objective was to implement in our country the operational *Conclusions* of the Montreux Conference. At that time, my Institution was reluctant to play any kind of role in measuring human rights or democratic governance. Nevertheless, this position started to evolve once the initiative of the Montreux-Manila Group matured in a more institutional form, under the leadership of our national Commission on Human Rights (CHR). In this context, we started to talk with institutions and persons we had never met until then: the CHR itself, the National Commission on Indigenous Peoples and several senior scholars working in the fields of human rights, democracy and governance. Thus we discovered highly qualified potential partners and started to explore with them how to work together. While the discussions on the possibility of measuring human rights and democratic governance were not always easy – as each partner had his own specific conceptual background, method of work and particular agenda – we realised that our Institution had a lot to gain and a lot to provide in this process of dialogue and incipient collaboration. We finally decided to provide a strong technical support to the design and implementation of the Metagora pilot in our country, aimed at measuring indigenous peoples' rights.

The Metagora pilot has been a success not only in terms of production of relevant and valuable information, but also – and perhaps mainly – in terms of the impact it had in transforming and empowering the relations between the many "actors of change" committed in this process. As a direct consequence of our involvement in the Metagora pilot, we reviewed the design of the national population census in order to make once and for all truly visible the demographic and social profile of indigenous peoples, who constitute a significant part of the total population of our country. Finally, we far overcame our initial reluctance to measure human rights and democratic governance issues, as this kind of work is now part of our regular working programme and we are producing, on a regular basis, indicators of local governance – an assessment tool that can be powerful in the hands of actors of change.

Dr. Romulo A. Virola
Secretary General, National Statistical Coordination Board of the Philippines

many as 57% among the Bugkalot/Ilongot. The largest two categories of violation, for all three tribes combined, were illegal entry (27%) and encroachment (20%). These violations were all the more severe among the Bugkalot/Ilongot (46% and 31% respectively).

About 13% of households reported having experienced dispossession of land. The majority of these cases involved fraud or deceit. In more than 50% of the instances the dispossession was reported to have been committed by private individuals and in about 10% by elders or leaders. About 5% of all households included in this study reported having been relocated: in most of the cases (if one adjusts for missing data) through natural calamity, but equally often by armed conflict in the case of the Bago, and to a lesser extent by mining exploration in the case of the Bugkalot/Ilongot. Only a few percent were compensated for relocation. The focus group discussions and the consultations confirmed the identification of these main kinds of violations and elaborated on them, notably on "land grabbing" and mining without indigenous peoples' consent. Findings on the nature and perpetrators of these violations are very valuable for defining and implementing policies and measures of redress.

Mechanisms for implementing rights

This pilot survey revealed that awareness of the government departments or agencies that deliver key services is uniformly higher amongst the tribes, with most services scoring between 65% and 85%. Similar proportions of households had availed themselves of their services, and were satisfied with what they had received: this was a welcome "eye opener" to the authorities. Of people or institutions contacted for help on land issues, political leaders were mentioned by a third of households on average across the tribes; NGOs and churches by a fifth each; professional groups by a tenth.

Figure 4.2. **Which organisations and institutions can address and settle land issues?**
(% distribution of households)

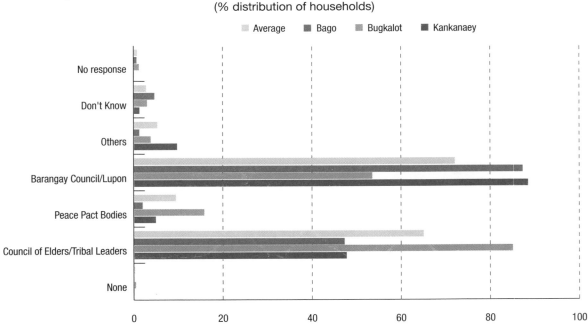

Source: NSCB in collaboration with CHR (Philippines).

Box 4.3. **Implications of the pilot experience in the Philippines**

Key policy implications

- The pilot experience on measuring the rights of indigenous peoples illustrates that combining the use of well-established statistical and qualitative methods is instrumental in making truly visible the expectations and problems of target or vulnerable groups.

- While the study showed impressive levels of awareness among indigenous peoples about their rights to ancestral lands and domains, such awareness was uneven among the tribes; as was awareness of the actual legislation, and of other human rights. There is therefore good reason for sustained implementation of the *Indigenous Peoples Rights Act* and capacity-building in human rights and advocacy.

- Possession of evidence of title to land (which was found to be empowering, and to lead to investment in improvements), was also uneven across the tribes; and two-thirds of those who did not have evidence of title had not taken any action to achieve it. There is room to improve these policies.

- While there was widespread awareness and use of institutions, both customary and statutory, for redressing violations, there was less confidence in their ability to tackle dispossession. While half of violations involved private disputes, private sector exploitation was also an issue. Moreover, customary institutions were used more often than statutory ones.

- The study would be worth replicating across other indigenous tribes and domains, to achieve - using more evidence-based findings - a well-defined operational concept of indigenous peoples in future population censuses, and thereby advance their recognition as a distinct sector of the Philippine society.

- The collaboration between the Commission on Human Rights, the National Commission on Indigenous Peoples and National Statistical Offices (in strong partnership with NGOs and academia), was highly efficacious and is being sustained so as to ensure a policy follow-up to the study and conduct further experiences.

Major methodological implications

- While this was a pilot survey with a small sample (750 households) and limited geographical and demographic scope (only three tribes in three provinces), it clearly illustrates the feasibility and relevance of collecting and analysing data on indigenous peoples with well-established statistical and qualitative methods.

- The multilateral organisational collaboration in conducting the project – of the national agencies responsible for human rights, indigenous peoples' interests, and official statistics – benefited from the project's legitimacy and technical soundness. Involvement of the National Commission on Indigenous Peoples greatly assisted access to respondents and their willingness and fairness in answering interviews, as did the employment and training of indigenous peoples as focus group moderators, field workers and supervisors.

- Multiple qualitative methods were used, not only in conceiving and designing the questionnaire, but also in interpreting and validating the findings (i.e. clarifying noteworthy variations among the tribes on specific issues), therefore ensuring that the investigation was aligned and responsive to indigenous conceptualisations, and focused on salient and meaningful priorities.

- The comparisons of various issues among the tribes highlighted the importance of sub-national specificities (such as specific groups or specific regions) for empirically monitoring the realisation of rights.

Almost 50% of Bagos and Kankanaeys, and some 85% of Bugkalot/Ilongot, reported that Councils of Elders exist in their communities (see Figure 4.2). Conversely, the Barangay Council or Lupon established by national legislation was reported by nearly 90% of Bago and Kankanaey respondents in the sample, and just over half of Bugkalots/Ilongots. The percentage of the community making use of such institutions was noticeably higher among the Bugkalots/Ilongots. The presence of such institutions may suggest that indigenous peoples still prefer to make use of customary institutions to resolve rights issues.

Finally, the survey established that the top five primary needs as prioritised by the three tribes in the survey were: **adequate food**, **housing**, **water system**, **livelihood** and **education**. The local consultations highlighted various needs and confirmed these priorities: particularly access to water, but also education and livelihood.

Disseminating results and enhancing their policy impact

Three workshops were held to present the findings of the pilot survey to the Bago, Kankanaey and Bugkalot tribes. Survey results were also presented for policy-oriented debate to a large group of national stakeholders in 2005 and 2006. On these occasions, stakeholders were unanimous in stressing that survey results call for continued and sustained IPRA implementation, human rights education, policy reviews and governmental delivery of services. It was stated that IPRA should be further reviewed to respond to and comply with rights-based norms in governance of indigenous peoples' affairs. Moreover, it was noted that gains in exercising rights are being hampered by on-going violations. Thus the government has a major role to play in empowering other governance stakeholders to respect, protect and fulfil indigenous peoples' rights to ancestral domains and land.

One of the main successes of this pilot experience resides in its transformation of the relations between various key domestic actors of change in the Philippines (see Box 4.2). The National Metagora Advisory Council succeeded, building on an integrated approach, to raise governmental and civil society attention on indigenous peoples' rights. As a follow-up to the pilot, budget was allocated within the national statistical programme to fund further official statistical work on indigenous peoples – and the design of the national census has been reviewed in order to better reflect their demographic, social and economic profile.

In the aftermath of the Metagora experience, the National Commission on Human Rights has been advocating, at the Asian regional level, for enhanced efforts of national Human Rights Institutions in assessing the situation of indigenous peoples – and a promising concrete project has been launched jointly by the Philippines and New Zealand, which will hopefully build further on the achievement and lessons of the Metagora pilot.

Chapter 5

Human Rights and Democracy Dimensions of Land Reform in South Africa

Metagora's pilot experience on land reform in South Africa is a case study for measuring the realisation of democracy and human rights in a complex practical context. This pilot designed and tested a survey methodology to take into account the varied nature of the South African land question, as well as the relevant but diverging views of a range of stakeholders. It addressed the particular needs of policy makers and civil society for evidence-based information on citizens' differing experiences, perceptions, attitudes and aspirations around land. The likely policy impact of this approach was to contribute with evidence-based information and analysis to the development of a land reform policy based on principles, standards and people's expectations of democracy, realisation of human rights and good governance.

Background

Measuring respect for human rights and effectiveness of the democratic process is particularly significant in South Africa; prior to the first non-racial democratic elections in 1994, the apartheid system emphatically negated these principles for the majority black population. The institutions and policies of post-apartheid South Africa have therefore largely been driven by the need to deepen the non-racial system of governance and democracy, and to establish a human rights culture. However, even before the 1994 turning point, there was a common awareness that political transformation had to be complemented by economic and social transformation, in particular to redress the material

This chapter was drafted on the basis of substantive reports, working documents and publications authored by:

Maxine Reitzes, Marlene Roefs and **Michael Aliber**

The Metagora activity in South Africa was conducted by the **Human Sciences Research Council**.

CEO: Dr. Mark Orkin, succeeded in September 2005 by Dr. Olive Shisana
Metagora Co-ordinator: Dr. Maxine Reitzes, in collaboration with Dr. Marlene Roefs and Dr. Michael Aliber
www.hsrc.ac.za

The pilot survey was designed with the assistance of Prof David Stoker (**Statistics South Africa**). Field work was conducted by a survey company, **Development Research Africa** (DRA).

deprivations and denial of opportunities experienced under apartheid. A clear expression of the inclusive nature of transformation was the 1993 framework document for ANC's Reconstruction and Development Programme (RDP), which set out a broad plan of transformation that, *inter alia*, touched on all sectors of the economy, improved access to health care, education, etc.

One of the areas highlighted in the RDP framework is land. Land ownership in South Africa has historically been a source of conflict and contention. Colonial and apartheid policies dispossessed millions of black South Africans of their land and moved them into overcrowded and impoverished reserves, homelands and townships. It is estimated that more than 3.5 million people and their descendants were victims of racially-based dispossessions and forced removals during the years of segregation and apartheid. These racially-based land policies were a cause of insecurity, landlessness, poverty and great hurt amongst black people, and also resulted in inefficient urban and rural land use patterns and a fragmented system of land administration. At the transition to democracy in 1994, blacks controlled only about 15% of land in private hands, mainly the rural so-called "homelands".

The RDP framework document urged land reform, and spelled out the three main elements of that reform, which were later provided for in the Constitution:

- **land restitution,** involving the restoration of land or cash compensation to victims of forced removals;
- **land redistribution,** through which people apply for grants with which to purchase land for farming and/or settlement; and
- **tenure reform,** which seeks to improve the clarity and robustness of tenure rights, mainly for residents of former homeland areas.

The RDP framework document furthermore expected that, "within five years the RDP will distribute 30% of the land through redistribution and restitution". In the event, in the decade following the end of the apartheid regime, no more than 2%-3% of the land was reallocated to Africans and Coloureds through redistribution or restitution. Of the 65,000 restitution claims lodged with the Commission on the Restitution of Land Rights, roughly one-third have been settled, but these have been mostly urban claims settled through cash compensation; the large, complex rural claims remain largely unresolved.

Success with redistribution has been even more limited, not only in terms of the number of people helped or amount of land involved, but in the quality and nature of redistribution projects through which land is accessed. Frustrated with the instability of early redistribution projects, in 2001 a new flagship redistribution programme was launched, called Land Redistribution for Agricultural Development (LRAD). This programme promotes black commercial farmers as the main beneficiaries of redistribution, the consequence being that much larger amounts of assistance are being made available to smaller numbers of households.

Tenure reform has perhaps been the most problematic of all the elements of land reform, with government struggling to develop a vision of what tenure reform should involve, especially in the light of resistance from traditional leaders who perceive tenure reform to be a threat.

One consequence of this generally unsatisfactory performance of land reform against government's own targets is the ascendancy over the past few years of the Landless People's Movement (LPM). The LPM has become the main voice for black people wanting to see a completely different vision of land reform and its motto is "Landlessness equal Racism. End Racism! Give Us Our Land Now!". Although LPM is rather weak as an organisation, it articulates aspirations and frustrations that do have great resonance for many black South Africans. There is a growing popular perception that the failure to deliver land reform is a failure to effect post-apartheid transformation, and thus a betrayal of the mandate entrusted to the new democratic state. But the task of land reform is difficult, complex, and expensive - it may be that popular expectations have outstripped what is possible.

Scope, aim and expected policy impact

In this context, the government, as well as civil society, lack sufficient information about the task that confronts them, but in particular about the precise breadth and intensity of people's expectations in terms of demand for land. Only one survey has ever been conducted on the demand for land in South Africa. When this Metagora pilot was initiated, not only was this survey already several years old, but the rather unsystematic manner in which it was conducted made policy conclusions based on it somewhat tenuous. Meanwhile, South Africa's land reform programme - and especially the land redistribution component - is proceeding without robust and detailed information about the demand for land amongst its target beneficiaries. With better information on the nature and extent of land demand, government and civil society would be better able to evaluate present policy and delivery trends, and to formulate new policy initiatives if necessary. This was the challenge for the Metagora pilot in South Africa.

Consultative process and survey design

The pilot began in the summer of 2003, when the Human Sciences Research Council (HSRC) started to consult different key stakeholders on their assumptions and expectations about land reform in general, and their views on the relationship of land issues to governance, human rights and democracy in particular. These stakeholders included government departments, the Human Rights Commission, NGOs (such as the National Land Committee, its affiliates, and the LPM), organised agriculture (such as white farmers), academics, and the National Statistics Council and Statistics South Africa. Consultations assumed different forms, including bilateral discussions between the HSRC-Metagora implementing team and stakeholders, and via a reference group. A literature review (with particular emphasis on the quantitative approach and potential applications of the democratic audit method) and in-depth analysis of the grey literature from various government departments helped identify the many different assumptions informing land reform policy.

The consultations and the literature review allowed building a broad picture of the issues at stake and related assumptions and expectations of the various groups and sectors involved in land reform. On this basis the survey was designed to explore five main dimensions of individuals and households' relationship to land:

- circumstances and situation (*e.g.* employment status and tenure status);
- experiences with land in general and land reform in particular;
- knowledge and understanding of land reform and land administration issues;
- attitudes towards land reform and land administration;
- needs and expectations in respect of land and land reform.

The key dependent variable in this study is land demand and was analysed in terms of: socio-economic circumstances, land loss and redress; current land access and use; knowledge about land reform; and perceptions of governance.

As with all Metagora's pilot experiences, the survey instruments were designed so that these five dimensions were not only covered with regard to the specifics of the South Africa land reform programme (restitution, retribution and tenure reform), but also in a broader perspective. The aim was to allow global lessons to be identified and possible further replication and extension in other countries and cultural contexts.

The survey sample was drawn from three of the more rural of South Africa's nine provinces (Limpopo, Free State and Eastern Cape) and focussed on the four most relevant categories of black respondents:

- 340 inhabitants of mainly white-owned commercial farms;
- 510 inhabitants of traditional communal land;
- 160 householders in urban formal areas; and
- 250 householders in urban informal settlements.

The results have been appropriately weighted. It is interesting to note that the study and sample includes two more groups: traditional leaders and farm owners, though as such the analytical work does not focus on them (e.g. 69 farm-owners, nearly all white, were also interviewed because of their obvious relevance to the processes, and these findings are also touched upon).

Among these four categories, women interviewees predominated on the communal land and in informal settlements, and men on the commercial farms and in formal areas. On average about half of respondents had post-primary education. However, this was true for only one-third of farm dwellers. On average about 60% of respondent households earned less than 1,000 South African Rand per month (approximately EUR 140 at the time of the survey); this proportion rose to around 70% on farms and in urban informal settlements. While landlines were scarce in all but urban households, nearly two-thirds of all respondent households included one or more members with a cell phone.

Results

Governance and democracy

The top three "important challenges facing South Africa today" identified by respondents were unemployment (74%), poverty (47%) and HIV/AIDS (42%). Such priorities overwhelm land reform, which was mentioned spontaneously by only 3%. However, appreciable proportions of respondents had considered views when they focussed on the issue, especially those who had been previously affected by it.

In a similar vein, 55% of those who expressed a view (nearly 90% of respondents) were satisfied with how South Africa is being governed in general. With regard to how government is handling land reform, only half the respondents expressed a view, generally because of a lack of knowledge about land reform. Of those who responded, an average of 38% were satisfied (see Table 5.1, row A – all rows are adjusted for "no answer" or "do not know"). This proportion rose to 52% among farm dwellers, who were also the most satisfied with their current life status compared to five years previously. Regarding the statutory land reform related institutions such as the Land Restitution Commission, Claims Court, and the Department of Land Affairs, around two-thirds of respondents either did not know of them or did not express a view. Among those who did express a view, about half were favourable on average, with lower scores in each case among informal-settlement residents.

However, 75% of respondents expressed views on land-related matters closer to home, e.g. trust in traditional leaders (see Table 5.1, row B). Of these, most communal-land dwellers and farm dwellers expressed trust, whereas only a small majority among urban formal residents expressed such trust, and a minority of informal residents trusted traditional leaders. More generally, respondents were politically aware: more than 75% of all four groupings had voted in the last election and planned to

Table 5.1. **Selected survey results for categories of black respondents**

	Response	% replying "yes", adjusted for "do not know"			
		Farm dwellers	Communal-land	Urban formal	Urban informal
A	Satisfied with how government is handling land reform?	52	35	44	31
B	Trust traditional leaders?	70	78	61	25
C	Perceive residence tenure to be secure?	35	13	19	35
D	The household does not own any fields	97	60	81	98
E	The household does not own any livestock	69	59	94	98
F	Household or ancestors known to have lost land through dispossession?	11	18	19	16
G	Lodged a land claim for restitution (among those aware of the programme)?	10	9	18	20
H	Household needs or wants (additional) land?	53	37	47	50

Source: Human Sciences Research Council of South Africa, HSRC.

vote in the next, even if few spoke frequently of political matters or engaged in political activism, including on land issues.

These findings are a reminder that certain aspects of rights issues may be highly salient to particular groupings, whilst other aspects are not; and that their views on these aspects may vary appreciably with their distinctive interests and contexts.

Land use and access

Though the survey exclusively targets respondents living in households - i.e. no homeless people were interviewed, an appreciable number do not feel their residence is secure (see Table 5.1, row C). More than a third of urban informal dwellers felt insecure, which was to be expected; but the proportion was similar for farm dwellers, since they reside on the owner's land.

A high proportion of respondents do not own land for cropping. This was especially surprising for respondents from communal areas, 60% of whom indicated owning no fields and no livestock (see Table 5.1, rows D and E respectively). The fields that are owned by respondents tended to be small. Among those who are using productive land to which they have access, the most important reason for engaging in agriculture is as "a main source of food for the household". Among those not having used such land in the previous year, lack of financial means was the most prominent reason given, especially if lack of seeds or fertiliser is taken as part of the same explanation.

The findings make clear that the right to land has important different connotations in practice: ownership versus secure ownership, access in principle versus access to an adequate area, and practical affordability.

Land dispossession

Up to a fifth of respondents, depending on the category, reported that they or their ancestors had been dispossessed of land (see Table 5.1, row F). Three-quarters of them indicated that whites were responsible, and another third (multiple answers were permitted) that it was the apartheid rule. A majority in each category, strongest among those on traditional communal land, felt that some form of redress is called for, arranged by government (82%) or white occupants, farmers or others (53%): notably in the form of financial compensation (59%) or restoration of the land (48%). Again, multiple answers were allowed.

However, only 29% of those who had experienced land dispossession could correctly describe the restitution programme. About one-tenth of these in rural areas and one-fifth in urban areas had lodged claims (see Table 5.1, row G). This suggests that lack of awareness was a serious obstacle to getting legal redress under the land reform programme. This is powerfully corroborated by the question of why respondents or their families did not lodge land claims; that is to say, by those respondents who demonstrated some knowledge of the restitution programme but who had not lodged a claim. The predominant answer was, rather obviously, that the household had never lost land, but the second and third most common answers are of true concern: almost 14% reported not knowing how to lodge a claim, and another 8% could not explain ("did not know") why they or their families had not lodged a claim.

Demand for land

The proportion of people wanting or needing land (as such or in addition to that currently available) varies between different settlement types (see Table 5.1, row H), but less so between different types of people (see Figure 5.1). The reason for wanting land was overwhelmingly food security (especially

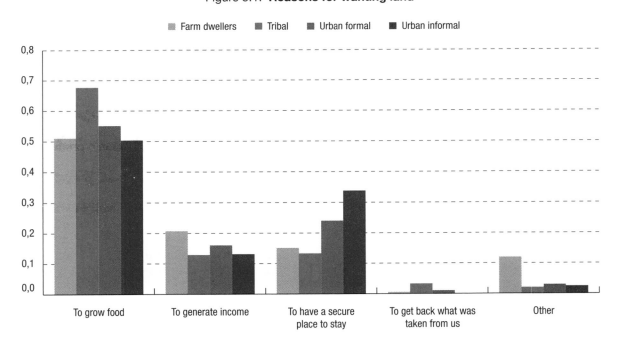

Figure 5.1. **Reasons for wanting land**

Source: Human Sciences Research Council of South Africa, HSRC.

Table 5.2. **Main reason respondent wants/needs land, by experience of land dispossession**

	Yes, household or ancestors dispossessed	No, household or ancestors not dispossessed	Do not know
To grow food	58.6%	63.2%	55.9%
To generate income	5.6%	14.9%	13.6%
To have a secure place to stay	12.8%	20.2%	27.8%
To use as collateral	2.2%	0.0%	0.0%
To get back what was taken from us	13.7%	0.1%	1.5%
Other	7.1%	1.6%	1.1%
Total	100.0%	100.0%	100.0%
N	104	396	89

Source: Human Sciences Research Council of South Africa, HSRC.

for those on communal lands or farms), followed by income generation and (for urban residents) tenure security. Wanting land for restitution received only a few percent of mentions by comparison, though it was slightly higher among those who have been dispossessed (see Table 5.2). This suggests that the views considered above take second place to economic considerations.

The demand for arable land among the majority of respondents is for very small amounts of land, enough to provide household food security. However, a small proportion of respondents would like to acquire much larger amounts of land. To give an idea of the extent of demand for land, the

Table 5.3. **"If you were to get the land you want or need, would you expect..."**
(% answering "yes")

	Farm dwellers	Communal	Urban formal	Urban informal
To have family members work on it?	83.2%	83.1%	86.1%	83.7%
To hire full time, regular workers to work on it?	70.8%	40.8%	76.6%	65.7%
To hire casual workers from time to time?	59.6%	42.0%	44.6%	56.6%
To operate it with other small-scale farmers?	68.0%	46.6%	46.1%	51.6%
To take out a loan to buy inputs, equipment, or livestock?	82.5%	46.7%	50.6%	72.9%
Your children to take it over from you when you get old/die?	97.6%	91.3%	100.0%	90.1%
To earn an income from it?	96.1%	80.9%	96.3%	92.0%
N	140	143	57	58

Source: Human Sciences Research Council of South Africa, HSRC.

estimated total area demanded would be double the amount of current commercial farm land within the three provinces studied. It would be half this amount if household demands were limited to 50 hectares per household.

Table 5.3 adds texture to the previous discussion of why people want land. Notwithstanding the overwhelming importance of land for the purpose of growing food, earning an income is also important (last row). Another important finding is that although there might be some employment created by land transferred through land reform, according to this survey, more people who want land envisage using family labour rather than hired labour.

Gender differences in land demand

Given the policy recognition that land reform should serve as a vehicle to benefit women, it is important to understand gender differences in land demand. Figure 5.2 compares the land demand of women and men in terms of the three main reasons identified above, i.e. to grow food, to generate an income, and to have a secure place to stay (tenure security). Women who want land are more likely than men to want it for growing good and for tenure security, than to generate an income. However, the differences are not stark. The main inference is that land for household food security is the predominant reason people want land, and this is especially true for women.

Blacks' and whites' views on land reform

There is both convergence and divergence between the attitudes to land reform of black and white respondents (whites comprise nearly all the respondents in the subgroup of commercial farm owners). Twenty attitudinal questions revealed that the main area of convergence was in broad support for a conservative approach to land reform, i.e. one that is careful not to disrupt the economy and that does not involve non-compensated land seizures. The main areas of difference include the following:

Figure 5.2. **Relationship between gender and reason for wanting land**

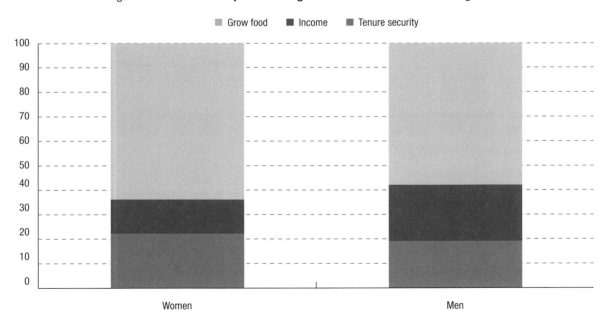

Source: Human Sciences Research Council of South Africa, HSRC.

- black respondents believe white farmers should make more of a sacrifice than the latter believe;
- black respondents favour a broad approach to land reform rather than one that focuses narrowly on certain beneficiary groups;
- black respondents are more optimistic about the benefits of properly conducted land reform for beneficiaries and for the economy;
- urban informal dwellers are more likely to agree with radical statements about how to conduct land reform; and
- farm dwellers are more likely to believe that land reform is important and to approach land reform from a commercial farming perspective.

Views differ as to who should be prioritised to benefit from land reform. Farm dwellers favour those who wish to farm commercially and, not surprisingly, farm workers; communal dwellers and urban formal dwellers mainly favour those from whom the land was taken; and urban informal dwellers most of all favour the poor. The (mostly white) commercial farm owners favour above all young people, followed by those with agricultural skills and those who wish to farm commercially. Views

---

Box 5.1. **Scaling up endogenous policy-oriented research**

Our Metagora experience has shown how important it is that endogenous institutions define and lead the policy-oriented research process in order to ensure that assessments of human rights and democratic governance issues are of genuine national significance.

The Human Sciences Research Council (HSRC) is a statutory research parastatal that forms part of South Africa's science council system. The HSRC's core mandate is to conduct and/or facilitate social science research that serves the public interest, with particular emphasis on the massive social challenges that characterise contemporary South Africa, and indeed the southern Africa region. Given the mission and ethos of HSRC, it was more than natural for it to share and own the main goals of the Metagora community: to promote the use of statistical methods for enhancing assessments of human rights and democratic governance, and to strengthen policy-oriented research in support of democratic dialogue and evidence-based policy-making.

The HSRC was well placed, as an endogenous institution, to conceptualise and carry out research of national significance, in consultation with a range of local stakeholders. The purpose of the Metagora study in South Africa was to shed light on people's aspirations and expectations in respect to redistributive land reform, as well as their general, less personal, attitudes as to what land reform means for the country. It thus sought to inform the debate about land reform and land reform policy in a particular way, *e.g.* not by assessing delivery performance relative to targets, nor by assessing its impact on those who have directly benefited from land reform, but rather by clarifying the targets themselves. As such, the study sought to go back to more fundamental questions: who wants land reform, what do they want it for, and what might be land reform's contribution to national goals such as development and reconciliation?

While the HSRC has a proven track record, its credibility in this particular endeavour was enhanced by its association with the Metagora community, from which it gained in various ways, both technical and non-technical. In the future, the HSRC hopes to partner with the nascent SADC Regional Land Reform Technical Support Facility, through which exercises similar to the South African pilot activity can be undertaken in various other countries in the region.

Udesh Pillay
Executive Director, Human Sciences Research Council, South Africa

---

are strongly polarised on land invasions: an average of about two-thirds of black respondents feel these would be justified under some circumstances, versus barely 3% of mainly white farm owner respondents.

Black respondents – only half of whom, it was noted, have any secondary education – had much less knowledge of the specifics of land reform than the predominantly white farm owners. Similarly, respondents who were financially better-off were generally much more knowledgeable (see Figure 5.3). This has an obvious bearing on who is likely to benefit from land reform measures. However, those who themselves or whose ancestors had experienced land dispossession are also significantly more likely to be aware of land reform, and in particular of land restitution.

White commercial farmers

Compared to the relatively high levels of satisfaction with the land reform process noted in Table 5.1, row A for black respondents, only 13% of the commercial farmers expressed satisfaction. They perceive a high incidence of corruption, and are inclined to distrust the government in general and the Department of Land Affairs in particular. However, white farmers also feel that most of them are supporting rather than impeding or exploiting land reform. Thus, relatively small percentages said they would try to discourage, or oppose, a neighbour wishing to sell his/her land to land reform beneficiaries. Though 42% indicated that their reaction "...would depend on who the beneficiaries are"; and 44% indicated that they think land reform does - or will - negatively affect them.

Figure 5.3. **Knowledge about land reform according to income level**

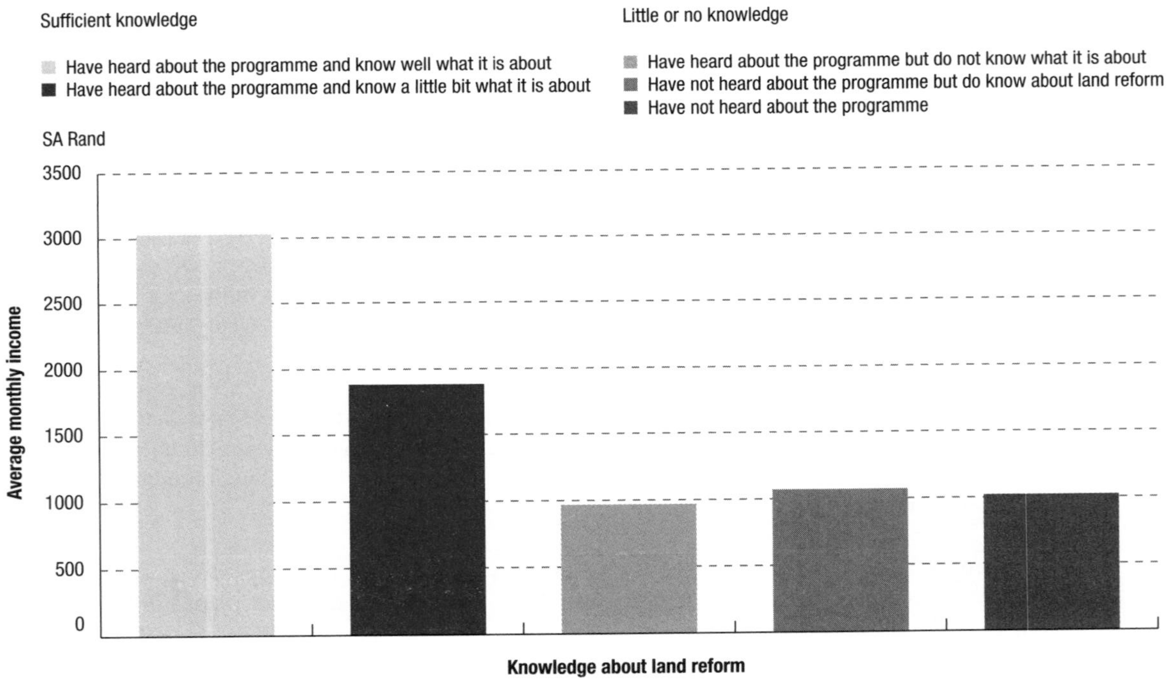
Sufficient knowledge
Have heard about the programme and know well what it is about
Have heard about the programme and know a little bit what it is about
Little or no knowledge
Have heard about the programme but do not know what it is about
Have not heard about the programme but do know about land reform
Have not heard about the programme
SA Rand
3500
3000
2500
2000
1500
1000
500
0
Average monthly income
Knowledge about land reform

Source: Human Sciences Research Council of South Africa, HSRC.

Box 5.2. **Implications of the pilot experience in South Africa**

Key policy implications

- The pilot experience confirmed the feasibility and relevance of measuring the realisation of democracy and human rights in the context of a land reform process.

- Although most black respondents were politically engaged to the extent of voting in elections, land reform featured low on their ranking of development priorities, and only a minority was aware of the actual land reform process and the associated government agencies, with particularly low awareness among rural dwellers. Low education levels and low income are predictors of lack of awareness of land reform, so that those who are already disadvantaged are less likely to seek the benefits of land reform. (e.g. almost three-quarters of those who said they had been dispossessed of land were unaware of the land restitution process and had not sought redress).

- The majority of black people seeking more land had small amounts of money in mind. But a minority of individuals who aspire to become commercial farmers accounted for the major share of land demanded. This calls for thoughtful policy choices.

- The majority of people who want land want it primarily to produce food for themselves. Demand for land mainly for tenure security and commercial purposes account equally for most of the balance. Demand for land "to get back what was taken" is a much more minor rationale.

- Though most of the people who have experienced land dispossession look to some form of restitution, in terms of land and/or financial compensation, only a small percentage had actually lodged claims, mainly because of a lack of awareness of the process. This points to the need for more efficient and targeted information and awareness campaigns on behalf of the institutions concerned.

- Blacks and whites tend to share a conservative attitude towards land reform, in that they believe it should be conducted carefully and non-punitively towards white land owners. However, blacks are far more optimistic about the economic benefits of the process, whether for individuals or the country as a whole.

Major methodological implications

- Measurement and analysis should attempt to encompass the diversity of relevant stakeholders involved in achieving human rights so that policy can take their views into account. This is especially the case, as in many post-colonial contexts, when redressing dispossession is involved.

- By using a six-part sample in each of three purposely chosen provinces, it is possible to address the multifaceted nature of the land question, and the diversity of views of relevant stakeholders. The survey thus covered, collected and analysed data on: rural households on traditional communal lands or residing in commercial farms, residents in formal or informal settlements in urban areas, and traditional leaders and commercial farmers, though a clear focus was put on the first four groups during the analysis. Moreover, whilst the first five groups were exclusively black, the sixth was predominantly white.

- Questionnaire design can highly benefit from being qualitatively informed by relevant policy documents and some exploratory piloting work, which shed light on and confirm the assumptions and issues at stake. This is especially the case through open-ended questions and scripted probes.

- A value-neutral approach is applicable to/and feasible for rights-related empirical investigations and, on the basis of the results, allows subsequent dialogue among the diverse stakeholders.

- This experience did not involve official statisticians; nevertheless future collaboration with the National Statistical Office could take different forms and enhance the quality and legitimacy of the results of studies of this kind.

- If relevant to respondents' concerns, topics that may appear sensitive are answered by respondents with enthusiasm and good will.

Chapter 6

Poverty, Governance and Democratic Participation in Francophone Africa and the Andean Region

One of the main contributions of statistical tools – and in particular of survey methods – to the enhancement of human rights and democratic governance assessments, is to allow to capture objective facts and subjective perceptions directly from people's experiences and views – without the intermediary of experts' opinions or theories. This is of the highest importance in developing countries, where sound knowledge and understanding of daily problems and the perceptions and expectations of the people – and in particular the poor – are essential preconditions for designing and implementing policies and programmes that are truly consistent with the issues at stake: extreme poverty, problematic access to basic services, social and political exclusion, widespread corruption or weak governance.

Two multi-country experiences carried out in Francophone Africa and the Andean region added significant value to the Metagora project, as they focused on "hearing the voice of the poor" on development priorities, democratic participation, social integration, corruption and governance. These experiences consisted of household surveys carried out by eleven National Statistical Offices (NSOs) using the *1-2-3 Survey* methodology developed by the DIAL, *Développement, Institutions et Analyses de Long terme* (Centre of the French Institute for Development Research). These multi-country experiences were implemented under the operational co-ordination of AFRISTAT and the General

This chapter was drafted on the basis of substantive reports, working documents and publications authored by:

Mireille Razafindrakoto, Javier Herrera and **François Roubaud**

The household surveys on subjective poverty, governance and democratic participation were conducted by National Statistical Offices in Francophone Africa and the Andean Community (see boxes p. 99 and p. 104), under the scientific co-ordination and with the technical assistance of the Metagora Partner Organisation:

DIAL, Développement, Institutions et Analyses de Long terme (Centre of the French Institute for Development Research, Paris),
www.dial.prd.fr

Director : Dr. Jean-Pierre Cling, succeeded by Dr. Jacky Fayolle
Metagora Co-ordinator: Dr. François Roubaud, in collaboration with Dr. Mireille Razafindrakoto, Mrs. Constance Torelli, Dr. Emmanuelle Lavallée and Dr. Javier Herrera.

Secretariat of the Andean Community, with scientific support, technical assistance and further in-depth analysis by DIAL.

These multi-country pilots explore the potential of official household surveys for measuring governance and democratic participation issues. Three modules (on different dimensions of poverty, governance and democracy) were added to existing official surveys on employment, the informal sector and poverty. The surveys have provided tangible answers to the following questions:

- How can relevant information on poverty, governance and democratic participation be collected, interrelated and integrated into a robust analytical framework?
- What kind of specific indicators can be produced when relating socio-economic variables to the assessment of democratic governance?
- How do these indicators mesh with indicators based on expert opinions?
- Is it possible, in fragile democracies or in non-democratic regimes, to measure governance issues, expectations for democracy or gaps between political expectations and reality?
- Can NSOs and official statisticians be involved in measuring democratic governance issues?
- Will people respond to sensitive political questions in a survey carried out by a governmental body?

Background and scope of the multi-country experiences

Building on the experience acquired since 1995 by DIAL and the NSO of Madagascar through the MADIO project, three questionnaires (*Multiple Dimensions of Poverty*, *Governance* and *Democracy*) were produced and appended to regular official surveys. The surveys have progressively conducted since 2001 in the capital cities of Benin, Burkina Faso, Côte d'Ivoire, Mali, Niger, Senegal and Togo and Madagascar; and at a national level in Bolivia, Ecuador and Peru.

Box 6.1. **An interactive multi-country experience**

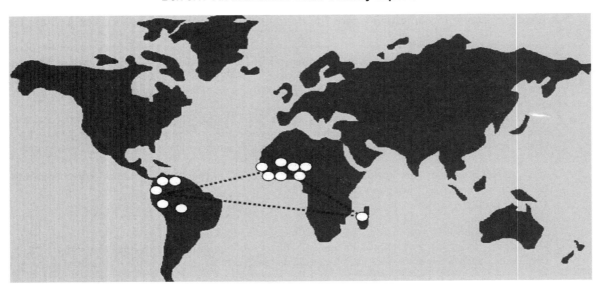

> Box 6.2. **Modules added to the questionnaires of regular official household surveys**
>
> The *Multiple Dimensions of Poverty* module proposes new poverty tracking indicators to inform and enhance poverty reduction policies. Despite recognition of the multifaceted nature of poverty, analyses of the different forms of this phenomenon and the links between them are scarce, mainly due to a lack of accurate data. The module is thus designed to bridge this gap, and also to pay particular attention to households' own subjective assessment of their living conditions and well-being.
>
> The *Governance* module focuses mainly (via questions on both objective facts and subjective perceptions) on the running and efficiency of the public institutions and the role of the state. The survey reflects people's perceptions of various institutions, and then seeks to identify the main sources of dysfunction, notably corruption and absenteeism among civil servants. The second part of the governance module looks at how much support there is among populations for the main economic policies. Lastly, a few more general questions explore the population's perception of the country's long-term trajectory: for example, the causes of underdevelopment, including governance; the country's strategic priorities, economic versus empowerment policies; and what principles a more just society should have.
>
> The *Democracy* module addresses three classic subjects in the field of political surveys: support for democratic principles (how individuals understand and perceive the democratic system compared with other systems), the actual running of democracy, the relations between citizens and polity and the integration to or marginalisation of significant sectors of the population from democratic processes.
>
> The three modules together make up some 200 questions used to gain new insights into these three key issues, about which little information has hitherto been available. The questionnaire is clearly far from being exhaustive: the aim was initially to define some strategic indicators and track them over time. The modules can also be used to identify some key issues – such as inept institutions, dysfunctional democratic principles, or rejection of a type of policy – for which detailed surveys with special focuses can subsequently be set up, for instance of the kind undertaken by the Mexican, Philippines and South African Metagora Partners

The three added modules were discussed, revised and agreed upon by the project's different national partner institutions. In general, the configuration of the questionnaires and the formulation of questions had to meet two criteria.

First, the total number of questions in each module has to be limited due to the fact that the modules were appended to existing surveys on employment, consumption, living conditions, etc.

Second, the project's comparative objective had to be balanced with the need to reflect national specificities and issues of interest. The former comparative objective was partly achieved by taking some of the questions from international initiatives (such as the *World Values Survey*) to be able to compare the answers with those obtained in other regions of the world; and partly by replicating some questions that had been specially designed to meet the survey's specific goals. The latter objective was achieved by some targeted questions corresponding to national centres of interest (for instance, the accountability of specific national public institutions).

The African questionnaires were all largely similar, allowing findings to be compared easily. In the Andean countries, however, individual country questionnaires were more varied, reflecting a greater weight of local considerations.

In Africa the three modules were appended to the *1-2-3 Survey* on employment, the informal sector and poverty. The surveys covered a representative sample of over 35,000 adults, accounting for 21,000 households in the eight African cities.

In Latin America, the survey mechanism was tailored to local particularities, but related to the common matrix designed for Africa. The modules were appended to the main household survey conducted by each NSO as part of the official statistics system: the survey on poverty and living conditions in Peru (ENAHO), the integrated system of household surveys and the survey on income and expenditure of households in Ecuador (SIEH and ENIGHU), and the survey on improved information on households and living conditions in Bolivia (MECOVI). Over 40,000 people were interviewed in the three Latin American countries, enabling a national as well as a regional level of statistical inference in Ecuador and Peru.

There are two main advantages of attaching modules to an existing official household survey. First, this reduces the cost of data collection substantially. Second, this allows to draw on the robust samples, regular collection of data and rich information provided by the master survey. Thus, in Peru the modules covered a sample of over 20,000 households with national, regional and even departmental representativeness; and it was possible to build in annual, quarterly and even monthly tracking indicators right from the start. In Ecuador the sample of 19,000 people also provided a sub-national level of statistical inference. However, this was a one-off effort, and the use of two different surveys for incorporating the modules ruled out any possibility of matching information, at the level of the individual, from the module on subjective poverty with the other two. The statistical properties of the survey were the most limited in Bolivia since the sample covered only 1,570 individuals, but it sample was designed so as to guarantee regional as well as national representativeness.

Surveys in Francophone Africa

Data collection in Francophone Africa (implemented before Metagora was launched) ended in 2003 and an in-depth analysis was then undertaken by the NSOs in collaboration with DIAL. Results are of great interest and allow for some comparisons among the eight capital cities.

Results

Measuring perceptions of poverty

The *1-2-3 Survey* module on the *Multiple Dimensions of Poverty* complements the usual objective criteria of poverty by **asking respondents to define what they consider to be basic needs**, and then to express their level of satisfaction as regards these needs. The minimum basket of needs is taken to be the top 6 of 26 listed items. In all eight countries, these six items were **health treatment, housing, education of children, access to water, electricity,** and **three meals daily** (employment was also mentioned, but not considered because of the lack of a corresponding subjective assessment). The basket is the same across all countries studied, but with some variation in the ranking and scoring. For example, less than half of inhabitants of Bamako and Ouagadougou viewed access to electricity as essential: an "attrition of preferences" due to the fact that electricity supply is only available to some 40% of households.

This approach makes it possible to compare the gap between aggregate satisfaction on each basic need with the level of importance attributed to it. Lomé and Antananarivo are notable for the large gaps between satisfaction and importance for the main basic needs, whereas Bamako and Niamey are striking for their generally small gaps. Dissatisfaction with the health supply was, to different extents, noticeable across all cities studied. A strong correlation was found between subjective and objective indications of poverty.

Another more general approach to subjective poverty is to look at **households' general perception of their well-being** or sense of "happiness". The proportion of those who *"find it hard to make ends meet"* — and who can therefore be categorised as poor from a subjective point of view — ranged from 25% in Bamako to 57% in Lomé. When this measure is compared with the level of satisfaction regarding the six basic needs, there is a close correlation in almost all instances. This makes a good case for including subjective approaches when studying and measuring poverty.

Indicators for monitoring governance: the example of corruption

This section summarises the analysis of questions relating to corruption in the *Governance* module. Corruption is seen as one of the main obstacles to administrative efficiency and is measured by a range of tools that monitor public service reforms. Across the eight cities, the vast majority of respondents, over 90%, believed that corruption was a major problem.

The surveys in capital cities in Francophone Africa were implemented by **eight National Statistical Offices**, with the involvement of the following experts: Mr. Alexandre Biaou (**INSAE, Benin**); Mr. Namaro Yago (**INSD, Burkina Faso**); Mr. Moïse Georges Enoh (**INS, Côte d'Ivoire**); Mr. Faly Rakotomanana (**INSTAT, Madagascar**); Mr. Mahmoud Ali Sako (**DNSI, Mali**); Mr. Djimrao A. Aboubacar (**INS, Niger**); Mr. Mamadou Matar Gueye (**DPS, Senegal**); and Mr. Komlanvi Afodah Eguida (**DGSCN, Togo**). These surveys were designed and implemented in close collaboration with **AFRISTAT,** the Economic and Statistical Observatory of Sub-Saharan Africa, (Director General: Mr. Martin Balepa; experts involved: Mr. Eloi Ouedraogo, Mr. Siriki Coulibaly, and Mr. Ousman Koriko).

Figure 6.1. **Levels of petty corruption and civil servants' wages in Antananarivo, Madagascar**

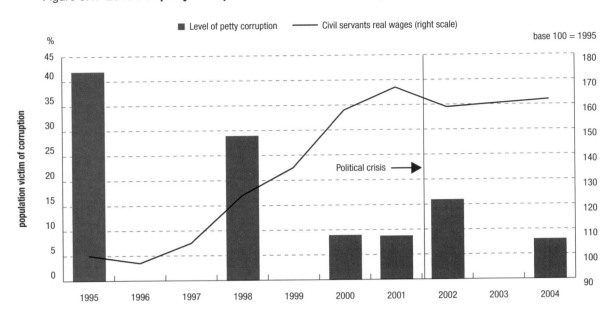

Source: INSTAT Madagascar and DIAL.

Note: The corruption module was not included in the survey in 1996, 1997 and 1999. Figures are derived from an objective indicator of the incidence of petty corruption (percentage of victims of corruption during the previous year).

An average of 13% of respondents in the eight cities reported being **direct victims of corruption** during the year before the survey. A time series from 1995 to 2004 showed an impressive decline in reported experiences of petty corruption (from 42% to below 10%) in Antananarivo, the capital city of Madagascar. Over this period, civil service wages rose in real terms by 50% (see Figure 6.1). This suggests that such time series may allow assessing the impact of public policies.

A nuance concerns measures for addressing corruption. There was widespread support for performance-based remuneration (93%), and coercive measures (82%). The survey revealed similar support for decentralisation to make the administration user-friendly (82%). Importantly, civil servants themselves were hardly less supportive of such measures. But there are revealing variations. The desire to see sanctions for serious misconduct was lower in countries with the most authoritarian regimes (Togo and, to a lesser extent, Burkina Faso), perhaps because citizens fear a fair principle being diverted for political use. And support for decentralisation was more circumspect in Niger and especially in Mali where the process is most advanced, perhaps because its negative effects had started to come to light.

Democracy indicators

The *Democracy* module of the *1-2-3 Surveys* provides information on the consolidation of the democratisation process embarked upon in many African countries at the beginning of the 1990s. The findings show that African citizens, and especially the poor, have embraced the principles of democracy - notably freedom of speech, transparent elections and equality before the law - despite breaches of such rights in different countries.

Figure 6.2. **Measuring dimensions of democracy: Are they fundamental? Are they respected?**

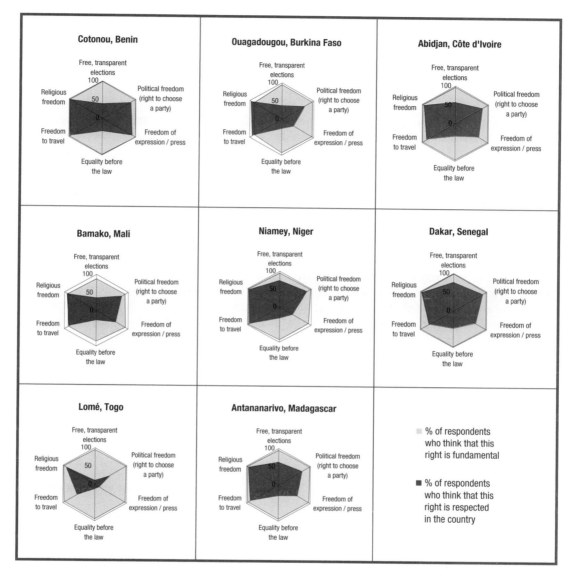

Source: NSOs of Benin, Burkina Faso, Côte d'Ivoire, Mali, Niger, Senegal, Togo and Madagascar and DIAL

Note: The value on each of the six axes is the percentage of respondents who answered "yes" to the questions "In your opinion, is the following right fundamental?" and "In your opinion, is this right respected in the country?"

What is understood by "democracy"? The survey explored whether democracy is a "western value" which may mean something different in other contexts. Respondents were asked whether a list of features traditionally associated with democracy were integral to this notion:

- free and transparent elections
- freedom of speech and the press
- political freedom (choice of political party)

- equality before the law
- freedom of worship
- freedom to travel

The finding was unequivocal. Some 95% of respondents approved each feature; and if the answers to all six are combined, 86% of the population across all cities surveyed felt that they are all **essential** to democracy, regardless of respondents' standard of living.

Respondents were then asked whether they felt each of the six features of democracy was actually **respected** in their country. Similarly to the analysis of basic needs, the gap between what respondents want in terms of rights and freedoms and how they feel the latter are actually respected, can be displayed in polar diagrams (Figure 6.2). While it is evident that religious freedom is generally widespread, other features vary considerably among the countries. For example, free, transparent elections and freedom of expression are low in Lomé (Togo) but high in both Dakar (Senegal) and Antananarivo (Madagascar); whilst in Cotonou (Benin), the press is considered to be much freer than elections, and the opposite is true in Niamey (Niger).

On average, 87% of the eight cities' inhabitants are "very much in favour" or "in favour" of democracy. Togo, which has a repressive political system, had the highest percentage of people expressing an unreserved yearning for democracy, with over 63% "very much in favour of democracy". Democracy is far more appreciated than other forms of government. Less than one in five respondents preferred an authoritarian regime, whether headed by a "strong man" (18%) or by the army (14%). Moreover, only 35% preferred "experts" to a democratically elected government, to decide what is right for their country. At the same time, around one-third of the population considered that democracy may have shortcomings: specifically that the economic system does not work well under democratic rule, and that democracies have problems maintaining order. Yet these shortcomings are seen as minor

Table 6.1. **The link between views on democracy and income**
(% of respondents answering "yes" to the following statements)

	ALL	Quartiles of income per capita			
		1st quartile (poorest)	2nd quartile	3rd quartile	4th quartile (wealthiest)
Assessment of the different political regimes :					
A. To have a strong leader	18	20	19	18	16
B. To live under military rule	14	14	16	15	12
C. To have experts decide on what is good for the country	35	36	34	36	33
D. To have a democratic political regime	86	88	86	86	87
Weaknesses of democracy :					
A. In democracy, the economic system does not work well	31	33	33	31	28
B. Democracies are unable to maintain order	34	35	35	35	32
C. Democracies have difficulties in decision-making	47	47	48	47	47
D. Democracy is better than other forms of government	81	81	80	80	82

Source: 1-2-3 Survey methodology, Democracy module, 2001/2003, NSOs, AFRISTAT, and calculations by DIAL.

Box 6.3. **Policy implications of the pilot surveys in Francophone Africa**

- These surveys shed light on phenomena which had hitherto received little (if any) attention.

- Despite gaps from country to country in the extent to which civil and political rights were respected, results showed massive support among African citizens, particularly among the poorest people, for principles of democracy such as freedom of expression, electoral transparency and equality before the law. This contrasts with received wisdom.

- The surveys' findings also illustrate the public's general disenchantment with the political class, whose role in the crisis in Côte d'Ivoire was particularly damaging.

- The urgent "need for state" was clearly and strongly expressed by the poorest groups.

- The surveys highlight the widespread nature of petty corruption, although proactive policies have been reducing it, such as in Madagascar where the number of cases of petty corruption halved between 2002 and 2004.

- Surveys in Africa (and also in the Andean region) provided precise information for evaluating local governance.

---

compared with the more than four in five people convinced that democracy - understood in the survey as a political process for appointing leaders via the ballot box - is the best system of government. Moreover, the survey revealed a massive support for democracy among both poor and rich (see Table 6.1).

Predicting crises?

Taken together, the range of indicators allows for an assessment of the country's social and political stability. For example, Lomé's population appeared glaringly dissatisfied with all the areas covered, and Togo was in last position for both governance and democracy. The results for Côte d'Ivoire are more mixed. Although the inhabitants of Abidjan were not particularly pessimistic about the way in which they were being governed, when findings were disaggregated a wider ethnic split appeared between the north and south, with the former being more distrustful of official institutions and national authorities and believing that the situation was getting worse. This finding is of particular interest given the crisis which broke out in Côte d'Ivoire after the data collection. This underlines the value of the surveys as a potential monitoring tool for anticipating crises, as well as the importance of proper data disaggregation.

Household surveys in three Andean countries

Over 40,000 people were interviewed in Bolivia, Ecuador and Peru in the framework of regular household surveys carried out by NSOs (see box below). As mentioned, the large samples of 20,000 households in Peru and 19,000 in Ecuador permitted regional as well as national analysis. The sample in Bolivia was 1,570, a sixth of the sample of the parent survey, but nationally and regionally representative.

Results

Perceptions of corruption

Governance is a high priority in Ecuador and Peru. While lack of jobs is perceived as "the number one priority" in both countries (31% and 44% of respondents respectively), corruption ranks second in Ecuador (29%), and third in Peru (8%) after poverty (28%). In both countries, lack of credibility of public institutions comes next (7%).

This diagnosis is directly reflected in citizens' poor confidence in institutions. In all three countries, the public distrusts the judiciary and the police most, though the main function of these two institutions is precisely to enforce the law. The trade unions and political parties, who are meant to defend rights and represent citizens in public debate, hardly fare better. The church, which often plays the role of mediator in serious social conflicts, receives greatest confidence. The public also remains confident in the public education and health services.

Table 6.2 illustrates, through the example of survey results in Peru, how disaggregation of information by institution allows for a precise diagnosis of the situation and can therefore inform focused policy interventions. Also, Figure 6.3 shows that lack of confidence in specific institutions - such as the police and the judiciary – correlates with households' actual experience of corruption with these precise institutions.

The household surveys on subjective poverty, governance and democratic participation were conducted by three National Statistical Offices of the Andean Community: **INE, Bolivia** (Director General: Mr. José Luis Carvajal, succeeded by Mr. Oscar Lora; leading expert: Mrs. Betty Pastor); **INEC, Ecuador** (Director General: Mr. Víctor Manuel Escobar, subsequently succeeded by Mr. Luis Alfredo Carrillo Jaramillo and Mr. Byron Villacís Cruz; leading expert: Mr. Claudio Gallardo); **INEI, Peru** (Director General: Dr. Gilberto Moncada, succeeded by Mr. Renán Jesús Quispe Llanos; leading experts: Mrs. Nancy Hidalgo and Mr. César Pantoja). A survey with a more delimited scope and coverage was also implemented by the National Statistical Office of **Colombia, DANE** (Director General: Mr. César A. Caballero, succeeded by Mr. Ernesto Rojas Morales; leading expert: Mr. Eduardo Freire). The experts of these National Statistical Offices gathered, together with experts of **INE, Venezuela**, in the Andean Community's **"Intergovernmental Group of Experts on Statistics on Subjective Poverty, Democracy and Participation",** convened and co-ordinated by the Metagora Partner Organisation:

General Secretariat of the Andean Community (Lima, Peru)
www.comunidadandina.org
Secretary General: Ambassador Allan Wagner Tizon
Metagora Co-ordinator: Mr. Guillermo Lecaros, in collaboration with Mr. César Correa and Mr. Javier Monterrey.

Table 6.2. **Public confidence in institutions in Peru**

(in % of respondents)

Do you have confidence in the following institutions?	A lot/more or less	A little/not at all	Do not know
Political parties	18	80	2
Congress	24	72	4
Judiciary	26	57	17
Trade unions	31	62	7
Police	31	65	4
Regional governments (CTAR)	37	50	13
Press	41	58	1
National Development Project Fund (Foncodes)	43	47	10
Local (municipal) government	44	53	3
Ombudsman	49	50	1
TV & radio	54	37	9
Social security (ESSALUD)	57	41	2
Civil registers (RENIEC)	59	35	6
Health Ministry	72	27	1
Education Ministry	74	25	1

Source: Estimation by DIAL, based on ENAHO 2002-IV.

Figure 6.3. **Incidence of corruption within public agencies in Peru**

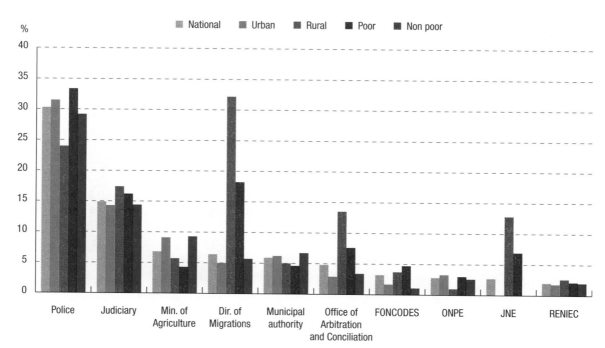

Source: INEI Peru and estimation by DIAL, based on ENAHO 2002-IV.

Note: Respondents were asked whether they "had been asked, felt forced, or gave voluntarily gifts, tips, gratuities, bribes".

Figure 6.4. **Importance of democracy in Ecuador according to respondents' education level**

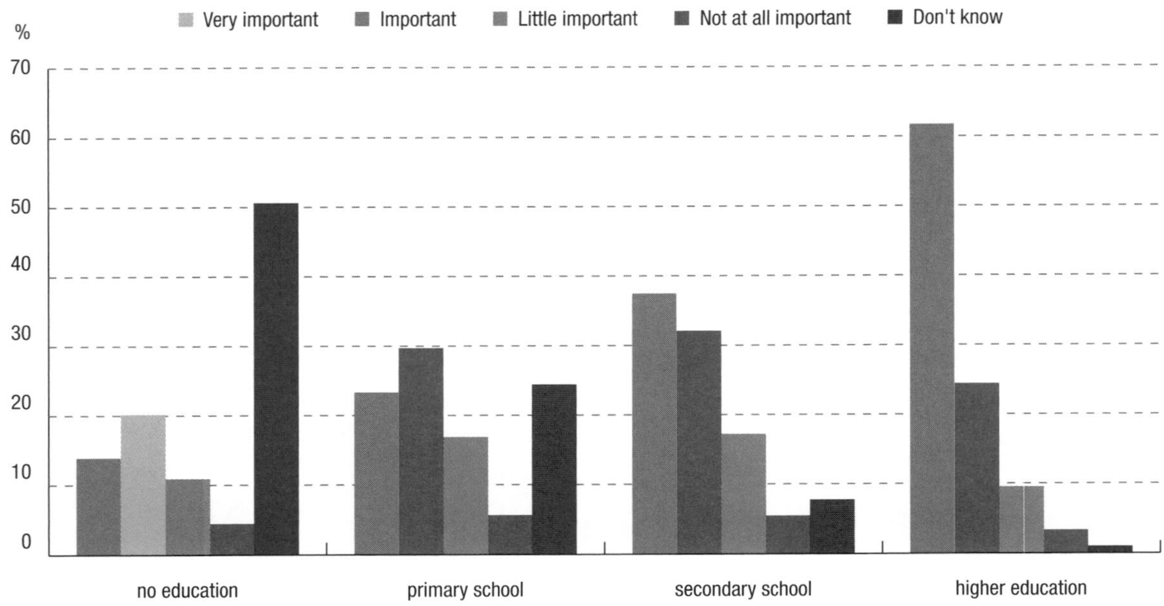

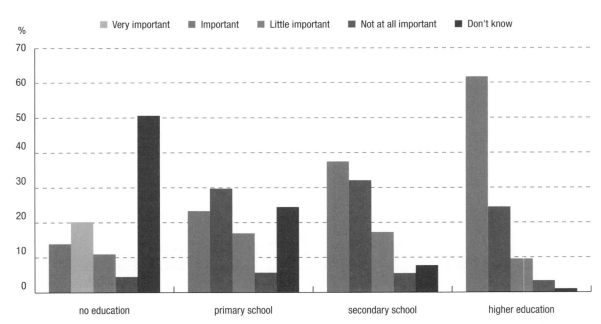

Source: INEC Ecuador, based on SIEH III, *Democracy* module, March 2004.

Figure 6.5. **Support for democracy across countries**

Source: INEC, Ecuador (SIE-ENEMDU-2004); INEI, Peru (ENAHO 2003-2004); INE, Bolivia (*Encuesta Continua de Hogares*, 2004) and calculations by DIAL.

Democracy indicators

As in Africa, most respondents attach high importance to the values of democracy and prefer it to other political systems, despite a rather lukewarm assessment of how well democracy works in their countries. In all three countries, over two-thirds of the population stated that they were "very much in favour" or "in favour" of democracy as a mode of government. But the proportion of individuals who responded with "do not know" was relatively high, particularly among women and in rural areas where adults have had little access to education, reflecting the exclusion of women and indigenous peoples from public life (see Ecuadorian example in Figure 6.4).

Again like in Africa, respondents considered "maintaining order" and "the economic system" as the most important shortcomings of democracy. There are telling differences among the countries in the level of public support for other forms of political regime (see Figure 6.5). Technocratic regimes come in second place behind democracy in the three Andean countries, reflecting the massive and extensive disfavour in which the political class is held (over 90% of interviewees felt that politicians only think of their own interests). In Ecuador and Peru, the population is somewhat lenient when it comes to military regimes, which have introduced land reforms and nationalised oil resources. This view is not shared in Bolivia, where military regimes are associated with the repression of the trade union movement and the suppression of individual freedom.

However, the population at large remains attached to democratic values. Only 13% did not vote in the municipal elections in 2002. The rate of non-participation rises among the poor, the rural, and the less-educated: groups that are also least likely to have the necessary voter's identification card (*libreta electoral*) or to be listed on the electoral registers. Economic factors, notably the cost of transport and

Figure 6.6. **Relationship between popular support for democratic regimes and perceptions of corruption and democracy performance, Peru**

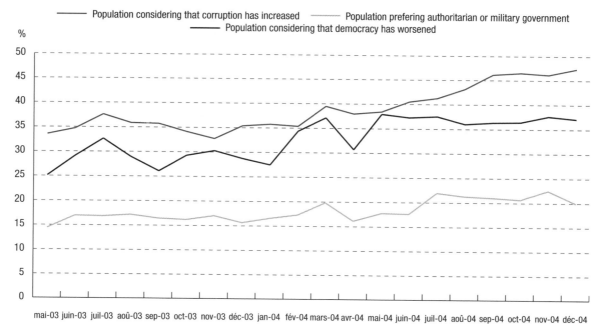

Source: Estimation by DIAL, based on ENAHO May 2003 - December 2004.

remoteness from the polling stations, rank second among the reasons for not voting. Only a couple of percent considered that "voting serves no purpose".

High public expectations of the virtues of democratic systems can be eroded over time. In Peru, the predominant feeling is that democracy has not improved since 1990, the beginning of the corrupt and autocratic Fujimori regime (the corresponding opinion is even more severe in Ecuador). Implementation of the surveys on continuous bases in Peru since May 2003 has led to the production of time series, thus allowing for views on democracy, corruption, and democratic performance to be compared over time. The finding is clear: as perceptions of corruption and democratic dysfunctions increase, preferences for an authoritarian or military regime gain ground (see Figure 6.6).

The population's "subjective" perception of corruption is that it has worsened over the period, whereas the "objective" incidence of actual experiences of petty corruption suffered by the households has not (see Figure 6.7). This shows the importance of combining both objective and subjective approaches. The difference, in Peru, may be because of increasing press attention to the issue; and also because stories of large-scale instances affect people's perceptions of the overall situation even though they themselves may be unaffected.

Reflecting the impact of social policies

Andean countries have introduced decentralisation to ensure more resources and participation for citizens in remote villages. Support for decentralisation was massive. However, more local corruption was a possible side-effect and the survey was designed to explore such issues. Data was disaggregated at the departmental level so as to capture existing differences – for instance, some regions may suffer

Figure 6.7. **Petty corruption in Peru: divergence between perception and actual incidence**

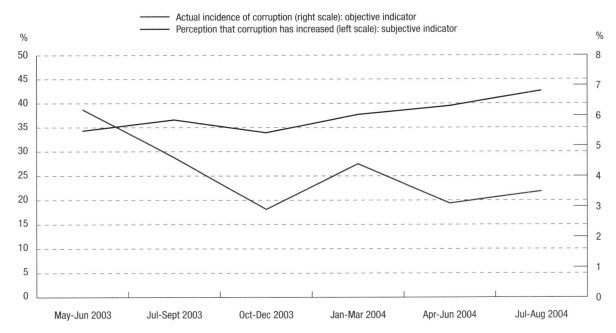

Source: Estimation by DIAL, based on ENAHO May 2003 - December 2004.

Table 6.3. **Perceptions of the impact of decentralisation in Peru**

Departments	...greater participation in decision-making?	...an improvement in public services?	...better attention to peoples' demands?	...more injustices and abuses?
Amazonas	38	42	42	40
Ancash	42	51	51	54
Apurimac	33	35	36	34
Arequipa	70	83	81	48
Cusco	56	61	63	40
Huancavelica	55	62	62	34
Huanuco	45	49	49	44
Ica	76	81	90	77
Junin	67	81	79	39
La Libertad	50	60	57	38
Lambayeque	48	66	76	82
Lima	43	50	55	38
Loreto	36	38	34	44
Pasco	77	70	77	27
...	...	...	...	...
Total	**51**	**57**	**59**	**44**

Source: Estimation by DIAL, based on ENAHO 2004.

Note: These percentages correspond to "a lot" and "more or less" mentions on a scale including: "a lot", "more or less", "little" and "not at all".

Table 6.4. **Are the poor less or more affected by corruption?**

Expenditure quintiles	Incidence (all individuals)	Incidence (individuals in contact with public services)	Average cost (soles per capita/year)	Weight of corruption (% of food expenditure)	Reason for not reporting: (fear of the consequences, don't know how to)
I (poorest)	2.6%	3.1%	4.8	0.8%	49%
II	4.4%	5.3%	8.4	0.9%	41%
III	5.0%	5.8%	7.2	0.7%	23%
IV	6.2%	7.1%	21.6	1.4%	31%
V (wealthiest)	7.9%	8.9%	33.6	1.2%	30%
Household condition					
Non Poor	6.8%	7.9%	69	1.3%	30%
Poor	3.9%***	4.6%***	15***	0.7%	37%***
Total	5.2%	6.1%	48	1.1%	32.3%

Source: Calculations by DIAL, based on INEI Peru, ENAHO 2002-IV.

Note: The incidence represents the ratio of individuals who live in households where at least one member has been victim of corruption. *** The differences between Poor and Non Poor are significant at 1%.

more than others from governance problems, and each region may face local specific governance issues, such as decentralisation or local accountability (see Table 6.3).

In the region of Arequipa in Peru, for example, 80% of inhabitants wanted decentralisation to be introduced and two-thirds expected that, as a consequence, local authorities would pay more attention to their needs. Only about 25% feared that decentralisation would generate more injustice and abuse by the local authorities. However, with the reforms now implemented, Arequipa has become the region where the population's *ex-post* evaluation of the process is the most negative. Less than 20% of respondents think that decentralisation has given the citizens a greater voice or has improved public services. Less than one-third consider that the population has a greater role in decision-making. Nearly half of the population even believes that decentralisation has brought greater injustice. It therefore comes as no surprise that, after the decentralisation process took place, there was a popular revolt in Arequipa that paralysed the economy for several days.

Data disaggregation reflecting the condition of the household in terms of expenditure quintiles is also highly informative. In Peru in 2002, the incidence of petty corruption was 6.1% (see Table 6.4). As in Africa, the non-poor are more concerned than the poor and frequency increases with the standard of living. The sums paid by the households to corrupt civil servants account for 0.4% of their total expenditure. This amount is not insignificant considering that it represents approximately one-third of state transfers received by households by way of social poverty reduction programmes.

Contrary to the findings from Francophone Africa, in Peru the relative cost of corruption in the household budget is generally lower for the poor than for the rich. Possible explanations of this difference could be that the questionnaire on household expenditure in Peru is more detailed and includes the various purchasing modes, or that the Peruvian ENAHO survey has a national coverage thus including both urban and rural households, and not just the capital city (see Herrera, Razafindrakoto, Roubaud, 2006). Also, the low presence of the state and the high incidence of poverty in rural areas tend to suggest that the rural Peruvian households are less "exposed" to the risk of corruption. Moreover, the costs of corruption probably have a dissuasive effect on many of them, hence increasing their marginalisation from state services.

Box 6.4. **Implications of the surveys in the Andean region**

Key policy implications

- In Bolivia, Ecuador and Peru, high levels of corruption are a major problem that is jeopardising the consolidation of democracy: support for authoritarian alternatives have increased as governments have appeared as dysfunctional to the population.

- Several survey questions on democracy and governance had high proportions of "don't know" answers, especially among women and in rural areas where levels of poverty are high and where most adults have had little access to education. This predominance of "don't know" answers constitutes significant information: it broadly reflects the exclusion of certain groups (such as women and indigenous peoples) from public life and society, and highlights the links between poverty, low levels of education and marginalisation from democratic processes.

- By disaggregating the data to reflect local specificities and concerns, or the behaviour and action of particular institutions, it is possible to inform – and better target – policies aimed to enhance governance at the local level or within specific national public agencies.

- The support for democracy over authoritarian alternatives, and the support for its key tenets, rebuts the assumption that democracy is less welcomed or differently understood in different parts of the world.

- Especially when data can be disaggregated by social and/or regional groups, the data collected through the household surveys potentially allow the prediction of crises.

- When surveys are repeated over time, the impact of policy interventions on the quality of governance can be monitored, and up-to-date information provided for decision-making processes and civil society engagement.

Major methodological implications

- Collaboration between NSOs and institutions specialised in applied research, such as DIAL, is highly productive. Official household surveys provide applied research and policy analysis with large and methodologically well-founded platforms. *Ad hoc* modules focusing on democracy, governance or economic and social rights can be added to regular official household surveys at modest additional cost and without compromising response rates.

- Large samples or time series led to invaluable extra insights. Survey-based indicators of democratic governance are technically feasible and analytically sound. The production of this kind of indicators could therefore be included in the National Statistical Development Strategies promoted by PARIS21 and supported by the UN family.

Methodological discussion

Do people answer "sensitive questions" on governance and democracy?

These multi-country surveys in Francophone Africa and the Andean countries dampened the widespread scepticism about whether democratic governance issues can be measured with official survey-based tools. The assumption had been that people would be very reluctant to respond to survey questions on "sensitive issues" such as corruption, political participation or support for democratic values. Such questions were thought to risk jeopardising the robustness of surveys by contributing to high non-response rates.

In fact, as shown in Table 6.5, in Francophone Africa, the non-response rate for questions on governance and democracy is generally lower than for questions on income (see detailed analysis in Amegashie *et al.*, 2005). This observation also holds for Latin America. For example, in the case of Peru where accurate calculations were made, the rate of non-response to the modules was low (from 2% to 4%) and was approximately half that for the entire standard ENAHO questionnaire (see Figure 6.8).

Thus, adding the modules onto existing official household surveys did not undermine the quality – or quantity - of responses to the basic survey. In some cases, the modules generated such interest among respondents that they were actually more inclined to answer these than the more classic socio-economic questions on consumption and income. Another reason why the added questions did not undermine the quality of the survey as a whole is that the time required for responding to the entire questionnaire remained reasonable. In Peru, the average length of an interview for all 3 modules was 31 minutes (9 minutes for the *Governance* module, 10 minutes for the *Democracy* module and 12 minutes for the *Multiple Dimensions of Poverty* module).

In the rural areas of the Andean countries, where the poor and relatively uneducated indigenous population is mainly found, some of the interviewees found it hard to understand the concepts used (such as democracy and references to other political systems), did not know that certain public institutions existed (especially institutions defending and protecting citizens' rights), and had trouble ranking their opinions (for instance, the country's main problems). As regards corruption, in particular, they tended to consider that the "gifts" to civil servants were part of the traditional (Andean) system of mutual assistance or they viewed corruption as "normal". These intrinsic problems are reflected by a percentage of "do not know" specifically in response to certain questions. However, this situation should not be confused with a refusal to answer all or part of the survey.

Table 6.5. **Rates of non-response to certain module questions in Francophone Africa**

%	Cotonou	Ouaga-dougou	Abidjan	Bamako	Niamey	Dakar	Lomé	Total
Running of the state	0	3.6	0.9	1.1	2.7	5.2	3.5	2.2
Opinion of democracy	0	2.8	0.5	0.9	1.9	3.1	0.3	1.1
Income stated in value	59.9	45.7	59	56.6	47.6	43.3	62.7	53.4
Income stated in value or brackets	97.7	93.4	96.8	93.3	84.8	90.2	98.3	93.6
Income not given	2.3	6.6	3.2	6.7	15.2	9.8	1.7	6.4

Source: 1-2-3 Surveys, Phase 1, *Governance* and *Democracy* modules, 2001/2003, National Statistical Offices, AFRISTAT, DIAL - calculations of DIAL.

Figure 6.8. **Peru: rates of non-response to (1) the overall survey and (2) the *Governance* and *Democracy* modules**

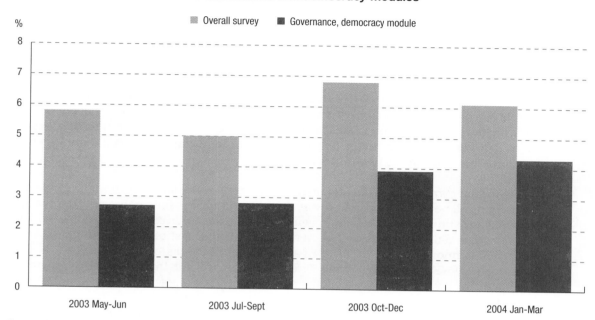

Source: ENAHO May 2003-March 2004, INEI, Peru, based on DIAL calculations.

In the case of the Andean countries, non-responses to certain questions were closely correlated with the level of education (language problems were ruled out in that interviewers speaking the local dialects conducted the surveys in areas with high indigenous population concentrations). Although it is hard to interpret refusal to answer the survey in the absence of information on the characteristics of the non-respondents, this type of non-response does provide some valuable information. It tells us exactly how integrated into citizenship the historically marginalised populations are. It provides an indicator on the ability of individuals to understand and express themselves, the extension of which should be one of the aims of the empowerment policies. The survey also helps further the expression of the "voice" of the poorest population groups, even if these groups have to make do with stating their lack of comprehension or ignorance when it comes to such issues as preferences for a political system, diagnosing the country's problems and assessing the running of democracy.

The Mirror Survey: comparing household survey results with expert opinion

To complement the survey on governance and democracy carried out in Francophone Africa, DIAL also surveyed experts to compare their perceptions with those of the general public. A total of 250 "experts" or "well informed persons" from both the Southern and Northern hemispheres responded to this *Mirror Survey* respondents included researchers, development specialists, decision makers, high-ranking public officials and politicians.

The "experts" were asked to select a country (out of the eight) that they knew well and then fill in the *Mirror Survey* questionnaire, which was actually a simplified version of the original questionnaire used in the household surveys. Two sets of questions were asked for each of the two modules (*Governance* and *Democracy*):

- Questions about the expert's opinion on the issues targeted by the household surveys. For example, experts were asked to give their personal opinion of how well democracy worked in the chosen country.
- Questions designed to gain an idea of what the experts would expect the public to answer. For example, for the question *"Does democracy work well in the country?"*, each expert respondent had to estimate the percentage of citizens who would answer *"Yes"* in the chosen country.

Not all the questions could work like this. For example, for the question, *"Which group do you feel proudest to belong to? 1. Your country, 2. Your ethnic group,"* only the experts' guesses about respondents' answers (*i.e.* the second set of questions) would be relevant. Lastly, to hone the analysis, experts were asked to provide a certain number of personal socio-demographic characteristics: gender, age, occupation, knowledge in the field, etc.

Sampling for the *Mirror Survey* was obviously complicated by the lack of a comprehensive sampling frame covering all potential "experts". It was therefore decided to follow the same approach as that used by most existing expert pools: *i.e.* drawing on DIAL's networks of correspondents worldwide, in both the North and the South, as well as on networks of other institutions working on these issues. These include, among others, Metagora partners, the networks of the OECD/DAC Network on Governance (GOVNET) and the French Directorate General for International Co-operation and Development. In addition, the questionnaire was applied during meetings of experts (CODI/ECA) and training sessions organised by various institutions for development experts (such as the courses of the InWent Centre). Finally, the questionnaire was sent to all recipients of DIAL's newsletter *Dialogue* and was also put online on the DIAL website. Although the representativeness of the *Mirror Survey* cannot be formally assessed due to the lack of a clearly defined reference population, the similarity between this database and the main international databases on this subject can be considered to be a form of *ex-post* validation of the survey.

As it has been highlighted in *Chapter 1*, existing governance indicators are mainly based on experts' assessments. The *Mirror Survey* therefore aimed to explore the extent to which views of experts – and indicators that aggregate these views – can be trusted. Results from the *Mirror Survey* revealed that experts seem to systematically overestimate the level of corruption suffered by citizens (see Razafindrakoto and Roubaud, 2005). Whereas an average of 13% of the population in the eight cities said that they had been direct victims of acts of corruption over the past year, experts estimated this rate to be 54%. Likewise, while barely 5% of the population considered that giving a bribe would be acceptable behaviour, experts reckoned this proportion would be 32%. In other words: experts have a much more negative view of the situation of petty corruption than the actual population, and current governance indicators may be, to a certain extent, erroneous and misguiding (for a detailed analysis of the profile of victims of corruption, see Razafindrakoto and Roubaud, 2004).

This extensive overestimation of actual corruption levels would not be so bad if at least it was consistent across the board. Yet major disparities in the relative ranking by experts of the countries show that this is far from being the case (see Figure 6.9). For example, experts have a relatively positive image of Burkina Faso ("the country of honest men"), giving it the lowest incidence of petty corruption in the *Mirror Survey*. It also received the lowest percentage of experts deeming corruption to be a major problem. Yet this is belied by the population's own perception and actual experiences. Conversely, Togo has a significantly lower level of daily corruption than the regional average, but was ranked the worst offender by the experts.

In fact, there is no correlation between the experts' estimates and the population surveys: the correlation coefficient is even slightly negative (-0.19). However, the *Mirror Survey* findings do correlate with indicators published in international databases and developed by experts. For example, the

Figure 6.9. **Significant findings of the *Mirror Survey***

a) Deviations between actual incidence of petty corruption and experts' assumptions about corruption in Francophone Africa

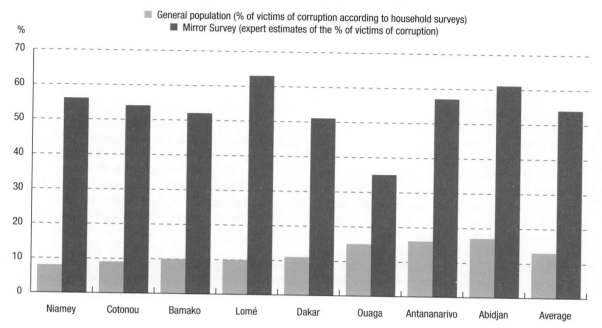

b) Do people consider giving a bribe to be acceptable behaviour?

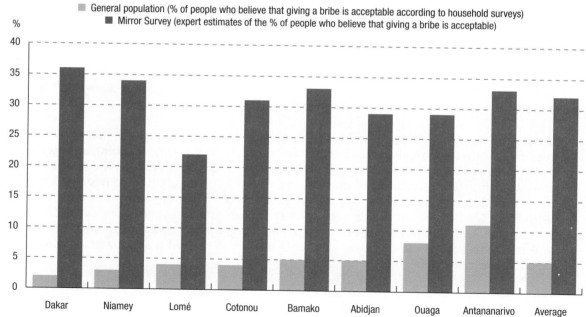

Source: 1-2-3 Surveys, Governance module, 2001/2003, NSOs, AFRISTAT, DIAL (35,534 persons interviewed; 4,500 on average in each country); *Mirror Survey* (246 experts surveyed; 30 experts on average in each country), DIAL. Calculations by DIAL.

correlation between the frequency of corruption from the *Mirror Survey* and the "control of corruption" indicator built by the World Bank Institute group (see Kaufmann, Kraay and Zoido-Lobaton 2002), which falls as corruption rises, is -0.52. This makes for a positive link. Indeed, the calculation of the Spearman coefficient of rank correlation produces similar findings: 0.02 between the *Mirror Survey* data and the population survey data; -0.50 between the findings of the *Mirror Survey* and the indicator from the base by Kaufmann, Kraay and Mastruzzi, 2005. On the other hand, the correlation between the real rate of corruption and the KKZ indicator is 0.48 (therefore indicating towards opposite directions), although this is not significant.

These observations raise doubts about the reliability of expert-based data and indicators, which are widely used by donors, especially to allocate official development assistance. Admittedly, this finding is limited to petty corruption in the eight countries studied. But it could reasonably be argued that it is precisely in those countries for which we lack information that the perception indices (produced by experts) will be furthest from reality. Yet the question remains as to what exactly the perception indicators based on expert pools measure. The findings of the *Mirror Survey* in no way undermine the relevance of such perceptions, and subsequent indicators, since such views of corruption are common, even if they do not reflect reality. But if corruption phenomena are to be understood in all their complexity, these indicators should be combined with a new generation of indicators based on objective measurements.

The surveys carried out in Francophone Africa and the Andean region show that it is possible to develop indicators for evaluating how well institutions and democracy are working, and for measuring the degree of support for policies among the general public. These indicators are generally less complex to implement than traditional socio-economic indicators, such as, for example, monetary poverty, and people are more likely to respond. A scientific comparison with other international initiatives (such as the Afrobarometer and Latinobarómetro projects) revealed both the strong convergence of results across the common fields — confirming the robustness of the indicators proposed here — and the areas in which the various instruments complement each other. Indeed, in June 2004, an international workshop co-organised by Metagora was held in Bamako, Mali, to compare the results and methods of three different survey-based tools that are being used in Africa to measure democratic governance: the Afrobarometer, the United Nations Economic Commission for Africa survey within the framework of the NEPAD peer review, and household surveys based on the *1-2-3 Survey* method. Similarly, Metagora organised a one-day workshop in March 2005 in La Paz, Bolivia, which allowed to compare on sound technical basis the surveys implemented by Latinobarómetro with those carried out within the framework of Metagora.

During the workshops, the different survey approaches were presented by senior experts and the results in different areas (access to public services, legitimacy of political representatives, corruption, etc.) were subject to comparative analysis. Discrepancies in the results served as a starting point for methodological discussions, thus leading to identify convergent and divergent aspects of the survey approaches as well as to assess the advantages and disadvantages of these. With these workshops, African and Latin-American experts and institutions currently involved in measurement of democratic governance gathered together in an atmosphere of mutual interest and transparency on the methods and tools used, and started a serious discussion on proper measurement methods.

Following the success of the African and Andean multi-country surveys in terms of both methodology (governance and democracy can be reliably measured) and analysis (results can shed light on public policies), a process has begun to institutionalise this approach as a regular official measurement tool. Some countries have started, or are planning, to incorporate this type of survey into their national statistical systems on a permanent basis. In Madagascar, the survey is now being carried out annually

---

Box 6.5. **Implications of the *Mirror Survey***

Key policy implications:

Today several governmental and non-governmental institutions produce data and develop international governance indicators on the basis of "expert pools" or the views of "well-informed persons". Many multilateral organisations, governments and development agencies often rely on these indicators in their internal analysis and decision-making processes as well as in their policy statements. Moreover, some countries are developing aid conditionality policies based on targets (such as levels of "good governance") that they intend to monitor using these indicators. In order to encourage proper interpretation of aggregates and to prevent misuse of these, a joint Eurostat/UNDP manual on sources of governance indicators, published in 2004, provided information on the sources, scope and methodological basis of existing indicators (as well as, in several cases, on their methodological opacity; see Eurostat/UNDP Oslo Governance Centre, 2004 and 2007). This raises a basic question: *How much can we trust expert opinions on corruption?*

A first evidence-based answer is provided by comparing the findings reported here, that while an average of 13% of the population in the eight cities said that they had been direct victims of corruption over the past year, experts responding to the *Mirror Survey* estimated the figure to be 54%.

While the *Mirror Survey* should still be further refined and replicated, its findings suggest that so-called "expert-based" surveys of corruption can systematically over-estimate the phenomenon, raising serious questions about decisions based on indicators derived from this kind of survey. Metagora therefore issues a warning to governments, development agencies and multilateral organisations: be cautious about relying only on indicators derived from expert opinion for making policy decisions.

---

by INSTAT, while the INEI in Peru is carrying it out on a monthly, quarterly and annual basis to build time-series indicators. The possibility of renewing the surveys is also being considered in other countries, such as Benin, Côte d'Ivoire or Ecuador.

The survey has great potential to be adopted on a wider scale:

- The approach offers all the advantages of statistical household surveys: transparency of measurement procedures, representative nature of collected information and quantification of phenomena, and allowing indicators to be compared over time.
- The richness of the information collected allows for better and more in-depth policy-oriented analyses to support the improvement of governance and democracy, than analyses based on international indicators and aggregates.
- The surveys allow combining objective information (behaviour, actual experiences) with subjective information (perception, satisfaction) on poverty, governance and democracy.
- Objective and subjective information obtained through the survey can also be combined with traditional variables on socio-economic characteristics of individuals and households (such as income, occupation, sex, age and ethnic group). It is thus possible to disaggregate the results and highlight the specific characteristics or disparities between different population categories, especially the most disadvantaged or those who suffer the greatest discrimination.
- The approach opens an interesting new perspective for comparing information internationally.
- Regional indicators (spatial disaggregation) can inform decentralisation processes and programmes aimed at enhancing local democracy.

The commitment of NSOs to measuring democratic governance, the accuracy of estimators and the intrinsic link with traditional economic indicators - particularly on issues related to poverty - were major assets in these Metagora experiences. Also, the wide diversity of political contexts, in terms of liberties and rights, in which the surveys were conducted shows that the approach can work in a vast range of developing countries, extending well beyond the new democracies. Furthermore, in countries which have experienced serious political upheaval (for example, the Côte d'Ivoire, Madagascar and Togo in Africa; Ecuador and Bolivia in Latin America), where the general public have shown particularly strong support for democracy, the surveys provide a better insight into the nature of the problems, and could probably be used to implement targeted preventive measures before identified tensions degenerate into open conflict.

It has often been argued that collection of data on sensitive democratic and governance issues by governmental statistical bodies – such as NSOs – can be severely biased because survey respondents will either not answer, or not answer honestly, by fear of possible retaliation. The pilot surveys conducted in 11 countries of Francophone Africa and the Andean region show this is not the case. As it has been mentioned, response rates illustrate the population is willing to answer so-called sensitive questions. Also, the internal coherence of the answers given by individuals, as well as the fact that many questions are rather negative towards the government, tends to attest to the general fairness of responses. Indeed, should individuals be afraid of answering sensitive surveys carried out by official bodies, one can imagine they would either not answer at all or provide answers which are favourable to, and not critical of, the government. Moreover, when comparing results obtained in the framework of these surveys with that of similar studies, clear parallels can be drawn; for example, this is the case in Peru with the survey on governance commissioned in 2007 by UNDP to a private firm.

The process for setting up the surveys is one of the tool's major advantages. The situation in Peru is a good example of this: there was national appropriation of the survey, under the joint co-ordination of the National Statistical Office (INEI), the Ministry of Finance and the Prime Minister's office. Civil society participated in the questionnaire design and data analysis, the process for revising the survey was institutionalised over time, and there were many co-operation opportunities for Peruvian experts with other countries in the region. Downstream, experience shows that in many cases there is greater demand for governance and democracy indicators than for traditional socio-economic ones – as was shown by the strong reaction of the public and the media at events for announcing results in the countries under study (in particular in Madagascar, Mali and Peru). Furthermore, by providing fuel for public debates over policies and major development issues, this type of surveys represents a force for strengthening democracy, revealing the wishes of the public and, lastly, empowering "voiceless" sectors of the population.

Chapter 7

The Right to Education in Palestine

T he Metagora pilot experience in Palestine focused on the right to education. It consisted in the development of indicators and a public information tool to enhance analytical capacities and evidence-based policy-making. The pilot was designed and implemented through a vigorous participatory process, involving a wide range of NGOs, governmental bodies and academic or independent research centres (see box below). It explored the following questions:

This chapter was drafted on the basis of substantive reports, working documents and publications authored by:

Mustafa Khawaja, Jamil Helal, Hadeel Qazzaz, Jana Asher and **Audrey Chapman**

This pilot experience was conducted by the **Palestinian Central Bureau of Statistics (PCBS)**
President: Dr. Loai Abdul-Hafiz Shabana
Metagora National Co-ordinator: Mustafa Khawaja, in collaboration with Amal Jaber, Khitam Al-Berzreh, Nafir Massad, Samar Khalid, Hama Zeidan, Maher Sbeih and Riziq Nazzal.
See: www.pcbs.gov.ps

PCBS worked in close collaboration with the **Al Haq Institution**, the **Bisan Center for Research and Development**, the **Teacher Creativity Center** and the **Ministry of Education** of the Palestinian National Authority, which provided relevant data and qualitative information for the database developed by the project. See: www.alhaq.org, www.bisan.org, www.teachercc.org and www.moe.gov.ps

The pilot was implemented in partnership with several civil society actors gathering together as the **Metagora-Palestine Steering Committee.** The members of this committee are: Dr. Moder Kassis (**Birzeit University**), Dr. Varsein Aghabekian (**Welfare Association**), Abed Arahman Abu Arafa (**Arab Thought Forum**), Izzat Abdel Hadi (**Bisan Center for Research and Development**), Dr. Sami Kilani and Samer Aqrouq (**Al Najah University**), Nina Atallah (**Al Haq Institution**), Lamis Alami (**The Palestinian Independent Commission for Citizens Rights**) Isam Younis (**Almizan for Human rights**), and Odeh Zahran (**Teacher Creativity Centre**).

Training and technical assistance were provided by Jana Asher (USA), Romesh Silva (Australia), Miguel Cruz (USA) and Richard Conibere (United Kingdom).

Palestinian experts on education and human rights drafted a *Conceptual Framework of the Right to Education Indicators and its Relationship with Development and Good Governance in the Palestinian Territory* (November 2005). In addition, Prof. Audrey Chapman, then Director of the Science and Human Rights Program at the **American Association for the Advancement of Science (AAAS,** USA) reviewed the experience and drafted a detailed report on *Candidate Indicators for Monitoring the Right to Education* (see Chapman, 2006 and *Chapter 11*).

- What kind of information is required to develop rights-based indicators?
- How can National Statistical Offices, policy actors, researchers and NGOs co-operate to define and design indicators and information tools on social and economic rights?
- What are the potentials and limits of involving official statistics in measuring human rights?

Background

As mentioned in *Chapter 1*, over the last 15 years or so, human rights organisations and UN Treaty Bodies have increasingly been calling for the development of indicators in order to effectively monitor economic and social rights. UN Special Rapporteurs on specific rights (such as education, health and housing), as well as the UN Committee on Economic, Social and Cultural Rights have, on several occasions, called strongly for a more systematic and comprehensive collection and analysis of relevant data both at the national and international levels.

Unfortunately, these appeals, whilst at times vibrant and solemn in form, were never duly addressed to the sole UN instance that could give a proper and consistent follow-up to them: the Statistical Commission, a subsidiary body of the UN Economic and Social Council that is precisely in charge of establishing standards, methods, guidelines and manuals for the production of statistics and indicators - and that provides advice to all organs of the UN system on general questions relating to the collection, analysis and dissemination of statistical information.

Also, during the last decade, international organisations and academic circles convened several workshops and expert meetings on indicators of specific social and economic rights. While these gatherings helped to maintain the impetus of international brainstorming, few were followed by concrete institutional or technical action. There are some visible outcomes of this process of exchange, but most of these are either academic papers on theoretical approaches and frameworks for building comprehensive "systems of indicators", or else grass-root calls for exhaustive series of both aggregated and disaggregated data, in particular concerning vulnerable groups, which "all countries must produce". This double unrealistic vein in the existing literature caused many professional statisticians and human rights experts to lose any hope of attaining concrete progress in the field of human rights indicators.

As a matter of fact, building an effective and exhaustive "system of human rights indicators" would require much more numerous, differentiated and reliable sets of data than are currently available in most countries. Rather than targeting such a utopian goal, a more pragmatic step-by-step approach could allow to progressively fill critical information gaps and to build a manageable number of indicators to be used for monitoring selected rights.

On the occasion of the 2000 Montreux Conference on *Statistics, Development and Human Rights*, concrete examples and case studies showed that significant aspects of social and economic rights can be properly measured (see IAOS, 2000). The *Conclusions* of that Conference stressed the need for a tangible follow-up to those pioneering efforts. The post-Montreux Task Force agreed that concrete work to produce and test pilot indicators should not be postponed until a beaming but remote future, when the conceptual cathedral of indicators is achieved and current statistical vacuum is refilled by generous flows of relevant data. This conviction led a Metagora Partner, the Palestinian Central Bureau of Statistics (PCBS), to pioneer an experience to produce indicators on human rights.

PCBS is the main supplier of statistical data on the Palestinian population. Since its creation in 1993 – and following a rigorous *Development Master Plan* – it has been progressively producing a wide range of national, regional and local socio-economic indicators. It conducted national population censuses

---

Box 7.1. Integrating the "rights element" into existing indicators

"A rights-based approach to development is a conceptual framework for the process of human development that is normatively based on international human rights standards and operationally directed to promoting and protecting human rights. Essentially, a rights-based approach integrates the norms, standards, and principles of the international human rights system into the plans, policies and processes of development. (…)

"The socio-economic indicators currently and broadly employed (…) will require a second look, from a rights perspective. The "right to health" is something quite different from "health." Because rights-based development focuses on accountability and incorporates notions of entitlement and obligation, simply measuring status, or degree of realization, is not sufficient. There is a need to ensure the existence of an express right, and to monitor and measure the effectiveness of institutions and mechanisms of redress and enforcement as well. In this sense, socio-economic indicators must also be supplemented if rights-based development is to be effective. Accountability means beginning with the identification of: (1) an explicit standard against which to measure performance; (2) a specific person/institution owing performance; (3) a particular right-holder (or claim-holder) to whom performance is owed; (4) a mechanism of redress, delivery and accountability. (…)

"Much work remains to be done in effectively integrating attention to the "rights element" in existing lists of socio-economic indicators. (…) In the end, if rights-based development means anything at all, it means moving development out of the vague and nebulous realm of charity, and into the measurable area of accountability, and progress."

Craig G. Mokhiber, OHCHR
Towards a Measure of Dignity: Indicators for Rights-Based Development
Contribution to the 2000 Montreux Conference on *Statistics, Development and Human Rights*
(Mokhiber, 2000)

---

in 1997 and 2007, both covering – in spite of particularly dramatic circumstances – the West Bank, Gaza Strip and Jerusalem East. The professional capacities of PCBS and its independence with regard to all domestic and foreign political actors has given it solid legitimacy and broad trust both within the Palestinian society and in the international arena.

On these bases, PCBS has been delivering statistical reporting on key issues, such as the status of the rights of the child, the situation of Palestinian refugees or the impact of the Wall on the living conditions of the population (see PCBS, 2004, 2005; Abu-Libdeh, 2007). Through these experiences, PCBS experts discovered possibilities and means to revisit and empower statistics and socio-economic indicators from a rights perspective (see Box 7.1). Nevertheless, they became also increasingly aware that, to be effective, shared and useful, rights-based indicators have to be developed and established through an inclusive multidisciplinary work, involving human rights practitioners, social scientists and relevant actors of the civil society. The PCBS therefore invited several leading Palestinian NGOs and research centres to undertake this work together.

Objectives and focus

In line with the Metagora overall strategic aim (see *Chapter 2*), the Palestinian organisations and experts who joined this initiative agreed that their common efforts should target five main objectives:

- to reinforce professionalism, accuracy and objectivity in human rights reporting;
- to encourage evidence-based research on democracy and human rights in Palestine;
- to progressively produce human rights indicators on a continuous basis, thus allowing comparisons over time;
- to enhance national participatory fora and promote interdisciplinary monitoring work involving official statisticians, experts from the academia and human rights practitioners;
- to contribute to a clearer analysis of accountability and governance issues in Palestine, and to a well-informed democratic dialogue.

The experience started with three national consultation workshops convened by the PCBS, each gathering 30 to 50 representatives from key stakeholder institutions, including human rights organisations, academic institutions, independent research centres and bodies of the Palestinian National Authority. Initial reactions to this consultation process revealed to be too ambitious, as the general expectation of stakeholders was to see the project produce, in the short and medium terms, robust indicators for all human rights. A first attempt to draft a comprehensive list of human rights indicators and related statistical needs however convinced everyone that such an ambitious project would quickly have become unmanageable. PCBS and its civil society partners therefore decided to restrict the pilot's focus to a single human right: the right to education.

The choice of this specific right as the thematic focus of the Metagora experience was guided by two kinds of considerations: first, by substantive arguments on the strategic importance of education for the fulfilment of other human rights, for enhancing national development efforts and for deepening democracy in Palestine; and secondly, by considerations on the availability of relevant data.

These arguments merit to be summarised briefly. The right to education is among the economic, social, and cultural rights that enjoy worldwide approval. All international human rights treaties and conventions recognise and guarantee this right and state signatories cannot express any reservation or cultural, religious, or political excuse for not complying with it (see Box 7.2). Hence, the right to education enjoys universal consensus; though, at the same time, the universal achievement of this right is also one of the most difficult challenges of the 21st century for reasons related to poverty, scarce resources, lack of democracy and poor governance.

Education has undeniable impacts not only in the form of economic growth, but also in terms of many other development outcomes (see Box 7.3). Experience has proven that spending a few years in education allows to improve age expectancy at birth, reduce the risks of infectious diseases, improve individual's income and limit the effects of harmful social norms. The importance of education has also been proven in maintaining alive peoples' cultural roots and traditions as well as in strengthening the values of tolerance, peace, and justice.

All these elements have particular importance in Palestine, where more than half of the population is under 18. Obviously, education is among the most immediate concerns of society at large, as well as of most political actors. On the occasion of the above-mentioned consultations, several stakeholders stressed the importance of the human capital factor for further building a truly independent, sustainable and peaceful Palestinian State. Others pointed out that it is only through increased effective enjoyment of the right to education that both the Palestinian National Authority and the Palestinian society can respond to several major challenges, such as the eradication of poverty or the empowerment of women.

From a technical point of view, the feasibility of a project aimed to build indicators largely depends on the existence of at least a few series of reliable data on the issue at stake. A preliminary overview of available sources of quantitative information revealed that official and non-official surveys on the

---

Box 7.2. **The right to education in international treaties and conventions**

Article 26 of the **Universal Declaration of Human Rights** stipulates that "Everyone has the right to education. Education shall be free, at least in the elementary and fundamental stages. Elementary education shall be compulsory. Technical and professional education shall be made generally available and higher education shall be equally accessible to all on the basis of merit."

Article 28 of the **Convention on the Rights of the Child** stipulates that "States parties recognize the right of the child to education and with a view to achieving this right progressively and on the basis of equal opportunity, they shall, in particular:

(a) Make primary education compulsory and available free to all;
(b) Encourage the development of different forms of secondary education, including general and vocational education, make them available and accessible to every child and take appropriate measures such as the introduction of free education and offering financial assistance in case of need;
(c) Make higher education accessible to all on the basis of capacity by every appropriate means;
(d) Make educational and vocational information and guidance available and accessible to all children;
(e) Take measures to encourage regular attendance at schools and the reduction of drop-out rates."

Article 13 of the **International Covenant on Economic, Social, and Cultural Rights** stipulates that: "The states parties to the present Covenant recognize the right of everyone to education. They agree that education shall be directed to the full development of the human personality and the sense of its dignity, and shall strengthen the respect for human rights and fundamental freedoms. They further agree that education shall enable all persons to participate effectively in a free society, promote understanding, tolerance and friendship among all nations and all racial, ethnic or religious groups, and further the activities of the United Nations for the maintenance of peace."

Article 50 of the **Geneva Convention relative to the Protection of Civilian Persons in Time of War** stipulates that "The Occupying Power shall, with the cooperation of the national and local authorities, facilitate the proper working of all institutions devoted to the care and education of children."

Article 34 of the **Arab Convention on Human Rights** stipulates that "Elimination of illiteracy is a compliance and duty. Education is a right to every citizen, primary education shall be minimum compulsory education and it shall be free. High education and university education shall be facilitated for all."

Article 9 of the **Cairo Declaration on Human Rights in Islam**, adopted and issued at the Nineteenth Islamic Conference of Foreign Ministers in Cairo on 5 August 1990, stipulates "(a) The quest for knowledge is an obligation, and the provision of education is a duty for society and the State. The State shall ensure the availability of ways and means to acquire education and shall guarantee educational diversity in the interest of society so as to enable man to be acquainted with the religion of Islam and the facts of the Universe for the benefit of mankind. (b) Every human being has the right to receive both religious and worldly education from the various institutions of education and guidance, including the family, the school, the university, the media, etc., and in such an integrated and balanced manner as to develop his personality, strengthen his faith in God and promote his respect for and defense of both rights and obligations."

---

living conditions of the Palestinian population have produced data that could be very relevant for assessing and further monitoring the right to education. Also, it appeared that a range of academic institutions, official bodies and NGOs collect various kinds of quantitative and qualitative information that could be useful. On these promising bases, it was agreed to steer the pilot experience towards the generation of a first tentative set of indicators on the right to education.

Assumptions and expectations

This pilot experience was based on three main assumptions. First of all, it was considered that rights-based indicators can only be relevant if they relate to the accountability of public authorities – and therefore allow to assess the quality of governance and the effectiveness of policies related to the right to education. In this respect, it is worth noticing that, while in Palestine numerous issues concerning this right have been assessed by academic research and NGO studies, this has been done quasi exclusively with the aim of highlighting the impact of the Israeli occupation on the territories (see for instance Al-Haq, 2005). The organisations and experts involved in the Metagora pilot experience agreed that the information to be collected and the indicators to be established should allow to identify and assess the accountability not only of Israeli authorities, but also of the Palestinian National Authority and key Palestinian social actors.

Indeed, as two leading Palestinian experts stated in a report on *The Conceptual Framework of Indicators on the Right to Education*, "*the right to education is the responsibility of individuals as well as the public responsibility of the authority and State.*" Individuals, social groups and public authorities are specifically accountable for respecting, protecting, meeting and promoting the right to education. Thus it is important that indicators "*contribute to providing the government agencies as well as the private ones with the necessary information for development planning, policy-making, and (…) society reforms*" (Helal and Qazzaz, 2005, p. 4).

The second assumption of this pilot was that information from various official and non-official sources – with different coverage, time span and structures – can be gathered and integrated within a single coherent framework. Such an assumption led the pilot towards important conceptual and technical challenges. It was expected that statisticians and substantive experts be able to select a wide range of quantitative data suited to build solid indicators, and to gather this information into a consistent statistical database.

As in other Metagora pilots – *i.e.* in the Philippines and Mexico – it was also expected that qualitative information be gathered and processed to complement quantitative data. Since the inception of the pilot, it was clear for involved stakeholders and experts that planned collection of narrative information should not aim at pre-determining what should be the "right" or "wrong" interpretation of particular quantitative data or indicators, but at allowing data users, analysts and researchers to relate quantitative indicators to their specific contexts.

The third main assumption of this pilot was that collecting data and developing human rights indicators only makes sense if this complex and costly work can deliver, as a final product, a sustainable information tool. It was therefore expected that the PCBS develop, on sound technical bases, a prototype database on the right to education, which could be further enriched over time with new information and expanded so as to progressively cover other rights. It was also expected that this database be of public access and serve as a reference tool for independent policy analysis and reporting by research centres, human rights organisations and policy actors.

An interactive multidisciplinary process

A Metagora-Palestine Steering Committee was formed by representatives of nine leading NGOs and academic or independent research centres, co-ordinated and serviced by the PCBS. This Committee examined the conclusions of the consultation process, discussed in-depth the above-mentioned assumptions and expectations, and agreed on the method of work and main steps of the pilot. It agreed in particular on a clear distinction of responsibilities and tasks between the PCBS and its partner organisations from academia and civil society.

Box 7.3. **The right to education in the development context**

The **UN Millennium Development Goals** connect the right to education with development, and in particular with the general objective of eradicating extreme poverty and hunger (Goal number 1).

Goal number 2 is to "ensure that all boys and girls complete a full course of primary schooling."

Goal number 3 is to "eliminate gender disparity in primary and secondary education preferably by 2005, and at all levels by 2015." (see: http://www.un.org/millenniumgoals/index.html)

In 1990, the **World Conference on Education for All**, held in Jomtien, Thailand, called for "meeting basic learning needs". Article V of the World Declaration on Education For All states that "primary education must be universal, ensure that the basic learning needs of all children are satisfied, and take into account the culture, needs, and opportunities of the community. (...) The basic learning needs of youth and adults are diverse and should be met through a variety of delivery systems. Literacy programmes are indispensable because literacy is a necessary skill in itself and the foundation of other life skills. Literacy in the mother-tongue strengthens cultural identity and heritage." (UNESCO, 1990)

In 2000, the **World Education Forum,** held in Dakar, Senegal, called for "the achievement of education for all goals and targets for every citizen and for every society", and adopted a Framework for Action" aimed at:

i.   Expanding and improving comprehensive early childhood care and education, especially for the most vulnerable and disadvantaged children;

ii. Ensuring that by 2015 all children, particularly girls, children in difficult circumstances and those belonging to ethnic minorities, have access to and complete free and compulsory primary education of good quality;

iii. Ensuring that the learning needs of all young people and adults are met through equitable access to appropriate learning and life skills programs;

iv. Achieving a 50% improvement in levels of adult literacy by 2015, especially for women, and equitable access to basic and continuing education for all adults;

v.   Eliminating gender disparities in primary and secondary education by 2005, and achieving gender equality in education by 2015, with a focus on ensuring girls' full and equal access to and achievement in basic education of good quality;

vi. Improving all aspects of the quality of education and ensuring excellence of all so that recognized and measurable learning outcomes are achieved by all, especially in literacy, numeracy, and essential life skills. (UNESCO, 2000)

Indeed, while for several years the PCBS has attested to its authoritative capacity to work with total technical and scientific autonomy, it remains an official body belonging to the Palestinian National Authority. In this institutional context, the PCBS wished to avoid undertaking policy-oriented activities which could, in one form or another, affect its independence and neutrality.

The scope of action of the PCBS within the pilot was therefore delimited to the collection, processing and quality analysis of data and indicators, as well as to the design, development, updating and maintenance of the database. Any other kind of activities, in particular aimed at enhancing the policy impact of the pilot, were of the sole responsibility of the partner academic and civil society organisations, as well as of other actors – such as the media or the various bodies of the Palestinian

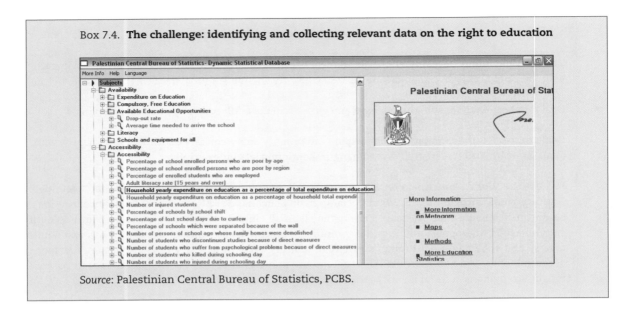

Box 7.4. **The challenge: identifying and collecting relevant data on the right to education**

Source: Palestinian Central Bureau of Statistics, PCBS.

National Authority – that may in the future use the indicators and the database on the right to education.

On these bases, the work of the PCBS and its partners truly followed the recommendations of the UN Statistical Commission on the production of statistical indicators for monitoring purposes. In particular, they bore in mind that "*identifying statistical indicators for monitoring purposes is neither a pure policy nor a pure statistical issue. The basic expression of the policy goal must drive the monitoring requirement, but turning that expression into a statistical indicator that will be relevant, reliable and acceptable to the various stakeholders is a statistical function. The tension between the policy view of what is needed and the statistical view of what is feasible and technically sound should be resolved by joint determination*" (UN-ECOSOC, 2002, p.8, para. 17).

It was indeed by joint determination that the actors involved in this pilot experience engaged in the interactive multidisciplinary process illustrated in Figure 7.1. Each partner organisation committed to contribute with its specific substantive competences or technical skills in the conceptual, implementing, assessing and reviewing steps of this process.

The PCBS established an internal Metagora technical team formed by experts in statistical indicators, database design and geographical information systems. The first task of this team was to establish a preliminary list of indicators, related definitions and measurement methodologies. It then identified, in collaboration with experts in the fields of education and human rights, available information in the databases of the PCBS, as well as other relevant data produced by official and non-official sources, including sets of data collected by research centres and NGOs on an *ad hoc* basis.

Once a tentative conceptual framework was agreed amongst all partners, quantitative information was collected from various official data sources, in particular from the *Education Census Database* of the Ministry of Education, and from several PCBS internal sources. The latter included in particular the databases of the surveys on demography and health, poverty, labour force, child labour, housing and housing conditions, as well as national accounts data, and the database on the impact of the Wall on the socio-economic conditions of Palestinian households.

Figure 7.1. **Interactive development of indicators and a public information tool on the right to education**

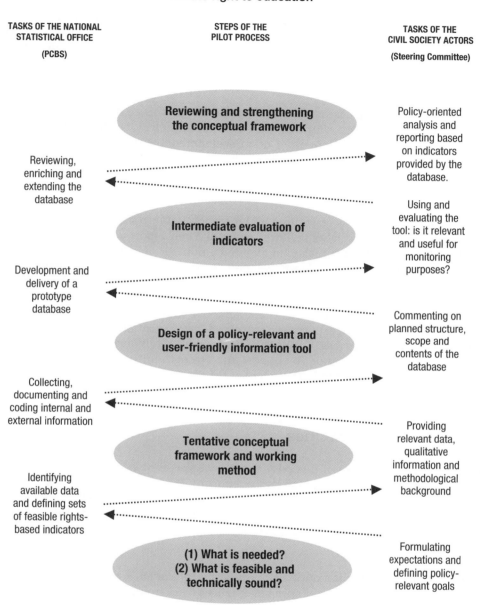

A team collected qualitative data, statements and narrative information, mainly from the Al-Haq Institution (database of demolished houses and statements archive), the Teacher Creativity Center (database for monitoring education), and the Bisan Center for Research and Development. The information provided by these NGOs often covered only part of the Palestinian territory (West Bank or Gaza Strip), given periods of time, or very particular aspects of the right to education. This kind of information was assessed both for its relevance with regard to the right to education and for its capacity to be quantified or to complement, in one way or another, the statistical information.

In parallel to the data collection process, PCBS experts, in collaboration with external Palestinian consultants, designed and developed a prototype database. The operational requirements, foreseen structure and functionalities and expected performances of this database were discussed in-depth with international consultants associated to Metagora. Several technical options were considered and a development scheme was finally agreed. A prototype of the database was then produced and nourished with the collected data, presented in tables as well as in graphical and geographical illustrations.

A first external technical assessment of the database confirmed its capacity to gather and interlink data collected from various sources. While this assessment identified a number of elements that would require further improvement or new developments, it recognised the appropriateness of the structure of the database, including three levels of information: main categories and subjects, indicators, and data sources and metadata. It also welcomed the flexibility and user-friendliness of the tool (see technical details in *Appendix 1*).

Once the collected data was structured and incorporated into the database, two Palestinian experts on education and human rights reviewed the tool. Their report acknowledged the achievements of the data collection process but also highlighted a number of information gaps and presented a list of indicators that still have to be developed for monitoring several of Palestine's very specific development and governance issues (see Helal and Qazzaz, 2005).

Thus, at the end of the first round of this interactive multidisciplinary process, the project cycle of this pilot led the Palestinian experts and stakeholders to revisit the two questions that gave the initial impetus to the whole process: (1) What indicators are really needed? and (2) What indicators are feasible and technically sound? To support and strengthen the conceptual framework developed, Prof. Audrey Chapman reviewed the content of the database and formulated a proposal for structural, process and outcome indicators on the right to education (see *Chapter 11*).

Enhancing national capacities

One of the main objectives of this pilot experience was to reinforce professionalism, accuracy and objectivity in evidence-based human rights reporting. Such an objective can only be reached through a strong enhancement of the capacities of statisticians, researchers and civil society actors to properly collect, process, understand and protect human rights data. Training was therefore a very important component of this Metagora pilot experience: it was intended to sustain the most crucial steps of the process described above.

A five-day training workshop on *The Use and Misuse of Human Rights Statistics* was attended by NGO staff – with no background in statistics but extensive background in human rights theory and practice – and PCBS and research centres staff, with extensive background in statistical techniques but no background in human rights. In order to provide this diverse audience with a common background, the trainer introduced basic concepts and methods of both human rights reporting and statistical work.

In the course of the workshop, several international examples of human rights data and analysis projects were presented. Attendants were invited to confront, through practical exercises, their own experience with the selected examples. This stimulated them to be increasingly involved in lively discussions on general methodological issues such as the definition of human rights data, how to work with "found data" or how to collect data. This training included basic information on issues related to sample design, questionnaire design, development of databases, data analysis, as well as

Figure 7.2. **A tool for monitoring progress**

(example: enrolment of young girls in secondary education, by region, 1999-2004)

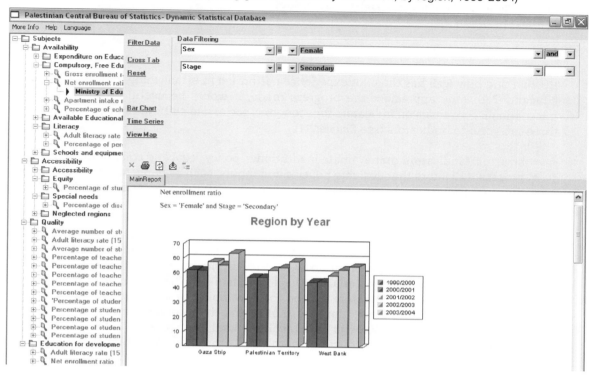

Source: Palestinian Central Bureau of Statistics, PCBS.

data misuse and misrepresentation. Attendants were also made aware of critical issues related to professional integrity of the statistical work and, in particular, of international standards and technical means to ensure protection of personal data.

This training workshop had a big impact in the establishment of a basic common ground among all actors involved in the pilot experience. Such a common ground considerably improved mutual understanding of each other's specific backgrounds, as well as the collective capacities to co-operate and make different complementary knowledge and skills converge towards a common end.

Several participants to the workshop attended a second round of training, more technically challenging, focusing on *Found Data and Coding Systems*. This second 5-day training workshop had a particular cross-fertilisation effect, as it revealed strong interest by staff from the PCBS and from its partner organisations in the *Controlled Vocabulary* and the methods for coding narrative information, as applied, for instance, in Sri Lanka (see *Chapter 8*). In the context of their collaboration in gathering human rights data, attendants discovered that should a "standardised" coding process exist across Palestinian NGOs, then the information gathered in the database on the right to education would be more consistent and of higher quality.

Thanks to this modest but accurately calibrated training scheme, Palestinian researchers, policy actors and NGO staff increased their capacities to play a double role as both providers and users of relevant information. Their knowledge and skills were empowered to better identify and interpret quantitative and qualitative data, to appropriately use indicators (and avoid their misuse), and to improve the accuracy, quality and effectiveness of evidence-based reporting by their institutions on human rights and democratic governance issues.

Gaps and perspectives

How far and how well has the pilot experience performed in establishing indicators on the right to education? To duly appreciate the progress made, it would be useful to refer to the evolving international consensus on indicators for economic, social and cultural rights, which has identified three categories of indicators (see *Chapter 11*):

- **structural indicators** that evaluate institutional, policy, legal and constitutional frameworks;
- **process indicators** that evaluate policies and inputs, such as budgetary allocations; and,
- **outcome indicators** that evaluate the extent to which the population enjoys a given specific right.

Most of the indicators provided by the prototype database are outcome indicators. These extensively inform on the status of enjoyment of the right to education – as well as on the many obstacles to its effective implementation. Nevertheless, the information collected so far does not allow to properly document and analyse the accountability of the main governmental, political and social actors. There is therefore a need for developing process indicators focusing on the performance of the Palestinian National Authority and the interventions of other key actors. As Palestinian and international experts have recommended, this work should take into account the *General Comments* on the right to education of the UN Committee on Economic, Social and Cultural Rights, as well as the recommendations on the right to education of the UN Committee on the Rights of the Child.

Moreover, while statistical data produced by the PCBS generally conform to international standards and are broadly documented through accurate metadata, the quality of the data collected from external sources – and the extent to which various data sources permit relevant disaggregation – has not yet been assessed in-depth. It is therefore necessary to further evaluate, document and improve the quality and coverage of the data gathered within the database. Also, as measuring progressive realisation of rights requires time series, a major challenge for future work will be to ensure consistency over time of data collected by NGOs and research centres.

Highlighting these limitations should however not occult the great achievements reached by this pioneering experience of collaboration between so diverse actors in building indicators and a public information tool on human rights. While the intermediary results of this experience can still appear as modest in their content and scope, they are opening new perspectives and providing significant lessons for future work on human rights indicators. In particular, this pilot experiment shows that:

- **human rights practitioners and professional statisticians can closely co-operate** in identifying indicators that can be relevant and shared, and in establishing, by joint determination, the conceptual framework, content and scope of those indicators;
- **a progressive approach to the long-lasting task of building human rights indicators** can allow to obtain, on the basis of available data, basic sets of indicators for monitoring selected rights, which can be further expanded;
- further efforts should aim at **generating data that may be relevant to assess the process** of implementation of public policies, in order to assess the accountability and performance of governmental authorities.

Box 7.5. **Implications of the pilot experience in Palestine**

Key policy implications

- Human rights analysis usually focuses on the degree to which a state is meeting its human rights obligations. In Palestine a "triple" framework is required: assessing the Palestinian National Authority's performance, taking into account the problems linked to the Israeli government's interference, and referring to specific responsibilities of various key Palestinian social and political actors.

- The experience has provided a key policy focus (and has given a strong impetus) to an effective cross-institutional partnership between the academia, independent research centres, NGOs, policy actors and the National Statistical Office. Appropriate training on data collection techniques, processing of data and uses and misuses of indicators substantially empowered the monitoring and advocacy capacities of civil society actors.

- Many stakeholders were involved in consultations and decisions. The participatory process is considered today at the national level to be one of the main policy achievements of the experience. It is often quoted by key actors and organisations as a valuable example to be followed by other major national initiatives and projects in Palestine.

- The scope and policy impact of the indicators on the right to education can be substantially enlarged by developing process indicators in addition to the existing structural and outcome indicators.

- More time and efforts will be required to build consensus around the project's outcomes and to progressively expand its focus to cover an increasing set of human rights and a range of issues more explicitly related to democracy and governance in Palestine.

Major methodological implications

- Integrative well-designed databases can provide a common framework for gathering, coding and analysing sets of information from different sources that otherwise may remain fragmented, anecdotal and irrelevant for large-scale analysis.

- To be effective, efficient and successful, a cross-institutional partnership for monitoring human rights and democratic governance has to be established on a solid and agreed basis, strong commitment of leading personalities and experts, light and flexible working mechanisms, and a clear distinction of responsibilities, roles and tasks between official institutions, research centres and NGOs.

- Training courses allowed experts from PCBS, researchers, policy actors and human rights practitioners from the civil society to advance together towards stronger skills and capacities, and to discuss the ways and means for applying the acquired knowledge to the identification, collection and analysis of relevant data and indicators.

The strong involvement of numerous stakeholders in the steering and implementation of this pilot experience is considered to be one of its main achievements. Throughout this experience, the PCBS has strengthened its links with civil society and the academia – and it has enhanced its own role and capacities as a provider of information, technical advice, support and training for those who wish to carry out evidence-based policy assessments.

Chapter 8

Massive Human Rights Violations in Sri Lanka

The Metagora project provided scientific and technical support to The Asia Foundation's project on *Mapping Political and Ethnic Violence in Sri Lanka* (see box below). This project focuses on the use of quantitative approaches and statistical tools and methods for empowering the documentation, analysis, reporting and advocacy work of non-governmental organisations committed to defending and promoting human rights. This project has enabled Sri Lankan human rights defenders to examine the patterns and magnitude of past and current violations. In light of Metagora's objectives, this innovative approach has provided concrete answers to the following questions:

This chapter was drafted on the basis of substantive reports, working documents and publications authored by:

Lakmali Dasanayake, Dinesha de Silva Wikramanayake,
Kohilanath Rajanayagam and **Romesh Silva**

The project *Mapping Political and Ethnic Violence in Sri Lanka* was managed and co-ordinated on an independent basis by **The Asia Foundation office in Colombo.**

Representative: Mr. Nilan Fernando
Assistant Representative: Mrs. Dinesha de Silva Wikramanayake
Project Co-ordinator: Ms. Lakmali Dasanayake
www.asiafoundation.org/country/overview/sri-lanka

The project was implemented by the **Human Rights Accountability Coalition (HRAC),** whose aim is to enhance collaboration and support among NGOs in collecting, encoding, analysing and sharing data on human rights violations in Sri Lanka. HRAC was established in November 2000 by four organisations: **Home for Human Rights (HHR),** the **Forum for Human Dignity (FHD),** the **Institute of Human Rights (IHR)** and the **Consortium of Humanitarian Agencies (CHA).** The project Co-ordinators in these organisations are: Mr. Kohilanath Rajanayagam (HHR), Mr. Chandralal Majuwana Kankanamge (FHD), Ms. Menaka Shanmugalingam (IHR), and Mr. Prabu Wedagedara (CHA). HRAC worked in close collaboration with the **National Human Rights Commission** of Sri Lanka (Mr. Mohomad Cassim Mohamad Iqbal).

In its early stages the project received technical assistance from the AAAS Human Rights Data Analysis Group (now part of Benetech) financed by The Asia Foundation. HRAC received technical assistance from Mr. Romesh Silva (Australia), co-financed in 2002 by the Swiss Federal Statistical Office and, in 2004, by the Metagora budget. HRAC field operations were supported by The Asia Foundation and, from July 2004, financed by a generous contribution from DANIDA, the Danish International Development Agency.

- What kind of statistical methods and tools can be used to improve systematic documentation and processing of data on human rights violations collected by civil society organisations?
- How can narrative information on human rights violations be translated into measurable data and consistently integrated into statistical-friendly frameworks and datasets?
- How can datasets from different organisations (each focusing on different aspects of human rights violations, geographical areas and reference periods) interlink within a common framework in order to provide a consistent record of abuse?
- What specific value does statistical analysis add to the current documentation, analysis, reporting and advocacy work of human rights organisations?
- How to ensure that scientific and technical assistance provided by international experts to civil society organisations is followed by the sustainable application of transferred technical and statistical skills?

A context of massive political and ethnical violence

The project is operating within a particularly challenging context, as Sri Lanka has still not left behind the most violent period of its post-independence history, a period in which human rights violations have been rampant. Since the late 1970s, government security forces have been guilty of widespread human rights abuses in their confrontations with an armed Tamil separatist movement in the north and east of the island, led since the late 1980s by the Liberation Tigers of Tamil Eelam, which has engaged in assassinations, mass killings, and suicide bombings. Between 1987 and 1989, the government also faced an armed insurrection in the south, led by the People's Liberation Front (*Janatha Vimukthi Peramuna*). Since 1979, the country has operated almost continuously under national security laws (the Public Security Ordinance of 1947 and the Prevention of Terrorism Act of 1979), supplemented by equally draconian emergency legislation. These laws have been used by successive governments to combat armed groups as well as to curb non-violent opposition.

Although almost every community and group in Sri Lanka agrees that there has been massive political and ethnic violence during the last two decades, there are tremendous inconsistencies in the facts and figures reported or estimated by the various actors involved in assessing the violence. For instance, by the end of 2006, the UN Commission on Human Rights had received 12,000 complaints of disappearances in Sri Lanka; Presidential Commissions of Enquiry into Disappearances report over 30,000 disappeared; and NGOs fear more than 60,000 people have disappeared.

In such a context, the expected policy incidence of this project was clear. Even if creating a mechanism for truth and reconciliation is not yet on the national agenda, it is now important to establish the truth about human rights violations over the past 25 violent years. Establishing a scientifically rigorous record of reported and estimated total numbers of violations, patterns of abuse, and the nature and identity of perpetrators and victims helps to clarify the past, assign responsibility for past violations and end perpetrators' sense of impunity. Furthermore, maintaining a record of current abuses helps to shape policies that promote greater human rights protection and accountability. Thus, the project's main objectives were:

- To provide NGOs with skills and tools (technical expertise, working procedures and advanced software applications) to improve the accuracy, objectivity, consistency and reliability of their reports and to ensure the security of their data on human rights violations.
- To facilitate the pooling and sharing of data on human rights violations among NGOs to support the development of a massive, objective and undeniable statistical record of human rights violations.

- To inject new, objective and scientifically rigorous evidence into the peace process once it is resumed and transitional justice mechanisms, as well as into local and international human rights debates about human rights violations connected to Sri Lanka's ethnic and political conflicts.

The project: ensuring rigour and responsibility

Each HRAC member organisation collects information about human rights violations from different sources, such as letters or oral testimonies of victims and witnesses, signed affidavits, field interviews, legal case files, newspapers clippings, rapid response emails and alerts. Thus, they each have huge archives containing thousands of pieces of detailed narrative information on human rights violations.

Each organisation has its own specific aims, fields of interest, geographic areas of action, independent strategies and specific expertise: the Consortium of Humanitarian Agencies aims to promote policy dialogue and information sharing between humanitarian agencies, whereas the Forum of Human Dignity, Home for Human Rights and the Institute for Human Rights primarily provide legal assistance to victims of human rights violations. Thus, the information on human rights abuses collected and archived by these organisations often reflects these factors. In other words, the records and reports of these organisations on human rights violations provide information that is partial or incomplete and fragmented in space and time.

The Human Rights Accountability Coalition (HRAC) was created in 2000 to overcome the incompleteness and fragmentation of the information and to improve the documentation and analysis of human rights violations by taking advantage of the complementary focus and geographic coverage of its four founding organisations. Since 2001, the HRAC initiative has involved three main phases:

- **Phase I (2001-2004)** aimed to build a common HRAC technical foundation through developing and implementing a standard documentation methodology. The HRAC organisations, with the support of international experts, developed a common systematic framework for collecting and processing data on human rights violations and established quality monitoring procedures for data encoding and processing. A *Controlled Vocabulary* (see below) was produced, as well as standardised data collection forms and processing/coding quality control measures. A detailed technical reference manual for the HRAC's documentation staff was produced to document guiding principles, technical methods and lessons learnt. Training workshops were held in 2001, 2002 and 2004 to ensure that the field work teams of HRAC member organisations are well-versed in implementing standardised data collection, processing and coding. Consequently, a major achievement is that, since the end of 2003, data collection and coding have been consistent across the coalition.
- **Phase II (2004-2005)** aimed to consolidate the HRAC's technical foundation and working methods, as well as to build institutional capacities. HRAC data processing increased in intensity by strengthening and expanding the field work teams of HRAC member organisations. With support from DANIDA, The Asia Foundation facilitated the translation of technical and reference manuals from English into Tamil and Sinhalese. In 2005 HRAC established a close partnership with the Department of Statistics and the School of Computing of the University of Colombo. This was a crucial strategic step, exemplary for the whole Metagora community, towards ensuring the sustainable follow-up of the project's achievements through more autonomous, nationally-based expertise. With hands-on training provided by the Statistics Department, HRAC member organisations were progressively able to produce descriptive

statistical analysis of their data and expand their programme to include sample survey-based studies. Also, due to the efforts of The Asia Foundation, close collaboration begun with the Human Rights Commission of Sri Lanka.

- **Phase III (2005-2008)** aimed to pool data across the HRAC and to build massive datasets in order to facilitate wide-ranging analyses of overall patterns, trends and levels of responsibility for human rights violations committed during Sri Lanka's 25-year ethnic conflict. Statistical analysis is helping uncover new evidence about the systematic nature, causes and effects of human rights violations. This phase includes: (1) collection of additional available information on human rights violations from sources such as official presidential commissions, the National Human Rights Commission and the UN Working Group on Disappearances; (2) identification of duplicate reporting and erroneous data by data editing and matching of datasets from different sources; (3) first attempts to apply multiple systems estimation and statistical modelling, in order to obtain statistical projections of the number of total violations; and (4) integration of qualitative, historical and legal analyses into statistical analyses to produce coalition-wide reports on the extent, patterns and trends and levels of responsibility for past violations.

The *Controlled Vocabulary*: a key tool

The project has established a large, objective and accurate statistical record of past and present human rights violations in Sri Lanka. In 2004, after two years of building technical foundations, HRAC was able to enter into a phase of high intensity data processing and coding. The main pillar of this work is the *Controlled Vocabulary* developed by HRAC.

Controlled vocabularies are used in "found data" projects to transform qualitative narrative text into structured quantitative data. They help transform narratives into countable units by specifying the classification rules and counting methods. The use of controlled vocabularies helps build consistent databases and allows human rights monitors to move beyond anecdotal case-by-case analysis of human rights violations to a more scientifically-defensible analysis of the extent and pattern of large-scale human rights violations.

To ensure a high level of data quality, every **violation definition** in the *Controlled Vocabulary* must be:

- **mutually exclusive:** no violation (or victim or perpetrator) can fit into any two definitions in the *Controlled Vocabulary*;
- **exhaustive:** a definition must exist for every possible violation that can occur in the situation being studied;
- **distinguished:** each definition must have an explicit characteristic which distinguishes this violation/victim/perpetrator from all others in the *Controlled Vocabulary*;
- **exemplified:** each definition must be accompanied by examples showing how to apply the definition in a specific situation;
- **countable:** each definition must contain a counting rule which explicitly states how violations, victims and perpetrators will be enumerated.

The HRAC *Controlled Vocabulary* (see Human Rights Accountability Coalition, 2006) uses the "Who did What to Whom, When and Where?" data model to structure the information for the purposes of statistical analysis (see Ball, 1996). It contains: (1) a violations coding scheme defining and describing violation categories and their related codes; (2) persons list codes referring to various institutional perpetrator types and specific perpetrators; (3) "where" codes referring to various types of places where violations occurred; (4) "when" codes referring to various periods of time when violations were perpetrated; (5) codes of legal and social contexts, referring to regulatory circumstances in which the violations occurred; (6) newspapers codes, referring to existing Sri Lankan newspapers reporting news on violations; (7) relationship codes referring to the familiar links of victims, witness or reporting sources; and (8) sources codes referring to various kinds of information sources (*e.g.* email, case file and letter).

The *Vocabulary* also contains a dual reference index for violation codes: an alphabetical index and a thematic index, both referring to very detailed categories of violations. In other words, this *Vocabulary* is a rigorous conceptual tool agreed by HRAC member organisations, which allows for standardised collection and processing of data. The structure, internal logic and practical application of this tool are analogous to those of internationally-agreed definition manuals aimed at harmonising statistical information.

The *Controlled Vocabulary* was periodically reviewed as experience developed and in order to take into account the problems examined and solutions found during weekly data coder meetings, in which HRAC teams controlled the data coding process. Special attention was paid to ensure there is a manageable number of violation categories which capture the nature of the most frequently reported violations in "found data" accessible to HRAC groups. The *Vocabulary* was also made available in local languages (Tamil/Sinhala) for easy reference by partner organisations.

Different violation categories were more precisely delineated by refining the boundary conditions in the HRAC *Controlled Vocabulary* (boundary conditions explicitly delineate between different categories of a controlled vocabulary). The counting rules were also reviewed to ensure more reliable data representation of the multiplicity of victims, violations and perpetrators (see Box 8.2). The vocabulary of institutions and the structured list of these institutions were completely revised to ensure that they

---

Box 8.1. Data coding: a major technical challenge for human rights defenders

In order to produce meaningful human rights statistics, it is necessary to transform narrative information on violations, victims and perpetrators into a countable set of data categories without discarding important information and without misrepresenting the collected information. This process of **transforming narrative information into quantitative data** is commonly referred to as **"coding"** and is guided by a **Controlled Vocabulary.**

Human rights organisations often have tens of thousands of documents which require several data coding specialists to process the data. For example, the Home for Human Rights, one of the founding HRAC member organisations, has over 45,000 individual documents which contain information about human rights violations connected to Sri Lanka's ethnic conflict. Their Data Coding Unit is staffed by 10 full-time data coding specialists.

In order to ensure the defensibility of their statistical analysis, human rights organisations must ensure that all data coders apply the *Controlled Vocabulary* consistently to each of the thousands of pieces of narrative information. In particular, in the case of human rights data projects, the organisations need to ensure that their data coding specialists identify, classify and count violations, victims and perpetrators in a consistent manner. One way to monitor the quality of the data coding process is to use Inter-Rater Reliability (IRR) measures to quantitatively measure how consistently different coders code the same raw data (how they treat narrative information according to the common coding frame provided by the *Controlled Vocabulary*. Such measurements, which are widely used in the social and behavioural sciences, help human rights statisticians evaluate the reliability of the data coding process, diagnose and address the underlying cause of any low reliability, via targeted training of data coding specialists or revisions of the *Controlled Vocabulary*.

Box 8.2. **The HRAC *Controlled Vocabulary*: some examples**

No.	Code	Violation Category	Definition	Boundary Condition	Counting Rule	Example
29	REFA	Restriction of Freedom of Association	Publication or issuance of a notification or instruction (verbal or written) that prohibits or limits the capacity of any person or group of persons to meet, gather or associate	1. Denial of a permit to hold a political meeting.	Each notification /instruction = 1 violation	• Prevention of persons from holding a political meeting by government security forces during the election period.
				2. Law/regulation that limits rights to associate.	Count period (imposed/lifted)	
30	FOMA	Forced Marriage	Forced/unwilling marriage of any couple by threat, intimidation, indictment, threats to family members, and/or violence by any person on the persons list.	Forced/unwilling marriage of any couple.	Each marriage = 1 violation.	• Muslim woman is forced to sign marriage certificates committing her to marriage with a Tamil man under a threat of torture.
					Each unwilling party = 1 victim	

Source: HRAC Symposium, December 2005, presentation handout.

accurately reflected the institutional relationships of the various parties to the Sri Lankan conflict. All these enhancements of the *Controlled Vocabulary* aimed at addressing four critical needs:

- to refer to the normative framework of relevant domestic law and international human rights standards;
- to fully reflect the nature and form of Sri Lanka's ethnic and political conflicts;
- to encompass the structure and form of the HRAC's found data sources;
- to ensure the reliability of the data coding process which is used to convert unstructured text into quantitative data on human rights violations.

HRAC member organisations also adopted standardised data collection forms referring to incidents, violations, persons (victims and perpetrators) and sources of information (Box 8.3). Each of the thousands of cases of human rights violations reported to the organisations (or found by them) is therefore now being documented in these harmonised forms and the characteristics of each violation are encoded following the agreed definitions provided by the *Vocabulary*.

Monitoring reliability of the data coding process

It is important to stress that the HRAC initiative is a truly collective work, not a simple addition of individual activities of each member organisation. As previously pointed out, implementing teams of HRAC member organisations gathered together once a week to review progress, discuss conceptual issues, and review the application of the *Controlled Vocabulary*. These weekly meetings allowed for consistency of data collection and documentation amongst the coalition and also ensured a high level of inter-rater reliability amongst coders (see Box 8.4).

Box 8.3. **HRAC harmonised violation form**

Source: HRAC Symposium, December 2005, presentation handout.

This is a very important element of the Sri Lankan experience. In most human rights data projects to date, inter-rater reliability is neither monitored nor measured, or only monitored anecdotally. In the HRAC initiative, inter-rater reliability measurements were developed, implemented and customised to suit the data model and *Controlled Vocabulary* (see a presentation of the underlying mathematics in Silva, 2002).

Input stratification

As part of the technical assistance provided to HRAC in the framework of Metagora, guidance was provided to two member organisations, the Forum for Human Dignity and Home for Human Rights, in developing detailed document indexes for their "found data". These document indexes were the first to identify a unique data source for each organisation, and they also listed information about the source, such as the date of the source document, where the data source was collected, and the type of data source. Such indexes are a necessary and valuable tool in randomising the data input stream in large-scale data analysis projects which use "found data". The randomisation of the data input stream, by stratifying on certain variables where notable variations exist in the underlying data, can assist analysts in developing representative statistical analysis of "found data" when the data processing work is only partially complete - if the sequential selection of documents for coding and data entry is based on a stratified random sample of the entire population of "found data".

Input stratification helps groups to develop interim statistical analysis which is representative of their entire dataset. This also provides a guarantee that if time and money run out before the coding is complete, the organisation will still be able to make reasonable quantitative statements about the entire body of collected testimonies.

The document index developed for Forum for Human Dignity spanned all its found data sources, namely legal case files, letters, lists and situation summaries. This amounted to indexation of all the

---

Box 8.4. **Measuring reliability of HRAC data coding process: an example**

A coding exercise completed during a weekly HRAC coders' meeting examined the reliability of data coding from the following narrative case (a newspaper article):

TEN CIVILIANS SHOT DEAD:

(1) *"Ten civilians, including children who had taken refuge in Kanahanthanai*
(2) *after shell attacks at Kiran and Pulypainthakal, were shot dead by the security forces*
(3) *and an injured person has been admitted to the Batticaloa hospital. In a separate incident at*
(4) *Thuraikutty a civilian who was assisting the army was shot dead by unidentified gunmen,*
(5) *the army had attacked the civilians who were near the place of murder*
(6) *and damaged the property in the villages of Sithandy, Santhively and Morokottanchenai.*
(7) *Further, Arunagiri Thurairaja and Sellathamby Siva, who were pulled out of their residences,*
(8) *were shot by persons in army uniform."*

(Virakesary, July 3, 2004)

This narrative case could refer to several categories of human rights violations defined in the *Controlled Vocabulary*, including in particular: forced displacement (FODI), death due to combat (DECO), injury due to combat (INCO), execution (EXEC), other killing (OTKI), destruction of property (DEPR) and assault (ASLT), or even general torture (GETO). The case was treated by **seven data coders** as follows:

Line	Coder A	Coder B	Coder C	Coder D	Coder E	Coder F	Coder G
1	FODI	FODI	FODI	X	FODI	FODI	FODI
2	DECO	DECO	DECO	DECO	X	DECO	DECO
3	INCO	INCO	INCO	INCO	X	INCO	INCO
4	EXEC	EXEC	X	EXEC	EXEC	EXEC	X
5	EXEC	EXEC	X	EXEC	EXEC	X	OTKI
6	DEPR	DEPR	DEPR	DEPR	DEPR	X	X
7	ASLT	ASLT	ASLT	ASLT	X	GETO	ASLT
8	X	X	EXEC	X	EXEC	EXEC	DECO

There was therefore notable variation in the way the different coders coded the violations reported by the newspaper article. For the entire coding case, the seven data coders agreed on the assignment of the violation classifications from their *Controlled Vocabulary* (known as the "overall level of agreement") 53.6% of the time:

Actual agreement	180
Possible agreement	336
Overall level of agreement	**53.6%**

The Inter-Rater Reliability measure reports this overall level of agreement and also the specific levels of agreement per violation category as follows:

Violation Category	Specific Level of Agreement
Forced displacement (FODI)	83.3
Death due to combat (DECO)	71.4
Injury due to combat (INCO)	83.3
Execution (EXEC)	52.8
Other killing (OTKI)	0
Destruction of property (DEPR)	66.7
Assault (ASLT)	66.7
General torture (GETO)	0

In this example, the relatively low level of overall agreement is driven by disagreement over the identification of some violations (mainly execution and destruction of property) and the classification of some violations (mainly fatal violations in the form of executions, assault and other killings). This can be seen by the relatively low levels of specific agreement observed for EXEC, DEPR, ASLT, OTKI and GETO, as reported in *Analyzer's* Inter-Rater module. The specific level of agreement for execution (EXEC) in this coding exercise is 52.8%. This is the estimated conditional probability that assuming one of the randomly selected coders assigns violation category EXEC to a certain violation object, the other coders will also assign violation category EXEC to the same violation object.

1,900 primary-source documents which the organisation has collected. The document index developed for Home for Human Rights indexed all of the organisation's legal case files, medical case files and affidavits: over 10,000 documents.

Identifying overlaps to avoid over-counting violations

When trying to calculate the magnitude of abuses, it is critical to determine where reports overlap so that violations are not over-counted. Overlaps must be identified by deciding which records are unique and which records describe the same participants and events. This process is called creating a "judgement layer" on top of many sources.

The *Analyzer* software - which is used to collect, maintain and analyse information on large-scale human rights violations - separates the source and judgement layers within the database. Identifying sources that refer to the same people and/or events is called "matching". *Analyzer* facilitates this process through an interface that enables data analysts to view fields from several records side-by-side. Decisions from the judgement layer link back to the source layer, providing an audit trail for all of the records and the decisions made about those records in the database.

The data fields and the order in which they appear on the screen are fully customisable. This enables the user to select the data fields that are the most relevant for making decisions about whether or not two records refer to the same person. The source and judgement layers together can be used to calculate statistics, while the judgement layer is the basis for Multiple Systems Estimation. *Analyzer* can combine data from multiple data collection projects, and it therefore facilitates matching within each project and then between the projects in order to perform Multiple Systems Estimation.

During its deployment to HRAC organisations, the *Analyzer* software was customised around the data model developed by HRAC and the particular structures of its *Controlled Vocabulary*. Staff of HRAC member organisations was trained in *Analyzer*'s data capture and data entry. Furthermore, a step-by-step training manual was provided to the staff to guide them through the various parts of the data capture tool (see Silva, 2006).

Data cleaning

A fundamental and necessary part of developing high quality statistical analysis is to sanity-check the data for processing errors and database representation errors. HRAC members were provided with datasets for error checking and data cleaning. This allowed important errors to be identified and corrected and thus avoid implausible or unfeasible data representation in the databases, or systematic misrepresentations of the underlying patterns of the violations phenomena under study.

Teams were also coached in identifying and correcting coding and/or data entry mistakes. Inconsistencies in the coding process included not only violation coding of raw information, but also the coding of victim affiliations and perpetrator institutions. Work was therefore carried out with each organisation to identify obvious coding and data entry errors in their databases and to develop data cleaning and correction processes to ensure that their first round of descriptive statistical analyses were valid representations of their coded data, and not artefacts of the data coding or data entry processes.

Enhancing statistical reporting capacities of civil society organisations

One of the main objectives of the Sri Lankan project is to support the reporting and advocacy work of civil society organisations by increasing their capacity to produce solid data and to use professional statistical analysis for making policy-oriented assessments of human rights issues. The road towards this goal has been long and challenging. At the beginning, organisations involved had difficulties understanding how to shape statistical analyses relating to human rights policy issues.

Indeed, while HRAC member organisations had considerable expertise in human rights defence through "case-by-case" analysis based on legal, qualitative and historical methods, staff initially found it hard to understand how best to answer policy questions using statistical tools and methods. They tended to view the data collection and data coding processes as being the same as their traditional "case-by-case investigation work", instead of understanding it to be a very different yet complementary method of analysis.

An important task was therefore to familiarise the staff and members of HRAC partner organisations with an evidence-based and policy-oriented form of analysis (see Box 8.6). All HRAC actors involved were coached by international experts in the policy-oriented interpretation and reporting of descriptive statistical analysis of data on human rights violations. Bilateral work with each organisation and workshops with all organisations focused on their own data, and guided them on how to ensure that they did not over-interpret their data and how to integrate statistical graphs and tables with qualitative analysis and narratives.

Seminars organised by The Asia Foundation allowed each HRAC member organisation to briefly present its descriptive statistical findings. Attendees included selected members of the national human rights community in Sri Lanka. These seminars marked significant steps towards effective

> **Box 8.5. Transferring skills to ensure sustainable work on an autonomous basis**
>
> In the past, projects that have attempted to train human rights defenders in advanced database design concepts or even basic techniques of statistical analysis have not been particularly successful. When technical work is done by inadequately trained personnel, the analysis can be wrong, and the results can be very problematic.
>
> People who receive "intensive" brief courses in complex technical matters often learn cookbook-style solutions. Similarly, non-technically-skilled users of off-the-shelf database software (*e.g. Microsoft Access*) can too easily create databases that simply do not model what the users think they are representing. Without extensive, advanced university-level training in technical matters, it can be difficult to convey the theoretical nuances which are essential for understanding how to apply a method appropriately. When the trainees of brief technical courses face real-world problems, minor changes in the conditions, assumptions, or even data formats can undermine their efforts. Worse yet, the trainee may attempt to apply the technique s/he learned in the course, but slightly changed conditions lead to inappropriate conclusions. Database design and statistical analysis have to be done correctly or the resulting analysis is likely to be wrong. In the worst case, bad analysis could completely discredit a project, and could raise doubts about human rights reporting more generally.
>
> Thus, the strategy behind the HRAC initiative in Sri Lanka was not to intensively train NGO activists to be statisticians. The strategy adopted here was to build locally-based sustainable capacities. This was done by:
>
> - providing technical assistance, training, coaching and tools to local non-governmental organisations (HRAC partners) so that well-trained staff and members become (1) skilled producers of solid and relevant data on human rights violations, and (2) skilled beneficiaries of statistical analysis carried out by professional statisticians;
>
> - ensuring a scientifically qualified and truly sustainable follow-up of the project's achievements on the basis of nationally-based statistical and technical expertise.

enhancement of analytical and reporting capacities of HRAC member organisations. Not only did they generate interest in evidenced-based statistical arguments about human rights violations patterns in Sri Lanka, but participants also had the valuable experience of discussing their data and analysis with other human rights practitioners and policy actors.

Reaching a critical degree of maturity

The tools developed within the project (such as the *Controlled Vocabulary*, the standardised encoding forms and the customised software) and the working methods adopted and promoted by HRAC with the support of The Asia Foundation have proved to be both solid and powerful. Moreover, proper and systematic implementation of each step within the working process ensured a very high quality of encoded data. This is a major achievement. International experts agree that the Sri Lankan experience represents one of the world's most accurate and rigorous constructions of datasets on human rights violations. Similar projects have been designed and implemented in Thailand, Timor-Leste and Colombia drawing on the data collection and data coding methods developed by the HRAC (see Silva and Ball, 2006).

It is worth noting that the project confirmed its potential for moving forward within a larger integrated methodological framework: while initially it focused only on encoding and analysis of "found data", it then integrated promising data capture with survey methods. Moreover, the monitoring scope was expanded from past to current human rights violations, with the project producing evidence-based preliminary assessments, for instance, on abuse of detainees by the police.

The descriptive statistical analysis of the data encoded between 2004-2007 shows that the project has reached a critical degree of maturity, producing highly relevant information but also highlighting the need for a deeper statistical analysis and fully reliable and incontestable results before delivering them to the public for advocacy purposes. In this context, HRAC partners have demonstrated remarkable responsibility and rigour.

Box 8.6. **Descriptive statistical analysis: integrating preliminary analysis into the human rights discourse**

This box provides a small example of the work carried out by HRAC partner organisations with human rights violations data coded and keyed into their *Analyzer* databases. The example is of a data series held by the Home for Human Rights (HHR), based on legal case files and testimonies collected by this organisation from 1977 to 2004.

The Prevention of Terrorism Act in Sri Lanka gave law enforcement officials and the state security apparatus wide-ranging powers to arrest and detain individuals on the grounds of "suspicion of terrorism". The graph below shows the reported patterns of (1) physical abuse and torture and (2) arrests and detentions committed by state forces between 1977 and 2004. The reported pattern of physical abuse and torture is strongly positively correlated with that of arrests and detentions: both phenomena tend to rise and fall together. This pattern is consistent with the hypothesis that arbitrary detentions and physical abuse by the Sri Lankan State are the result of the same cause.

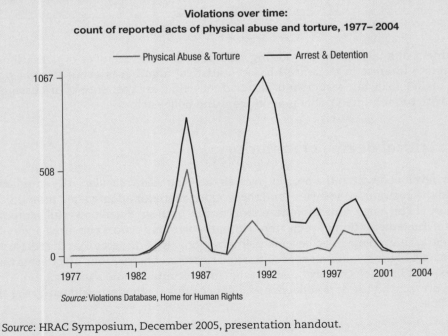

**Violations over time:
count of reported acts of physical abuse and torture, 1977– 2004**

Source: Violations Database, Home for Human Rights

Source: HRAC Symposium, December 2005, presentation handout.

Box 8.7. **Implications of the experience in Sri Lanka**

Key outcomes and policy implications

- Establishing a scientifically rigorous record of reported and estimated total numbers of violations, patterns of abuse, and the nature and identity of perpetrators and victims helps to clarify history, assign responsibility for past violations and will put an end to perpetrators' sense of impunity.

- Maintaining a record of current abuses effectively assists in monitoring human rights over the country and helps to shape policy in ways that promote greater human rights protection and accountability.

- Analysis of datasets has been confirming the correlation between patterns of various forms of massive human rights violations, which is consistent with the hypothesis that these violations have been the result of specific causes and perpetrators that can be identified over time. This kind of analysis is invaluable for the work of future truth and reconciliation mechanisms.

- Decisions on the timing and form of release of findings must be taken with a high sense of responsibility and rigour. While the experience produced highly relevant information, it also underscored the need to deepen the statistical analysis and ensure results are fully reliable and incontestable before delivering them to the public for advocacy purposes.

- The experience has not only provided new technical skills and knowledge to civil society organisations, but it has also substantially enhanced their role, profile and capacities in policy-oriented analysis and action.

- To be effective, fruitful and sustainable, these kinds of projects require a long-lasting effort by local implementing organisations and domestic experts, sustained by long-term commitment and consistent funding from international donor institutions.

Major methodological implications

- Several factors contributed to the success of this experience: (1) the effective ownership of the project by local civil society actors; (2) the authoritative role of The Asia Foundation as facilitator, co-ordinator and overall manager of a project involving many actors and instances with diverse individual constituencies, agendas, interests and skills; (3) the technical assistance, training, coaching and tools that were provided to the HRAC member organisations; (4) the generous funding from DANIDA, allowing the project to embark on increasingly intensive work, with larger teams and appropriate equipment - and therefore to achieve ambitious targets in terms of both volume of encoded data and capacity of analysis; and (5) the partnership with the Department of Statistics of the University of Colombo.

- The design and implementation of a clear and coherent strategy to transfer skills and enhance domestic capacities - including transmission of different skills to different kinds of local actors involved in the project - are essential to ensure effective local sustainability of the work on an autonomous scientific and technical basis.

Chapter 9

Main Lessons and Products from Metagora

The Metagora pilot experiences were each planned, designed and implemented as part of a coherent whole. Their local processes therefore converged into common achievements. This chapter summarises the lessons formulated collectively by the Partners Group. It also highlights two key products of the project: the *Inventory of Initiatives* and the *Training Materials*.

Feasibility and relevance

Measuring human rights and democratic governance is technically feasible and politically relevant: data on human rights and democratic governance can be collected and indicators produced that are of central relevance for policy makers and for society at large.

None of the pilot experiences aimed to provide an exhaustive assessment of the human rights and democratic governance issues at stake. Rather, they sought to produce sets of limited but robust and relevant information to efficiently address specific policy needs.

The surveys and studies conducted in Francophone Africa and the Andean Community show that it is possible to collect relevant data and develop indicators for evaluating how well institutions and democracies are working, and for measuring the degree of support for policies among the general public (see *Chapter 6*). Measuring such indicators is generally less complex than measuring traditional socio-economic indicators such as, for example, monetary poverty. The response rate to questionnaires on the functioning of democracy and on governance issues was generally higher than for questions on income and revenue. Moreover, a scientific comparison with other similar international initiatives (*e.g.* the Afrobarometre and Latinobarometre projects) revealed both the strong convergence of results across the common fields - thus confirming the robustness of the proposed indicators - and the areas in which these various instruments are complementary.

This chapter was drafted on the basis of both the preliminary lessons formulated by the Partners Group on the occasion of its meeting in Oaxaca (20-22 April 2005), and the conclusions of the Metagora Methodological Workshop held on January 2007 and gathering together the members of the Partners Group and of the Independent Panel of Experts.

The three pilot surveys carried out in Mexico, the Philippines and South Africa showed that well-established statistical survey methods can be applied to measure sensitive human rights and democratic governance issues (see *Chapters 3, 4* and *5*). As with all surveys that intend to capture sensitive or complex data, proper questionnaire design and testing are basic preconditions for obtaining reliable relevant data. This is particularly crucial for ensuring that a survey appropriately addresses the issues at stake in specific national political, social and cultural contexts. Although non-response is a serious problem, here further study and articulation of assumptions and models can improve statistical estimates. These three surveys were designed and implemented as pilot experiences. Short timeframes and few available resources resulted in a number of sampling and technical limitations. In spite of this, the data collected provided significant information on the nature, dimensions and magnitude of the issues at stake.

The surveys' findings showed the high incidence of abuse by law enforcement authorities in Mexico City; the centrality of ancestral land protection for the effective implementation of indigenous peoples' rights in the Philippines; and the true expectations of the South African black population with regard to land reform. These findings were particularly relevant for addressing key governance issues, for confirming or correcting stakeholders' perceptions and policy assumptions, and also for using evidence-based analysis in the appropriate design of policies and programmes to redress rights and enhance accountability.

The methodology used in Sri Lanka to document, encode and analyse sensitive information on massive human rights violations helped create a scientifically rigorous record of reported and estimated total numbers of violations, patterns of abuse, and the nature and identity of perpetrators and victims. This, in turn, is helpful to clarify history, assign responsibilities for past violations, and put an end to perpetrators' sense of impunity. Analysis of datasets is contributing to confirm the correlation between patterns of various forms of massive human rights violations that is consistent with the hypothesis that these violations were the result of specific causes and perpetrators that can be identified over time. This kind of analysis is invaluable for future truth and reconciliation work. Moreover, in spite of the severe deterioration of the situation in the country, the development of records and survey-based estimates of current abuses could help shape processes and policies to promote greater human rights protection and accountability.

In other words, these pilot experiences - deliberately conducted in different cultural, political and development contexts and based on different survey approaches and data collection methods - attest to the feasibility, relevance and fruitfulness of applying professional statistical tools and methods in assessing and monitoring human rights and democratic governance.

Quantitative and qualitative data

Quantitative and qualitative data can and should interrelate to properly inform democracy, human rights and governance assessments.

Metagora has shown that the assessment of democracy, governance and human rights can build on the solid rock of proper quantitative reporting. However, it has also confirmed that accurate qualitative research and documentation of the situation, perceptions of target populations and the assumptions and expectations of a variety of stakeholders must also inform the process. Qualitative information is essential not only to ensure proper design of survey questionnaires, but also to focus statistical analysis on relevant issues and to provide appropriate contextual frameworks for an effective policy-oriented interpretation of quantitative data.

The design of the Mexican pilot survey questionnaire was based on extensive qualitative consultation with experts, as well as on systematic records of qualitative information gathered through in-depth narrative interviews with victims of abuse by law enforcement authorities. In the Philippines, multiple qualitative methods were used (including focus group discussions with target populations, substantive reports by local experts as well as broad consultations and thematic discussions with all relevant stakeholders). These were invaluable, not only in conceiving and designing the questionnaire, but also in interpreting and validating the findings (i.e. clarifying significant variations among the indigenous tribes on specific issues), therefore ensuring that the investigation was aligned and responsive to indigenous conceptualisations and focused on salient and meaningful priorities.

The pilots also explored new ways of better matching quantitative and qualitative sources of information. For example, the Sri Lankan experience has been building statistically-friendly series of data encoded from records of narrative reports on human rights violations (see *Chapter 8*). In Palestine, official statisticians and researchers have been integrating quantitative and qualitative information on the right to education within a single database (see *Chapter 7*).

The outcomes of the different activities show that relating survey results with qualitative and contextual information provides a solid comprehensive basis for policy-oriented reporting on human rights and democratic governance issues.

National ownership and participatory processes

In order to be truly shared and to have effective policy impact, assessments of human rights and democratic governance have to be based on domestic ownership, involve a wide range of national stakeholders through participatory processes, be driven by authoritative national actors and be implemented on a multidisciplinary basis.

The main characteristic and most powerful asset of Metagora has been its original bottom-up approach (see *Chapter 2*). The project has been conducted following firmly the principles of ownership and participation formulated in the *Paris Declaration*. Through a variety of pilot experiences, the project has clearly shown how assessments of human rights and democratic governance can be launched and driven by authoritative domestic actors – and how they can contribute to enhance national capacities and institutional monitoring mechanisms.

International indicators and most assessments driven by international organisations, donor agencies or academic experts from the global North have little or no impact on the domestic processes and national policies of the target countries. While this kind of indicators and assessments can powerfully inform a number of national stakeholders, most often they are ignored or not shared by society at large. As a matter of fact, national ownership of assessments cannot be materialised if national actors are merely passive recipients of the results obtained or if, as it often happens, they are "associated" *ad post* to discussions on these results. It is up to an inclusive community of domestic stakeholders to take the decision of conducting an assessment, formulate its rationale, identify the key issues to be measured, and define the assumptions and expectations that have to guide the design of measurement tools such as survey questionnaires and survey samples.

It is only through wide domestic participatory processes that the measurement and assessment of human rights and democratic governance can be of interest for society at large – and thus produce shared knowledge of the policy issues at stake. This is the way in which the Metagora Partners have been addressing, in their countries, national needs for reliable data and indicators on human rights and democratic governance. Indeed, participatory processes have been a cross-cutting mark of the

Metagora pilots. The form of these processes varied from one pilot experience to another. They have been based on strong inter-institutional mechanisms (like in the Philippines), on national steering committees involving the civil society and policy actors (such as in Palestine), or on *ad hoc* groups of experts and key stakeholders (such as in Mexico, Peru and South Africa). They have included large workshops, training sessions, focus group discussions with target groups, or narrative interviews of relevant actors concerned by the specific issues at stake.

As mentioned in the *Chapter 1*, the Metagora Partner Organisations have also mobilised, in the course of the last four years, an impressive number of domestic stakeholders and local qualified consultants both in the design and implementation of the pilots and in related participatory processes. More than 300 stakeholders and experts were involved in local advisory bodies and steering mechanisms, and around 1,000 stakeholders and experts have been attending, at the national and international levels, consultative meetings and workshops.

Most pilots were conducted by local multidisciplinary teams consisting of human rights practitioners, policy actors, statisticians, social scientists and stakeholders from the civil society. Discussions on the possible ways and means for measuring human rights and democratic governance were not easy, as each of these actors had a different background, interest and working methods. In most cases, it took these teams a long time to establish a common ground and start working together based on the complementarity of their skills. In some countries, the Metagora pilots had a strong impact in transforming and empowering the relations of the many "actors of change" involved in the measuring processes. This tends to suggest that, in this bottom-up approach and in a long-term perspective, the process behind the assessments might actually be more important than the results themselves.

Involvement of National Statistical Offices

National Statistical Offices can be efficiently involved in the measurement of human rights and democratic governance issues.

Contrary to a deep prejudice still ingrained within the international official statistical community, Metagora's pilot experiences show that National Statistical Offices can: (1) conduct large sample surveys on governance and democracy issues; (2) provide qualified technical assistance and field logistics to other governmental agencies or Human Rights Institutions; and/or (3) develop, in collaboration and interaction with civil society actors, proper tools for systematic evidence-based monitoring of social, economic and cultural rights.

As evidence of the feasibility of measuring democracy and governance issues with official statistical tools, survey questionnaires on these issues have, to date, been attached as a supplement to regular household surveys conducted by eleven National Statistical Offices in Francophone Africa and the Andean region (see *Chapter 6*). This experience develops and promotes a very promising tool, as using well-established official surveys has obvious advantages: the size and quality of the sampling frames, the effectiveness of proper data collection, the analytical potential of the data collected, as well as the marginal additional costs incurred by appending specific modules to the questionnaires of existing surveys. Analysis of the resulting data is enriched by information on respondents collected from both the regular and supplement questionnaires, making it possible to focus on governance issues in relation to major social and development problems such as poverty and exclusion. In Francophone Africa and the Andean countries, disaggregated data also proved invaluable for the evidence-based assessment of local governance. In Madagascar, Peru and Ecuador, the survey has become a routine measurement tool that allows for time series to be built. The institutionalisation of this tool within the national official statistical information systems must be further enhanced, deepened and included in the National Strategies for the Development of Statistics (NSDS) promoted by PARIS21 and supported by the UN family.

In the Philippines, the National Statistical Coordination Board provided sound expertise on the design of the survey and on the analysis of the results on the rights of indigenous peoples, the study of which was organised by the Commission on Human Rights (see *Chapter 4*). It also co-ordinated the training, sampling work and field support, which were provided by the National Statistical Office and the Statistical Research and Training Centre. Experts from these statistical offices were involved throughout the whole process, from the participatory consultation of stakeholders and communities of indigenous peoples, to the statistical analysis and presentation of findings to the stakeholders and the media. This involvement not only helped to ensure that the survey conformed to well-established professional standards, but also enhanced the culture of evidence-based assessment among the other main institutional partners: the Commission for Human Rights and the National Commission for Indigenous Peoples. All this undoubtedly contributed to reinforce the specific role of the various official statistical agencies, their technical independence, as well as their capacity to interact as qualified partners with other public institutions and with organised civil society.

In Palestine, the Central Bureau of Statistics (PCBS) co-operated intensely with civil society actors to develop indicators and a prototype database on the right to education (see *Chapter 7*). This co-operation was based on a clear and rigorous distinction of roles and tasks. PCBS was responsible for the identification, collection and processing of relevant data, as well as for the design, development, updating, maintenance and public access of the database. The analysis and interpretation of the information provided by the database, however, was the sole responsibility of the users (NGOs, academic and independent research centres, the media and bodies of the Palestinian National Authority) on a strictly independent basis.

All these experiences show that NSOs can efficiently and successfully be involved, in various ways, in the measurement of human rights and democratic governance. Nevertheless, the decision for a NSO to conduct or support measurement exercises in these areas must be based on sound consideration of the feasibility, suitability and usefulness of doing so in each national particular context.

In this perspective, the Metagora community would like to share with all concerned actors - and in particular the UN Statistical Commission, the UN Regional Conference of Statisticians, the PARIS21 Steering Committee, and the OECD Committee on Statistics - its appreciation of the basic conditions that are required to (1) decide whether a National Statistical Office can participate in measuring human rights and democratic governance, and (2) obtain relevant information on governance and democracy through official statistical surveys.

The Metagora community considers that the decision of a National Statistical Office to be involved or not in measuring sensitive human rights or democratic governance issues must take two criteria into account: its legitimacy and its capacity.

The legitimacy of official statistics fundamentally depends on public trust in the office responsible for generating and disseminating the information. Such trust is normally based on the recognised technical skills and professional standards of the NSO, as well as on its technical independence – that is reflected in independent (and not in politically influenced or biased) information. In this sense, legitimacy results from the history of the NSO, the public perception of its work, and from its effective capacity to work with recognised and respected technical independence when it comes to measuring sensitive issues.

Depending on the specific national context, some NSOs may be widely considered as legitimate, whereas others may be perceived to be "too close" to the political authorities or as potentially vulnerable to pressure. One might assume that this latter scenario is particularly likely in countries with poor human rights and democratic governance records. In such circumstances, it seems unlikely that the NSO will positively contribute to the assessment and monitoring in these fields. However, the Metagora experience in Francophone Africa shows that other factors can palliate weak legitimacy (for instance, a regional or supranational dimension of the surveys). Moreover, it is worth noting that when a NSO is successfully involved in evidence-based assessment of democratic governance, this can in turn help its public image, thereby increasing its legitimacy.

The criteria of capacity relates to an institution's ability to undertake proper collection of data, statistical analysis and dissemination of results. Well-trained field staff, as well as tools and expertise for designing samples and translating the key issues (i.e. the interests and preoccupations of various stakeholders) into clear and pertinent survey questions are important factors for deciding whether an institution can take on the responsibility for collecting, processing and analysing data. In many countries, besides NSOs, other institutions (whether private or public) may also have the required skills. The question to ask is, therefore, what makes (or does not make) the NSO the most suitable institution for measuring human rights or democratic governance issues?

Another issue to consider when involving NSOs in this kind of assessment is that the information produced will be labelled "official statistics". Though this may not always be important, it can have two major implications for some stakeholders. In some cases, information with an official label is more likely to hold the attention of government, whilst in other cases, experience has shown that, though NSOs collect relevant data and produce significant information on democratic governance issues, the sensitive nature of such data may prevent their dissemination, thus hindering their use and impact.

Ultimately, it is up to the top management of each NSO to evaluate if and how its involvement in measuring human rights and democratic governance can be feasible, suitable and fruitful in its specific national context. The Metagora community strongly recommends that this decision be taken within NSO's global National Strategy for the Development of Statistics (NSDS).

The Metagora community considers the following preconditions to be necessary for obtaining reliable information on governance and democracy through official statistical surveys:

- *a political environment which allows for the technically independent implementation of field operations and data processing, secure and free mobility of interviewers, and free and confident responses by interviewees;*
- *an in-depth dialogue with the various stakeholders on the survey's assumptions is highly desirable;*
- *the content of the survey should take into account the existing knowledge as well as the assumptions and expectations of a wide range of stakeholders;*
- *particular attention should be paid to the structure, content, clarity and respondent-friendliness of the questionnaire;*
- *high statistical competency of those conducting the survey and analysing the results is indispensable;*
- *legitimacy of the institution co-ordinating the survey and disseminating the results is a decisive characteristic.*

Moreover, the implementation of the survey, the documentation of methods and the dissemination of results must conform to the UN Fundamental Principles of Official Statistics (UN-ECOSOC, 1994).

Box 9.1. Measuring democratic governance with official statistical tools

In the development context of Ecuador, my institution can't escape the duty of informing the public debate on democracy performances and key governance issues. The National Institute of Statistics and Censuses of Ecuador is part of the Metagora community and is proud of having implemented a pioneering survey on governance, citizenship, participation and subjective poverty. This experience was very challenging for my institution for two main reasons: first, such a survey required us to review and upgrade our working structures and processes; and second, the nature of the survey pushed us to engage in important innovations to ensure not only the statistical quality of the information produced, but also its relevance for policy design and decision-making processes. Indeed, the objective of the survey was very ambitious, as it aimed to provide data for informing the design, implementation and evaluation of our national strategy for poverty reduction, as well as various development supporting programmes.

This survey was part of our Integrated Household Survey System, and was carried out through a special module attached to the questionnaire used for the survey on employment, unemployment and underemployment. The core conceptual element underlying the design of this survey is "democratic governance", which covers the dimensions of governance, legitimacy and participation. The survey questionnaire included four series of questions related to governance and democracy, corruption and trust in institutions, decentralisation and public participation, and subjective poverty. Human rights, democracy, social and political participation were among the key variables studied.

Respondents' socio-demographic profiles, as well as the data gathered on the perception of standards of living and concrete problems faced by households allowed us to analyse interesting data and obtain important findings. For instance, in the development and political contexts of Ecuador it is today important to consider dramatic facts such as the relation between people's levels of education and the importance they attach to democracy, the general mistrust towards "the political class" (85% of respondents think that it represents only private interests), or the scarce credibility of parliamentary and judicial systems among the population. Furthermore, one of the survey's main contributions has been to highlight the sheer dimension of the social and institutional exclusion of the many people with little or no education.

No doubt, these and many other findings are of the highest importance not only for policy makers, but also for the Ecuadorian society at large. We have therefore decided to follow a three-fold strategy aimed at: (1) ensuring the legitimisation of this statistical project through a broad dissemination and socialisation of the data; (2) enhancing and conducting the survey on a regular basis with the aim of building a formal system of democratic and governance surveys; and (3) generating indicators to support democratic dialogue and decision-making, in particular within the framework of the implementation of our national development plan. For a country like Ecuador, reliable statistics and indicators on democratic governance are of the highest importance today. My institution is therefore firmly committed to addressing and taking this challenge onboard.

Byron Villacís Cruz
Director General, National Institute of Statistics and Censuses of Ecuador

---

Value added for Human Rights Institutions

Statistical analysis and quantitative indicators bring a significant value-added to the work of national Human Rights Institutions.

Current human rights monitoring mechanisms are mainly based on reporting of individual cases (or series of cases) to Human Rights Institutions (HRIs), as well as on judicial decisions. This form of monitoring is certainly invaluable for purposes of advocacy on individual cases, but it does not provide relevant information on the real dimension and wider trends of major human rights issues considered as collective, social and political phenomena. As HRIs are primarily concerned with promoting and protecting human rights on the basis of international norms and standards, they are particularly aware of the lack of such information in a reliable form. However, HRI agents are often unfamiliar with quantitative analysis and may consider statistics to be an overly reductive approach unable to capture the multiple complex dimensions inherent in human rights issues.

The Metagora experience in the Philippines, conducted by the Commission on Human Rights, has proven that working mechanisms involving different institutions with the appropriate substantive and technical skills can facilitate the measurement of complex problems such as indigenous peoples' rights (see *Chapter 4*). This experience has shown that strong leadership by HRIs, political commitment of relevant institutions in charge of protecting target populations, proper technical assistance and field support from NSOs, and wide consultation with all relevant stakeholders are essential for the success of this kind of initiative.

This experience also showed that a long process of dialogue and mutual learning is required to overcome prejudices as well as the unfamiliarity of the various actors with the approaches and skills of the others. The results of the pilot survey and complementary qualitative analysis prove that, on the basis of shared analysis, statistical figures and indicators can effectively inform HRIs' regular reporting and powerfully back their recommendations to the executive and legislative powers, in particular on the implementation of economic, social and cultural rights.

In a different context, the pilot survey on ill-treatment and abuse in Mexico City also emphasised the value-added of statistical methods to the work of HRIs, not only in identifying the specific forms and mechanisms of abuse by law-enforcement authorities, but also in constructively promoting and supporting governmental policies and programmes for enhancing governance structures and measures to eliminate and prevent such abuse (see *Chapter 3*).

Alongside the Metagora experience, other initiatives and plans undertaken by HRIs were identified, namely in Kenya and South Africa. A network of such HRIs has been developing to allow more frequent and efficient exchanges, as well as the transmission of lessons to the international human rights community. In this context, the AAAS Science and Human Rights Program and the Metagora Co-ordination Team elaborated, in collaboration with some national HRIs, two outlines of structured work to ensure a more shared, replicable and sustainable involvement of HRIs in evidence-based assessment of human rights issues.

Empowerment of civil society

Statistical methods can substantially enhance the research and advocacy of civil society actors in the fields of human rights and democracy.

In the framework of the project *Mapping Political and Ethnic Violence in Sri Lanka* supported by The Asia Foundation, technical expertise was provided to the Human Rights Accountability Coalition (HRAC) in which different NGOs joined efforts to systematically collect, collate, analyse and share data on human rights violations (see *Chapter 8*). The objective of HRAC was to develop a massive, objective and undeniable statistical record allowing NGOs to inject scientifically rigorous evidence into the search for truth about the patterns, magnitude, and responsibility for past and current violations connected to Sri Lanka's ethnic and political conflicts. Technical foundations were established with the adoption of harmonised forms to register events and of an agreed *Vocabulary* on human rights violations to ensure standardised coding and processing of comprehensive physical records. On this basis, this pilot experience developed and expanded further to ensure rigorous data processing and quality control, and to build an impressive electronic record of human rights violations. All this demonstrates that well-established methods for ensuring harmonised data collection and coding help to reinforce the capacity of NGOs and open promising prospects for proper evidence-based analysis of massive human rights violations.

An important objective of the Sri Lankan project was to build locally-based sustainable capacities through (1) the provision of technical assistance, training, coaching and tools to local civil society organisations (HRAC partners) in order that well-trained staff and members produce solid and relevant data on human rights violations, and (2) the running of the project on the basis of national statistical and technical expertise.

This experience shows that to enhance the capacities of civil society to conduct evidence-based assessments, different skills must be built among the different local actors involved in the collection, analysis and policy-oriented interpretation of human rights data. This is essential to ensure the local sustainability of the work on an autonomous scientific and technical basis.

In a different context, the Metagora experience in Palestine explored, through a broad participatory process, options for involving civil society actors, together with the Palestinian Central Bureau of Statistics (PCBS), in measuring human rights and democratic governance issues (see *Chapter 7*). The experience focused on developing indicators on the right to education based on official statistical data as well as on information collected by NGOs and academic or independent research centres. Quantitative and qualitative information was integrated into a dynamic database developed and managed by the PCBS. This prototype is being further developed and will become a public information tool allowing for independent policy-oriented analysis and reporting by research centres, human rights organisations and political actors. This prototype database thus provides a common basis for gathering, coding and analysing sets of information of different sources that otherwise would remain fragmentary, anecdotal and of little use for comprehensive analysis.

As in Sri Lanka, the Palestine pilot experience confirmed that appropriate training in data collection and data processing, as well as appropriate skills-building, can substantially empower NGOs' monitoring and advocacy capacities. Thanks to this training, NGOs can now play a double role as providers and users of relevant information. Moreover, the Metagora experience has provided a key policy focus to (and has given a strong impetus for) an effective cross-institutional partnership between academia, independent research centres, NGOs, policy actors and the NSO. This illustrates the power of Metagora's bottom-up approach - jointly conducted here by NGOs and a technically and professionally skilled institution. The experience also shows, however, that to be effective the implementation of this approach requires a clear distinction of roles and tasks among NGOs and statistical and other governmental bodies.

Emerging initiatives worldwide

Many initiatives in different regions of the world, with approaches and objectives similar to those of Metagora, have been identified and documented in the form of an online database.

The Montreux Conference revealed for the first time an emerging need worldwide for evidence-based assessments of human rights and democratic governance. More than half of the 300 written contributions to that Conference came from developing countries. To get a better picture of on-going field work and existing expertise in this field, Metagora carried out a worldwide survey. Its main objective was to identify relevant initiatives by local, national and regional organisations, with a particular emphasis on developing countries.

The survey was based on an open-ended questionnaire developed by a task team of leading experts and reviewed in-depth by the whole Metagora community (see *Appendix 2*). This questionnaire was sent out in 2004 to about 3,000 potential respondents registered in a database provided by the organisers of the Montreux Conference. These potential respondents included national institutions, NGOs, research centres, government bodies and experts worldwide. From the hundreds of responses received, some 250 were considered relevant by the task team.

The survey was extremely useful in providing basic information on the objectives, methods of work, experts and sources of funding of these relevant projects. The information gathered was recorded in an *Inventory of Initiatives aimed at Enhancing Evidence-based Assessment of Human Rights and Democratic Governance*, made public in the form of an online repository and Internet search tool (see Métagora, 2006).

The *Inventory* aims to share information and to facilitate exchanges and networking among organisations and experts worldwide. Thanks to a user-friendly search engine users can find detailed descriptions of initiatives (topics, methods, budget, etc.), information and addresses of institutions and experts involved, and links to related publications and available documents (see selected examples in *Appendix 3*).

The *Inventory* has contributed to uncover numerous efforts around the world to measure democratic governance and human rights, largely unheard of by the international human rights and statistical communities until then. It provides information on these efforts and gives an interesting picture of local and national needs and priorities in on-going assessments of human rights and democratic governance. It covers a wide range of initiatives: from well-known institutions working at the global level, to small civil society organisations interested in measuring one particular aspect of democratic governance or human rights in their local contexts. It highlights the diversity of institutions involved, objectives sought and themes addressed, geographical scope covered, and methodological approaches used. Last but not least, it also reflects a wide variety of assessment approaches, though most combined qualitative and quantitative approaches - thereby underlining one of Metagora's main features: the complementarity of quantitative and qualitative methods.

Information gathered in the *Inventory* shows that academia and the international community are not the only ones to call for a more rigorous use of quantitative methods in the collection, production and analysis of data in the field of human rights and democratic governance. A strong demand is also coming from the field, in particular in the South. The survey revealed that over 40% of the organisations implementing relevant initiatives are based in developing countries. About 28% of initiatives were identified as "global initiatives" due to their cross-country scope which involves more than one continent.

The *Inventory* reveals that, most often, national and local initiatives are modest in scope, conducted with few resources and based on rudimentary methods, thereby attesting to a major need for technical assistance, transfer of know-how and financial support. Finally, the heterogeneity of initiatives speaks to the richness of existing work and calls for enhanced co-operation and exchanges between the various producers of data on human rights and democratic governance. This would allow initiatives to feed into each other, thereby complementing and enhancing their comprehensiveness and impact wherever possible.

The *Inventory* paves the way for exploring many feasible ways of bringing statistical analysis into the heart of monitoring human rights and democratic governance. It is not only a reference information tool, but also a means for building on and further deepening the worldwide network that has been growing around Metagora in the course of the last four years. This useful tool is part of the concrete legacy of Metagora to the international community; it will be handed over to the Oslo Governance Centre (UNDP), which will update and further expand it.

Training Materials

Metagora has documented the experiences, problems encountered and lessons learnt to produce a substantive set of Training Materials. These Materials - available online - aim at informing individuals, groups and organisations interested in measuring human rights and democratic governance, and at helping them to adapt and apply the tested methods and participatory working approaches in their own national and cultural contexts (see Métagora, 2007a).

There is a close relationship between the *Inventory of Initiatives* and the web-based *Training Materials*. The rationale behind the development of the *Training Materials* is that, by documenting activities in a structured form, Metagora could enable others to learn from its experience, mistakes and good practices - and thus to gain from and build on existing work. This transfer of know-how and lessons learnt addresses one of the main needs identified through the *Inventory of Initiatives*.

The *Training Materials* are intended to serve as a reference tool for producers of data and indicators on human rights and democratic governance. These materials cover a wide range of data collection techniques, with a particular focus on survey methods. They highlight the role and value of data and indicators in the measurement of human rights and democratic governance. These data and indicators can stem from two different processes: pre-existing data or the collection of new data – and therefore the *Training Materials* provide information on the various steps and considerations inherent to both processes. How to get started, address and find the right people, or create a questionnaire, are among the issues tackled.

The *Training Materials* powerfully articulate statistical methods and policy-making when it comes to assessing issues related to human rights and democratic governance. They also highlight some of the challenges linked to the use of data and indicators in these complex and sensitive fields. The information and concrete examples provided throughout these materials serve as a strong basis for identifying good practices.

The *Training Materials* also aim to inform and guide relevant stakeholders - such as policy and decision makers, civil society actors, analysts, journalists or donor institutions - on the approaches, conditions and methods for measuring human rights and democratic governance. The technical vocabulary used in elaborating these materials has therefore been adapted to fit the different levels of knowledge and needs of this wide range of users of data and indicators – including those who are totally unfamiliar with statistical methods and mathematics. Indeed, information is presented at different levels of detail and various entry points have been developed. Thus, depending on individual's particular knowledge or interest in a specific topic, it is possible, for selected issues, to choose the level of depth one wishes to go into. Thanks to this, the *Training Materials* allow:

- policy and decision makers to understand how appropriate quantitative and qualitative methods of data collection and analysis can inform the formulation of policies related to democratic governance and human rights;
- civil society actors, Human Rights Institutions and other potential users of data to understand the complementary roles of quantitative and qualitative information in their work, and how to create statistically rigorous projects for data collection and analysis; and

- professionals working with data to understand the policy processes related to democratic governance and human rights as well as the particular information needs of policy makers, and to grasp the specific challenges inherent to conducting projects like Metagora.

The *Training Materials* therefore facilitate the creation of a common ground of understanding. They include *Guidelines for Informing Policy via Data*, definitions in the form of an *Encyclopaedia of Terms*, a *Case Study*, and a collection of documents and tools from the Metagora project that can be used as potential examples for future projects. These documents include training manuals for interviewers, sample analyses and selected technical and narrative reports on the Metagora pilots.

The *Training Materials* are therefore one of the more tangible, useful and innovative results of the Metagora project. They are the result of a collective work by the Metagora community. Their structure and content were subject to an extensive international peer-review process, involving not only Metagora partners but also external scholars, including statisticians, social and political scientists, and experts in human rights monitoring. This process was key in validating and further enriching the content of these materials.

The *Training Materials* are accessible through the Internet. As for all other elements that the project has handed over to the international community at large, the Metagora community hopes that its efforts will serve as a basis for other projects and initiatives aimed at measuring human rights and democratic governance. May these new projects further complement, enrich and expand these materials with new documented experiences and lessons.

Part II

Chapter 10

Indicators for Monitoring Compliance with International Human Rights Instruments

The work on indicators at the Office of the United Nations High Commissioner for Human Rights (OHCHR) was initiated at the request of the Inter-committee meeting of the human rights treaty bodies to help them make use of statistical information in states parties' reports in assessing the implementation of human rights. OHCHR undertook an extensive survey of literature and prevalent practices among national and international organisations on the use of quantitative information in monitoring human rights (see Fasel and Malhotra, 2005). Having taken stock of the state of the art, steps were taken to develop a conceptual and methodological framework, in consultation with a panel of experts, for identifying operationally feasible human rights indicators. The first outline of the framework was presented to the Inter-committee meeting of human rights treaty bodies in June 2006 (see UN-HRI, 2006b).

This chapter was contributed by the

Office of the United Nations High Commissioner for Human Rights

Since the establishment of the United Nations in 1945, promoting and encouraging respect for human rights for all without distinction as to race, sex, language, or religion, as stipulated in the UN Charter, has been one of the fundamental goals of the organisation. As the principal UN office mandated to promote and protect human rights for all, the Office of the UN High Commissioner for Human Rights (OHCHR) acts as the focal point of human rights research, education, public information, and advocacy activities in the UN system. The method of work of the OHCHR focuses on three major dimensions: standard-setting, monitoring and implementation on the ground.

This chapter is based on a report submitted by the OHCHR at the seventh Inter-committee meeting of the human rights treaty bodies and at the twentieth meeting of chairpersons of the human rights treaty bodies held in Geneva, respectively on 23-25 and 26-27 June 2008.

The text was edited for the purposes of this publication. Its original official source is the UN document HRI/MC/2008/3, available at: http://www2.ohchr.org/english/bodies/icm-mc/docs/HRI.MC.2008.3EN.pdf

Additional information on the current work of OHCHR on human rights indicators can be requested to Mr. Nicolas Fasel at: nfasel@ohchr.org

---

Based on the articulated approach, lists of illustrative indicators were elaborated on 12 selected human rights - both civil and political, as well as economic, social and cultural. These indicators were then subjected to a validation process involving, at the first stage, discussions with an identified panel of experts from treaty bodies, human rights special procedure mandate-holders, academia, non-governmental organisations and relevant international organisations. At the second stage, discussions were held with national stakeholders, including national Human Rights Institutions, policy makers and agencies responsible for reporting on the implementation of the human rights treaties, National Statistical Offices responsible for data collection and representatives from non-governmental organisations.

These consultations were held in the context of regional and country level workshops. The workshops provided a platform for sensitising the stakeholders on the potential use of available statistical information for promoting and monitoring the implementation of human rights at the country level. It also helped in collating the feedback from the stakeholders on the relevance of and the application of the work undertaken by OHCHR at the country level.

The first section of this chapter outlines the adopted conceptual and methodological framework for identifying the relevant quantitative indicators as it has evolved over the last two years (though qualitative and quantitative indicators are both relevant in the work of treaty bodies, this section focuses on quantitative indicators and statistics in view of the specific request of the Inter-committee meeting of UN treaty bodies).

The second section discusses the relevance of using the configuration of structural-process-outcome indicators for the said framework and highlights some considerations in the selection of the illustrative indicators on different human rights.

The third section outlines the results from regional and country level consultations and feedback from the validation exercises undertaken for this work. It also reflects on some issues relevant for taking this work forward at country level. A concluding box sums up the current status of the work and suggestions for a follow-up on this work for the consideration of the treaty bodies (see Box 10.2).

The conceptual and methodological framework

The basic objective in developing a conceptual and methodological framework was to adopt a structured and consistent approach for translating universal human rights standards into indicators that are contextually relevant and useful at country level. The need for an adequate conceptual basis for this work lies in having a rationale for identifying and designing the relevant indicators and not reducing the exercise to a mere listing of possible alternatives. It is important that such indicators are explicitly and precisely defined, are based on an acceptable methodology of data collection and presentation, and are or could be available on a regular basis. It is also important that indicators are suitable to the context where they are applied. In the absence of these considerations being addressed, it may not be feasible or even acceptable to the states parties as well as the Committees to use quantitative indicators in the reporting and follow-up process.

Conceptual concerns

To begin with, for the framework to be conceptually meaningful, it is necessary to anchor indicators identified for a human right in the normative content of that right, as enumerated in the relevant articles of the treaties and General Comments of the Committees. Secondly, the primary objective of human rights assessment is in measuring the effort that the duty-holders make in meeting their obligations - irrespective of whether it is directed at promoting a right or protecting it. While it is this facet of measurement that helps in bringing out the value-added of the approach, it is equally important to get a measure of the "intent/commitment" of the state party, as well as the consolidation of its efforts, as reflected in appropriate "result" indicators. Such a conceptualisation also helps in putting all the human rights on an equal footing, thereby emphasising the interdependence and indivisibility of civil, cultural, economic, political and social rights. Thirdly, the adopted framework should be able to reflect the obligation of the duty-holder to *respect, protect* and *fulfil* human rights. Finally, it is necessary to recognise and reflect cross-cutting human rights norms and principles (such as non-discrimination and equality, indivisibility, accountability, participation and empowerment) in the choice of indicators, as well as in the process of undertaking an assessment. These concerns were addressed in the following manner.

Identifying attributes

As a starting point for each human right, the narrative on the legal standard of the right was translated into a limited number of characteristic attributes that facilitate a structured identification of appropriate indicators for monitoring the implementation of that right. Indeed, the notion of attributes of a right helps in concretising the content of a right and makes explicit the link between identified indicators of a right, on one hand, and the normative standards of that right, on the other. Often, one finds that the enumeration of the standards on a right in the relevant articles and its elaboration in the concerned *General Comments* are quite general and even overlapping, not quite amenable to the process of identifying indicators. By selecting the attributes of a right, the process of identifying suitable indicators or cluster of indicators is facilitated as one arrives at a categorisation that is clear, concrete and, perhaps, more "tangible" in facilitating the selection of indicators.

For most human rights for which indicators were identified, it was found that, on average, about four attributes were able to capture reasonably the essence of the normative content of those rights. Thus, in the case of right to life, taking into account primarily article 3 of the *Universal Declaration of Human Rights* (UDHR), article 6 of the *International Covenant on Civil and Political Rights* (ICCPR) and *General Comment* 6 of the Human Rights Committee, four attributes of the right to life, namely "arbitrary deprivation of life", "disappearances of individuals", "health and nutrition" and "death penalty" were identified. In addition, articles 10-12 of the *International Covenant on Economic and Social Rights* (ICESCR), articles 5(b) and 5(e-iv) of the *International Convention on the Elimination of All Forms of Racial Discrimination* (ICERD), article 12 of the *Convention on the Elimination of All Forms of Discrimination against Women* (CEDAW), articles 1-16 of *Convention against Torture and Other Cruel, Inhuman and Degrading Treatment or Punishment* (CAT), article 6 of the *Convention on the Rights of the Child* (CRC), article 9 of the *International Convention on the Protection of the Rights of All Migrant Workers and Members of Their Families* (ICRMW) and article 10 of the *Convention on the Rights of Persons with Disabilities* (CRPD) also informed the selection of the attributes on the right to life.

Similarly, in the case of the right to health, five attributes were identified: namely, sexual and reproductive health, child mortality and health care, natural and occupational environment, prevention, treatment and control of diseases, and accessibility to health facilities and essential medicines were identified. These attributes were based primarily on a reading of article 25 of the UDHR, article 12 of the ICESCR and *General Comment* No. 14 of the Committee on ESCR, *General Recommendation* No. 24 of the Committee on the Elimination of Discrimination against Women, and *General Comments* No. 3 and 4 of the Committee on the Rights of the Child. Articles 6, paragraph 1, of ICCPR, articles 5(e-iv) of ICERD, articles 12 and 14 (2-b) of CEDAW, article 24 of CRC, articles 28 and 43(e) of ICRMW and article 25 of CRPD were also useful in identifying these attributes.

Thus, the relevant articles from the *Universal Declaration of Human Rights* and the core international human rights treaties, as well as the elaborations in respective *General Comments* of the committees were used for reading the normative content of 12 selected human rights on which indicators were enumerated, namely:

- the right to life
- the right to liberty and security of person
- the right to participate in public affairs
- the right not to be subjected to torture or cruel, inhuman or degrading treatment or punishment
- the right to freedom of opinion and expression
- the right to a fair trial
- the right to the enjoyment of the highest attainable standard of physical and mental health
- the right to adequate food
- the right to adequate housing
- the right to education
- the right to social security
- the right to work

The choice of these 12 rights (see *Appendix* 4), in the first instance, was guided by their recognition in the UDHR and the consideration that these rights would be major building blocks for putting together, in due course, a treaty specific list of illustrative indicators. In that context, there may be a need for further refinement or re-clubbing of the identified attributes of human rights to better reflect the treaty-specific concerns.

Measuring human rights commitment-efforts-results

A key concern in developing the conceptual and methodological framework was to ensure that it did justice in reflecting the inherent complexity of human rights, particularly in the context of their implementation and, at the same time, had a sufficiently operational structure for supporting the identification of quantitative indicators. It was necessary to measure the commitment of the duty-bearer to the relevant human rights standards, the efforts that were undertaken to make that commitment a reality and results of those efforts over time as reflected in appropriate summary indicators. Accordingly, the framework opted for using a configuration of structural-process-outcome indicators, reflecting the need to capture a duty-bearer's commitment, efforts and results, respectively. In other words, by identifying structural-process-outcome indicators for each attribute of a human right, it becomes possible to bring to the fore an assessment of steps taken by the states parties in meeting their human rights obligations. The rationale for the three categories of indicators and the logic of selecting indicators in each category is elaborated in the next section.

A related issue is the extent to which the use of structural-process-outcome indicators for each human right attribute reflects the state obligations to **respect, protect** and **fulfil** human rights, and whether the use of such a configuration of indicators in "unpackaging" the narrative on the normative content of a right is a better option than identifying indicators for the three obligations outlined in respect of each right. There are at least two good reasons for choosing the former categories of indicators in the framework.

First, these are categories of indicators that have a wide use already in the development policy context and are likely to be more familiar to policy makers/implementers and development/human rights practitioners who are, in some sense, the main focus of this work. In fact, the use of structural, process and outcome indicators in promoting and monitoring the implementation of human rights will help demystify the notion of human rights and take the human rights discourse beyond the confines of legal and justice sector discussions, but also facilitate the mainstreaming of human rights standards and principles in policy making and development implementation.

Second, it may not always be possible to identify a quantitative indicator that reflects uniquely one of the three types of obligations. Often, an indicator based on the commonly available administrative and statistical data, may end up reflecting more than one kind of obligations, which may not be very desirable if the intention is to build a structured, common and consistent approach for elaborating indicators across all rights, covering the different human rights treaties. Having said this, in the selection of indicators for each attribute of a human right, attempt was made to include all such indicators that reflect explicitly and uniquely the state obligations to respect, protect and fulfil human rights. In addition, an appropriate combination of structural, process and outcome indicators, particularly the process indicators were identified with a view to facilitate an assessment of the implementation of the said state obligations.

Indicators for cross-cutting human rights norms

The indicators that capture the cross-cutting human rights norms or principles cannot be exclusively identified with the realisation of a specific human right, but are meant to capture the extent to which the process to implement and realise human rights is, for instance, participatory, inclusionary, empowering, non-discriminatory or accountable. It is worth noting that there is no easy way to reflect these cross-cutting norms and principles explicitly in the selection of indicators.

In capturing the **norm of non-discrimination** and equality in the selection of structural, process and outcome indicators, a starting point is to seek disaggregated data by prohibited grounds of discrimination such as sex, disability, ethnicity, religion, language, social or regional affiliation of people. For instance, if the indicator on the proportion of children enrolled in primary school, given that primary education should be available free of costs, is broken down by ethnic groups or religious minorities for a country, it would be possible to capture some aspect of discrimination faced by the concerned groups or minorities in accessing education and enjoying their right to education in that country. In some instances, this cross-cutting norm, like some others could be addressed as a "procedural right" that has a bearing on the realisation of a specific "substantive right", hence is defined in reference to that right. In this context, it is worth noting that substantive rights have a relatively clear content and may also have a "level/progressive" component in realising them, such as the right to education or the right to life. More procedural rights like the right not to be discriminated or the right to remedy are critical to the process of realising the substantive rights and may be easier to define in the specific context of substantive rights.

Compliance with the norm of non-discrimination in the context of the right to education, as a substantive right, could be captured using an indicator like the proportion of the girls in school-going age-group enrolled in school to the proportion of the boys in the same age-group enrolled in the school. Similarly, the proportion of the accused who are requesting/availing themselves of legal aid, if broken down by ethnic groups or minorities, could help in capturing non-discrimination and equality in the implementation of the principle of effective remedies and procedural guarantees. More importantly, in reflecting the cross-cutting norm of non-discrimination and equality the emphasis has to be on indicators that capture the nature of access, and not just availability, to such goods and services that allow an individual to enjoy her rights.

Similarly, in the case of the human rights **principle of participation**, the attempt is to reflect whether the vulnerable and marginalised segments of population in a country have been consulted in the selection of indicators included in the reporting procedure of country, or the extent to which they have participated in identifying measures that are being taken by the duty-holder in meeting its obligations. At a more aggregative level, indicators like the Gini coefficient, which expresses the distribution of household consumption expenditure or income, to assess whether the development process in a country is encouraging participation, inclusion and equality in the distribution of returns, have been used.

Indicators on work participation rates and educational attainment of the population, in general, and of specific groups, in particular (for instance women and minorities) also help in providing an assessment of the extent to which the **principle of empowerment** is being respected and promoted by the duty-bearer.

Finally, the first steps in the implementation of the **principle of accountability** are already being taken as one translates the normative content of a right into quantitative indicators. Indeed the availability of information sensitive to human rights, and its collection and dissemination through independent mechanisms using transparent procedures, reinforces accountability. Moreover, as we shall see in the next section, by identifying a process indicator as a measure that links a state's effort to a specific "policy action - milestone relationship", the framework takes an important step in enhancing a state's accountability in implementing human rights.

Methodological concerns

To be useful in monitoring the implementation of human rights treaties, quantitative indicators have to be explicitly and precisely defined, based on an acceptable methodology of data collection, processing and dissemination, and have to be available on a regular basis. The main methodological issues relate to the sources of data and data generating mechanisms and the criteria for selection of indicators. There is also the issue of amenability of the framework to support contextually relevant indicators.

Sources and data generating mechanisms

In the context of this work it was found useful to focus on two complementary sources of data, namely socio-economic and other administrative statistics and events-based data on human rights violation. **Socio-economic statistics** refers to quantitative information compiled and disseminated by the state, through its administrative records and statistical surveys, usually in collaboration with National Statistical Offices and under the guidance of international and specialised organisations.

For the treaty body monitoring system, this category of indicators are of primary importance given the commitment of states, as parties to international human rights instruments, to report on their compliance and the fact this data source is based on the record of administrative authorities (duty-bearer) at the level of their interface with the public (rights-holders). Socio-economic statistics provide information on issues not only related to economic, social and cultural rights, but also on civil and political rights, such as on issues of administration of justice and rule of law (e.g. executions carried out under death penalty, prison population and incidence of violent crimes).

The use of a standardised methodology in the collection of information, whether it is through census operations, household surveys or through civil registration systems, and usually with high level of reliability and validity, makes indicators based on such a methodology vital for the efforts to bring about greater transparency, credibility and accountability in human rights monitoring.

Events-based data consists mainly of data on alleged or reported cases of human rights violations, identified victims and perpetrators. Indicators, such as alleged incidence of arbitrary deprivations of life, enforced or involuntary disappearances, arbitrary detention and torture, are usually reported by

NGOs and are or can also be processed in a standardised manner by, for instance, national Human Rights Institutions and special procedures of the United Nations.

Though events-based data has been mainly and most effectively used for monitoring the violation of civil and political rights, recent attempts have shown that it can also be used for monitoring economic, social and cultural rights. In general, such data may underestimate – or, in certain circumstances, overestimate – the incidence of violations (thus indications on error margins or confidence intervals would be required for using it as a valid and reliable indicator). Events-based data may also prevent valid comparisons over time or across regions; yet it could provide some indication to the treaty bodies in undertaking their assessment of human rights situation in a given country.

Two other data generating mechanisms have been identified: data based on expert judgements, and household perception and opinion surveys (see Fasel and Malhotra, 2005 and *Chapter 6* for some insight on their strengths and weaknesses).

Criteria for the selection of quantitative indicators

The foremost consideration in adopting a methodology for identifying and building human rights indicators, like any other set of indicators, is its relevance and effectiveness in addressing the objective(s) for which the indicators are to be used. Most other methodological requirements follow from this consideration. In the context of the work undertaken by the treaty bodies in monitoring the implementation of human rights, quantitative indicators should ideally be:

- relevant, valid and reliable;
- simple, timely and few in number;
- based on objective information and data-generating mechanisms;
- suitable for temporal and spatial comparison and following relevant international statistical standards; and
- amenable to disaggregation in terms of sex, age, and other vulnerable or marginalised population segments.

The formulation of this criteria lead to three particular methodological considerations. First, the information content of the indicators should be objects, facts or events that can, in principle, be directly observed or verified (for example, weight of children, number of casualties, and nationality of the victim), as against indicators based on perceptions, opinions, assessments or judgements made by experts/individuals.

Second, indicators should be produced and disseminated in an independent, impartial and transparent manner and based on sound methodology, procedures and expertise (in this regard, see, for instance, the UN Fundamental Principles of Official Statistics in UN-ECOSOC, 2002).

Third, the production of any statistical data also has implications for the right to privacy, data protection and confidentiality issues, and may, therefore, require appropriate legal and institutional standards.

In the context of the present conceptual framework, the above-mentioned criteria and methodological considerations in the selection of indicators are being addressed through the preparation of a **meta-data sheet** that is being prepared for each indicator included in the illustrative lists. *Appendix 5* to this publication presents some examples of meta-data sheets that cover different categories of indicators across civil and political rights as well as economic, social and cultural rights.

Contextual relevance of indicators

The contextual relevance of indicators is a key consideration in the acceptability of indicators among potential users. Countries and regions within countries differ in terms of their level of development and realisation of human rights. These differences are reflected in the nature of institutions, the policies and the priorities of the state. Therefore, it may not be possible to have a set of universal indicators to assess the realisation of human rights.

Having said that, it is also true that certain human rights indicators, for example those capturing realisation of some civil and political rights, may well be relevant across all countries and their regions, whereas others that capture realisation of economic or social rights, such as the rights to health or adequate housing, may have to be customised to be of relevance in different countries. But even in the latter case, it would be relevant to monitor the minimum core content of the rights universally. Thus, in designing a set of human rights indicators, like any other set of indicators, there is a need to strike a balance between universally relevant indicators and contextually specific indicators, as both are needed.

Relevance and selection of structural, process and outcome indicators

In opting for the use of structural, process and outcome indicators in the conceptual framework adopted for this work, the primary objective has been to consistently and comprehensively translate the narrative on human rights standards with the help of indicators that can reflect the commitment-effort-results aspect of the realisation of human rights through available quantifiable information. Working with such a configuration of indicators simplifies the selection of indicators, encourages the use of contextually relevant information, facilitates a more comprehensive coverage of the identified attributes of a right, and, perhaps, also minimises the overall number of indicators required to monitor the realisation of the concerned human right standards.

Structural indicators

Structural indicators reflect the ratification and adoption of legal instruments and existence of basic institutional mechanisms deemed necessary for facilitating realisation of a human right. They capture commitments or the intent of the state in undertaking measures for the realisation of the concerned human right. Structural indicators have to focus foremost on the nature of domestic law as relevant to the concerned right - whether it incorporates the international standards - and the institutional mechanisms that promote and protect the standards.

Structural indicators also need to look at policy framework and indicated strategies of the state as relevant to the right. This is particularly important from the human rights perspective. A national policy statement on a subject is an instrument that is expected to outline a government's objectives, policy framework, strategy and/or a concrete plan of action to address issues under that subject. While providing an indication on the commitment of the government to address the concerned subject, it may also provide relevant benchmarks for holding the government accountable for its acts of commission or omission concerning that subject. Moreover, a policy statement is a means to translate the human rights obligations of a state party into an implementable programme of action that helps in the realisation of the human rights. Thus, while identifying structural indicators on different rights and their attributes, an attempt was made to highlight the importance of having specific policy statements on issues of direct relevance to that human right attribute. It was seen that many potential structural indicators were common to all human rights and that others were relevant to specific human rights or even to a particular attribute of a human right.

Process indicators

Process indicators relate state policy instruments with milestones that cumulate into outcome indicators, which in turn can be more directly related to the realisation of human rights. State policy instruments refers to all such measures including public programmes and specific interventions that a state is willing to take in order to give effect to its intent/commitments to attain outcomes identified with the realisation of a given human right.

By defining the process indicators in terms of a concrete "cause and effect relationship", the accountability of the state to its obligations can be better assessed. At the same time, these indicators help in directly monitoring the progressive fulfilment of the right or the process of protecting the right, as the case may be for the realisation of the concerned right. Process indicators are more sensitive to changes than outcome indicators and hence are better at capturing progressive realisation of the right or in reflecting the efforts of the state parties in protecting the rights.

Two considerations guided the selection and formulation of process indicators. The first was to ensure that the articulation of process indicators reflected a causal relationship with the relevant structural as well as outcome indicator. Thus, for instance, a process indicator of the right to health - proportion of school-going children educated on health and nutrition issues - was chosen so that it could be related to the corresponding structural indicator, namely "time frame and coverage of national policy on child health and nutrition", as well as with the outcome indicator "proportion of underweight children under 5 years of age".

The second consideration in giving shape to a process indicator was to bringing out explicitly some measure of an effort being undertaken by the duty-holder in implementing its obligation. Thus, indicators such as "proportion of requests for social security benefits reviewed and met in the reporting period" or "proportion of the population that was extended access to improved sanitation in the reporting period" were included in the category of process indicators. At times, this meant reformulating a commonly available indicator (in the latter case an MDG indicator), and/or requiring some additional estimation on the basic information of the indicator.

Outcome indicators

Outcome indicators capture attainments, individual and collective, that reflect the status of realisation of human rights in a given context. It is not only a more direct measure of the realisation of a human right but it also reflects the importance of the measure in the enjoyment of the right. Since it consolidates over time the impact of various underlying processes (that can be captured by one or more process indicators), an outcome indicator is often a slow-moving indicator, less sensitive to capturing momentary changes than a process indicator would be (see Box 10.2). For example, life expectancy or mortality indicators could be a function of immunisation of the population, education or public health awareness, as well as of availability of, and access of individuals to, adequate nutrition.

It is therefore instructive to view the process and outcome indicators as "flow" and "stock" variables, respectively. A stock variable is measurable at one particular time (for example, the number of persons in detention at the end of the reporting period), whereas a flow variable is measured over a prolonged amount of time (for example, the number of entries into detention during the reporting period). Nevertheless this illustrative analogy has to take into account a caveat that often more than one process may be responsible for the same outcome and on other occasions the same process may be impacting more than one outcome.

It is important to note that process and outcome indicators may not be mutually exclusive. It is possible that a process indicator for one human right can be an outcome indicator in the context of another right. The guiding concern being that, for each right or rather attribute of a right, it is important to identify at least one outcome indicator that can be closely related to the realisation or enjoyment of that right or attribute. The process indicators are identified in a manner that they reflect the effort of the duty-holders in meeting or making progress in attaining the identified outcome. Having said this, there is an attempt in the list of illustrative indicators (see *Appendix* 4) to use a consistent approach to differentiate process indicators from outcome indicators.

Additional common indicators

The illustrative list of indicators has to be seen in the context of some background information that each state party to the international treaties is expected to provide as a part of their general reporting guidelines. This background information, reflected through appropriate indicators, is expected to cover population and general demographic trends, the social and economic situation, the civil and political situation, and general information on the administration of justice and the rule of law (see the compilation of guidelines on the form and content of reports to be submitted by states parties to the international human rights treaties, in UN-HRI, 1994).

In addition, it is envisaged that information on certain structural indicators such as the proportion of international human rights instruments ratified by the state (from a list of selected human rights treaties, protocols, relevant articles, ILO conventions, etc.), the existence of a domestic bill of rights in the Constitution or other forms of superior law, the type of accreditation of national Human Rights Institution by the rules of procedure of the International Co-ordinating Committee of National Institutions, and the number of non-governmental organisations and other personnel (employees and volunteers) formally involved in the protection of human rights at domestic level is relevant for monitoring the implementation of all human rights. Hence this information needs to be reflected in the preamble to the tables on the illustrative indicators in *Appendix* 4. Some of these indicators have been reflected in the 12 tables to make them self-explicatory.

Some other consideration in indicators selection

In general, for all indicators it is essential to seek disaggregated data on the human rights situation of **vulnerable and marginalised population groups** vis-à-vis the rest of the population *General Comment* 19 of the Committee on Economic, Social and Cultural Rights sets out an exhaustive listing of grounds for non-discrimination, which may require disaggregation of data, if feasible. Thus, it argues for prohibiting any discrimination, whether in law or in fact, whether direct or indirect, on the grounds of race, colour, sex, age, language, religion, political or other opinion, national or social origin, property, birth, physical or mental disability, health status (including HIV/AIDS), sexual orientation, and civil, political or other status, which has the intention or effect of nullifying or impairing the equal enjoyment or exercise of human rights (UN-HRI, 2008a, advanced draft, para. 29).

A second consideration relates to the **principle of the indivisibility of human rights**, and makes it necessary to look at indicators in their totality across all rights and not merely in terms of sectoral frameworks anchored in the normative content of the specific human rights. This is notwithstanding the fact that, in the course of identifying indicators, for instance for the right to life, it may be necessary to identify indicators on the health attribute of that right within the confines of its normative content and not in the light of the normative content of the right to health. At the same time, some aspects related to the right of an individual to control one's health and body may have to be elaborated in indicators on the right not to be subjected to torture or to cruel, inhuman or degrading treatment or punishment, and not in the context of the right to health, both for analytical

---

Box 10.1. **Identifying process and outcome indicators**

There is some similarity in process and outcome indicators which comes from the fact that any process can either be measured in terms of the inputs going into a process or alternately in terms of the immediate outputs or outcomes that the process generates. Thus, a process indicator on the coverage of immunisation among children can be measured in terms of the public resources or expenditure going into immunisation programme (which is the input variant) or in terms of the proportion of children covered under the programme (which is an outcome or impact variant). Both are process indicators: they inform on the process of lowering child mortality – which is an outcome indicator as it captures the consolidated impact of the immunisation programme over a period of time and it can be more directly related to the realisation of the right to health attribute on the child mortality and health care. It is desirable that the process indicator be measured in terms of the physical milestone that it generates rather than in terms of the resources that go into the concerned process. Indeed, experience across countries and across regions within the same country reveals that there is no monotonic relationship between public expenditure and the physical outcome that such expenditure generates. The physical outcome is a function of resources and other institutional and non-institutional factors that vary from place to place and thereby make it difficult to interpret indicators on public expenditure. For instance, it is possible that a lower per capita public expenditure produces better outcomes in one region in comparison to another region within the same country.

---

convenience and overall manageability of the number of indicators. Ultimately, at the level of a convention or in the context of theme-based assessment of human rights (*e.g.* violence against women or rights in early childhood), one may need to rationalise the list of indicators in view of the need to respect the principle of indivisibility and interdependence.

In certain instances, as in the case of the right to health, it may not be possible to have outcome indicators exclusively dependent on efforts within the framework of state obligations under the right to health. However, it may still be worthwhile to include such indicators because of their importance to the realisation of that right and to facilitate priority-setting and targeting of effort.

Selection of all indicators has to be guided by the **empirical evidence** on the use of those indicators. If identified indicators do not fare well on the criteria of empirical relevance, they will not be useful as monitoring tools. An important consideration in this regard has been to put the selected indicators on a technically rigorous foundation. Accordingly, **meta-data sheets** highlighting key information on identified indicators, including terminology and common name of the indicator, standard international or national definition, data sources, availability, level of disaggregation and information on other related and proxy indicators are being prepared. A sample set of these meta-data sheets is provided in *Appendix* 5 of this publication.

It is important to note that a generic formulation was adopted for the indicators reflected in the **illustrative tables** provided in the *Appendix* 4 of this publication. Where applicable, an alternative or a more specific formulation that may be relevant to only certain contexts, like the developing countries or the developed countries, has been indicated in the relevant meta-data sheet for the concerned indicator. Similarly, a general terminology of "target group" was adopted to refer to specific population groups, like women, children, ethnic or religious minorities or vulnerable and marginal segments of the population, which may require a focused attention in keeping with the country context.

Finally, while putting together the illustrative tables, care was taken to highlight the role of the primary duty-holder in the implementation of the right concerned. In this context, besides indicators that reflect the scope and recourse to judicial remedy, the framework identifies indicators on potential role of non-judicial (administrative), judicial and quasi-judicial (*e.g.* national Human Rights Institutions) actors in implementing human rights. Attempt was also made to identify, through suitable structural and process indicators, the role of NGOs and international cooperation in furthering the implementation of human rights.

Validation and feedback on the work

In undertaking this work, OHCHR had set up an informal expert group in 2005 with part of its membership changing as per the requirements of the agenda for the consultations. This expert group peer reviewed all proposals made by the secretariat on the concept, methodology, the choice of illustrative indicators, as well as the process for validating the results at country level. It brought together experts and practitioners from the academia, international agencies, NGOs, human rights treaty bodies as well as special procedures mandate-holders – and it included Metagora Partners. This was done with a view to developing a common understanding of the conceptual and methodological approach to identifying indicators for monitoring compliance with international human rights instruments and benefit from each other's expertise and experience.

Experts from a number of international organisations participated in these consultations or were consulted. These included the World Health Organisation (WHO), UN-Habitat, UNESCO, the United Nations Economic Commission for Europe (UNECE) statistical division, the Food and Agriculture Organisation of the United Nations (FAO), the World Bank, the United Nations Office on Drugs and Crime (UNODC), and more recently, the International Labour Organisation (ILO) and the United Nations Statistics Division (UNSD).

A number of workshops were organised with a view to consulting and validating the work undertaken with national stakeholders. It included participants from national Human Rights Institutions, policy makers and agencies responsible for treaty reporting or with implementation mandates related to specific rights, National Statistical Offices responsible for data collection and dissemination, NGOs and staff from United Nations country teams.

OHCHR collaborated with FAO to validate illustrative indicators on the right to adequate food in country-level consultations at regional workshops in Uganda (October 2006) and Guatemala (December 2006). As part of follow-up workshops on the implementation of treaty bodies' concluding observations at the national level, a module on illustrative indicators on the right to health and the right to judicial review of detention was presented in a workshop in Uganda in November 2006. In 2007, OHCHR organised sub-regional validation workshops in Asia (New Delhi, July 2007) and Africa (Kampala, October 2007), gathering national stakeholders and experts from 22 countries. A national workshop took place in Brazil (Rio, 5-6 December 2007). In addition, the work on indicators was presented and discussed in several international conferences, workshops and forums, as well as within the Metagora Partners Group (see more detailed information in UN-HRI, 2008b).

Moreover, during 2007 and 2008, OHCHR organised briefings on this work for the Committee on Economic Social and Cultural Rights, the Committee against Torture, the Committee on the Rights of a Child, the Committee on the Elimination of Racial Discrimination, the Human Rights Committee and the Committee on Migrant Workers.

Based on the reactions this broad consultation process there has been a continuous attempt at refining the framework and improving the selection of illustrative indicators. The stakeholders consulted at country level were very supportive of OHCHR work. The relevance of the adopted framework and the identified indicators were repeatedly emphasised. The participatory methodology adopted for the workshop sessions helped in overcoming the initial scepticism of some participants.

In the course of these working sessions attendants were requested to identify: (1) the main content or characteristic attributes of the rights considered; and (2) contextually relevant indicators on the attributes of the rights, to capture aspects of commitments and efforts on part of the states parties, as well as outcomes of those efforts. This enabled an assessment of the implementation of human rights obligations of the duty-bearer(s) in the realisation of these rights in the respective countries. The result of this exercise was a striking consistency between the attributes and indicators identified by the participants for the rights concerned and the tables prepared by OHCHR (tables that were circulated to the participants only at the end of each working session) and helped, thereby, in validating the OHCHR framework and the list of illustrative indicators.

The participants at the various workshops endorsed the conceptual and methodological framework presented by the OHCHR. They highlighted the practicality and transparency of the approach in unpackaging the normative content of the rights. The illustrative indicators were seen as concrete tools to promote accountability and appropriate policy response from the duty-bearers in furthering the implementation of human rights. Most of indicators identified to assess the implementation of the rights, derived primarily from administrative records, were considered as being generally available, although occasionally lacking sufficient coverage. Participants welcomed the application of the human rights indicators framework and its value added to the Millennium Development Goals (MDGs). They often stressed a certain arbitrariness in the choice of MDG indicators, the insensitivity of the corresponding targets and indicators to capture contextual concerns, the fixation with averages rather than inequality or distribution adjusted indicators, as well as a general lack of attention to strategies and the processes for meeting the targets.

As this broad consultation has shown, there is a need to further simplify the conceptual framework and to improve its communication and accessibility so that it can be appreciated by a wider audience of stakeholders, including human rights, development and statistical practitioners. In this context the proposal to develop a user's manual and a tool-kit for national stakeholders found an across the board support. Interests were expressed by several participants to organise follow-up country-specific events, including workshops and training courses.

Moving forward at country level

During consultations, an issue that was raised by stakeholders more than once related to the nature of the process envisaged for applying and developing this work further at the country level. And whether the indicators identified in the context of this work for the treaty bodies could also help in building and refining the methodology for undertaking rights-based monitoring.

Rights-based monitoring (RBM) is not divorced from other existing monitoring approaches such as those followed by any administrative agency at national or sub-national level to monitor, for instance, agricultural production and food security, administration of justice, or even project level outcomes and impacts. It, however, necessitates a certain institutional arrangement for collection of information and a focus on specific data that embodies and reflects realisation of human rights for the most vulnerable and marginalised population groups, referred to as target groups in the context of this work. A shift in focus from national averages to status of target groups, ideally going down to the individual level, permits an assessment of the extent of discrimination or lack of equality or even violation of the right for some - a principal concern in monitoring the realisation of human rights. This, however, does not mean that RBM is all about disaggregated information and indicators. Indeed, RBM requires use of an appropriate set of indicators that are explicitly embedded in the human rights normative framework, as tools to facilitate a credible assessment of the realisation of human rights. It is the objective of the work undertaken by OHCHR for the treaty bodies to identify relevant quantitative indicators that could be used in undertaking human rights assessments. To that extent this work can help build and strengthen a rights-based approach to monitoring in general.

It is essential that the RBM process be country-owned and implemented, and is sufficiently decentralised as well as inclusive for the different stakeholders to reflect their concerns. In setting up an RBM at the country level or strengthening an existing mechanism to monitor the realisation of a particular human right, one can identify, among others, the following considerations.

Identification of monitoring stakeholders

As a first step, it would be necessary to identify the various institutional and non-institutional stakeholders who would be contributing to the monitoring process either as information providers, or as independent interpreters of the available information, or as the ultimate users of that information for articulating their claims and monitoring the realisation of human rights. This may involve, *inter alia*, the national Human Rights Institution, the administrative agencies including the relevant line ministries as data providers, relevant non-governmental organisations engaged in monitoring human rights, consumer groups, other social groups, including parliamentary committees and claim-holders at large. Once the monitoring stakeholders have been identified at the country level, it would be necessary to bring them together in a participatory process where their respective competencies and perspectives, based on complementarities in objectives (such as a focus on different aspects of the right) and methods of information collection, contribute to the monitoring process. An important element of this process is the identification of an independent institution that takes a lead in interpreting the available information from a human rights perspective and perhaps also co-ordinating the assessment of other partners. It could well be a national HRI or human rights non-governmental organisation. This would facilitate the creation of a country-owned monitoring mechanism.

Identification of major vulnerable groups

It is possible that one could identify different segments of the population as target groups who are vulnerable on different attributes or elements of the core content of a specific human right. For instance, considering the right to adequate food, in some cases children could be more likely to suffer from dietary inadequacy or malnutrition, whereas a working or migrant population may be more vulnerable to food safety and consumer protection issues. Thus, in each country, it would be desirable to assess the population groups and regions for identifying the target groups. The process of identifying the target groups using appropriate criteria also has to be based on cross-cutting human rights norms and principles of participation and transparency, allowing for potential self-identification by individuals, if required. This would yield the target group for RBM and, at the same time, help in assessing the disaggregation requirement of information for the identified indicators.

Focus on non-discrimination and accessibility indicators

Given that human rights are universal and inalienable, it is imperative in the context of undertaking RBM that special attention be given to indicators that capture the extent to which discrimination of individuals and population groups influences the level of realisation of their human rights. Thus, the notion of "accessibility" as against mere "availability" has a particular importance in the human rights framework and in the context of RBM. Accordingly, in undertaking RBM or human rights assessments it is necessary to identify relevant information on discrimination and tailor the data generating mechanisms to collect, compile and present such information as appropriate indicators.

Box 10.2. **Main features of the conceptual and methodological framework**

There are several features of the conceptual and methodological framework that has been adopted to elaborate indicators for different human rights. First of all, it follows a common approach to identify indicators for promoting and monitoring civil and political rights, and economic, social and cultural rights, thereby strengthening the notion of the indivisibility and interdependence of human rights.

Secondly, the framework comprehensively translates the narrative on the normative content of human rights (starting with the related provisions of international human rights instruments and *General Comments* by treaty bodies) into a few characteristic attributes and a configuration of structural, process and outcome indicators. The identified indicators bring to the fore an assessment of steps taken by the state party in addressing its obligations - from commitment to international human rights standards (structural indicators) to efforts being undertaken by the primary duty-bearer, the state, to meet the obligations that flow from the standards (process indicators) and on to the results of those efforts from the perspective of rights-holders (outcome indicators).

Thirdly, the framework facilitates an identification of contextually meaningful indicators for universally accepted human rights standards. It seeks neither to prepare a common list of indicators to be applied across all countries irrespective of their social, political and economic development, nor to make a case for building a global measure for cross-country comparisons on the realisation of human rights. Rather it enables the potential users to make an informed choice on the type and level of indicator disaggregation that best reflects their contextual requirements for implementing human rights or just some of the attributes of a right, while recognising the full scope of obligations on the relevant human right standards. Indeed, the framework allows a balance between the use of a core set of human rights indicators that may be universally relevant and at the same time retain the flexibility of a more detailed and focused assessment on certain attributes of the relevant human rights, depending on the requirements of a particular situation.

Fourthly, the framework focuses on two categories of indicators and data generating mechanisms: (a) indicators that are or can be compiled by official statistical systems using statistical surveys and administrative records; and (b) indicators or standardised information more generally compiled by non-governmental sources and human rights organisations focusing on alleged violations reported by victims, witnesses or NGOs. The intention being to explore and exhaust the use of commonly available information, particularly from objective data sets, for tracking human rights implementation. Finally, the framework focuses primarily on quantitative and some qualitative indicators, to support a transparent assessment of the implementation of human rights. Efforts have been made to keep the identified indicators simple, based on standardised methodology for data collection and, to the extent feasible, with an emphasis on disaggregation of information by prohibited grounds of discrimination and by vulnerable or marginalised population groups, who have to be the target for public support in furthering the realisation of human rights.

Discussions with the potential users of this work, in particular the country-level stakeholders, has highlighted considerable unmet demand for appropriate resource materials, including a users' manual and other tool-kits on the application of quantitative information in supporting the implementation of the human rights obligations of states parties. This work undertaken by OHCHR for the treaty bodies could potentially meet a large part of this demand and help stakeholders in promoting and protecting human rights at the country level. While there is a need to further validate and pilot this work, especially among users who are as yet not fully informed of this initiative, it would be desirable to consider ways and means to help improve dissemination of the results of this work.

Reporting periodicity, publication, access to information and follow-up

Given that the realisation of human rights is not a onetime event, both protection and promotion of human rights have to be continuously pursued, it would be necessary to have information to monitor the concerned human right, at least, at different points of time or ideally through an appropriate time series of observations. This would facilitate monitoring of the progressive realisation of the right and the incidence of violation of the right over time. An RBM mechanism also requires access of all stakeholders, in particular the claim-holders, to available information and data relevant to the enjoyment of human rights. This necessitates a framework with a schedule of publication and dissemination of relevant information. As a follow-up to the monitoring process, it also implies a framework that enables use of available information as an advocacy tool - to raise awareness on entitlements and duties, help in better articulation of claims by the rights holders and in monitoring the progress in discharge of obligations by duty bearers.

Chapter 11

Candidate Indicators for Monitoring the Right to Education

There has been increasing awareness in recent years that the development of indicators is central to effectively monitoring human rights, particularly economic, social, and cultural rights, and evaluating the performance of countries in implementing these rights. Effective monitoring requires the systematic collection and analysis of appropriate data. To determine which data are relevant, it is first necessary to translate the abstract legal norms in which various human rights are framed into operational standards. This process involves conceptualising specific enumerated rights, for example the right to education, and developing standards by which to measure implementation and identify violations of state obligations. These standards or indicators can then provide yardsticks to assess compliance. Human rights indicators offer a tool for the following: making better policies and monitoring progress; identifying the unintended impacts of laws, policies and practices; determining which actors are having an impact on the realisation or non-realisation of rights; revealing whether the obligations of these actors are being met; giving early warning of potential violations so as to enable prompt preventive action; enhancing social consensus on difficult trade-offs required in the face of resource constraints; and exposing issues that had been neglected or silenced (UNDP, 2000, p.89).

For more than ten years human rights advocates and UN human rights bodies acknowledged the need for indicators. *General Comments* conceptualising the scope of obligations related to specific rights prepared by the UN Committee on Economic, Social and Cultural Rights, including the Committee's *General Comment* on the right to education (UN-HRI, 1999), called for the development of indicators. So have many of the rights-specific special rapporteurs appointed by the Commission for Human Rights, including the former Special Rapporteur for the Right to Education (UN-HRI, 1998).

In 2002, Paul Hunt was appointed as the first Special Rapporteur on the right to the highest attainable standard of physical and mental health by the Commission for Human Rights. While specifically directed to indicators for the right to health, he proposed an approach to indicators with relevance to other economic, social and cultural rights. He identified three types of indicators: structural indicators, process indicators, and outcome indicators (UN-HRI, 2003):

This chapter was contributed by **Audrey Chapman**

University of Connecticut, former Director of the Science and Human Rights Program at the American Association for the Advancement of Science (AAAS).

- **Structural indicators** address whether or not the requisite infrastructure is in place that is considered necessary for, or conducive to, the realisation of a specific right. Specifically, structural indicators evaluate whether a country has established the institutions, constitutional provisions, laws, and policies that are required. Most structural indicators are qualitative in nature and are not based on statistical data. And many can be answered by a simple yes or no.
- **Process indicators**, along with outcome indicators, monitor the variable dimension of the right to health that arises from the concept of "progressive realisation." Their key feature is that they can be used to assess change over time. Specifically, process indicators assess the degree to which activities that are necessary to attain specific rights-related objectives are being implemented and the progress of these activities over time. They monitor effort and not outcome. The types and amounts of governmental inputs are one important kind of process indicator. Unlike structural indicators, process indicators require statistical data.
- **Outcome indicators** assess the status of the population's enjoyment of a right. They show the "facts" and measure the results achieved. Many of the Millennium Development Goal indicators are outcome indicators. Like process indicators, outcome indicators are variable and require statistical data.

In 2005, the joint meeting of chairpersons of the then eight UN human rights treaty bodies requested that the UN Secretariat provide assistance to the treaty bodies in analysing statistical information in state parties' reports and to that end asked the Secretariat to prepare a background paper for the next inter-committee meeting on the possible uses of indicators. In response, the Office of the High Commissioner for Human Rights (OHCHR) organised an expert working group to develop indicators for monitoring compliance with international human rights instruments in Geneva on 29 August 2005. This author is a member of that group. At the time of writing the group has met five times and developed candidate indicators for 12 human rights, 6 of which are civil and political rights and 6 of which are economic and social rights.

The salient features of the framework of the expert working group on indicators are as follows. It is using a common approach to identifying indicators for monitoring civil and political rights and economic, social and cultural rights. Like Paul Hunt's approach, it uses the three categories of structural, process, and outcome indicators. Unlike Paul Hunt, who used both qualitative and quantitative indicators, the mandate of the expert working group is to focus on quantitative indicators to assess the implementation of human rights. The process is focusing on indicators that can be used by the UN human rights treaty bodies. It is also trying to provide a relatively small number of indicators for each right. Thus the working group is not seeking to prepare a comprehensive list of indicators to be applied across all countries irrespective of their social, political, and economic development (United Nations High Commissioner for Human Rights, 2005 and 2008).

In 2005 when I was serving as the Director of the American Association for the Advancement of Science (AAAS) Science and Human Rights Program, the Metagora Partners Group requested that I develop a set of candidate indicators for the right to education based on the interpretation by the Committee on Economic, Social and Cultural Rights. The right to education is one of the most affirmed and best conceptualised economic, social and cultural rights. There are provisions recognising the right to education in the Universal Declaration on Human Rights (1948) and a series of human rights instruments based on the Universal Declaration: the *International Covenant on Economic, Social and Cultural Rights* (ICESCR) (1976), the *International Convention on the Elimination of All Forms of Racial Discrimination* (1965), the *Convention on the Elimination of All Forms of Discrimination against Women* (1979), and the *Convention on the Rights of the Child* (1989). The right to education is also dealt with in such documents at the UNESCO *Convention against Discrimination in Education* (1960), the ILO *Convention Concerning Indigenous and Tribal Peoples* (1989), regional human rights instruments, including the *American Declaration of the Rights and Duties of Many* (1948) and the *African Charter on Human and*

Peoples' Rights (1986), and some national constitutions. Educational attainment also affects the capacity to enjoy many other human rights.

The following list of candidate indicators is intended to be a contribution to the process of identifying the requirements of human rights indicators. The indicators follow the approach proposed by Paul Hunt and include both qualitative and quantitative indicators. Given the number and comprehensive nature of the proposed indicators, they can best serve as a menu from which a monitoring organisation can select the most appropriate indicators for its specific purposes and goals. The usefulness of the indicators will also depend on the availability of relevant data in disaggregated form.

Structural indicators

Structure

Which levels of the political system have responsibilities for the provision of education?

(a) National (yes/no)
(b) Regional, state, or provincial level (yes/no)
(c) Local, town, or municipal level (yes/no)

Constitutional provisions

Does the Country's constitution include access to education as a right? (yes/no)
If so,

(a) Is the provision of universal education a directive principle of state policy? (yes/no)
(b) Is the right to education an entitlement?
  • for universal primary education (yes/no)
  • for universal secondary education (yes/no)
(c) Does the Constitution specify the right of access to education without discrimination? (yes/no)
(d) Does the Constitution recognise the right of adults without primary schooling to a basic education? (yes/no)

Legislation

Does the state have legislation expressly recognising the right to education? (yes/no)

Is there legislation specifying the right of children to a place in primary school? (yes/no)

Is there legislation making primary education compulsory? (yes/no)

If there is legislation making education compulsory, specify the ages and/or number of years:

(a) Compulsory beginning at age _____
(b) Compulsory ending at age _____
(c) Compulsory for _____ number of years

Is there legislation making primary education free to all? (yes/no)

Is there legislation expressly prohibiting local governments or schools from charging supplementary fees for:

(a) Books (yes/no)
(b) School supplies (yes/no)
(c) Construction or maintenance of school buildings (yes/no)
(d) Teacher's salaries (yes/no)

Is there legislation providing for the right of access to public educational institutions and programmes on a non-discriminatory basis? (yes/no)

Is there legislation expressly prohibiting any form of discrimination for students on the basis of:

(a) Sex (yes/no)
(b) Race or colour (yes/no)
(c) Language (yes/no)
(d) Religion (yes/no)
(e) Political or other opinion (yes/no)
(f) National or social origin (yes/no)
(g) Financial resources (yes/no)

Is there legislation expressly prohibiting discrimination in the recruitment and promotion of teachers on the basis of:

(a) Sex (yes/no)
(b) Race or colour (yes/no)
(c) Language (yes/no)
(d) Religion (yes/no)
(e) Political or other opinion (yes/no)
(f) National or social origin (yes/no)
(g) Financial resources (yes/no)

Is there legislation recognising the right of handicapped persons with disabilities to education? (yes/no)

If so,

Does the legislation make provision for the necessary equipment and support to enable handicapped students to attend school? (yes/no)

Is there legislation prohibiting early marriages (below the age of 16) that would interfere with girls' school attendance? (yes/no)

Is there legislation restricting or prohibiting child labour so as to encourage children to attend school? (yes/no)

Private schooling

Is there legislation expressly recognising the liberty of individuals and groups to establish and operate educational institutions, subject to the requirement that the education given in such institutions shall conform to such minimum standards as may be laid down by the state? (yes/no)

Is there legislation expressly recognising the right of parents and, when applicable, legal guardians, to choose for their children schools, other than those established by the public authorities, which conform to the minimum educational standards as may be laid down or approved by the state? (yes/no)

Is there legislation expressly recognising the right of parents and, when applicable, legal guardians to ensure the religious and moral education of children in conformity with their own convictions? (yes/no)

Treaty ratification

Has the state ratified the following international treaties?

   (a) ICESCR (yes/no)
   (b) CRC (yes/no)
   (c) CEDAW (yes/no)
   (d) ICERD (yes/no)

Has the state ratified any regional human rights instruments recognising the right to education? (yes/no)

National strategy and plan of action

Does the state have a national educational strategy and plan of action? (yes/no)

   (a) Does the national educational strategy include a timeline for achieving the goals? (yes/some/no)
   (b) Does the national educational strategy have a monitoring mechanism for assessing the attainment of the goals? (yes/some/no)

If yes, does the national educational strategy and plan of action expressly include the goals of:

   (a) Universal, compulsory, and free primary education? (yes/no/not relevant because already achieved the goal)
   (b) Progressive introduction of free secondary education (yes/no/not relevant because already achieved the goal)

Gender issues

Does the state have a policy to protect girls' access to education? (yes/no)

Have public policy measures been taken to:

   (a) Remove gender bias from primary education primers? (yes/no)
   (b) Remove gender bias from teachers' educational strategies? (yes/no)
   (c) Remove gender bias in terms of male and female roles in school? (yes/no)
   (d) Remove gender bias in terms of gender- targeted optional subject? (yes/no)
   (e) Train teachers in gender issues? (yes/no)

Are there opportunities for pregnant girls to continue their education? (yes/no)

Curriculum

Does the state establish minimal standards regulating the curriculum and the quality of study programmes and educational methods? (yes/no)

If so,

    (a) Are these national standards for the entire country? (yes/no)
    (b) Are the standards set by provincial, regional, state and/or municipal governments? (yes/no)

Is there an inspection system to monitor and evaluate the quality and content of education? (yes/no)

Does the official curriculum include human rights education and/or values, such as respect for human dignity, non-discrimination, and equal status before the law:

    (a) In primary school? (yes/no)
    (b) In secondary school? (yes/no)

Does the official curriculum include units on the constitution and democracy:

    (a) In primary school? (yes/no)
    (b) In secondary school? (yes/no)

Is there legislation mandating respect in the educational system for the culture and religious practices of various groups and communities in the society? (yes/no)

Human Rights Institutions

Does the state have human rights institutions (commission or ombudsperson) mandated to monitor the right to education?

If yes, does the human rights institution collect data and issue regular reports on the status of the achievement of the right to education? (yes/irregularly/no)

Participation

Does the state have a mechanism to consult representatives of teachers and parents in the formation of educational policy, other than normal political institutions, at the:

    (a) National level ?(yes/no)
    (b) Provincial, state, or regional level? (yes/some/no)
    (c) Local level? (yes/some/no)

Process indicators

Basic financial context

Percentage of GDP devoted to education:

(a) Total all sources
(b) Public sources
(c) Private sources

Percentage of budget allocated overall to education by:

(a) National government
(b) Regional, state, or provincial governments
  • Regional government by name
  • State government by name
  • Provincial government by name
(c) Local governments

Percentage of national budget allocated to:

(a) Primary education
(b) Secondary education
(c) Vocational training
(d) Higher education
(e) Teacher training
(f) Special disbursements to improve the gender balance
(g) Targeted aid to poor localities and areas of the country

Percentage of total spending by regional, state, or provincial governments allocated to:

(a) Primary education
(b) Secondary education
(c) Vocational training
(d) Higher education
(e) Teacher training
(f) Special disbursements to improve the gender balance
(g) Targeted aid to poor localities and areas of the country

Percentage of each region, state, or provincial government – listed by name – allocated to:

(a) Primary education
(b) Secondary education
(c) Vocational training
(d) Higher education
(e) Teacher training
(f) Special disbursements to improve the gender balance
(g) Targeted aid to poor localities and areas of the country

Percentage of total spending by local governments allocated to

(a) Primary education
(b) Secondary education
(c) Vocational training
(d) Higher education
(e) Teacher training
(f) Special disbursements to improve the gender balance
(g) Targeted aid to schools serving poor and vulnerable groups

Amount of educational funding received from foreign bilateral and multi-lateral funding sources:

(a) Total amount for most recent year_____
(b) Percentage of total public educational budget _____

Was there overspending by more than 10% of the amount allocated for education in the last fiscal year by the:

(a) National government? (yes/no)
(b) Provincial, regional, or state governments? (yes/some/no)
   • *If some or yes,* by how much cumulatively? _____
   • *If some or yes*, list the provinces, regional, or state government in ascending order of overspending:

_____

_____

_____

_____

Was there underspending by more than 10% of the amount allocated for education in the last fiscal year for which data are available by the

(a) National government? (yes/no)
   • *If yes*, by how much? _____
(b) Provincial, regional, or state governments? (yes/some/no)
   • *If some or yes*, by how much cumulatively? _____
   • *If some or yes*, list the provinces, regional, or state governments in ascending order of underspending:

_____

_____

_____

Charges payable in public education

Specify whether or not there are charges for each of the following components in public primary education:

   (a) Enrolment fees (yes/no)
   (b) Tuition fees (yes/no)
   (c) Uniforms (yes/no)
   (d) Schools supplies and educational materials (yes/no)
   (e) School meals (yes/no)
   (f) School transport (yes/no)

Total average cost per year per family for a student in a public primary school: _____

Is there a special funding system to offset the costs of primary education for students from the following population groups:

   (a) Low income groups
   (b) Female students
   (c) Persons with disabilities
   (d) Displaced persons
   (e) Groups living in dispersed rural areas

Specify whether or not there are charges for each of the following components in public secondary education:

   (a) Enrolment fees (yes/no)
   (b) Tuition fees (yes/no)
   (c) Uniforms (yes/no)
   (d) School supplies and educational materials (yes/no)
   (e) School meals (yes/no)
   (f) School transport (yes/no)

Total average cost per year per family for a student in a public secondary school _____

Is there a special funding system to ensure access to secondary education for students from the following population groups:

   (a) Low income groups
   (b) Female students
   (c) Persons with disabilities
   (d) Displaced persons

School facilities

Primary schools (infrastructure)	Total	Rural	Urban	Private	Public
Total number of schools					
Number of schools with buildings in a state of disrepair					
Number of schools that have a shortage of classrooms					
Number of schools with inadequate textbooks					
Number of schools with no water within walking distance					
Number of schools with lack of access to sanitary facilities					
Number of schools with no electricity					
Number of schools with no telephones					
Number of schools with inadequate toilet facilities					
Number of schools with lack of access to library facilities					

Secondary schools (infrastructure)	Total	Rural	Urban	Private	Public
Total number of schools					
Number of schools with buildings in a state of disrepair					
Number of schools with inadequate textbooks					
Number of schools with no water within walking distance					
Number of schools with no electricity					
Number of schools with inadequate toilet facilities					
Number of schools with lack of access to computers					
Number of schools with lack of access to library facilities					
Number of schools with lack of access to recreational and sporting facilities					

Physical accessibility

Percentage of children having to travel more than 1 kilometre to reach primary school:

(a) Nationally
(b) In rural areas
(c) In urban areas

Monitoring

Does the national government collect data adequate to evaluate performance under the strategy/national action plan, particularly in relation to vulnerable groups? (yes/no)

   (a) Through educational statistics collected through school reporting (yes/no)
   (b) Through national household surveys (yes/no)
   (c) Through national census surveys (yes/no)

Are data collected at the primary level that disaggregate on the basis of students'

   (a) Age (yes/no)
   (b) Sex (yes/no)
   (c) Urban/rural location (yes/no) (yes/no)
   (d) Income of family (yes/no)
   (e) Linguistic or ethnic group (yes/no)
   (f) Disabilities (yes/no)

Are data collected at the secondary level that disaggregate on the basis of students'

   (a) Age (yes/no)
   (b) Sex (yes/no)
   (c) Urban/rural location (yes/no)
   (d) Income of family (yes/no)
   (e) Linguistic or ethnic group (yes/no)
   (f) Disabilities (yes/no)

Are data collected at the higher education level that disaggregate on the basis of students'

   (a) Age (yes/no)
   (b) Sex (yes/no)
   (c) Urban/rural background (yes/no)
   (d) Income of family (yes/no)
   (e) Linguistic or ethnic group (yes/no)
   (f) Disabilities (yes/no)

Are reports issued annually analysing these data that cover trends at the:

   (a) National level (yes/no/sometimes)
   (a) State/regional, or provincial levels (yes/no/some)

Are disaggregated data publicly available related to:
   (a) Primary education (yes/no/some)
   (b) Secondary education (yes/no/some)
   (c) Higher education (yes/no/some)

Reporting

Number of reports the state has submitted to the UN treaty-based bodies monitoring the following treaties that include the status of the right to education:

(a) ICESCR
(b) CRC
(c) CEDAW
(d) ICERD

Participation

Did the state consult with a wide range of representatives of the following groups in the past year about issues relating to formulating, implementing, and/or monitoring national educational policy:

(a) Non-governmental organisations? (yes/no/ some)
(b) Educational professional organisations? (yes/no/ some)
(c) Local governments? (yes/no/ some)
(d) Community leaders? (yes/no/some)
(e) Representatives of vulnerable groups? (yes/no/some)
(f) Private sector? (yes/no/some)

In the past year, did the state disseminate information on its educational policies and relevant educational data to:

(a) Non-governmental organisations? (yes/no/ some)
(b) Educational professional organisations? (yes/no/ some)
(c) Local governments? (yes/no/ some)
(d) Community leaders? (yes/no/ some)
(e) Representatives of vulnerable groups? (yes/no/ some)
(f) Private sector? (yes/no/ some)

Teacher availability and qualifications

Number of years of education for primary school teachers to meet certification requirements:

(a) for lower primary school teaching: _____years
(b) for upper primary school teaching: _____years
(c) for lower secondary school teaching: _____ years
(d) for upper secondary school teaching: _____years

Percentage of teachers meeting the minimum certification requirements:

(a) in lower primary school classes (grades 1-3)
   • in urban areas _____
   • in rural areas _____

(b) in upper primary school classes (grades 4 and above)
   • in urban areas _____
   • in rural areas _____

(c) in lower secondary school teaching (first three years)
- in urban areas _____
- in rural areas   _____

(d) in upper secondary school teaching (fourth year and above)
- in urban areas _____
- in rural areas   _____

What is the learner/educator ratio:

(a) in lower primary school classes (grades 1-3)
- in urban areas
- in rural areas
- in public schools
- in private schools

(b) in upper primary school classes (fourth year and above)
- in urban areas
- in rural areas
- in public schools
- in private schools

(c) in lower secondary school teaching (first three years)
- in urban areas
- in rural areas
- in public schools
- in private schools

(d) in upper secondary school teaching (fourth year and above)
- in urban areas
- in rural areas
- in public schools
- in private schools

What is the percentage of public schools with a sufficient number of qualified teachers:

(a) primary schools
- in urban areas
- in rural areas
- in sex segregated schools catering to girls

(b) secondary schools
- in urban areas
- in rural areas
- in sex segregated schools catering to girls

Complaints and court cases

Number of administrative complaints that considered educational rights in the last five years regarding:

(a) Availability or accessibility of primary education
(b) Funding of primary education
(c) Availability or accessibility of secondary education
(d) Accessibility of higher education
(e) Discrimination issues
(f) Registration or closing of private schools
(g) Parents' rights to ensure the religious and moral education of their children in conformity with their own convictions

Number of court cases that considered educational rights in the last five years regarding:

(a) Availability or accessibility of primary education
(b) Funding of primary education
(c) Availability or accessibility of secondary education
(d) Accessibility of higher education
(e) Discrimination issues
(f) Registration or closing of private schools
(g) Parents' right to ensure the religious and moral education of their children in conformity with their own convictions

Number of complaints filed in the past five years regarding:

(a) Availability or accessibility of primary education
(b) Funding of primary education
(c) Availability or accessibility of secondary education
(d) Accessibility of higher education
(e) Discrimination issues
(f) Registration or closing of private schools
(g) Parents' rights to ensure the religious and moral education of their children in conformity with their own convictions

Number of court cases filed in the past five years regarding

(a) Availability or accessibility of primary education
(b) Funding of primary education
(c) Availability or accessibility of secondary education
(d) Accessibility of higher education
(e) Discrimination issues
(f) Registration or closing of private schools
(g) Parents' rights to ensure the religious and moral education of their children in conformity with their own convictions

School registrations

Number of schools that the government has refused to register in the past year:

(a) primary schools
(b) secondary schools
(c) vocational schools
(d) institutions of higher learning

School closings

Number of schools that the government has temporarily closed in the past year

(a) primary schools
(b) secondary schools
(c) vocational schools
(d) institutions of higher learning

Number of schools that the government has permanently closed in the past year

(a) primary schools
(b) secondary schools
(c) vocational schools
(d) institutions of higher learning

Outcome indicators

Literacy rate	Urban			Rural	
	Total	Females	Males	Females	Males
Ages 12 - 18					
ages 19 and over					

School attendance

(a) percentage of eligible children of primary school age attending school (net enrolment ratio)
  - total
  - females
  - males
  - in urban areas
  - in rural areas
  - among low income groups
  - with disabilities
  - by provinces/states (with full listing)

(b) percentage of total primary school population who are older than the official primary school age
- total
- in urban areas
- in rural areas
- by provinces/states (with full listing)

(c) percentage of total students in primary school who are enrolled in private schools
- total
- in urban areas
- in rural areas
- by states/provinces (with full listing)

(d) percentage of eligible children of secondary school age who attend secondary school
- total
- females
- males
- in urban areas
- in rural areas
- by states/provinces (with full listing)

(e) percentage of total students in secondary school who are enrolled in private schools
- total
- in urban areas
- in rural areas
- by states/provinces (with full listing)

(f) percentage of total students in primary school attending single sex institutions
- total
- in urban areas
- in rural areas
- by states/provinces (with full listing)

(g) percentage of total students in secondary school attending single sex institutions
- total
- in urban areas
- in rural areas
- females
- males
- by states/provinces (with full listing)

Educational attainment

Percentage of children entering primary school who complete the full number of years prescribed for the primary school cycle:

(a) total
(b) urban
(c) rural
(d) females
(e) males
(f) by states/provinces (with full listing)

Percentage of primary school leavers who pass the primary school leaving exam if one is given:

(a) total
(b) urban
(c) rural
(d) females
(e) males
(f) by states/provinces (with full listing)

Percentage of number of primary school leavers who enter secondary school

(a) total
(b) urban
(c) rural
(d) females
(e) males
(f) by states/provinces (with full listing)

Percentage of secondary school students in their final year who pass the requisite examinations

(a) total
(b) urban
(c) rural
(d) females
(e) males
(f) by states/provinces (with full listing)

Chapter 12

Measuring Economic and Social Rights to Hold Governments Accountable

Developing rigorous monitoring tools has been a persistent challenge for human rights NGOs working on economic and social rights. Article 2 of the *International Covenant of Economic, Social and Cultural Rights* obliges each state party to take steps toward "*achieving progressively the full realisation of rights*" to "*the maximum of its available resources.*"

At the same time, governments have various obligations which are of immediate effect. *General Comment 3* of the UN Committee on Economic, Social and Cultural Rights states that these include minimum core obligations to ensure the satisfaction of, at the very least, "*minimum essential levels*" of access to essential foodstuffs, basic health care, primary education and other needs. This also includes the obligation to guarantee the exercise of rights without discrimination, and to take deliberate, concrete and targeted steps to protect society's most vulnerable members.

Any adequate economic and social rights monitoring methodology must therefore take into account both resource availability and the notion of the "*progressive realisation*" of these rights, while providing tools for assessing compliance with minimum and immediate obligations. Such a monitoring mechanism requires quantitative tools and analytical skills that are typically not part of the research toolkit of human rights organisations (a few notable exceptions include the work of several NGOs that have been engaged in assessing economic and social rights using budget analysis, such as Fundar in Mexico, the Children's Budget Project at the Institute for Democracy in South Africa, ICEFI in Guatemala and DISHA in India, as well as the use of epidemiology in research conducted by Physicians for Human Rights).

Responding to this challenge, the Centre for Economic and Social Rights (CESR) has been engaged in the development of quantitative tools to strengthen the monitoring and advocacy of economic and social rights. This paper sets out a blueprint for the development of these tools.

This chapter was contributed by **Eitan Felner**

Executive Director, **Centre for Economic and Social Rights (CESR)**

The author would like to thank: Edward Anderson of the University of East Anglia for challenging him with basic questions about key human rights concepts; Jeremy Perelman of CESR for helpful research assistance; and Ignacio Saiz and Sally-Anne Way of CESR, for countless helpful conversations and invaluable editorial input.

Using indicators to monitor economic and social rights

In recent years, there has been a growing recognition of the value of using indicators for human rights monitoring. This has been the subject of numerous international academic conferences and a myriad of articles. Meanwhile, the UN human rights machinery has increasingly called for the production and use of human rights indicators and a number of initiatives have been launched to put such indicators into practice to measure human rights (see review of some of the literature in Fasel and Malhotra, 2005).

Clearly, the incorporation of indicators into the human rights field has come in many different forms. This is partly the result of conceptual and methodological differences between the various initiatives, but also in large part because of the different end goals of each of these initiatives. In the field of economic and social rights, as in other fields, indicators and data are often used for more than one purpose and by more than one type of user (be it an organisation or an individual). In short, **there is no single "right way" to use indicators to monitor human rights - different users, with different motivations, may utilise the tools at their disposal in different ways** (see *Chapter 1*).

For example, the quantitative tools that a UN Human Rights Treaty Body would use to monitor compliance with an international convention would probably be very different than those used by an international development agency interested in assessing human rights progress by individual countries to help them determine their aid priorities. Furthermore, the use of quantitative tools by a government committed to integrating human rights principles into its public policies would be quite different than that of an advocacy human rights NGO that is interested in exposing, and perhaps "naming and shaming," a government that is unwilling to adopt policies in line with its human rights obligations.

As an advocacy organisation, CESR is primarily interested in developing tools that would help various actors (UN mechanisms, development agencies and NGOs) hold governments – particularly recalcitrant ones – accountable for violations of economic and social rights. While data collection and analysis can be time-consuming and may appear overly academic and removed from the front line of advocacy, the use of indicators can provide an effective advocacy tool to address government noncompliance (UNDP, 2000). Therefore, the quantitative tools the organisation is developing are primarily designed to strengthen monitoring which, in turn, could be used for more effective advocacy efforts. Nevertheless, it is our hope that the tools will also serve other users and might be adapted for different purposes.

Obviously, quantitative indicators cannot give the full picture of the enjoyment of any right. There are many unquantifiable dimensions to human rights, which are not concerned solely with access to more housing, more clinics and more teachers but, also how such goods and services are provided, whom they reach, what the implications are for others, and whether people affected by the decisions participate in making them (Rubenstein 2004). Therefore, a rigorous monitoring mechanism requires combining quantitative tools with qualitative research based on methodologies developed by human rights experts (see *Chapters 1, 10 and 11*).

A focus on accountability for avoidable deprivations

There is a general agreement among human rights and human development experts that one of the key contributions of human rights to development is the focus on accountability (Sen, 2000; Robinson, 2005). However, what is often not elucidated is accountability for what and by whom.

There are a number of reasons why millions of people around the world are deprived of basic education, health care, shelter and food. Many of them, such as natural disasters, scarcity of material resources or technical means, often cannot be directly deemed as the responsibility of anyone in particular. Nonetheless, using a human rights approach calls attention to the fact that widespread deprivations are all too often not inevitable; rather, they are frequently generated or exacerbated by the lack of political will of various actors, whether national governments, international financial institutions, or developed countries.

For instance, in asserting a right to free primary education, we are claiming that this is something to which all are entitled. Therefore, if someone avoidably lacks access to it, there must be culpability somewhere in the social system (Sen, 2000). A human rights approach puts the focus on the accountability of relevant institutions for failing to prevent or rectify avoidable deprivations, whether through such factors as discrimination, corruption, abuse of power or the wilful indifference of political and economic elites.

By exposing arbitrary cutbacks in social services or discriminatory policies depriving wide sectors of the population access to basic goods, problems related to poverty can be exposed and challenged as the results of intentional actions (or inactions) of governments and other powerful actors. The creativity and added value of international advocacy networks is in finding "intentionalist frames" within which to address structural problems (Keck and Sickink, 1998).

Effectiveness of governmental efforts: structural and institutional issues

The overarching challenge is how to determine whether governments have made all possible efforts in good faith to realise the economic and social rights of those under their jurisdiction. Thus, we need to develop tools that would help us identify cases of avoidable deprivation, where government policies are a major contributing, if not causal, factor.

Moving beyond indicators

Most of the current literature on the use of quantitative data to monitor economic and social rights has focused either on a theoretical plea to use quantitative indicators for human rights monitoring or on setting out lists of indicators. However, so far, there is surprisingly little work on how to use these indicators to assess government compliance with its specific human rights obligations.

Recent efforts by various UN human rights mechanisms have begun to set out a set of indicators to monitor compliance with human rights norms pertaining to economic and social rights. As early as 1990, Danilo Türk, the UN Special Rapporteur on economic, social and cultural rights noted that, "*without the availability of a measurement device based on some form of statistical data, there is little chance of obtaining an overall picture which shows the extent which these rights are realised.*" (Türk, 1990) More recently, the UN Office of the High Commissioner for Human Rights (OHCHR) developed a set of indicators to monitor compliance with international human rights instruments (see *Chapter 10*). Additionally, the UN Special Rapporteurs have been involved in developing key indicators for their areas of focus, which include indicators to monitor the right to education or the right to health (see for instance Tomaševski, 2002; Hunt, 2006).

Regional bodies that monitor compliance with human rights have also begun exploring the potential use of indicators in their work. For instance, The Inter-American Commission for Human Rights recently prepared a paper on measuring the progress of economic, social and cultural rights with quantitative indicators (see Inter-American Commission, 2007).

So far, these UN and regional efforts have focused primarily on: (1) outlining a conceptual framework for the development and selection of human rights indicators such as analysing the differences between development indicators and human rights indicators; (2) establishing a typology of human rights indicators, distinguishing between "outcome," "process" and "structural" indicators; and (3) proposing various sets of indicators related to specific rights. However, to date, the UN human rights system has not made significant progress towards the integration of these proposed indicators into the ongoing work of its various monitoring mechanisms.

In order for a set of quantitative metrics to be useful for monitoring state obligations pertaining to economic and social rights, it is necessary not only to propose a set of human rights indicators, but also to develop quantitative tools that use these indicators in an integrated form. Indeed, in much the same way as having a grocery list is not sufficient to make a meal, **having a list of human rights indicators is not sufficient to assess compliance.** As with cooking, **what is needed is a set of recipes, or a box of analytical tools that tell you how to combine and analyse the indicators.**

Without such tools, a set of human rights indicators will never be able to sufficiently assess the multiple dimensions of state obligations pertaining to economic and social rights, including monitoring "progressive realisation" of rights according to available resources, identifying obstacles to fulfilment, revealing information about the extent of enjoyment of "minimum thresholds" of rights and of shortcomings of states in fulfilling their "minimum core obligations," and analysing when disparities in social and economic outcomes can be construed as forms of discrimination.

Without developing new analytical tools that form the basis for an analysis of the various indicators, it will be impossible to define whether states' human rights obligations are being met. Without such tools or recipes, it is not clear how indicators will be used, and therefore there remains the potential for the indicators to be misused or altogether avoided by the human rights movement. As Michael Ignatieff and Kate Desormeau point out, "*Even where relevant data is available over time we are uncertain how to interpret it, how to use it to guide our human rights arguments. Many practitioners are unsure how to conduct their own studies; many too are uncertain where to find relevant statistics and unsure what to do with them once they have found them*" (Carr Center for Human Rights Policy, 2005).

Dimensions of state obligations pertaining to economic and social rights

CESR's work has therefore aimed to take this next step and to move beyond collecting indicators and towards developing a toolbox of analytical and methodological tools that provide a framework (or recipe, to take the cooking analogy further) that help us understand how the indicators measure government efforts to realise economic, social and cultural rights. This project does not require devising new methodological tools as such, but rather adopting tools used by social scientists and the development community for purposes of human rights monitoring and, when necessary, adapting them for these purposes.

CESR is focusing primarily on those dimensions of government obligations that can be identified and critically assessed most usefully through the use of socio-economic tools and quantitative methods. These areas are: (1) the obligation to fulfil, and its constituent elements; (2) the obligation to satisfy minimum essential levels of rights; (3) the duty to move progressively and expeditiously towards full realisation of rights within the constraints of maximum available resources; and (4) the obligation to ensure that no discrimination in the enjoyment of rights (particularly, on ensuring that resource allocations are not discriminatory).

In concrete situations these different dimensions are often inter-related. A significant proportion of a country's population may be deprived of basic health care or education because of their gender, race or ethnicity. Or, despite growth in available resources, a state may fail to meet its minimum core obligations. Nevertheless, each dimension may require different monitoring methods, and will therefore largely be treated separately.

This work also seeks to inject substantive meaning into these concepts, so that they can be translated into more concrete policy prescriptions. It aims to contribute to making more operationalised the normative frameworks developed by the UN Human Rights Treaty Bodies to assess compliance with the right to health, education, housing and food. It also aims to measure the essential elements of the rights to health and education set out by *General Comments* 13 and 14 of the UN Committee on Economic, Social and Cultural Rights - including *availability, accessibility, acceptability* and *adaptability* or *quality*.

Measuring "progressive realisation" according to available resources

The *International Covenant on Economic, Social and Cultural Rights* obliges states to take steps progressively towards the full realisation of economic, social and cultural rights according to the maximum available resources. The language of the treaty thus implicitly recognises that the obligations of state parties are not uniform or universal but are relative to levels of development and available resources (Chapman and Russell, 2001). A country's economy must be taken into account when determining the level of obligations it can be expected to fulfil.

Neither the *Covenant*, nor the UN Committee that monitors states' compliance with it, provides specific guidance or benchmarks to judge the sufficiency of resources made available to realise rights, making it difficult to assess whether governments have met this obligation.

The simplest method to measure "progressive realisation according to available resources" in a single country is to compare its GDP per capita (as a proxy of available resources) over time with an outcome social indicator, such as primary completion rates or child malnutrition (as a proxy for the enjoyment of some aspects of a specific right). This very simple method might be helpful in cases where a country had an actual regression of some of these outcome indicators during a period in which that country benefited from a significant economic growth. Such a regression in outcome indicators during a period in which overall resources have increased might prima facie indicate that a state is not complying with its obligation to progressively realise key rights according to available resources.

But the application of this simple tool is quite limited, since in most cases countries do make progress over time over most outcome indicators, although this progress may be very slow. We then need a methodology for determining whether progress is adequate or whether it is too slow relative to the change in resources. One way to measure this is to look at a cross country comparison of per capita incomes with health or education indicators in order to provide an objective benchmark against which actual performance may be judged.

Using this simple method, some authors have illustrated the inadequacy of using income indicators as the most common method of measuring quality of life in a state, showing that in many countries there is no correlation between GNP (or GDP) per capita and education or health attainments (*e.g.* Sen, 1999). Others have used cross-country regressions of per capita income and health or education outcome indicators such as life expectancy to identify poor performers on basic needs (Stewart, 1985, ch. 4) or to *"capture the relative efficiency of national political economies in converting national material resources into human development"* (Moore, Leavy and White, 2003).

Using a similar method to measure progressive realisation of economic and social rights could serve as a **first step** towards identifying outliers that appear not to be making progress on health or education in accordance with their available resources. A complementary exercise would be comparing a country's Human Development Index (HDI) ranking with its ranking of GDP/per capita: "*For 26 countries, the HDI rank is 20 or more places lower than per capita income rank, showing that they have considerable potential to improve their human development levels and spend their national incomes more wisely*" (UNDP, 1991).

A **second step** could be to track the progress of each of these outliers over time, both in terms of GDP per capita and the relevant health or education indicator. This could reveal, for instance, countries where there was a decrease in the rate of children enrolled in primary school in a given period despite economic growth.

When comparing GDP (or other proxies for "available resources") with social outcomes, the methodology would have to consider which factors should be controlled for. For instance, when studying the effect of governance on poverty, Mick Moore controlled for population density, figuring that a country with a higher population density can more efficiently provide services than a larger country with small population density. (Moore, 2003) In another similar study, Frances Stewart controlled for whether or not a country was heavily dependent on oil extraction for its economic well-being (Stewart, 1985).

These quantitative methods will clearly not be sufficient to assess whether a state is violating its obligation to use the maximum available resources for the realisation of economic, social and cultural rights. Still, these simple methods could serve as a preliminary means to flag issues worth exploring further in this regard. Thus, these methods would need to be complemented by contextual qualitative studies (or quantitative studies based on household surveys and other data sets) to understand the contributing factors to complex issues (such as why in a given country there was an increase in under-5 mortality or of children not finishing primary school despite an economic windfall).

Beyond the question of which specific method is used, some conceptual/normative issues regarding the exact meaning of the principle of "progressive realisation" need to be elucidated if we hope to make this principle truly operational. For instance, the obligation speaks only of progressive realisation of economic, social and cultural rights according to available resources - but what if a country suffers an economic slowdown or retrogression in its economic performance? In such a case, could a country justify retrogression in its realisation of economic and social rights inasmuch as its economy regressed?

The notion of "progressive realisation" assumes that progress must be continuous, and that it is never acceptable for policy makers to "go backwards" at one point in order to move forward later on. While development economists take it for granted that most development programmes cause damage en route, either for a minority or for the majority of long-term beneficiaries, human rights analysts are often uncomfortable dealing with differential advantage (Robinson, 2005).

Similarly, if the principle of progressive realisation in a key indicator is measured only by tracking its relative change (compared to GDP growth) over time, should we expect less improvement in the indicator for a country with high GDP but low GDP growth (the US, for example) and more improvement for a low-GDP country with high GDP growth (like Viet Nam)? This dilemma highlights the problem with assessing a country's performance based solely on the relative change of its key indicators over time.

Measuring discrimination of public policies

The concept of non-discrimination, like the concept of equality, is a foundational principle of international human rights law, and is reflected in Articles 2, 3 and 26 of the *International Covenant on*

Box 12.1. **Discrimination in international covenants**

The *International Covenant on Civil and Political Rights* states that:

Article 2.1: Each state party to the present Covenant undertakes to respect and to ensure to all individuals within its territory and subject to its jurisdiction the rights recognised in the present Covenant, without distinction of any kind, such as race, colour, sex, language, religion, political or other opinion, national or social origin, property, birth or other status.

Article 3: The states parties to the present Covenant undertake to ensure the equal right of men and women to the enjoyment of all civil and political rights set forth in the present Covenant.

Article 26: All persons are equal before the law and are entitled without any discrimination to the equal protection of the law. In this respect, the law shall prohibit any discrimination and guarantee to all persons equal and effective protection against discrimination on any ground such as race, colour, sex, language, religion, political or other opinion, national or social origin, property, birth or other status.

The *International Covenant on Economic, Social and Cultural Rights* states that:

Article 2.2: The states parties to the present Covenant undertake to guarantee that the rights enunciated in the present Covenant will be exercised without discrimination of any kind as to race, colour, sex, language, religion, political or other opinion, national or social origin, property, birth or other status.

Article 3: The states parties to the present Covenant undertake to ensure the equal right of men and women to the enjoyment of all economic, social and cultural rights set forth in the present Covenant.

Civil and Political Rights, as well as in Articles 2 and 3 of the *International Covenant on Economic, Social and Cultural Rights* (see Box 12.1). Non-discrimination constitutes an immediate obligation that is not subject to progressive realisation, and nor is it contingent on available resources.

Non-discrimination is a relatively precise concept that is therefore not subject to the argument that state obligations related to economic, social and cultural rights are indeterminate. However, although conceptually this principle is clear, the measurement of discrimination in terms of indicators and in quantitative terms is less clear.

The most obvious place to start is to look at the distribution of government spending in relation to the prohibited grounds of discrimination (for example, between ethnic groups or between men and women). We can look at, for instance, how much of the resources to provide a certain education or health service is allocated to one group compared to another group. This can give us an important initial indication of which groups are being actively discriminated against in government expenditure.

However, quantitative tools to monitor discriminatory public policies in the areas of education and health cannot exclusively focus on assessing the distributional aspects of government spending. This is because many discriminatory policies are related to the failure of a government to allocate adequate resources to a health or educational service which a specific group needs (and others groups don't need), which an analysis would not capture if it focuses exclusively on assessing the distributional aspects of existing government spending on particular services.

For instance, governments are culpable of gender discrimination not only when they allocate more public resources to men than women for the same good (providing more resources per person to school for boys than school for girls, for example), but also when they do not allocate sufficient resources to services that inherently are necessary to fulfil women's rights (*e.g.* reproductive health services). Similarly, in countries where HIV infection is associated with sexual behaviour, stigma against homosexuality may keep governments from devoting the necessary resources to address this health catastrophe.

Discrimination in the allocation of resources is not the only form of public policy intervention that has an effect on disparities among groups in education and health outcomes. As O'Neil and Piron note, "*An examination of the social, economic and political processes that produce and maintain unequal access to services, assets, income, power and opportunities is required to address the discriminatory roots of inequality*" (O'Neil and Piron, 2003). For instance, it is important to examine the evidence on the effects of institutional reforms and economic policies to promote greater gender equality (King and Mason, 2001) or the ways that retrenchment policies may disproportionately affect minority or excluded groups.

Inequality between groups

Persistent inequality between groups in health status or educational outcomes may also be the result of a cumulative impact of past discrimination, whether or not direct discrimination continues to play a role. Thus, our analysis should also enable us to expose indirect forms of discrimination, such as persistent socio-economic disadvantage and unequal distribution of power due to the cumulative effects of historical discrimination. O'Neil and Piron write, "*Such indirect discrimination creates an uneven playing field, impeding the equal enjoyment of civil, political, economic, social and cultural rights*" (O'Neil and Piron, 2003). Thus, while differences in pay can be a reflection of different educational achievements and skills, and therefore not a result of direct discrimination, these differences in human capital can themselves be an outcome of indirect discrimination (that is, past discrimination that has produced inbuilt disadvantage due to factors such as unequal service provision).

It is also essential to analyse systematic differences between the benefits of public expenditure received by different groups who are socially, economically and politically disadvantaged, whether on grounds of gender, ethnicity, caste, membership of a linguistic minority or another specific characteristic. Thus, the unit of analysis for assessing discrimination needs to be differences between these groups rather than differences between households. Although households as such are not the relevant unit for an analysis of discrimination, we may need to rely on them since various data sets, such as household surveys, are based on household characteristics (see *Chapter 6*). This of course will be a major methodological problem when these data sets are not disaggregated by the relevant groups on which we want to focus the analysis.

Given that some forms of discrimination are related to policies that ignore the needs of particular people, we need to take into account the specific ways in which discrimination on these grounds manifests itself and is perpetuated. That is, in constructing models for assessing whether government policy is discriminatory, we need to identify the particular demand and production functions that shape, for example, women's access to sexual health information or indigenous people's enrolment in secondary education. A discrimination-sensitive methodology would also take into account the fact that certain health/education inputs may only be needed by women or by indigenous groups, such as access to reproductive health services or teaching in indigenous languages.

It may make sense, for example, to focus on gender, race and ethnicity, in view of the systemic gender, racial and ethnic disparities that exist almost universally in the enjoyment of health and education benefits, the fact that these are the three group-based identities that appear to have the most pronounced influence on the disproportionate chance of experiencing poverty (O'Neil and Piron, 2003), and taking into account the greater availability of data disaggregated on these grounds.

At the same time, we should also investigate the interactions between these three key forms of group-based identities (Burchardt, 2006). Such interactions can help us detect the discriminatory patterns contributing to some of those inequalities and set out accordingly the type of policy interventions the government can undertake to eliminate those patterns.

For instance, in a country where we find that the gap between male and female education rates varies by ethnic group, we should explore whether cultural institutions and beliefs of the ethnic groups with greater gender disparities are contributing to the inequality between men and women's access to education. In such a case, the policy interventions that the government could undertake to address gender discrimination might be geared toward changing the attitudes about women within that ethnic group. In other cases, there might be a close link between one of those three key forms of group-based identities and poverty. For example, gender disparities tend to be greater among the poor (King and Mason, 2001). This would require other types of policy interventions to address the gender disparities.

Inequality of what? Outcome and input indicators

Although observations of inequalities of outcome in health or education can highlight issues of concern, they are not, in themselves, evidence of discrimination. A multiplicity of factors account for differential outcomes across different social groups, including lifestyle, personal choices and genetic makeup; in some cases these disparities might exist in spite of a government's genuine efforts to close these gaps. Therefore, our primary concern when measuring discrimination would be with unequal access among relevant groups on the access to policy inputs that have an effect on the relevant health or education outcomes.

Nonetheless, although inequalities of outcomes are not in themselves proof of discrimination, such inequalities are still relevant for our purposes. As noted above, we are interested in both the enjoyment and the obligations aspects of rights. Moreover, an analysis of outcome indicators over time can also show inadequacy of current policy inputs, as underscored above regarding the sluggish decline of child undernourishment in India. Finally, persistent inequalities in levels of rights enjoyment may be indicative of policies or practices that perpetuate or fail to redress long-standing patterns of systemic discrimination against certain groups. Thus, they could serve as "red flags" to identify potential problems of discrimination that call for a contextual assessment of all relevant data and policy inputs.

Conceptual and methodological challenges

There are various measurement issues and challenges that need to be addressed in order to develop tools for measuring various forms of discrimination.

– Measuring racial or ethnic discrimination

Often relevant data sets (household surveys, government budgets) are not disaggregated by race or ethnicity. In such cases, which methods can be used to infer the relevant data to make a case of discrimination? For instance, if there is a region in a country where the majority of the population belongs to a minority ethnic group and that region gets disproportionably less resources for health or education, would this be sufficient proof of a discriminatory policy? Are there other methods that can be used to measure racial or ethnic discrimination in government spending, if there is no detailed disaggregated data available?

– Measuring gender discrimination

Measuring gender discrimination has its own challenges because, as noted above, in contrast to discrimination of ethnic or racial groups, gender discrimination often occurs within a household. If a girl is not schooled because her parents refuse to send her to school, then the responsibility for the failure can be placed on the parents. However, the government may share responsibility if it failed to combat discriminatory practices against women within the household, which often are embedded in traditional attitudes and practices (Sen, 2000).

In other situations, the discrimination may be more complex. For instance, the decision to send only boys to school when parents cannot afford the school fees for all their children may indeed be a reflection of the parents' gender biases, but it could also be because economic returns for education might be higher for boys than for girls. In such a case, although the parents may be directly responsible for sending the boys rather than girls to school, the governments may still share responsibility by not providing affordable schooling for all children (either by cancelling school fees, providing subsidies for poor families, etc) and for not undertaking economic and social programmes to provide job opportunities for women equal to men.

Other times, governments are directly responsible for gender discrimination. For example, governments often allocate disproportionately insufficient resources to services for women (emergency obstetric care clinics, for example). Other policy interventions that seem neutral but have discriminatory effects can also be classified as discriminatory policies; after all, the definition of discrimination includes actions or omissions with discriminatory effects, regardless of whether there is discriminatory intent. For instance, building schools with co-ed bathrooms in a traditional society may discourage parents from sending their daughters to school because of traditional customs about modesty.

A methodology to measure gender discrimination will need to take into account all these (and possibly other) situations, developing relevant tools for the multiple aspects in which governments have direct or indirect responsibility of commission or omission.

– Resolving the tension between maximisation of resources for the fulfilment of economic and social rights and ensuring special attention for the most marginalised communities

Are differential levels of benefits from government spending among groups justified if they can be attributed to differences in effectiveness? This is a crucial issue for assessing government policies that prioritise urban over rural areas. For instance, in a country with limited resources, where both the urban and rural poor may be deprived of basic health services, it might be more efficient to prioritise giving services to the poor in the urban areas (where the greater density may increase the scope of an intervention). On the other hand, the rural poor might be more deprived than the urban poor and have less ability for social mobility, implicitly exacerbating rural-urban disparities by reducing their access to some of those services. Does it make a difference if there are no such disparities in outcome indicators before the policy intervention? These are clearly normative questions that must be addressed with reference to the human rights framework. However, there may be methods that could help determine how to solve these policy dilemmas by drawing from other professional fields.

Is it legitimate to prioritise urban areas over rural areas to benefit a greater number of people? Can we distinguish between regional marginalisation (which would under this circumstance be considered legitimate) from ethnic or racial discrimination, when there is a correlation between ethnic or racial minorities and the concentration of a population in rural areas?

Measurement methods and tools

In order to identify and measure the multiple forms of discrimination described above, there is clearly a need to create a range of new quantitative tools. However, existing methods used by economists and other social scientists to analyse development issues can be applied.

First, for example, we could explore the various methods proposed in the literature for measuring inequality between groups (*e.g.* Stewart *et al.*, 2005; Justino, 2005; Justino *et al.*, 2004; Roemer, 1998; Bourguignon *et al.*, 2003). There are also various tools in existing literature for measuring gender inequality (*e.g.* UNDP, 1995; Dijstra and Hanmer, 2000). Furthermore, it may be worth exploring the relevance of a new tool developed by the OECD Development Centre's Gender, Institutions and Development Data Base (GID–accessible at www.oecd.org/dev), "*whose aim is to determine and analyse obstacles to the economic development of women. The GID covers a total of 162 countries and comprises a comprehensive array of 50 indicators on gender discrimination from various sources. Its true value-added is the innovative inclusion of institutional variables that range from intra-household behavior to social norms that determine endemic discrimination in poor countries. Examples are young (mainly forced) marriages, genital mutilation, and restrictions on inheritance as well as property rights.*" (see Jutting et al., 2006)

Second, in order to measure policy inputs that affect horizontal inequalities, we could apply various tools that are already used in the development field, such as benefit incidence analysis, public expenditure tracking surveys, poverty mapping, or budget analysis. We should examine what each of these tools is usually used for, and whether they could be used to measure patterns of discrimination.

With regards to budget analysis, we can learn from the growing experience of analysing public expenditure programmes from a human rights perspective (International Budget Project; see Elson, 2006, section II). There has also been significant analysis of budgets from a gender perspective, including work on monitoring government budgets for compliance with the *Convention on the Elimination of All Forms of Discrimination against Women* (Elson, 2006).

Measuring minimum core obligations

The concept of "minimum core obligations" was put forward by the UN Committee on Economic, Social and Cultural Rights in response to the perception that states' obligations with respect to economic, social and cultural rights were too indeterminate and contingent on available resources to make possible the identification of clear violations. The Committee posited the idea of an intangible baseline level that must be guaranteed for all persons in all contexts - a minimum below which no government should perform, even in unfavourable conditions and regardless of resources (see Box 12.2).

The notion of minimum core obligations is an important safeguard against the risk of complacent governments evading accountability by blaming dire levels of deprivation on economic constraints and merely pledging to do better if and when resources allow. But how useful is the term in practice as a guiding instrument of policy making? Can it be refined and fleshed out in light of more recent thinking on human capabilities and the quest for minimum universal norms in the fields of health and education? (Buchanan, 1984; Acharya, 2004, 2005). Or is the ambiguity of the concept such that it cannot meaningfully be made operational in the real world of ever-shrinking public coffers and tough policy trade-offs? What social science tools are available to quantify minimum core obligations and verify their fulfilment?

Box 12.2. **Minimum core obligations of states**

The **UN Committee on Economic, Social and Cultural Rights** "is of the view that a minimum core obligation to ensure the satisfaction of, at the very least, minimum essential levels of each of the rights is incumbent upon every state party. Thus, for example, a state party in which any significant number of individuals is deprived of essential foodstuffs, of essential primary health care, of basic shelter and housing, or of the most basic forms of education is, prima facie, failing to discharge its obligations under the Covenant. If the Covenant were to be read in such a way as not to establish such a minimum core obligation, it would be largely deprived of its raison d'être. (...) In order for a state party to be able to attribute its failure to meet at least its minimum core obligations to a lack of available resources it must demonstrate that every effort has been made to use all resources that are at its disposition in an effort to satisfy, as a matter of priority, those minimum obligations" (*General Comment 3*, paragraph 10 see UN-HRI, 1990b).

The UN Committee developed the concepts of minimum core content and minimum core obligations for two related reasons: (1) the need to circumvent the difficulties inherent in assessing progressive realisation; and (2) the Committee's concern that the content of article 2:1 of the *Covenant* (in particular the concepts of "progressive realisation" and the obligations being subject to the availability of resources) provides an escape hatch to let recalcitrant states with dismal human rights outcomes off the hook and that therefore a "floor" had to be established. This minimum obligation recognises that elements of economic, social and cultural rights create an immediate duty on the part of the state, and therefore are not subject to progressive realisation.

The term "minimum core obligations" refers to the things a state must do immediately to realise the most essential elements of a right, those that should be addressed as a priority. A state may still claim that it cannot meet even those most minimal obligations. If it does, however, the burden of proof shifts to the state to justify its claim.

Basic deprivations as violations of minimum core obligations

The pitiful failure of many governments, and of the international community as a whole, to make significant strides in eradicating abysmal levels of poverty, inequality and deprivation, demands that renewed efforts be made to demonstrate when and how these phenomena can be traced back to specific actions or omissions of state policy, and how these can be categorised as violations of internationally recognised human rights obligations.

Unless fulfilment of core obligations is made a pressing political priority, and unless governments are held to account for their efforts to address these obligations, whole generations will continue to be consigned to lives of misery, indignity and preventable brevity. For instance, in India "*if the child undernourishment figures continue to decline at the sluggish rate of one percentage point per year, it will take another forty years before India achieves nutrition levels similar to those of China today*" (Dreze, 2005).

Measuring outcomes or inputs?

Development organisations use socio-economic indicators primarily to measure the condition of people's lives and gauge the extent to which states have improved their level of development. In measuring human rights, outcomes are also crucial; they are the ultimate goal in terms of rights enjoyment. From a methodological point of view, outcome indicators serve as a first step in the monitoring process, in that they identify significant avoidable deprivations. Yet, for human rights organisations, this cannot be the purpose of using statistical indicators. As noted above, the purpose

---

Box 12.3. Categorising a good as a right

The significance of categorising a good as a right is illustrated by Philip Alston, former Chair of the UN Committee on Economic, Social and Cultural Rights:

"If we are told that girl children have very limited access to primary education in a particular country – Nepal, Pakistan, Afghanistan, or wherever – or that, despite formally equal access, only very few girls actually attend school, do we immediately say 'This is a clear violation of their human right to education'? Or do we say, 'This is a great pity and we really hope that social programmes over the next fifty years will address the problem so that their great grandchildren will benefit'? By contrast, if the same girls were being forced or sold into prostitution, we would immediately be outraged and say, 'Why isn't something being done? This is a violation of their human rights" (Alston, 1997).

---

of the human rights framework is to hold governments accountable for their policies and priorities. Therefore "*to capture the additional features of human rights – and to create policy and advocacy tools – indicators are needed that can help create a culture of accountability*" (Human Development Report, 2000).

For this purpose we need to focus on inputs, which can measure the extent to which governments as duty holders are complying with their obligations to make every effort to ensure access for all to the level of goods, services and resources deemed essential to prevent people from falling below these outcome thresholds.

Accordingly, the UN Committee on Economic, Social and Cultural Rights appears to understand minimum core obligations as being primarily about inputs, such as access to essential foodstuffs or to essential primary health care (see *General Comment 3*, as well as *General Comment 13* on education, and *General Comment 14* on the right to health, which also describe core obligations in terms of necessary inputs).

Thus, when monitoring human rights, although we are interested in whether people are enjoying the objects of the rights – the enjoyment aspect of rights – the primary focus is on monitoring whether governments (and possibly other duty bearers) are meeting their human rights obligations – the obligation aspect of rights (Raworth, 2001).

Beyond these normative issues, there are also methodological problems in using outcome indicators as the basis for monitoring minimum core obligations. Often, the outcome to be monitored is quite clear but there are great difficulties in actually measuring it. This is the case with maternal mortality, for example; according to the relevant international agencies, there are huge methodological problems with measuring maternal mortality because of: (1) the relative infrequency of maternal deaths; (2) a significant under-reporting of maternal deaths in most developing countries; and (3) many maternal deaths that are incorrectly misreported as if they were deaths that do not fall in this category (WHO, UNICEF and UNFPA, 1997).

Even if the measurement of an indicator is not problematic, it is often difficult to establish a minimum threshold of enjoyment below which a country would be deemed to be violating its minimum core obligations. For instance, it may be difficult to determine what illiteracy rate would constitute a violation of minimum core obligations. Initially, one would say that anything below 100% literacy is a violation of minimum core obligations. But in practice, that may be imposing too heavy a burden on states, particularly developing countries.

Despite these problems, outcome indicators are not to be discarded in monitoring economic, social and cultural rights in general and minimum core obligations in particular. Rather, outcome indicators could serve as an initial rule of thumb to identify red flags, where it is worth delving into input data. For instance, if we find that country X consistently shows lower rates of literacy or higher maternal mortality rates than other countries with similar characteristics (such as GDP per capita) it would give us a clear indication that there is a problem worth exploring further, even if we could not quantify the exact scope of the problem.

Inputs relating to core obligations in health and education

As noted above, the UN Committee on Economic, Social and Cultural Rights basically frames minimum core obligations as inputs. The first sources to select relevant inputs are its *General Comments* themselves. Given that the key core obligation for the right to education is to provide primary education for all, the relevant indicators of *direct* inputs are obvious: primary enrolment and children reaching grade 5 or primary school completion.

In the case of the right to health, as noted above, the core obligations have different degrees of specificity and not all of them are easily quantifiable. Thus, it may be quite clear which direct input indicators are related to core obligations such as providing essential drugs, "*as from time to time defined under the WHO Action Program on Essential Drugs;*" or providing "*immunisation against the major infectious diseases occurring in the community.*" But there are other core obligations that are broad categories of health care (such as, "*to ensure reproductive, maternal – pre-natal as well as post-natal – and child health care*" and to provide "*essential primary health care*"), which are not specific enough to serve as a basis for monitoring governments' compliance.

Human rights law does not specify what a number of key terms actually mean; for example, "*essential primary health care,*" nutritionally *adequate* food or *basic* shelter, housing and sanitation are not clearly defined. To inject specific meaning to these concepts and identify relevant indicators, we need to rely on what public health experts say are the main components of each of those broad categories. For instance, Alicia Yamin points out that the guidelines developed by WHO, UNICEF and UNFPA to monitor the availability and use of obstetric services delineate a set of "process indicators" that inject substantive meaning into the normative concepts of availability, accessibility and, to some extent, quality set out under Article 12 of the *International Covenant on Economic, Social and Cultural Rights*, as well as provisions under the *Convention for the Elimination of All Forms of Discrimination Against Women* (Yamin, 2005). The WHO, UNICEF and UNFPA guidelines recommend specific indicators to measure the availability and use of obstetric services and corresponding minimum acceptable levels for each of these indicators (see Box 12.4).

Furthermore, similar guidelines outlining indicators and minimum essential levels of inputs for aspects of the right to health (*e.g.* infant health) and the right to education should be integrated into the methodological toolbox.

Regressive spending policies as a violation of human rights

The combination of having a significant proportion of the poorest segment of the population deprived of minimum essential levels of economic and social rights with regressive spending patterns that disproportionably benefit the more affluent groups in society is quite common in developing countries. As a UNICEF study notes, "*More is spent on highly specialised hospital care than on basic health care, even though substantial numbers of people have no access to the most basic health clinic. The same applies*

Box 12.4. **Indication of the availability and use of obstetric services**

Indicator	Minimum acceptable level
Amount of essential obstetric care (EOC): Basic EOC facilities Comprehensive EOC facilities	For every 500,000 population, there should be: At least 4 Basic EOC facilities At least 1 Comprehensive EOC facility.
Geographical distribution of EOC facilities	Minimum level for amount of EOC facilities is met in sub-national areas.
Percentage of all births in Basic or Comprehensive EOC facilities	At least 15% of all births in the population take place in either Basic or Comprehensive facilities
Met Need for EOC: women treated in EOC facilities as a percentage of those estimated to have obstetric complications	At least 100% of women estimated to have obstetric complications are treated in EOC facilities
Cesarean sections as a percentage of all births	Cesarean sections account for no less than 5% nor more than 15% of all births in the population
Case fatality rate: deaths among women with complications in EOC facilities	The case fatality rate among women with obstetric complications in EOC facilities is less than 1%

Source: WHO, UNICEF and UNFPA: *Guidelines for monitoring the availability and use of obstetric services*

to the continuing emphasis on secondary and university spending in countries where most children do not complete even five years of formal schooling." (UNICEF, 1996).

Twelve years ago, a UNICEF report showed how the equity of social spending was strongly related to overall outcomes. UNICEF studied the distribution of public spending on primary education in 19 countries. It found that the impact of regressive spending patterns on basic deprivations was striking. Where net enrolment at primary level is less than 70%, it was observed that the poorest 20% of the population received less than 20% of the benefits of public spending on education. In contrast, countries with enrolment above 70% devoted a much larger share of public money to the bottom quintile. Families from the richest quintile can and did send their children to private schools, which is why their "share" of public spending on education was less than 20%. Nevertheless, the equity of primary spending was more apparent in countries where primary net enrolments were higher (UNICEF, 1996).

At that time, UNICEF found a similar correlation in the area of health. In countries with under five mortality rates below 70, the poorest 20% of the population received more than 25% of the benefits of public spending on primary health care, while those countries where the poorest 20% of the population received less that 15% of the health benefits, had an average under-five mortality rate of over 140.

Taking into account empirical evidence about the impact that spending distributional patterns on basic health and education has on the ability of a country to ensure the satisfaction of minimum essential levels of each economic and social right for the whole population, it could be concluded that regressive policies in spending on education or health (that is, spending more on tertiary education than on primary education when a large proportion of the population is deprived of primary education) is a violation of minimum core obligations. Therefore, identifying regressive spending patterns could serve as one method for assessing whether a government is making every effort to use all resources that are at its disposal to satisfy, as a matter of priority, its minimum core obligations.

As Philip Alston points out, in a country with very limited resources the maxim that "poverty is a denial of human rights" would be often valid in legal terms if the government "*has failed to take possible steps to improve the situation and instead has opted to devote scarce resources to other objectives that do not address directly the realisation of basic rights*" (Alston 2005). This is precisely what is happening in many poor countries, where the most impoverished people lack primary health care and basic education, but the state allocates most of its social spending on the non-poor.

Impact of macroeconomic policies on economic and social rights

In order to determine whether governments have made all possible efforts to realise their obligations related to economic and social rights, it is necessary to go beyond an analysis of the public policies specifically related to particular social sectors, such as health or education, and analyse the multiple arenas of state policy in which a government should take into account the basic rights of all, and in particular of deprived groups, but fails to do so.

One aspect would be the fiscal policies of the country – both the amounts of money raised in taxation as well as the pattern of taxation. Another key aspect would be the patterns of public social spending. For the latter, it would be worth exploring how to use or adapt the set of ratios that UNDP proposed for designing and monitoring public spending on human development (UNDP, 1991; UNDP, 1996) - comparing the "public expenditure ratio" (government share of GNP) with the "social allocation ratio" (social services share of government spending) and "social priority ratio" (human priority share of social sector spending) – as well as any other tools for locating failures in public spending.

Macroeconomic policies also have a significant impact on people's ability to acquire basic goods and services. Laws and regulations that would prevent foreseeable systemic deprivations are often lacking at the national and international level. Undernourishment and other forms of deprivation are often "systemic" deprivations resulting from the confluence of many factors, often accidental and unpredictable, none of which by itself caused the harm (Shue, 1996). Therefore realising economic, social and cultural rights may not always involve transferring commodities to people, but may require preventing people from being deprived of these commodities or ensuring the means to grow, make or buy them.

A whole set of structural and institutional issues therefore play a role in excluding some groups from access to services or resources the state makes available. As Pogge points out, "*in the modern world, the rules governing economic transactions — both nationally and internationally — are the most important causal determinants of the incidence and depth of poverty. They are most important because of their great impact on the economic distribution within the jurisdiction to which they apply. Thus, even relatively minor variations in a country's laws governing tax rates, labor relations, social security, and access to health care and education can have a much greater effect on poverty than even relatively large changes in the policies of a major corporation or in the habits of individual economic behaviour*" (Pogge, 2003).

In an era of significantly increased global economic interdependence, macroeconomic policies and institutions have a considerable impact on the capacity of countries in the global South to guarantee the fulfilment of economic and social rights for poor and marginalised populations. For instance, a study of the national expenditure patterns of 17 developing countries showed that the countries in the sample are carrying a heavy debt burden of, on average, 23.6% of national expenditure, surpassing the average public expenditure on basic social services of 12.3% (Harrington *et al.*, 2001).

Therefore, these structural and macroeconomic issues will need to be taken into account as well as analysing the role of developed countries, international finance institutions and transnational corporations in influencing governments' efforts and capacity to realise economic and social rights.

Visualising rights: an example of CESR work

As part of CESR's efforts to strengthen the monitoring of human rights, the organisation began publishing a new fact sheet series on individual countries, called *Visualising Rights*. The series collects relevant socioeconomic indicators from both international and national sources, analyses them based on applicable international human rights standards, and displays the results in innovative visual forms.

The overall goal of this project is to strengthen the monitoring and advocacy capabilities of the human rights movement - particularly of international human rights mechanisms (such as the Universal Periodic Review of the Human Rights Council or UN Treaty Bodies) and NGOs.

CESR's *Visualising Rights* are not meant to give a comprehensive picture, nor provide conclusive evidence, of states' failure to comply with their obligations under international law. Rather, they flag some possible concerns that arise when statistics are analysed in light of the various dimensions of a state's obligations related to economic and social rights, including its core obligation to satisfy minimum essential levels, to realise rights progressively (in accordance with the duty to allocate to this purpose the maximum available resources), and to ensure no discrimination and equal treatment in access to and enjoyment of these rights.

CESR's *Visualising Rights* therefore constitute evidence-based contributions to a more focused, substantive and fruitful discussion between the UN Committee and a given state party – as well as to enhance the capacities of national and international NGOs to make national governments accountable for their obligations pertaining to economic, social and cultural rights.

The first issue of the *Visualising Rights* focused on India, with particular emphasis on the right to education and the right to health – and more specifically on two areas of particular concern to CESR: India's high rates of child mortality and some specific issues related to primary education (see figures below and, for more information, ftp://cesr.org/pub/india%20web.pdf). It highlighted, among other important findings:

- **Little public investment in health.** India accounts for 2.5 million child deaths annually, one in five of the world total (UNDP, 2005). Figure 12.1 shows that, while India has one of the highest child mortality rates in Asia, it still has one of the lowest per capita government expenditures on health (as a percentage of GDP per capita). The under-five mortality rate in India is the same as Nepal and higher than Bangladesh, two of the poorest countries in Asia. Despite their meagre resources, these two countries spend significantly more per capita on health than India.
- **Slow reduction in child mortality despite rapid economic growth** (see Figures 12.2 and 12.3). While India had an income growth of 58% between 1995 and 2005 - one of the highest in the world - its reduction in child mortality during the same period was one of the lowest in South Asia. India's underperformance in the reduction of child mortality becomes apparent when compared with Bangladesh, which has reduced under-five child mortality significantly more

Figure 12.1. **Under-5 Mortality Rates and Per Capita Government Expenditure**

Mortality rate, under-5 (per 1,000) 2005		Per capita government expenditure on health as % of GDP pc PPP, 2004	
Cambodia	143	Mongolia	5,2%
Pakistan	99	Korea, Rep.	3,2%
India	74	Thailand	2,5%
Nepal	74	Malaysia	2,5%
Bangladesh	73	Vietnam	1,9%
Mongolia	49	China	1,9%
Indonesia	36	Sri Lanka	1,9%
Philippines	33	Philippines	1,8%
China	27	Cambodia	1,6%
Thailand	21	Singapore	1,5%
Vietnam	19	Nepal	1,4%
Sri Lanka	14	Indonesia	1,2%
Malaysia	12	Bangladesh	1,0%
Korea, Rep.	5	India	0,6%
Singapore	3	Pakistan	0,5%

Source: World Bank 2008 and WHO 2008

Figure 12.2. **Rapid Economic Growth, 1995-2005**

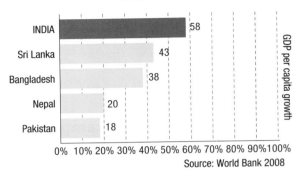

Source: World Bank 2008

Figure 12.3. **Decrease in Under-Five Mortality Rates, 1995-2005**

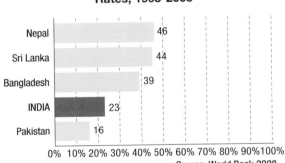

Source: World Bank 2008

Figure 12.4. **Gender Disparity in School Attendance**

Proportion of female to male children of primary school age who are out of school, 2005

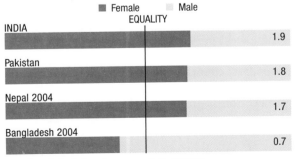

Note: Data indicate females as a multiple of males.
Source: UNESCO, 2008.

Figure 12.5. **Less Investment on Primary Education – The Cost for Education Quality**

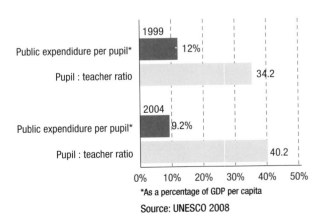

*As a percentage of GDP per capita
Source: UNESCO 2008

Box 12.5. **Formulating relevant questions on states' accountability**

Evidence-based analysis of key issues related to the rights to education and health in India led CESR to suggest the UN Committee on Economic, Social and Cultural Rights to address the following questions to the government of this state party:

On little public investment in health:
- What accounts for the high rate of child mortality in India?
- Why does India have such a low commitment to public spending on health, when it has a high rate of child mortality?
- In light of such low spending on health—proportionally lower than many countries that are significantly poorer (per capita) than India - how does the state party demonstrate that every effort has been made to use all resources at its disposition in an effort to satisfy, as a matter of priority, its minimum obligations regarding the right to health?

On slow reduction in child mortality:
- Why has the rate of decline in child mortality been so slow in India compared to poorer neighbouring countries such as Bangladesh and Nepal, especially when contrasted with its impressive economic growth?
- How is this slow reduction in the child mortality rate, especially during a period of economic windfall, compatible with India's duty, as a state party to the *Covenant*, to progressively realise the right to the highest attainable standard of physical and mental health?

On gender disparity in school attendance:
- Why is the rate of primary school age girls who are out of school much higher than the rate of primary school age boys out of school?
- How is this situation compatible with India's duty, as a state party to the *Covenant*, to ensure the equal right of men and women to the enjoyment of all economic, social and cultural rights set forth in the present *Covenant*?
- Which measures is India taking to ensure that fewer girls will be out of school?

On decreasing public investment in primary education:
- Although the increase in enrolment is to be welcomed, why has this not been accompanied by a corresponding increase in human and financial resources, to prevent a deterioration of the quality of education?
- Both the percentage of total government spending on education and the expenditure per pupil as a percentage of GDP per capita has decreased in recent years. Why is this?
- What is India planning to do to reduce the increasing pupil-teacher ratio?
- How is the current high pupil-teacher ratio and its increasingly lower expenditure on education compatible with India's duty, as a state party to the *Covenant*, to ensure quality of education for all?

---

despite far lower levels of income per capita and economic growth than India These differences matter - had India matched Bangladesh's rate of reduction in child mortality over the past decade, 732,000 fewer children would have died in 2005 (UNDP, 2005).
- **Gender disparity in school attendance.** Figure 12.4 shows that girls in India are nearly twice as likely to be out of school as boys. This represents a higher rate of gender inequality than other countries in South Asia. In 2005, there were over 4.7 million primary school age girls out of school in India (UNESCO, 2008), while 37% of "lowest caste" girls aged seven to fourteen do not attend school (compared with 26% of other Indian girls the same age). School attendance for tribal girls is 9% below that of tribal boys (Lewis and Lockheed, 2007).

- **Less public investment in primary education.** Figure 12.5 shows that from 1999 to 2004 (the most recent year for which data is available) the pupil/teacher ratio in primary schools in India increased from 35 to 40 pupils, while the public expenditure per pupil as a percentage of GDP per capita in primary schools decreased over the same period from 12% to 9.2%. This is probably the result of the welcome increase in primary enrolment rates over this period (net primary enrolment in India increased from 81percent in the year 2000 to 89% in 2005, according to 2008 World Bank figures). However, unless accompanied by a corresponding increase in human and financial resources, an increase in enrolment increases the pupil-teacher ratio, with serious consequences on the quality of education. According to UNESCO, while the impact of class size on educational outcomes remains a matter of debate, the very large class sizes observed in primary schools in many developing countries are clearly not conducive to adequate learning. In general, low pupil-teacher ratios are associated with high survival rates to the last grade of primary school (UNESCO, 2004). Although significantly increasing the number of teachers in the school system obviously has budgetary implications, India has decreased, as shown in Figure 12.5, its expenditures on primary school education per student (as a percentage of its GDP per capita). Furthermore, public spending on education also decreased from 13% of total government expenditure in 1999 to 11% in 2003 (World Bank, 2008).

These findings have obvious significance in terms economic and social rights and India's obligations to provide these rights. Box 12.5 summarises the questions that CESR suggested the Committee pose to India on these specific issues.

These fact sheets are just one example that concrete progress can be made in measuring economic and social rights and in using such measurement for influencing policy dialogue and policy-making. The response to CESR's emerging approach from human rights advocates, development economists, and other social scientists has been overwhelmingly positive. Experts consulted believe that is precisely the type of work that the human rights movement should be doing in order to adopt the "measurement revolution" that has been underway in the fields of development and governance.

As it is developed, tested and refined, CESR's innovative approach could resonate well beyond the organisation's own work. For example: other NGOs could adopt it for monitoring and advocacy on a range of issues; the UN Committee on Economic, Social and Cultural Rights, and other UN treaty bodies, could use it to promote more substantive dialogue with countries that claim not to have enough resources to address an issue; and public interest legal advocates could make use of this sophisticated methodology in national and regional courts to enforce economic and social rights.

Even in the early stages of this new methodology, local NGOs and advocates have emphasised the importance it could have for their own work. For instance, Mahama Ayariga, Chairperson of the Ghana Legal Resources Centre in Ghana and a member of Parliament, wrote: *"I believe that the methodology CESR is developing could have tremendous benefits to the work we are engaged with on the ground. I realise that the process of integrating development economics and other social sciences to a human rights analysis will require time and skill, but I think this cutting edge work is desperately needed"* (for other expressions of support for CESR's methodology, see http://cesr.org/about/methodology/support).

Chapter 13

Capacity Development for Assessing Democratic Governance: a UNDP Global Programme

Reflecting the critical outcome of the Millennium Declaration and the World Summit 2005 which highlighted democratic governance as a requirement for inclusive development and the achievement of the Millennium Development Goals, countries are increasingly pressed to assess and measure their progress towards democratic governance as both end and means. As a direct effect of this encouraging trend, UNDP Country Offices register a rising demand to assist national counterparts develop their capacity to engage in nationally owned and driven democratic governance assessments.

In response, capacity development for country-led governance assessments and measurements are a priority in UNDP strategic plan for 2008-2011, and they are also a flagship support area for the UNDP Democratic Governance Group and its Oslo Governance Centre. The Centre has been supporting national initiatives for monitoring and measuring governance focused on the development of national governance indicators since 2003.

The *Global Programme on Capacity Development for Democratic Governance Assessments and Measurements* addresses the need to better understand various methods and approaches to assess and measure democratic governance and its links to pro-poor planning, budgeting, and delivery of the MDGs. Operationalised through country, regional and global level windows, the *Global Programme* thus provides a comprehensive response to related concerns and demands among national partners and develops an effective agenda for targeted support in this area.

This chapter was contributed by the **UNDP Oslo Governance Centre** and authored by

Noha El-Mikawy, Marie Laberge, Joachim Nahem, Ingvild Oia and *Alexandra Wilde*

The UNDP Oslo Governance Centre was established in 2002 as part of the UNDP's global policy network for democratic governance. Its main objective is to promote principles of democratic governance that are critical for meeting the Millennium Development Goals. The Centre is part of the Democratic Governance Group of UNDP's Bureau of Development Policy. It facilitates knowledge sharing and networking on democratic governance, and provides policy guidance and technical support to UNDP Country Offices around the world. See: http://www.undp.org/oslocentre/

Evolving approaches to democratic governance assessment

Democratic governance is central to human development in general and the achievement of the Millennium Development Goals, providing in particular the "enabling environment" for reducing poverty. The critical importance of democratic governance in the developing world was highlighted at the Millennium Summit of 2000, where the world's leaders resolved to "*spare no effort to promote democracy and strengthen the rule of law, as well as respect for all internationally recognized human rights and fundamental freedoms*". The Summit reached a consensus that improving the quality of democratic institutions and processes, and managing the changing roles of the state and civil society in an increasingly globalised world, must underpin efforts to reduce poverty and promote human development (see UNO, 2000).

An increasing number of organisations are giving greater priority to the need to assess democracy, governance and human rights as part of their development assistance programmes. Assessment tools, frameworks and global datasets enable comparisons over time and across countries and regions. However, while this data is a rich source of information for a range of analyses, it does not necessarily point to particular institutions or institutional arrangements as the cause of governance challenges, nor does it help identify appropriate operational solutions and performance improvement processes. It can thus be of only limited help in policy-making processes.

Furthermore, donor assessment tools and global databases often lack national ownership and engagement in the assessment process and rarely include the necessary elements of disaggregation to capture the impact, experiences and perceptions of marginalised, vulnerable and discriminated people in society, especially the poor and women. Such assessment tools also do not identify the capacity deficits that exist and how to address these if improvements are to be made and effectively monitored.

Most assessments to date serve a muddled list of purposes:

- Taking stock of the wider political economic context of governance;
- Identifying democratic deficits of governance;
- Understanding the factors and drivers of policy reform;
- Providing governments with a tool for further democratisation;
- Providing donors with a tool for governance performance-based aid allocation;
- Providing a tool for advocacy and civic engagement by facilitating domestic debate;
- Designing, monitoring and evaluating progress of development.

The 2005 *Paris Declaration on Aid Effectiveness* has changed the parameters by which governance is to be assessed in at least three identifiable ways: through a shift from external to local or national assessments; through relying less on international experts and more on national institutions and local expertise; through the adoption of a more political, rather than a managerial approach (see OECD, 2005). Thus, the *Paris Declaration* has had major implications for the work of UNDP and other development actors as it requires development assistance to be aligned with priorities and needs as expressed in national development plans, and to focus on strengthening capacities.

Over the last decade, UNDP has gradually shifted its policy and programming support on governance from a traditional emphasis on public administration reform to a broader agenda of democratic governance for human development which entails fostering inclusive participation, building accountable and responsive state capacity and advocating and integrating well established international principles of human rights and gender equality into the technical and policy support that UNDP provides to national partners. UNDP emerging approach to democratic governance assessments is meant to support its understanding of democratic governance as anchored in the 2008-2011 strategic plan.

A new challenge for National Statistical Offices and other domestic actors

There is an explosive growth in the production and use of governance "indicators" by domestic stakeholders, including state and non-state actors in developing countries, as well as international investors, donors of official development assistance, development analysts and academics. New global standards of democratic governance are emerging. Citizens of developing countries are demanding better performance from governments, and they are increasingly aware of the costs of poor management and corruption. Furthermore, scarce resources, especially resources from external donors, are increasingly being allocated to governments that will use them most effectively, and countries are asking for help in diagnosing governance failures and in finding solutions.

The role of National Statistical Offices (NSOs) in governance assessment and monitoring has increasingly been debated and explored in recent years. Many official statisticians have shied away from generating and disseminating indicators on democratic governance for various reasons, including principally for lack of existing data, a perceived and real lack of experience in this field and in some countries because of the potential sensitivity of such an undertaking.

There are currently multiple initiatives addressing national statistical capacity through national statistical development strategies, *e.g.* PARIS21, Marrakech Action Plan for Statistics, and Regional Strategic Framework for Statistical Capacity Building in Africa. The objective is to enhance country data systems, statistical methodological rigor and analytical capacity. Within that context, it is apt to consider NSOs as likely anchor institutions for governance measurement and indicators (see *Chapter 9*).

Official statistics are vital to public policy and to the democratic process itself. The range of official statistics, including in the field of democratic governance and the ways in which they are used have become increasingly important. For example, there is a growing use in developed and developing countries of statistical performance indicators. NSOs have an important contribution to make to both producing and co-ordinating the production of governance statistics and in working with others to investigate the most appropriate choice of indicators, their compilation and the setting of realistic targets for future performance that are challenging and susceptible to realistic policy intervention.

However, there are other national and sub-national actors alongside statistical offices who contribute to the evidence base on governance, producing and disseminating non-quantitative evidence using qualitative and participative methods. The challenge is to triangulate evidence and bring together official statisticians with other in-country producers and users of evidence in order to better address trends and respond to societal needs.

National and regional on-going efforts

Countries' willingness and interest to use and develop governance indicators is catalysed by different sets of circumstances. The following are a few examples:

- **Mongolia** is a case where a 9th Millennium Development Goal on human rights, anti-corruption and democracy has been adopted at the national level. This pioneering MDG-9 initiative was developed out of the hosting of an International Conference on New and Restored Democracies

(ICNRD, which is a process that, unlike the Community of Democracies, is open to all UN member states and has encouraged countries to develop their own databases on governance indicators). A phase of institutionalisation of the MDG-9 analysis and linkage thereof to national plans is now to be explored (see a brief outline of the Mongolia case in Box 13.1, at the end of this chapter).

- **Zambia** is a case where a Governance Secretariat has been set up in the Ministry of Justice to monitor and evaluate the implementation of the governance commitments made in the 5th National Development Plan at a time when the country's governance is being assessed from the outside with national stakeholder involvement/co-ordination.
- **Malawi** is a case in which numerous donors are conducting governance assessments (*e.g.* Millennium Challenge Account, World Bank, a group of donors monitoring the conditions for Direct Budget Support and a number of bilateral donor initiatives). This has resulted in a huge drain on the capacities of national partners, duplication in data collection and a lack of national participation and ownership.

On a continent-wide basis, Africa is pioneering a peer review mechanism that includes an assessment of countries' democratic governance based on in-country reports. The Africa Peer Review Mechanism (APRM) has triggered the process of nationally owned democratic governance assessments which holds potential for enhancing capacity development in the future. UNDP has been very much engaged in supporting the APRM initiative, primarily through the Regional Bureau for Africa.

Countries of various sizes and political economic legacies, but with a common claim to successful economic performance, question how to combine governance measures with development measures, how to benchmark institutional progress towards democratic governance and monitor its economic and political risks and rewards (*e.g.* Tunisia and China).

In this context, four challenges arise at the country level:

- **conceptual** challenge for countries to arrive at a definition of governance for the purposes of measuring the quality of it and monitoring changes to it;
- **political** challenge for countries to arrive at a consensus over what "ownership" of governance assessments means and its implications;
- **institutional** challenge related to who is to undertake governance assessments; and finally
- **operational** challenge related to the guiding principles of governance assessments.

In the latter case the issue is one of choosing one's approach to be parsimonious or holistic, analytical or catalytic for activism, methodologically cumulative or inventive, relying on secondary or primary data, costly or cost effective, etc.

Most governance assessments to date have not adequately resolved these challenges. Furthermore, it is still pre-mature to know how and if the peer review assessments undertaken in Africa have been able to respond adequately to these challenges

UNDP and democratic governance assessments

A *Global Programme* which distils acquired knowledge on the aforementioned challenges, documents country experiences and develops tools to assist national capacity development would fill a sizeable void. There are few organisations that have a remit or an expertise in this area. UNDP is one of those very few organisations that have prioritised developing the capacities of national actors to measure and monitor the quality of governance as a critical support area in its governance programmes.

UNDP strategic plan constitutes a multi-year funding framework – a compact among donors, host governments and UNDP to implement results-oriented programmes at the country, regional and global levels. The UNDP strategic plan of 2008-2011 makes capacity development one of the drivers of development and a corporate principle. The strategic plan also makes enhancing national capacity for governance assessments a corporate strategic initiative on which UNDP commits to deliver. The first indicative activity for such commitment is planned in 2008 to explore a common understanding on governance assessments among UNDP and UN agencies.

During 2006, 134 UNDP Country Offices were engaged in supporting governance programmes. UNDP's comparative advantage in the provision of support for democratic governance cooperation is due to the organisation being viewed as a neutral but principled and committed partner working to apply internationally agreed norms and standards to nationally determined policies and programmes, rather than seeking to impose arbitrary conditionality. Therefore, UNDP is often invited to play an important co-ordination and resource mobilisation role on sensitive democratic governance issues including on measuring and assessing governance. To further strengthen this niche, in 2001, the Democratic Governance Thematic Trust Fund was established as a new instrument to address UNDP's development priorities. The democratic governance work of UNDP is further supported by the Democratic Governance Practice network and the Oslo Governance Centre.

For UNDP, the value of a nationally owned governance indicator system is that it serves as a critical accountability mechanism for local stakeholders, especially the citizens of a country and non-state actors, rather than donors. A nationally owned governance assessment provides upward internal rather than external pressure for reform. And through the transparency of information stemming from it, it also provides a catalyst for greater citizen engagement in democracy processes and for demanding greater effectiveness of governance actors. As part of UNDP assistance to supporting democratic governance in the countries in which we work, Governance Indicators provide support to nationally owned processes for assessing and monitoring democratic governance within those countries.

Research, policy development and advisory support on governance assessments have been flagship activities of the UNDP Oslo Governance Centre since 2003. For the last five years, UNDP through its Oslo Governance Centre and in partnership with selected country offices and UNDP Regional Service Centres, has been developing tools and providing support to national partners wanting to assess the quality of democratic governance in their countries (see UNDP, 2008).

Technical support and 'seed' financial assistance to catalyse national assessment processes have been provided to more than 15 countries in most regions including Mongolia, Malawi, Tunisia, Egypt, Zambia, Afghanistan and the Philippines. The Africa Peer Review Mechanism (APRM) and the International Conference on New and Restored Democracies (ICNRD) are important entry points for UNDP to provide assistance. UNDP, for example, has actively been supporting Mongolia's follow-up of the ICNRD–5 in 2003 by providing technical support and expertise to the development of a national democratic governance indicator system (see ICNRD, 2003).UNDP has held a number of international events and workshops bringing together a wide array of national actors, experts and donor community practitioners on the technical dimensions and policy implications of governance assessments and their impact on national ownership. UNDP has also facilitated workshops to enhance national capacity development in Mongolia (see Box 13.1), Philippines, Malawi, Tunisia, Egypt and China in cooperation with UNDP country offices, national statistical bureaus, ministries and research centres in those countries.

In 2007, a training workshop on governance indicators was held for over 50 country office staff and national counterparts to present methods of developing governance indicators, assessing data ownership and sources, data quality, uses and impact on development. Also in 2007, over 80 UN senior management and bilateral donors were brought together in a seminar on governance assessments, to discuss with national counterparts the different experiences in participative nationally driven governance assessments (see UNDP and CMI, 2007).

The Oslo Governance Centre also responds to queries on the UNDP knowledge networks and direct requests for technical assistance on integrated poverty and governance measurement methods and tools. UNDP has also produced various publications mapping sources and methods of governance assessments as well as policy and programmatic guidance on gender and poverty sensitive democratic governance assessments (see Eurostat and UNDP, 2004; UNDP, 2005a, 2005b, 2005c, 2006a, 2006b).

The Democratic Governance Group's (DGG) and its various thematic areas will continue to inform and strengthen the work on governance assessments. Knowledge products from the various DGG thematic areas (parliamentary development, electoral systems and processes, justice and human rights, e-governance and access to information, decentralisation and local governance, public administration reform and anti-corruption) will also support future training and capacity development as set forth in this *Global Programme*.

Focus on nationally owned processes

For UNDP, governance assessments are most effective as a tool to bring about better democratic governance when they are grounded in nationally owned processes, are based on nationally and locally developed indicators and are designed with policy makers and policy reform in mind. In this regard, assessments that are disaggregated to show differences within countries across geographic areas and across social economic categories will help to make governance reforms more sensitive to poverty and gender issues and to the needs of vulnerable groups.

UNDP has a distinct approach to democratic governance assessments and indicators that emphasises (1) national ownership, (2) capacity development and (3) harmonisation with national development planning instruments:

- **National ownership** – governance assessments and the development of governance indicators need to be nationally owned which is achieved through an inclusive and consultative process involving government, civil society, elected representatives, and other key stakeholders about what should be assessed and how.
- **Capacity development** – governance assessments are a critical entry point and opportunity for developing the capacities of national stakeholders (including statistical offices, government and civil society) in the production and application of governance related data. This entails support to national and local participative processes of assessing and monitoring governance with a focus on building national and local capacities to collect, analyse, and share governance data.
- **Harmonisation** – nationally-owned governance assessments and monitoring systems, as well as sector specific plans, must be harmonised and aligned with national development plans and related instruments where relevant, such as the PRSPs, MDG progress reports and local development plans.

Competitive advantage

UNDP's comparative advantage in promoting and nurturing nationally owned governance assessments derives from its position as the lead UN agency on democratic governance, its focus on long term capacity development, its expertise and experience base on democratic governance, its experience with human development indicators through the *National Human Development Reports*, its engagement in MDG monitoring, and importantly the trust it enjoys among UN member states. In particular, UNDP has proven strengths in the following areas:

- Facilitating and convening of national dialogues involving state and non-state stakeholders on national democracy and democratic governance assessments.
- Encouraging and facilitating through its relationship with government, efforts to harmonise multiple governance assessments within a country.
- Helping ensure that democratic governance assessments are linked with national development.
- Providing support to the undertaking of capacity assessments and identifying what parts of the capacity development cycle need to be strengthened. This should focus on both state and non state actors in governance data collection and governance data analysis.
- Brokering knowledge through electronic networks, facilitating country-transfer of knowledge, identifying lessons learned and best practices, and building communities of practice.

Scaling up support to nationally driven assessments

Understanding progress, clarifying the relevance of democratic governance for inclusive development and enhancing domestic accountability are some key positive effects of nationally driven assessments and measurements of democratic governance especially when the process by which assessments are conducted and measurements are developed is transparent, participative and sustainable over time. However, some challenges with respect to assessments and measurements require attention.

A recent Nils Boesen *Survey of Donor Approaches to Governance Assessment* describes 38 different governance assessment tools being used by selected bilateral and multilateral donor institutions (see OECD, 2008). With such a proliferation of donor led governance assessments there is an increasing need to address the problem of duplication and overlap in aid disbursement which puts the burden on already strained developing country capacities. Although it is unlikely that a single unifying OECD/DAC-endorsed assessment methodology is either feasible or desirable, improved harmonisation and closer working on governance assessments are needed. A set of governance indicators agreed to by national stakeholders and institutionalised within the country, provides an initial basis for donors to harmonise their governance assessments and at the least draw on locally produced data. One set of data collected nationally to feed into these assessments will strengthen countries ability to respond and engage with donors, harmonise data collection and improve the evidence base for national as well as donor assessments.

There is a growing awareness amongst donors of the need to enhance local participation and ownership of governance assessment processes. National ownership of assessments is not a zero sum game, but rather a continuum. Some donors are promoting a more national based assessment approach including prioritising the use of local data that is available in the public domain to avoid new research and encourage triangulation of information from various local sources. For UNDP, national ownership goes beyond that to include locally driven, deliberative processes of rigorous data collection and analysis and locally driven, institutionalised systems of bringing evidence into policy. Moreover, as for the Metagora initiative presented in the first part of this publication, for UNDP the processes of developing governance indicators are as important as the governance indicators themselves. An assessment process that respects the democratic principles of transparency, inclusiveness, accountability and equality can be an effective tool for bringing about better democratic governance.

With respect to measurements and indicators, a real problem that many developing countries face is a lack of reliable data on key governance issues. They have limited capacity to rigorously define indicators, collect and interpret data. Existing indicators often provide inadequate measures for assessing changes in governance or for formulating and implementing reforms in specific countries. Indicators that are sensitive to country context would help provide countries with:

- Information for assessing key governance challenges
- Information and ideas for institutional reform
- More reliable, systematic and nuanced data for specific policy initiatives
- Greater capacity to track changes in governance over time
- Disaggregated evidence for advocacy efforts
- Participative agenda-setting processes

The field of governance indicators is new and in its infancy compared to the level of maturity of socio-economic indicators. Compared to the limited international standardisation in the use of governance indicators, knowledge related to developing and using governance indicators at the national level is very rudimentary especially in terms of how governance indicators and variables should be defined and how the capacities of national statistical systems and participative processes can be developed to work with governance indicators in order to support country-led governance assessments.

Civic engagement has the potential to expand the knowledge base in any society by havingNGOs, a professional media, academic institutions and think tanks collect and analyse a wide range of information about governance, unmet needs and unheard concerns. Evidence based policy, however, often relies primarily on official data. There is a need to make governance policy more sensitive to the perceptions of women and the poor and other marginal groups whose concerns are often not well represented in official data.

Poverty and gender sensitive governance indicators are of priority concern for UNDP and constitute also an area of considerable interest to national development partners. Governance indicators should include a focus on poorer groups in society and the different impacts and experiences that men and women have of government institutions and governance processes (see UNDP, 2006a). The ability of countries to develop pro-poor and gender-sensitive evidence bases is crucial. How best to do that, using which approaches and processes are key questions in any national governance assessment.

The *Global Programme* will seek to build on and leverage the pioneering work carried out by the community of Metagora Partners, presented in the *First Part* of this publication. Of particular relevance for the *Global Programme* are the household surveys on poverty, democratic governance and participation, conducted by eleven National Statistical Offices in Africa and Latin America with the technical support and further sound analysis of DIAL (see *Chapter 6* and DIAL, 2005). In this context, particular emphasis will be given to the enhancement of national statistical capacities. This work will benefit from PARIS21 which supports National Strategies for the Development of Statistics (NSDS; see PARIS21, 2004, 2006, 2007).

The number of countries that have requested support from UNDP for assistance in developing governance indicators and indicators that can be disaggregated has been steadily increasing: it grew from three requests in 2003 to 40 requests in 2007. The latter consist of requests for policy and technical support made directly to the Oslo Governance Centre from UNDP Country Offices on behalf of national partners as well as proposals submitted for funding under the UNDP Democratic Governance Thematic Trust Fund and the UN Democracy Fund.

Strategy and objectives of the Global Programme

Recognising the need for more meaningful and operational tools for assessing governance, the *Global Programme* ultimately aims **to strengthen the capacities of national actors (both state and non-state) to develop and apply methods and approaches for measuring and monitoring governance**. The total budget of the *Global Programme* is approximately ten million US dollars.

A rights-based approach

The strategy of the *Global Programme* is anchored in a rights-based approach. The favoured UNDP approach to nationally led democratic governance assessments – which the *Global Programme* is meant to support- emphasises methods and processes that foster capacity of state and society institutions alike; such an approach enhances the provision of disaggregated governance evidence that captures discriminatory effects and thus helps in advocacy for inclusive, responsive policy. The UNDP approach to nationally driven democratic governance assessments/measurements is meant to foster domestic accountability of the state through transparency, participative, inclusive and non discriminatory methods and processes of data collection, analysis and uptake into policy.

Windows and outcomes

The *Global Programme* intends to approach capacity development with a holistic strategy which goes beyond the provision of training. As initiatives of capacity development in various fields have demonstrated, building communities of practice and enhancing peer-learning tend to be effective mechanisms of capacity development. The *Global Programme* will do that among the country beneficiaries as well as among regions and at the global level. Indeed, the *Global Programme* will be operationalised through **three windows**:

- **Country level window** which includes financing for four activities within 10 target countries: (1) mapping existing governance indicators; (2) developing governance assessment frameworks; (3) collecting data; and (4) developing governance databases and applying governance indicators to development plans.
- **Regional level window** which includes financing for three activities: (1) regional based training; (2) developing regional specific knowledge products; and (3) regional conferences.
- **Global level window** which includes financing for three activities: (1) knowledge services; (2) capacity development; and (3) policy development and advocacy.

The *Global Programme* strategy is designed to contribute to **six principal outcomes**:

- Increased transparency about the overall national democratic governance situation and increased government accountability for the quality of democratic governance in the country.
- Enhanced capacities of the national statistical system, academia and research institutes in using governance indicators.
- Increased uptake of governance indicators in policy making processes.
- Improved global awareness and knowledge on governance measurement methods and approaches.
- Improved harmonisation of national and international donors based on nationally produced governance assessments.
- Increased capacities of UNDP to facilitate and provide technical and advisory support for national partners.

Objectives and action at the country level

The country level window of the *Global Programme* has four objectives:

- Enhance **national ownership** through facilitating multi-stakeholder engagement on governance measurement and monitoring.
- Support **capacity development** initiatives focused on defining and selecting governance indicators and data collection.
- Promote the **sustainability** of national governance monitoring through supporting the development of a governance database and facilitating its institutionalisation.
- Increase the **policy relevancy** of governance indicators by promoting and supporting processes and methods that (i) enable country contextualisation and (ii) increase the uptake and use of governance indicators in policy-making processes.

These objectives will be met through the provision of support for four activities: (1) mapping existing governance indicators; (2) developing governance assessment frameworks; (3) collecting data; and (4) developing governance databases and using governance indicators.

The country level window is expected to directly support activities in **at least ten countries** over the four-year period beginning in 2008. The selection of beneficiary countries will be decided on by UNDP Oslo Governance Centre, Regional Bureaux and Centres. Important criteria for selecting countries include:

- The government's commitment to actively support an inclusive and participatory governance assessment initiative.
- Countries that have Least Developed Country status, especially those from the Sub-Saharan Africa and Asia-Pacific regions. This category of countries should be prioritised.
- Existing UNDP support to governance assessments initiatives in the country *i.e.* through an existing UNDP supported governance programme or through a project supported by the UNDP Democratic Governance Thematic Trust Fund (see www.undp.org/governance/ttf.htm).
- The timing of a governance indicators initiative, for example, in relation to important political events taking place in the country.
- Existing and future pilot countries in the *Delivering as One* pilot initiative. The volunteering pilot countries of this initiative currently include: Albania, Cape Verde, Mozambique, Pakistan, Rwanda, Tanzania, Uruguay and Viet Nam. The *Global Programme* should include at least one of these pilot countries.
- The level of democratic development in the country (*i.e.* the *Global Programme* should target a mix of mature democracies and democratic transitioning countries).

For the selection process an invitation of becoming a beneficiary country of the *Global Programme* will be sent to Country Offices. Final selection of countries by the Project Board, in consultation with the Consultative Group, will be based on relevant factors demonstrated by Country Offices in consideration of the criteria listed above. It should be noted that interested countries which would not be selected could still be eligible to be supported through the regional and global windows.

Objectives and action at the regional level

The regional window will evolve and will be developed in close cooperation with UNDP Regional Bureaux/ and Centres and their regional partners. It has **two primary objectives**:

- Enhance understanding of nationally driven governance assessments within the regions through regional training events and regional conferences.

- Produce knowledge products responsive to regional priorities and contexts.

The regional window will focus on **three activities**:

- Regional based training
- Developing regional specific knowledge products
- Regional conferences.

The *Global Programme* will aspire to engage - for the delivery on these objectives - with regional think tanks and NGOs that are active in the field of assessments and measurement of various areas of democratic governance. The UNDP Oslo Governance Centre has established linkage to several such institutions, *e.g.* in India, Philippines, Mongolia, Ghana and South Africa. In order to further enhance ownership and sustainability, capacity development of regional institutions will be considered under this regional window. Within this window, a strategy for partnership building with clear criteria on types of institutions to partner with will be developed in cooperation with regional centres.

The *Global Programme* will have two regional programme officers housed by UNDP Regional Centres (locality to be determined) in the second, third and fourth years of the *Programme* as demand increases. The first year of the *Programme* will be mainly engaging in advocacy in co-ordination with the regional centres to establish demand in UNDP offices, develop regional knowledge products and capacity development tools.

Objectives and action at the global level

The global window has **four main objectives**:

- Establish and maintain a high quality and dynamic depository of knowledge on governance indicators and governance assessment for access/use by national/international organisations.
- Develop knowledge products (primers, guidance notes, discussion papers) on priority governance measurement/assessment themes including on sector-based governance assessments *e.g.* water sector, health sector, education sector.
- Develop and make available a menu of capacity development services including training that is tailored to individual country needs.
- Produce research and policy recommendations for a global audience of development practitioners including international agencies, academia, and international organisations on nationally-owned governance assessments.

The *Global Programme* will benefit from and build upon a network of global partners such as the OECD-DAC, the North/South community of Partners of the Metagora project, International IDEA, DIAL, Global Integrity, Global Barometer, Institute of Development Studies, World Bank Institute, the World Governance Assessment etc. This will form the basis for a south-south network to enhance exchange of knowledge and capacity development.

Building on partnership bases

UNDP has prioritised partnership building on governance assessments and measurement. This is crucially important because UNDP does not have the capacity or the specific technical expertise to be able to provide national partners with the resources that they want. Partnerships have been developed in all dimensions of governance assessment support i.e. research, policy development, advocacy, and implementation. The *Global Programme* will provide a much stronger basis for developing new partnerships, focusing in particular on identifying and supporting potential partners in developing countries as well as prioritising partnerships with regional organisations.

The modalities for establishing and maintaining partnerships that support in-country assessment efforts have been flexible in nature without needing to enter into a formal Memorandum of Understanding. This flexibility enables UNDP to choose partners that are more responsive and in-tune with the country and regional setting in terms of linguistic capabilities, regional experience, familiarity with the governance issues of the county etc. At the global level, and in the area of policy development and advocacy, UNDP has worked especially closely with the International Institute for Democracy and Electoral Assistance (IDEA) and the Metagora project, which comprises a strong network of organisations and leading experts in developing countries, and shares UNDP views on the approach, purpose and ways to measure and assess democratic governance.

Box 13.1. **A case study: Assessing the state of democratic governance in Mongolia**

Beginning in 2004, the Government of Mongolia with assistance from UNDP embarked on a process of conducting a democratic governance assessment as a follow-up to the *Fifth International Conference of New or Restored Democracies* (ICNRD-5) which was hosted in Mongolia in 2003.

The Mongolian assessment was a full-scale and comprehensive process that included consultations with civil society, country contextualisation of methodology, capacity development of local research institutions and political institutionalisation of governance indicators.

Approximately 130 indicators were developed, including a set of satellite indicators designed to capture the national characteristics of democratic governance in Mongolia. The first round of results was published in 2006 and provided a legitimate evidence base to formulate a National Plan of Action to Consolidate Democracy in Mongolia (see Mongolia Government and UNDP, 2006). This Plan of Action identified the most urgent governance challenges and the reforms needed to overcome them. After extensive national consultations around the assessment results and the proposed Plan of Action, it was formally adopted by the Mongolian Parliament.

The selection of indicators in Mongolia was the result of a highly participatory process led by the Government and an independent research team, and supported by UNDP. Consultative meetings with international experts (such as International IDEA, Human Rights Centre at the University of Essex, UK and the Centre for the Study of Developing Societies, New Delhi) also played an important role in refining the conceptual framework for the assessment and the methodology for collecting data.

In addition to strong media coverage and numerous awareness-raising events, the highly participatory Mongolian assessment methodology included the following components:

- Over 100 participants of a national conference on *Democracy in Mongolia - Challenges and Opportunities* were interviewed to clarify key issues related to the research;
- Over 1000 citizens in 6 *aimags* and 6 districts of Ulaanbaatar were given a governance questionnaire;
- 36 focus group discussions were held and 12 free dialogues for data collection were organised in 6 aimags and 6 districts;
- The questionnaire used for surveying public opinion was also used to study and compare the opinion of parliament members.
- Other methodologies used included UN-Habitat's *Urban Governance Index* (to measure the quality of urban governance in Mongolia's capital, with a particular focus on the urban poor) and a *Civil Society Index* based on a methodology developed by CIVICUS.

"Satellite" indicators reflecting Mongolia's specificities along with "core" indicators reflecting the general attributes of democratic governance (drawn from the IDEA's State of Democracy Assessment framework) have become an important methodological novelty of the Mongolian Assessment. Satellite indicators, for instance, were developed to account for the predominant importance of social relations, traditions and customs over the rule of law in Mongolian society, given the country's small and partially nomadic population unevenly dispersed over a large territory.

One method used to ensure that the governance assessment would be pro-poor and gender sensitive was the use of focus group discussions with vulnerable subsets of the population, including herders, gold diggers ("ninjas"), migrants, unemployed men and women, etc.

The second phase of the project (2007-2008) aimed to institutionalise the Democratic Governance Indicators (for enhancing the evidence base for policy-making.

Indicators are means rather than an end, and they will be useful as a tool for promoting governance reforms only to the extent that are well-embedded in a country's long-term political process.

In this context, a subset of the 130 Democratic Governance Indicators were selected by the local research institute, in consultation with various stakeholders, and approved by the Parliament to **measure progress in achieving a 9th Millennium Development Goal adopted by the Mongolian government on human rights, anti-corruption and democracy** (this MDG-9 has 3 targets and 12 indicators).

The institutionalisation of an independent monitoring and reporting system on the implementation of MDG 9 points to the real impact of the governance assessment on democratic governance in Mongolia: the opening of formal channels to direct assessment results in national policy-making processes in a systematic and sustainable manner. The results compiled by this monitoring system are also published in a chapter on MDG-9 in the statistical yearbook prepared by the National Statistical Office, and are shared and discussed in nation-wide dialogues on MDG 9-related issues.

The democratic governance assessment in Mongolia can make a significant contribution towards consolidating democracy and developing a culture of evidence-based decision-making. The bottom-up approach adopted by the national Steering Committee ensured that public opinion from diverse social groups would be reflected throughout the assessment process. Finally, the several national consultations and the active involvement of the local media were very effective in raising public awareness on governance issues. Such transparency and inclusiveness in the assessment process will make it possible for Mongolia's governance indicator system to perform its most important function: to serve as a critical accountability mechanism for local stakeholders, especially for marginalised groups, and to provide upward internal rather than external pressure for reform.

Since 2004, significant synergies were developed between the UNDP Oslo Governance Centre and Metagora. As this project is now being steered towards its conclusion, it has been agreed that all relevant materials, documentation and resources generated by Metagora - including in particular the *Inventory of Initiatives* and the *Training Materials* (see *Chapter 9*) - be handed over to the Centre. Moreover, the UNDP *Global Programme* will actively work with the network of Metagora Partners. The chairperson and the general co-ordinator of Metagora will be part of the consultative group of the *Global Programme*, and the various project Partners will be invited to join a broad knowledge network: the Community of Practice on Governance Assessments and Measurements.

The *Global Programme* will place a premium on fostering south-south partnerships where national stakeholders and actors can share knowledge and experiences on governance assessments. It will build on the existing network of the Oslo Governance Centre, *e.g.* in Mongolia, Zambia, Malawi, Ghana, Philippines, India, South Africa, Egypt, China, Paraguay.

Regional partnerships including the New Partnership for Africa's Development (NEPAD) and its Africa Peer Review Mechanism will be important for the *Global Programme* especially at the country level (*i.e.* linking governance assessments to national APRM secretariats in Africa). Considering the centrality of governance assessments and indicators to this initiative and the countries in which they are operating, the *Global Programme* will enable UNDP and its partners in the *Global Programme* to reach out and engage with the APRM more substantively.

The UN *Delivery as One* pilot initiative offers an opportunity for enhancing UN cooperation on governance assessments that will serve as a basis for joint programming on governance as well as contribute to in-country efforts to improve harmonisation of governance support where there are many active donors on governance. The *Common Country Assessments* of the United Nations Development Assistance Framework will benefit immensely from being able to draw on a nationally driven and owned governance assessment framework with indicators.

Conclusion

Eight years after the 2000 Montreux Conference on *Statistics, Development and Human Rights*, much progress has been made thanks to considerable work carried out by many actors. As the international community is celebrating the 60th anniversary of the *Universal Declaration of Human Rights*, this publication attests to effective steps towards a robust monitoring of its implementation. Indeed, the Metagora project has been a successful materialisation of the Montreux North/South commitment to enhance national capacities to apply proper methods and tools in assessing human rights and democratic governance.

A fruitful partnership

Over the last four years, both the strong individual engagement of the numerous Metagora Partners and their efficient collective work within the Partners Group – the true engine of the project – have been determinant for ensuring the quality and timeliness of planned results, analysis and reports. Thanks to this, the project was able to deliver, within a tight schedule, **six types of products:**

- **documented multidisciplinary and participatory working methods** for integrating well-established quantitative methods and proper qualitative approaches;
- **measurement tools and methodologies**, including data collection techniques, survey-based assessments, and dynamic databases;
- **selected examples of good practices** of evidence-based assessment of human rights and democratic governance;
- **examples of relevant information and indicators on key national issues and policies**, which empower the analysis and concrete action of policy makers, parliamentarians, civil society, human rights defenders and other actors of change;
- **national policy-oriented reports** that, based on the information collected and analysed, highlight the relevance of assessments' findings and have been instrumental for enhancing democratic dialogue and evidence-based policy-making;
- **online resources**, including a substantive set of *Training Materials* and a worldwide *Inventory of Initiatives Aimed at Enhancing Evidence-based Assessment of Human Rights and Democratic Governance* (both available at: www.metagora.org).

A tangible impact

Through these products Metagora has had a tangible impact in the field. Various chapters of this publication have highlighted how human rights champions, committed stakeholders and policy actors are using the tools generated by the project to take policy action aimed at improving the situation of human rights and democratic governance in their countries. This publication has also shown that the original bottom-up approach of Metagora has resulted in enhanced interlinking and further empowerment of domestic actors of change.

The tools and materials generated by the project are creating common ground among national stakeholders and policy makers on the conditions and opportunities for developing solid evidence-based monitoring tools. Also, as it has been mentioned, in some countries household surveys on democratic participation and governance issues – conducted by National Statistical Offices – are now being institutionalised as routine tools and are therefore generating time series that shall soon serve as a basis for true monitoring of progress.

An encouraging independent assessment

To guarantee the rigour and robustness of the methods and tools generated by Metagora – and in line with one of the main *Conclusions* of Montreux concerning the principle of scientific transparency and the need for external supervision –, the implementation and results of the project have been scrutinised in-depth by a panel of senior experts who worked with strict independence from both the steering and implementing bodies of the project. This Independent Panel of Experts (IPE) delivered an *Assessment Report*, in which it stresses, *inter alia*, that:

"Metagora has made a major contribution in showing, through its various pilot experiences, that measuring human rights, democracy and governance is technically feasible and policy-oriented. (…) The IPE appreciated the remarkable progress accomplished by Metagora in a very short time, including the rich body of important and useful substantive results produced by several of the national pilot projects and (…) the impressive capacity gained by the project to generate tools that are informative, rigorous, innovative and useful. (…) The original multidisciplinary approach and the synergies among official and academic statisticians, human rights practitioners, social and political scientists and other stakeholders constitute a considerable value-added of the project" (see full text of this Report in *Appendix 6*).

A strategic reflection on next steps

On the strength of these achievements, as well as the many perspectives opened by the project (see *Chapter 9*), the Metagora Partners were ready to deepen the project's lessons, and expand the methods and tools. The IPE itself strongly recommended that the community of donors back the continuation and enhancement of Metagora. Some donor institutions reacted positively to this recommendation and expressed their readiness to support a new phase of the project.

In this context, the possibility of further continuing the Metagora efforts had to be assessed both in terms of the availability of the extensive funds that would be required to implement a significant number of field operations, and with regard to the strategic orientation defined since the inception of the project by the Metagora Partners Group and the Steering Committee. As affirmed on various occasions in both arenas, Metagora had no vocation to become a new institution: the project was intended to have a beginning and an end. The target goal has always been to allow institutional project Partners and relevant international organisations to inherit and further expand, by their own, the results, lessons, methods and tools generated by Metagora.

Emerging initiatives in the international arena

As the IPE notices in its *Assessment Report*, *"the Metagora community has been increasingly extending and deepening its international network, integrating new partners and promoting, through many means, dialogue and exchanges among the various actors involved in measuring human rights and democratic governance over the world"*. Indeed, over the last four years, Metagora has been strongly advocating in the international scene, enhancement of proper assessment methods. It has also facilitated exchanges among key international actors, and developed close ties of collaboration with institutions that play a leading role in monitoring human rights and assessing democratic governance. These include, for instance, the Office of the UN High Commissioner for Human Rights or the UNDP Oslo Governance Centre. Through these actions, Metagora had a significant influence on the evolving international approaches and plans in these areas.

At present, several international programmes on human rights and democratic governance assessment, with national, regional and global scopes, are being designed and shall soon be launched by well-established international organisations. Some of them – such as the UNDP *Global Programme on Democratic Governance Assessments and Measurements*, presented in *Chapter 13* of this publication – are firmly based on the bottom-up approach and the principles promoted by Metagora: domestic ownership, participation, policy focus, professional rigour and enhancement of national capacities.

Thus, as the *Second Part* of this publication has shown, the main goals targeted by Metagora are becoming central to actions planned by key international organisations that have prominent voices, efficient funding mechanisms and worldwide operational structures – such as national representative offices in most developing countries. These organisations have therefore the capacity to effectively continue the work initiated by Metagora and to closely link it with on-going major UN initiatives, policies and programmes in the fields of development, human rights, democracy and governance.

Handing the task over

In this evolving environment, the Metagora community at large – including not only its Partners but also the donor institutions and the many personalities who have been providing wise advice and strong support to the implementation of the project's pioneering work –therefore had to consider, in line with the original aim and strategy of the project, how to best serve and facilitate the enhancement of methods, tools and national capacities for measuring human rights and democratic governance.

Following a joint proposal of the Chair of the Partners Group and the Co-ordination Team, the Metagora community agreed to steer its pioneering work to a conclusion, by intensifying and accelerating the handing over of its network, products, resources and lessons to relevant organisations and emerging programmes.

Thus, at the closing of this publication, the documentation and online resources generated by the project – the *Training Materials* and the *Inventory of Initiatives* – are being transferred to the UNDP Oslo Governance Centre, which will continue to update, enrich and expand them. While Metagora comes to a conclusion, the community of organisations and individuals, which was born in Montreux and further expanded around Metagora, will continue to grow and work within the Community of Practice that will sustain the UNDP *Global Programme on Capacity Democratic Governance Assessments and Measurements*.

Commitment of national Partners

Recent and current initiatives taken by several Metagora Partners attest to their commitment and capacity to continue to play a pioneering role after the conclusion of Metagora. For instance, Fundar has found ways and means for extending to the City of Queretaro the survey-based study on abuses and ill-treatment originally implemented in Mexico City. In the Philippines, the Commission on

Human Rights has established a joint project with New Zealand to continue to explore issues related to indigenous rights. Also, the National Statistical Coordination Board of the Philippines is now regularly producing indicators of governance at sub-national level.

The institutionalisation of household surveys as a routine tool for measuring issues of governance and democratic participation is also in good way in a number of Andean and African countries – and, despite some reluctance, this new domain of official statistics will sooner or later be on the international statistical agenda. This will most probably be a medium and long term effect of Metagora efforts: a process that – while based on true national ownership – will progressively lead to a broad and firm international appropriation.

A legacy of lessons, resources and expertise to the international community

In the perspective of future developments based on the Metagora seminal efforts, it is important to record here six elements that can be of particular relevance for any emerging initiative aimed at enhancing evidence-based assessments of human rights and democratic governance.

The first resides in the need for cumulative documentation of experiences. As a matter of fact, the measurement experiences conducted within Metagora are still too few. More experiences – to be conducted under proper external scientific review – are needed to duly validate robust measurement tools. In this perspective – and as suggested by the IPE –, particular attention has to be paid to the methodological reporting of measurement experiences, including information on quality control of field work and data processing, estimates of sampling variability for all major survey estimates and analytical conclusions – as well as information on data limitations.

The second relevant element to be taken into account in future work regards the entire set of lessons learnt through Metagora. As the *Assessment report* of the IPE points out, any future action in this field *"must take into account both the achievements and the identified weaknesses of Metagora. The technical shortcomings identified by the independent review have to be duly addressed when planning, budgeting, designing and implementing activities."* The weaknesses identified by the IPE are duly documented in the *Appendix 6* of this publication and are of the highest importance for whoever will intend to engage in evidence-based assessment of human rights and democratic governance.

A third element relates to one of the main lessons emerging from Metagora, extensively commented in this publication: the various forms that the involvement of official statistics in measuring human rights or other aspects of democratic governance can take (see *Chapter 9*). This is a very important finding for the Development Assistance Committee of the OECD and the European Union. Both leading international institutional actors are strongly committed, through vigorous initiatives, to promoting human rights and democratic governance as an inherent part of genuine development efforts, and to enhance national statistical capacities for ensuring proper monitoring of development goals. Given this double political commitment, it would make sense for both institutional actors to give a serious follow-up to the Metagora lessons concerning official statistics – in particular in their policy guidelines and within existing regional frameworks for international co-operation, such as the Strategic Partnership between the European Union and Latin America, or even within statistical co-operation programmes such as MEDSTAT or MERCOSUR.

The fourth element concerns appropriate funding of evidence-based assessments – and is of highest importance both for implementing organisations and for donor institutions. The expenditure related to the 54-months of Metagora work roughly amounts to four and a half million euros. This amount has been relatively limited with regard to the scope of the whole project and the needs of the various

---

Box C.1. **A policy conclusion: encouraging domestic actors to develop their own assessment tools**

"Measuring progress in democratic governance has recently proved to be feasible. This development, which must not lead to a mechanistic approach, is politically important in that it permits the development of useful indicators to help identify the reforms needed and compare countries at international level. Having both national and international/global indicators is useful because they serve different purposes. The international indicators permit comparison at world level. National indicators help establish national standards based on the country's priorities for improving governance. The indicators developed by the partner country itself have a greater incentive effect in that they encourage politicians to be accountable to citizens and institutions and enable civil society and the media to get involved in a monitoring process. The different types of indicator must not be seen as competing but as a set of complementary tools to be used according to the situations or problems that arise.

"It is important to encourage governments, politicians, independent public bodies and civil society to develop their own tools and capabilities for identifying the reforms needed and for gauging the situation and the progress made. These national indicators must comply with the principles of ownership, participation and transparency and permit the necessary reforms to be identified (see footnote: *the Metagora project illustrates this process*). This approach is likely to stimulate demand for reform and thereby reinforce the processes of democratic governance."

Governance in the European Consensus on Development:
Towards a Harmonised Approach within the European Union
(communication from the European Commission to the Council, the European Parliement
the European Economic and Social Council and the Committee of the Regions
Brussels, 30 August 2006
(European Commission, 2006, p. 8)

---

pilot experiences. As the IPE stresses in its *Assessment report* on Metagora, the implementation of a measurement project on solid scientific, technical and operational bases "*will cost money to be implemented properly. In these circumstances, donors will have to weigh expected costs against expected benefits*". Indeed, to be robust, assessments have to be conducted on a professional basis, with professional experts, at professional rates. "Voluntary work" or "cheap labour force" in this domain can entail considerable risks of weak scientific, technical and operational quality.

The fifth element for future action has to do with the independence that underlies the original bottom-up approach of Metagora. None of its pilot experiences was undertaken with prior authorisation or agreement by governmental authorities. Policy dialogue and collaboration with political authorities developed in the course of the experiences, but in most cases had activities been subject to prior governmental approval the experiences would probably never have started. Therefore there is a relevant lesson in this: UN agencies or other international organisations which would like to engage in the path opened by Metagora may encounter operational limitations inherent to their own intergovernmental status. There is therefore floor for creative informal collaboration between these international organisations and other independent academic, research or non-governmental organisations that would be better suited to promote, prepare and start assessment processes based on a genuine bottom-up approach – and not on bureaucratic bases.

The sixth and last significant element of the Metagora legacy lies in its potential to influence and modify current dynamics of transfer of knowledge and know-how in measuring human rights and democratic governance. As a matter of fact, a critical mass of expertise and cumulated experience has been gathered through the effective commitment and substantive work of institutions and experts of the Southern hemisphere. This qualified knowledge and experience on issues - that are also of importance for industrialised countries - suggest a possible inversion in the usual North-South relations. As François Roubaud stated on the occasion of the 2005 Metagora Forum: *"let's share a dream together: let's imagine that, for the first time, methodological transfers will not follow the traditional route from the North to the South, but could flow from the South to irrigate the North. (…) This will not only be a big step forward for statistics, but also one giant leap for mankind – and for enhancing more balanced relations between rich and poor countries."*

With these achievements, lessons and elements for future action in mind, the Metagora community is glad and proud to transmit the legacy of its seminal efforts to the international community. The results of this work are not yet – as expected by Mary Robinson in her 2000 opening address in Montreux – an achieved *science of human dignity*. They are however a fair part of what is today required to be put in place and in movement for seriously assessing and monitoring progress of human rights, democracy and governance.

Appendices

Appendix 1

Methodological and technical outlines of Metagora pilot experiences

This appendix presents succinct descriptions and information on the methodological basis of the following Metagora activities: the pilot surveys carried out in Mexico, Philippines and South Africa, the pilot experience of attaching modules to regular household surveys in Francophone Africa and in the Andean region, as well as the development of a dynamic database on the right to education in Palestine.

The content of these brief outlines results from a trade-off between the requirements of professional statisticians for exhaustive scientific and technical descriptions of each pilot – that would be better suited in a scientific statistical journal – and very general technical information that would not provide much value-added to the texts of the various chapters.

The outlines therefore present technical information at a level of detail that will hopefully fill the basic documentation needs of individuals and organisations willing to engage in measurements of human rights and democratic governance following the path opened by Metagora. This information focuses both on the qualitative and quantitative work carried out, and provides a fair description of questionnaire and sampling design, field work operations, data processing and configuration and structure of databases.

Each outline includes the contact details of the national organisations and individual experts who were in charge of the pilots (including e-mail addresses) and who will be glad to provide, upon request, more extensive technical information as well as guidance on design, planning and budgeting of statistically-based measurement exercises.

Metagora pilot experience in Mexico

Brief description of the project

The Metagora pilot in Mexico focused on abuses by law enforcement authorities in the Federal District of Mexico. The study covered a wide range of irregularities, abuses of power, and acts of ill-treatment. Although the degree of severity of these abuses varies, all such abuses have in common that, by being carried out by law enforcement agents, they weaken the police and justice systems and do not allow Mexico to reach higher levels of democratic governance and respect for human rights. Following stakeholder consultations, and exploratory research that included in-depth interviews with individuals and police officers as well as focus groups with experts to explore the issue at stake, two test surveys were conducted: one to test the draft questionnaire, and another to refine it and fix the necessary sample size. The ensuing survey consisted of 3,666 interviews in a multi-stage sample from 362 census enumerator-areas. A subsequent policy-oriented report based on the results obtained aims to enable stakeholders to identify the context in which abusive behaviour on behalf of public authorities occurs, the specific forms and patterns of contact and abuse, and the characteristics of the victims. The study may also provide a baseline to analyse trends and track the impact of remedial measures (Naval and Salgado, 2006).

Implementing organisations and leading experts

The Metagora pilot in Mexico was implemented under the leadership of Fundar, Centre for Analysis and Research (Cerrada de Alberto Zamora No. 21, Col. Villa Coyoacán, Del. Coyoacán, C.P. 04000, México DF, Mexico, Tel: +52 55 55543001) in collaboration with:

- Pearson Research (Homero 223, piso 4, Col. Polanco, C.P. 11560, México D.F., Mexico)
- Ms. Gloria Labastida from Probabilística (gloria@probabilistica.net)
- Dr. Ignacio Méndez from the *Institute for Applied Mathematics, National University of Mexico*, IIMAS-UNAM (imendez@servidor.unam.mx)

Preliminary qualitative work

Fundar first held reduced focus groups with key stakeholders: selected experts and practitioners in the fields of human rights and security issues, penal lawyers, and the Human Rights Commission of the Federal District, in order to define the scope of the study, shape and enrich the project.

From then on, a grid of possible contacts between individuals and public authorities working within the local police and justice systems, as well as a thematic guide for interviews to address the issue of irregularities, abuses of power and ill-treatment in the Federal District were drafted. Special emphasis was attached to the conceptual aspects of the survey and to the expectations of stakeholders regarding the future use of the data.

The next stage of the "qualitative work" consisted of in-depth interviews with individuals and police officers to test the thematic guide to serve as a basis for the development of the questionnaire. In collaboration with Pearson, which recruited the interviewees, a range of cases were selected to get as comprehensive a view of the question as possible. Twenty-three in-depth interviews were completed: 6 of police officers and 17 of victims of abuse. These interviews contributed to identify the terminology used by both police officers and victims of abusive behaviour on behalf of the authority; the most frequent acts of abuse committed; as well as the general attitudes of the population towards police officers and public security authorities. Thus, the whole consultation process contributed to the ongoing redefining of the "working definition" to be used throughout this study. This working definition covered a wide range of irregularities, abuses of power, and acts of ill-treatment.

Finally, when a preliminary version of the questionnaire was ready, cognitive interviews were carried out to further test its validity before finalising the questionnaire.

Quantitative work

The quantitative work consisted of a random sample household survey applied to the open population (aged 15 or more) of the Federal District of Mexico.

Questionnaire and sample design

In addition to the contribution of the qualitative work to the design of the questionnaire, two test surveys were conducted. For an initial testing of the questionnaire, 49 households were chosen randomly in one of Mexico City's basic geo-statistical areas (AGEBs). Following feedback meetings with interviewers, changes were made to the format and content of the questionnaire for it to be as clear and easy to use as possible.

Subsequently, a full test was carried out in October 2004, reaching 216 dwellings in 18 AGEBs. The main objective of this test was to define the desired size of the sample, by calculating the variance of the main estimators (*e.g.* percentage of people with contact with public authorities, percentage of people suffering some form of abuse on behalf of forces of public security, etc.), the design effect, and the estimated refusal rate in different socio-economic levels. The pilot test revealed a higher refusal rate within high-class sectors, indicating the need for special measures in subsequent field work to improve this rate.

The *Sistema de Consulta para la Información Censal* (SCINCE) from the National Statistical Office (INEGI) was used for the sampling frame. This software provides a list of AGEBs, each of which represents in the Federal District a basic unit area including around 2,500 inhabitants and between 25 and 50 blocks. The AGEB maps include information obtained from the population census and which relate to: number of dwellings, education levels, income levels, etc. The maps allow for the geographical reference of the blocks and their random selection in the office.

For sample selection, a multi-stage sampling was carried out. Twenty strata were created from the AGEB maps, based on the socio-economic classification of the AGEB as well as on a group of relevant socio-economic variables from the SCINCE. Within each stratum, the AGEBs were selected by probability proportional to the size of the population aged 15 or over living in the AGEB (PPT). A secondary stage consisted in selecting blocks within the AGEB maps by enumerating the blocks and randomly selecting six blocks with equal probability. This was done in the office.

Further sample selection occurred during the field work. Within each selected block, a field census was carried out by interviewers to count the total number of dwellings there. Then, a random selection of 4 dwellings was done using a random number table. In cases where more than one household was found within a dwelling, the interviewers were instructed to carry out a pre-established random selection of the household (using the possession of separate cooking facilities to distinguish households.) Finally, for the chosen household, a list of the members aged 15 or more was elaborated. The list included several variables: gender, age and date of birth. The member who had the most recent birthday was chosen as informant.

The final sample size, determined on the basis of the findings from the test survey, was of 8,688 dwellings from 362 AGEBs to obtain an expected number of effective interviews ranging from 2,567 to 3,726, depending on the final response rate. This variation can be explained by the fact that substitution was never included as part of the field procedures. Indeed, at no stage in the field work were any substitutions made: neither for final respondent nor for household, block or geographical area (AGEB).

Implementation

Prior to the field tests of the questionnaire, Fundar and Pearson organised training sessions for interviewers to present the aim of the Metagora study; clarify the notion of abuse, as well as the situation of public authorities working in police and justice in the Federal District; and explain the content and format of the questionnaire, the target population, sampling procedures, etc. Interviewers then participated in mock interviews. As a result, a document was written on the specificities of the study and on the application of the questionnaire, and was provided to all members of the field staff.

During and after the testing of the questionnaire, meetings were arranged to obtain interviewer feedback on the questionnaire, and answer any problems and doubts among interviewers. Moreover, the Pearson team produced a manual for the interviewers and the latter were provided, at the beginning of the field work, with a set of all necessary documents.

The field work was carried out from November 2004 until the end of January 2005. Although the initial coverage of the study was the entire Federal District of Mexico, Fundar decided during the field work to reduce its coverage, excluding the southern borough of Tláhuac. Indeed, in late November 2004, an angry crowd killed two police officers there, and the event was transmitted live on television. The decision to exclude this borough was taken partly so as not to put at risk the security of the interviewers in light of the high levels of violence which surrounded this event, and partly because the information provided by inhabitants of the area might be biased by the event and strongly affect the study and its results.

Field work was supervised at all times. Every supervisor was responsible for a team of 3 or 4 people. Their activities ranged from supervising the census work, to verifying the authenticity of the response rate, to checking that interviewers had indeed carried out their visits to the selected dwellings.

The survey in Mexico was subject to a relatively high refusal rate. This had already been identified during the test survey and is due to Mexico City's overall living conditions: highly urbanised, long transportation periods and subsequent long periods of absence in the dwellings, weakened social cohesion, high levels of insecurity and crime, limited access to certain residential areas, etc. However, it should be stressed that the refusal rate for this survey (33% of the total selection) is not, as such, higher than refusal rates in most private and public household surveys carried out in the Federal District. Recent examples of this include leading surveys on voting preferences for which reported refusal rates went up to 52%.

Data processing

Weights were created to adjust the surveyed population to have the same distribution as the target population on gender, age and socio-economic level. The data from the study exists in the form of four databases: one containing all effective interviews (representing some 6.4 million individuals), one containing only interviews in which contact with authorities was reported (representing some 1.5 million individuals), one containing only interviews in which the respondent was subject to one or more abuses (representing some 800,000 individuals), and a final database in which the primary unit is the contact with the authority (accounting for some 2.3 million contacts) and not the respondent him/herself. Moreover, the databases are such that it is impossible for anyone to identify individual respondents.

Metagora pilot experience in the Philippines

Brief description of the project

The Metagora pilot in the Philippines was led by the Commission on Human Rights in partnership with the National Commission on Indigenous Peoples and the National Statistical Coordination Board. It aimed at developing methods and statistical tools to monitor the rights to ancestral domains and lands of three purposely identified tribes of indigenous peoples: the Bago, Bugkalot/Ilongot, and Kankanaey. The investigation covered indigenous peoples' perceptions and awareness of their rights to ancestral domains and lands, enjoyment or violations of these rights, the associated measures provided by the government as well as customary institutions, and the measures actually used in redressing grievances or fulfilling rights. Qualitative methods – focus group discussions and structured consultations with stakeholders – were extensively applied not only in conceiving and designing the survey questionnaire but also in interpreting and validating the statistical findings. Multi-stage systematic cluster sampling for the 750-household survey was based on the population census, and field work and data-processing were subject to very thorough training and monitoring.

Implementing organisations and leading experts

The pilot study was implemented under the leadership of the Commission on Human Rights of the Philippines, CHR (U.P. Complex, Commonwealth Avenue, Diliman, 1101 Quezon City, Philippines, Tel: +63 2 928 5655) in collaboration with:

- National Commission on Indigenous Peoples of the Philippines, NCIP (2nd Floor N. dela Merced Building, Cor. West and Quezon Avenues, Quezon City, Metro Manila, Philippines, Tel: +63 2 373 9787)
- National Statistical Coordination Board of the Philippines, NSCB (2/F Midland Buendia Building 403, Sen. Gil. Puyat Ave., 1200 Makati City, Philippines, Tel: +63 2 895 2767)
- National Statistics Office of the Philippines, NSO (Solicarel Building 1, Ramon Magsaysay Boulevard, Sta. Mesa, Manila 1008, Philippines, Tel: +63 2 716 0807)
- Statistical Research and Training Centre of the Philippines, SRTC (J&S Building, 104 Kalayaan avenue, Diliman, Quezon City, Philippines, Tel: +63 2 433 1745).

Qualitative work

Two types of qualitative work were carried out: focus group discussions (FGDs) with three categories of respondents, and in-depth consultations with stakeholders. This qualitative material was used to complement and inform the quantitative findings.

Focus Group Discussions

Three tribes were selected to provide case comparisons for the study: Bago, Bugkalot/Ilongot, and Kankanaey. Three focus groups were selected per tribe: tribal leaders, women and youths.

Indigenous peoples were trained to recruit, moderate, record and analyse FGDs, supported by CHR and NCIP field workers as monitor-supervisors. 41 participants attended the training. One of the outputs of the training was an FGD Guide for the use of the moderators. In each tribe 24 indigenous peoples - approximately 8 per group - were the key informants. The findings were organised according to the key questions in the Guide and summarised in a narrative report.

Local Consultations for both quantitative and qualitative work

Local consultations with various groups of stakeholders were undertaken to derive from the target tribes their prevailing issues and concerns. These consultations also served to substantiate or clarify analysis of the responses made in the survey and FGDs. They were conducted in the following forms:

- Ancestral domain consultations: to obtain the informed consent of the three tribes in conducting the Metagora pilot activity.

- Consultative workshops: to present the project to stakeholders for comments.
- Technical consultations: to present the survey design and questionnaire to major stakeholders and the three tribes.
- Consultations cum livelihood training and site visits: to conduct site visits, livelihood training and consult tribal and Barangay leaders of the tribe.
- Local users' forums: to consult tribes on findings of the study and validate the findings.
- National stakeholders' forums: to present the findings of the study to stakeholders.
- The recorded issues were categorised and summarised in a comprehensive report.

Quantitative work

The quantitative work consisted of a random sample survey within each of the three purposively chosen tribes.

Questionnaire Design

An orientation-workshop was conducted in June 2004 to agree on the survey objectives, adopt a conceptual framework, inform the development of the questionnaire and build a shared awareness of issues relating to human rights and indigenous peoples. It was attended by experts and staff of partner agencies involved in the project. The attendants agreed that this was a pilot experiment meant to develop and test the methods and tools for measuring human rights in the Philippines that can be used in conducting a full survey in the future.

The NSCB project staff designed and drafted the questionnaire. During a technical consultation in September 2004, this draft questionnaire was scrutinised by representatives of indigenous peoples' organisations, NGOs, local government units, and the Implementing Group of Experts. Based on these consultations, the draft questionnaire was reviewed and then pre-tested to determine the effectiveness and appropriateness of the translation. Two interviewers and four respondents from each of the three tribes were selected to do so. Resource persons from the CHR and NCIP were also involved. As a result, and based on the feedback obtained from the NSO field staff during training sessions, the questionnaire was further improved.

The questionnaire featured a series of vignettes or simplified stories formulated to reflect indigenous peoples' own awareness and perceptions of their rights. The final questionnaire consisted of eight parts, and included 78 questions containing 197 data items.

The questionnaire was initially developed in English and translated into the relevant local dialects by first-language speakers. Back-translations to English were then reviewed for accuracy.

Sampling Design

The survey covered the three ancestral domains in the northern part of the country: the Bago tribe, the Bugkalot/Ilongot tribe, and the Kankanaey tribe. An ancestral domain is defined as all areas generally belonging to an indigenous people, comprising not only the ancestral land, but also inland waters, coastal areas and natural resources therein, held under a claim of ownership, occupied or possessed by the indigenous people.

The sampling frame was the listing of households per barangay based on the 2000 Census of Population and Housing. A limitation of this sampling frame was that the tribal identity of the heads of households is based on ascribed rather than self-ascribed ethnicity.

In each of the three northern regions (Regions I, II/III and Cordillera) an ancestral domain was selected according to three main criteria: the domain had to be inhabited by one main tribe (thus guaranteeing common language and culture), accessible and located in areas where the survey can be conducted safely (thus not in areas suffering from insecurity or endemic political violence). The selected tribes of indigenous peoples are: the Bago, the Bugkalot/Ilongot and the Kankanaey. The total sample of 750 households for the pilot survey was designed by experts of the National Statistical Coordination Board after consultations with the other members of the Philippines team and Metagora experts. After discussing the nature of each of the tribes in the chosen ancestral domains, it appeared that the Bago can be considered as the most "mainstream" of the 110 indigenous peoples in the Philippines and the Kankanaey as the most "literate". In view of the specific and less "mainstream" nature of the Bugkalot, it was decided to oversample it and include 350 households. The other two tribes, on the other hand, were more proportionally sampled and included 150 and 250 respondents respectively. A random sample of respondents in each ancestral domain ensured representativeness of the indigenous peoples in these areas.

The sample size for each barangay was established by proportional allocation from the predetermined sample size for each tribe. The households in a barangay were grouped into clusters of five. Systematic sampling was utilised in the selection of the clusters. All the households in the sample clusters were enumerated.

Survey operations

An *Interviewers' Manual* was drafted by the NSCB project staff and then reviewed on the basis of the pre-test. With each revision of the questionnaire, the manual was adapted accordingly. It covered concepts and terms in the survey, as well as its objectives, design, and organisation, and instructions on how to properly ask questions and record answers.

Two levels of training were conducted by the NSO. The first level consisted in the training of trainers and involved a two-day session in February 2005 on how to conduct training for the enumerators. The 29 trainees learnt about the Metagora project, concepts and definitions used in the survey and the various procedures to follow. The interviewers' manual was used as reference material. In the course of the training, participants suggested additional changes to the questionnaire, which was then subject to final scrutiny and revision by the NSCB project staff.

The final survey questionnaire, the sampling design and the *Interviewers' Manual* were approved and cleared through the Statistical Survey Review and Clearance System of the NSCB. The latter ensures conformity of surveys conducted by official organisations with standard definitions, concepts and classifications, thus enhancing comparability and accuracy of statistics generated.

The second level of training was conducted by the NSO for three days in selected training centres. It was attended by team supervisors, enumerators and NCIP observers. The training focused on the concepts and definitions used in the questionnaire, field enumeration procedures, and how to fill in the questionnaire and administrative forms. Procedures for supervision were also tackled and mock interviews conducted.

Right after the second level of training, field data collection was undertaken for four days in March 2005, through face-to-face interviews. Two more days were allotted for checking the completeness and correctness of administered questionnaires. A total of 80 enumerators were sent to the field with 11 team supervisors assigned to oversee and monitor their work for the whole duration of the survey. Two interviewers, one from the NSO and one from the NCIP, were assigned to enumerate a sample area with 15 to 20 households. One was in charge of conducting the interview while the other recorded the response. Each team was requested to complete its interviews in the assigned sample area within five days.

The head of household or any responsible member of the household was interviewed. Given the difficult access to the pilot areas, undertaking call-backs revealed to be too costly and time-consuming. Therefore, for all the tribes, a 100% replacement list of households was prepared from the beginning. Replacement was done if the sample household refused to answer; was absent; if there were no Kankanaey, Bago or Bugkalot in the sample household; if the sample household was no longer the occupant; or if the housing unit was vacant or destroyed.

Interviewers visited the sampled household. If it was the right one and qualified to be covered, the location of the household was plotted on the area map, and the interview conducted with any responsible member who could provide accurate answers. Out of the 750 households in the final sample, 270 accounted for replacements.

Close supervision of the enumerator's work and regular review of completed questionnaires were carried out to ensure quality control of the data collected at various levels. Regional or provincial statistical officers or assistant officers of the NSO occupied the function of supervisors throughout the survey operations. Each team supervisor was responsible for four teams of interviewers.

Data processing

The data processing encompassed data entry, checks for certification/completeness, editing, and generation of summary tables. The data entry system on MS Access simulated the format of the questionnaire and allowed for automated data validation. Further data verification and completeness checks were applied by reviewing the summary tables, and immediate corrections made when required. The individual household records stored in the database allowed for the generation of summary tables and graphs in various formats.

The statistical tables and charts generated from the survey produced mainly descriptive statistics. No further statistical inferences were attempted in this pilot study.

Metagora pilot experience in South Africa

Brief description of the project

The project in South Africa involved a survey of the land reform process, as a case study on measuring the realisation of democracy and human rights in a complex practical context. The multifaceted nature of the land question, and the variety of stakeholders with relevant views, were confronted by using a six-part sample in each of three purposely chosen provinces, which include Limpopo, Free State and Eastern Cape:

- rural households on traditional communal lands (referred to in the study as communal areas) or residing on commercial farms (referred to in the study as farm dwellers)
- residents in formal or informal settlements in urban areas (respectively referred to as urban formal and urban informal groups)
- traditional leaders (referred to as the traditional group)
- owners of commercial farms (referred to as the farm owners group)

The first five groups were exclusively black, whereas the sixth was predominantly white. Sampling was multi-stage, based on census enumeration areas; and questionnaire design was qualitatively informed by relevant policy documents and an open-ended pilot survey.

Implementing organisations and leading experts

The Metagora pilot in South Africa was implemented under the leadership of the Human Sciences Research Council, HSRC (Private Bag X41, Pretoria 0001, South Africa, and 134 Pretorius Street, Pretoria 0002, South Africa, Tel: + 27 12 302 2000).

Qualitative work

Qualitative work consisted in an initial exploration of core documents, and in a pilot survey using open-ended questions. The former extracted the underlying hypotheses or assumptions which inform land policies and legislation from three key sources: the "Policy Framework" document of the Reconstruction and Development Programme (RDP) of 1993, the Constitution, and the 1997 "White Paper on South African Land Policy". One assumption, for example, was that land reform is a personal priority of most rural dwellers.

A brief pilot questionnaire was developed to explore the shape that the household questionnaire/survey might later take, deliberately using open-ended questions and cognitive probes to identify the respondents' frame of reference. Some 33 such interviews were conducted, of which 16 were in Zulu and 17 in Northern Sotho. Among other things, the pilot highlighted the fact that different household members have not only different attitudes towards land issues but also different levels of awareness. Rather than being seen as a methodological problem, however, this observation led to a decision to ensure representation of different types of household members by randomly selecting a single adult respondent per selected household. This, for instance, enabled the perspectives of women and men, heads of household and other members of the household, and older and younger adults to be adequately captured and compared.

Quantitative work

Questionnaire Design

In addition to the qualitative inputs described, experts were consulted via the Metagora Partner's group in finalising the questionnaire structure. In order to address, with relevance, the particular situations of prospective land reform beneficiaries versus farm owners, it was decided to draft two distinct questionnaires. The questionnaire aimed at farm owners was translated into Afrikaans, while the questionnaire designed for black respondents was translated into Sepedi, Xitsonga, Tshivenda, and IsiXhosa.

Sampling Design

The key components of South Africa's land reform policies concern land tenure, redistribution and restitution. In order to select geographical areas on which all three elements impact, three out of the nine provinces of South Africa were selected purposely – Limpopo, Free State, and the Eastern Cape – because they are predominantly rural, also encompass urban areas, and are spread out across South Africa.

Within the confines of the selected provinces, the study sought to ensure a fair representation of different possible "land reform constituencies" among black South Africans, in particular among:

- communal dwellers, meaning blacks residing in a former homeland area;
- farm dwellers, which for our purposes was understood as blacks residing on commercial farms owned by someone else and located in former "white" South Africa;
- urban formal dwellers, meaning those residing in areas designated by Statistics South Africa as urban or peri-urban, and who reside in areas characterised by formal housing structures; and
- urban informal dwellers, meaning those residing in areas designated by Statistics South Africa as urban, but who reside in settlements predominately consisting of informal housing ("shacks").

Within the provinces selected, and in order to get an appropriate level of representation among the different "settlement types" across the provinces, multistage stratified cluster (probability) sampling was employed. The sampling frame that was used was largely based on the 2001 census, which contains descriptive statistics (e.g. total number of people or total number of households) for all the enumerator areas (EAs) in South Africa. The census-based sampling frame was slightly adjusted by a renowned, South African statistician, Professor Stoker, and used for the purpose of this study. The value of using this sample frame is that a representative sample could be drawn of all of the target groups and geographical areas and the results of the survey could thereafter be properly weighted to the 2001 census-based population figures. It is important to note that the samples of commercial farm owners and traditional leaders were not large enough to allow for generalisability.

Within each of the explicit strata, EAs from the 2001 census were selected and formed the primary sampling units (PSUs). Within the PSU or EAs, households were randomly selected based on an interval applicable to the EA, i.e. number of households divided by number of households to visit in the EA. At the visiting point the respondent was randomly selected from the present adult household members, on a one respondent per household basis. The purpose of this was to ensure that the survey covered a range of adult household members (aged 18 and over) and not only heads of households. This strategy implied that it was particularly important to approach households when there was a greater likelihood of all adult members being at home, i.e. during evenings and over weekends.

Various intricacies had to be taken into account. The EAs in formal and informal urban areas are predominantly located in metropolitan municipalities, but also in some other urban areas. Predominantly black African households were selected with a few coloured households (none Indian or white). Regarding commercial farm owners and dwellers, field worker supervisors had to investigate how many farms there were in each farming-area and whether sufficient farm workers were living on the farm. To ensure diversity in the farm sample, farms were selected that were not too close to one another. If there were no farms in the selected EA, the EA could be substituted with one from a list.

Implementation

Phase 1 of the field work was conducted in late November 2004, involving all interviews apart from those with commercial farm owners and farm dwellers. Training for the field work took place in three locations. Field work started immediately afterwards, and finished in early December 2004. Phase 2 of the field work started in January with the finalisation of the farm owners' questionnaire, followed by training in late February 2005 and field work until early March.

There was a field manager for each team of four field workers, and a quality-control manager per province. For Phase 1 nearly all the field workers were black to ensure correspondence between ethnicity of respondents and interviewers. For Phase 2, white field managers were necessitated by the fact that the farm owners who were to be interviewed were predominantly white. The South African commercial farmers' union, Agri-SA, was informed about the study, to assist access to farm owners that is otherwise somewhat difficult. Regional representatives of Agri-SA were contacted to collect information on farm names and contact details in the selected EAs. There were nevertheless a few problems, generally solved after further explanation about the study was provided by the HSRC office in Pretoria.

Completed questionnaire schedules were checked by field workers, and by field managers whilst in field. Call-back personnel from the field work agency, DRA, performed telephonic and physical call-backs on a target of 10% of randomly selected questionnaires. However, in practice it was not possible to reach so many respondents. Additionally, staff both from the HSRC and DRA conducted spot visits in the field. No major problems were encountered.

Given the predominantly rural sample, problems included understanding the EA boundaries from the maps, reaching distant EAs, and the time to be invested with traditional authorities or police to achieve access. In Phase 1, 971 out of 985 interviews were realised. Most of the unrealised interviews related to interviews with traditional leaders, who were not necessarily resident in sampled EAs. In Phase 2, 380 out of 440 interviews were realised. Most of the shortfall related to an inability to get permission to visit commercial farms. Most selected households and respondents were co-operative and supportive. Households that refused to be interviewed (and vacant stands) were replaced with the adjacent households to the left.

Data Processing

Two data capturers working independently captured the same questionnaires, to eliminate punching errors. The software ran checks, allowing errors to be rectified by returning to the original questionnaire schedule.

Indicator Development

An approach to indicator development would entail three main stages: identify desirable characteristics of government policy in general and land policy in particular, with an emphasis on democratic governance and human rights; identify variables from the survey that would appear to relate to these characteristics; and where more than one such variable relates to a particular characteristic, determine whether there is a rationale for combining them. On this basis, seven main "indicator categories" were identified, though some indicator categories contain more than one indicator: trust/distrust (in public institutions), efficacy (in influencing government decisions), participation (in democracy), land demand, awareness of land reform, satisfaction with land reform, and land reform policy preferences.

One problem encountered was that so few respondents had knowledge of the components of land reform, making it impossible, on the basis of the present survey, to construct indicators related to the perceived performance of these components. Another perceived problem was that as respondents are exposed in the interview to various aspects of land reform, their answers may not be consistent.

Metagora pilot experience in countries in Francophone Africa and in the Andean Community

Brief description of the project

DIAL worked in partnership with eight African and four Latin American National Statistics Offices (NSOs), and with two regional institutions (respectively AFRISTAT and the General Secretariat of the

Andean Community, SG-CAN), in using official household surveys as a platform for additional modules on subjective aspects of poverty, democracy, governance and human rights. An additional *Mirror Survey* of the assessments of experts on democracy, governance and human rights was also implemented in Africa for comparison purposes. In the African countries, samples of 2,500 households or more were used in the capital cities; in some of the Andean countries, samples of up to 20,000 households allowed for sub-national analyses.

Implementing organisations and leading experts

The two multi-country Metagora Activities in Francophone Africa and in the Andean Community were facilitated and supported by DIAL, *Développement, Institutions et Analyses de Long terme* (Centre of the Institute for Development Research, 4 rue d'Enghien, 75010 Paris 10, France, Tel: +33 1 53 24 14 50) in close collaboration with:

- AFRISTAT, *L'Observatoire Économique et Statistique d'Afrique Subsaharienne* (The Economic and Statistical Observatory of Sub-Saharan Africa, Rue 499, Porte 23, Quartier Niaréla, Bamako, Mali, Tel: +223 221 55 00).
- *Secretaría General de la Comunidad Andina*, SG-CAN (Secretariat General of the Andean Community, Paseo de la República 3895, esq. Aramburú, San Isidro, Lima 27, Peru, Tel: +51 1 411 14 00).

The surveys were organised and implemented by:

- *Institut National de la Statistique et de l'Analyse Économique*, INSAE (BP 323, Cotonou, Benin, Tel: +229 30 82 44)
- *Institut National de la Statistique et de la Démographie*, INSD (555, avenue de l'Indépendance, BP 374, Ouagadougou 01, Burkina Faso, Tel: +226 50 32 49 76)
- *Institut National de la Statistique*, INS (Plateau Cité administrative, BP V55 01, Abidjan, Côte d'Ivoire, Tel: +225 20 21 05 38)
- *Institut National de la Statistique*, INSTAT (Jules Ranaivo Anosy, 101 Antananarivo Anosy Tana 101, Antananarivo, Madagascar, Tel: +261 20 22 216 52)
- *Ministère du Plan et de l'Aménagement du Territoire, Direction Nationale de la Statistique et de l'Informatique*, DNSI (Rue Archinard, Porte 233, BP 12 Bamako, Mali, Tel: +223 222 24 55)
- *Institut National de la Statistique*, INS (BP 13 416 Niamey, Niger, Tel: +227 207 23 560)
- *Direction de la Prévision et de la Statistique*, DPS, now *Agence Nationale de la Statistique et de la Démographie*, ANSD (Rue de Diourbel et rue de St-Louis Point E, BP 116 Dakar RP, Senegal, Tel: +221 33 824 36 15)
- *Direction de la Statistique et de la Comptabilité Nationale*, DGSCN (Avenue de la Kozah Quartier Administratif, Immeuble CENETI, BP 118 Lomé, Togo, Tel: +228 221 27 75)
- *Instituto Nacional de Estadística*, INE (Carrasco n°1391 Miraflores, Casilla 6129, La Paz, Bolivia, Tel: +591 2 222 2333)
- *Instituto Nacional de Estadística y Censos*, INEC (Juan Larrea n° 15-35 José Riofrío, Quito, Ecuador, Tel: +593 2 529858)
- *Instituto Nacional de Estadística e Informática*, INEI (Gral. Garzón 658, Jesus María, Perú, Tel: +51 1 433 8284)

Quantitative work

Questionnaire Design

The main quantitative work consisted of three modules – *Multiple Dimensions of Poverty*, *Governance* and *Democracy* – to be used as add-ons to existing household surveys. The modules were developed by the researchers, drawing upon their experience in the MADIO project in Madagascar since 1995. The modules were then discussed and revised by the project's different partner institutions, bearing in mind that, at the end of the day, the choice of questions was decided on at a national level through a process of development and consultations in each country.

In general, the configuration of the questionnaires and the formulation of questions had to meet two criteria. Firstly, the total number of questions put in the modules had to respect the fact that the modules were appended to existing surveys on employment, consumption, living conditions, etc. whose length differed from that of the modules and from one country to another. Secondly, the project's comparative objective had to be balanced with the need to avoid glossing over national particularities and centres of interest.

The questionnaires put in Africa resembled the generic model very closely, ensuring a maximum comparability of findings. In the Andean countries, however, there was more of a departure from the basic structure, reflecting a greater weight of local considerations.

The *Multiple Dimensions of Poverty* module proposes new poverty tracking indicators to inform and enhance the content of poverty reduction policies, paying particular attention to households' own subjective assessment of their living conditions and well-being. The *Governance* module focuses mainly (via factual responses and perceptions) on the running and efficiency of public institutions and on the role of the state, and seeks to identify the main sources of dysfunctions, notably corruption and absenteeism among civil servants. It also looks at the population's perception of the country's long-term trajectory. The *Democracy* module addresses three classic subjects in the field of political surveys: support for democratic principles, the actual running of democracy, and the nature of the link between citizens and polity. The questions in this module seek to test the universality of the concept of democracy, and study the level of support to democracy by comparing the opinion of democracy with other types of political systems and by asking questions about perceived advantages and disadvantages of democracy.

Taken together, these three modules make up a total of some 200 questions, used to gain insight into these three key issues: poverty, governance and democracy, about which little information is available. The questionnaire is clearly far from exhaustive: the aim was initially to define some strategic indicators and track them over time. The modules can also be used to identify some key issues (inept institutions, dysfunctional democratic principles, rejection of a type of policy, etc.) for which detailed surveys with special focuses can subsequently be set up, *e.g.* of the kind undertaken by other Metagora Partners.

It is important to note that all questionnaires were subject to both partial content tests and full pre-tests so as to ensure the surveys are feasible and that the questions are well-understood and accepted.

Sample design and implementation

The statistical operations were conducted in seven economic capitals in West Africa (Benin, Burkina Faso, Côte d'Ivoire, Mali, Niger, Senegal and Togo), in Madagascar, and in four Andean countries (Colombia, not reported here, and Bolivia, Ecuador, Peru) from 2001 to 2005.

In **Francophone Africa** the three modules were appended to the regular surveys on employment, the informal sector and poverty carried out by the NSO. The surveys covered a representative sample of over 35,000 adults (aged 18 years or over), accounting for 21,000 households in the eight African cities.

The survey approach to measuring governance, democracy and poverty is based on the 1-2-3 model developed by DIAL to track the trends in employment, the informal sector and poverty in developing countries. The first phase is a survey of household employment, unemployment and working conditions. The second phase concerns the head of informal production units. The third phase is a household consumption survey designed to estimate household's standard of living and analyse the determinants of poverty. To this basic structure are added the subject-specific modules appended to one of the phases in line with the statistical unit studied (household, individual or informal production unit). Given that the statistical unit for the *Multiple Dimensions of Poverty* module of this project was the household, it was appended to the phase 1 household sheet. The *Governance and*

Table A.1. **Main characteristics of the modules in selected economic capital cities of Francophone Africa**

	Cotonou	Ouaga-dougou	Abidjan	Bamako	Niamey	Dakar	Lomé	Antana-narivo	Total
Phase 1 sampling plan:									
Total number of basic units	464	713	2483	993	368	2041	129	1330	8521
Number of basic units in sample	125	125	125	125	125	125	125	108	983
Initial number of households in sample	3000	2500	2500	2500	2500	2500	2500	3019	21019
Final number of household in sample	3001	2458	2494	2409	2500	2479	2500	3019	20860
Subjective Poverty module:									
Survey date	oct-01	oct-01	juin-02	oct-01	sep-02	oct-02 fév-03	sep-01	déc-02 jan-03	-
Unit of analysis	Househld	Househld	Househld	Househld	Househld	Househld	Househld	Househld	Hhld
Number of households	3001	2458	2494	2409	2500	2479	2500	2734	20575
Questionnaire	Full	Full	Full	Full	Full	Full	Full	Full	Full
Number of questions	78	78	78	78	78	78	78	78	78
Governance and Democracy modules:									
Survey date	oct-01	oct-02	juin-02	oct-01	sep-02	oct-02 fév-03	oct-01	avr-03	-
Unit of analysis	Adult	Adult	Adult	Adult	Adult	Adult	Adult	Adult	Adult
Survey phase	Phase 1	Phase 3	Phase 1	Phase 1	Phase 1	Phase 1	Phase 3	Phase 2	-
Number of individuals	6328	2023	4794	4482	6431	6829	1840	2807	35534
Questionnaire	Full	Partial	Partial	Partial	Partial	Partial	Full	Partial	-
Number of questions	124	119	117	117	124	113	114	120	-

Source: *1-2-3 Surveys*, Phase 1, Phase 3, *Multiple Dimensions of Poverty, Governance and Democracy* modules 2001/2003, National Statistical Offices, AFRISTAT, and estimations by DIAL.

Democracy modules focused on the opinions of individuals aged 18 and over, and were therefore essentially incorporated into phases 1 or 3 depending on the country (see Table below).

In the Andean countries, the survey mechanism was tailored to meet local particularities, but based on the common matrix designed for the African case. The more advanced development of the national statistical system in the Andes meant that the three modules could be appended to the main household survey conducted by each NSO as part of the official statistics system: the ENAHO survey in Peru, the SIEH (for the *Governance* and *Democracy* modules) and ENIGHU surveys (for the *Multiple Dimensions of Poverty* module) in Ecuador, and the MECOVI survey in Bolivia. The surveys in all three countries took in large-scale national samples. Over 40,000 people aged 18 years or over were interviewed in the three Latin American countries, with a national as well as a regional level of statistical inference in Ecuador and Peru.

To date, the experiment in Peru is the most complete: the modules form an integral part of the ENAHO survey along with the employment, income and consumption modules. Under the ENAHO sampling scheme, the modules cover a sample of around 20,000 households (annual average) with national, regional and even department representativeness. Moreover, the fact that ENAHO is an ongoing survey meant that it was possible to build annual, quarterly and even monthly tracking indicators right from the introduction of the modules in May 2003. Like Peru, the sample of 19,059 people in the *Governance* and *Democracy* module (GD) and 11,256 in the *Multiple Dimensions of Poverty* module (MP) in Ecuador provided a sub-national level of statistical inference (four major cities, as well as other urban and rural areas). However, this was a one-off survey and not an ongoing one (March 2004 in the

Table A.2. **Main characteristics of the modules in the Andean countries**

	Peru	**Ecuador**	**Bolivia**
Sample size	18,918 households (ENAHO) 18,918 in GD module 18,918 in MP module	19,059 households (SIEH) 11,270 households (ENIGHU) 19,059 in GD module 11,256 in MP module	9,433 households (MECOVI) 9,196 in MP module 1,570 in GD module
Survey Period	May 2003- Oct. 2005 Continuous	March 2004 (GD, SIEH) 2003-2004 (MP, ENIGHU)	Nov. 2003-Nov. 2004 (MP) Sept-Nov 2004 (GD)
Geographic scope	National, regional, department	National, regional, 4 biggest cities	National, regional
Subject coverage	Demographic + socio + economic + GDMP modules	Demographic + socio + economic + GDMP modules	Demographic + socio + economic + GDMP modules
Questionnaire harmonisation process	SG-CAN	SG-CAN	SG-CAN
Participatory process, institutionalisation	INEI (NSO) NGOs Academics Public agencies	INEC (NSO)	INE (NSO)
Governance, democracy indicators	Objective (process & outcomes) and perceptions	Objective (process & outcomes) and perceptions	Objective (process & outcomes) and perceptions
Policy impact	Institutional & poverty gender disaggregation	Institutional & poverty gender disaggregation	Institutional & poverty gender disaggregation

Source: ENAHO, SIEH, ENIGHU and MECOVI surveys, Multiple Dimensions of Poverty, Governance and Democracy modules, 2003/2005, National Statistics Offices, SG-CAN, and estimations by DIAL.

case of SIEH survey and 2003-2004 in the case of ENIGHU survey). The survey's statistical properties were the most limited in Bolivia since the sample covered only 1,570 individuals in the GD module, which corresponded to one-sixth of the data collection by the MECOVI survey (from September to October 2004) and 9,196 in the MP module over the whole survey period (November 2003-October 2004). The sample was drawn so as to guarantee national and regional representativeness. It is worth noting here that the different survey characteristics of the countries under study reflect the levels of development of their national statistical systems.

Mirror Survey for the African countries

As a complement to the survey tool of households in the areas of *Governance* and *Democracy*, a survey of experts was conducted in the eight African countries. This survey, which aims to compare the responses given by the general public with those of experts on a number of common questions, was answered by a total of 250 specialists from the South and the North (researchers, development specialists, decision makers, high-ranking public officials, politicians, etc.).

Based on their own individual knowledge, experts were asked to select one country (out of the eight) and to fill in the *Mirror Survey* questionnaire. This survey consisted of two sets of questions: a simplified version of the *Governance* and *Democracy* modules, requiring experts to provide their own opinion on the particular items, and a second set of questions asking the experts what they think the interviewees answered on these particular items. Experts were also required to provide their personal socio-demographic characteristics: gender, age, occupation, knowledge in the field, etc.

Metagora pilot experience in Palestine

Brief description of the project

This experience consisted in building indicators on human rights and developing a prototype of a public information tool. It targeted five main objectives: (1) to reinforce professionalism, accuracy and objectivity in human rights reporting; (2) to encourage evidence-based research on democracy and human rights in Palestine; (3) to allow the production of human rights indicators on a continuous basis, with possible comparisons over time; (4) to enhance national participatory fora and promote interdisciplinary monitoring work involving official statisticians, experts from the academia and human rights practitioners; and (5) to contribute to a clearer analysis of accountability and governance issues in Palestine, and to a well-informed democratic dialogue.

The pilot explored, through a large participatory process, possibilities for involving National Statistical Offices, together with research centres and NGOs, in measuring human rights and democratic governance issues. The experience focused on the development of indicators on the right to education based on official statistical data as well as on information collected by NGOs. Quantitative and qualitative information was integrated into a dynamic database developed and managed by the Palestinian Central Bureau of Statistics (PCBS). This tool is intended to serve as a reference tool for independent policy-oriented analysis and reporting of research centres, human rights practitioners and policy actors.

Integration of data from a wide range of sources took place on two different levels: first, data from different in-house statistical databases of PCBS (intra-organisational matching) were gathered; second, this set of data was completed with quantitative and qualitative information from other organisations (inter-organisational matching). The pilot experience included a strong training component aimed at enhancing the capacities of the members and staff of civil society organisations,

PCBS and Palestinian National Authority bodies in terms of collecting, processing, analysing and interpretating data.

Implementing organisations and leading experts

The Metagora Activity in Palestine was implemented under the leadership of the Palestinian Central Bureau of Statistics, PCBS (P.O. Box 1647, Ramallah – West Bank, Palestine, Tel: +972 2 240 6340) in collaboration with:

- the Bisan Center for Research and Development (P.O. Box 725, Ramallah, West Bank)
- the Palestinian National Authority (Ministry of Education, P.O. Box 576, Ramallah, West Bank, Tel: +972 2 298 5555)
- the Teacher Creativity Centre (P.O. Box 1948, Ramallah, West Bank, and Mahkamat Al-Suluh Street, Rayyan & Imsih Building, 3rd. Floor, Ramallah, West Bank, Tel: +972 2 295 9960)

Data collection and processing

PCBS established an internal Metagora technical team formed by experts in statistical indicators, database design and geographical information systems. This team: (1) drafted a preliminary list of indicators, related definitions and measurement methodologies; (2) identified relevant data sources; (3) prepared forms and required tools for data collection; (4) processed data available in PCBS internal databases and collected data from various external sources; (5) designed and tested the database to meet the needs of the project objectives; (6) periodically reviewed the consistency of the methodological framework (including the definitions and coding); and (7) prepared the dynamic maps used in the database.

Quantitative data was collected from internal PCBS databases and other official and non-official sources to cover the list of indicators prepared by PCBS. These data sources included the partner organisations listed above. Qualitative information was also gathered from these partner organisations as well as from other sources.

A trained team worked on collecting narrative statements. Such qualitative information was identified and assessed on the basis of its relevancy (with regard to the right to education) and ability to be quantified or to usefully complement or put into context the statistical data. As a pilot exercise, some of the indicators were created using data that covered part of the territory (West Bank or Gaza Strip), covered only a particular period of time, or referred to particular cases of violations or rights.

PCBS experts in information technologies developed prototype databases for the Metagora project. The team of experts spent about two months actively studying the problem, and developing and improving coding to handle data entry, storage and reporting. The prototype databases were implemented using the Dot Net Framework utilising XML and XSLT. The XML/XSLT solution follows industry trends to standardise data dissemination via XML. This solution allows for data and indicators to be added or modified easily, and web services can be used to connect the database to online data sources. The Crystal Reports engine is used to dynamically generate charts and graphs based on filtered data within the database.

The design of the database foresees further incorporation of tools to enable subject matter specialists to update the data independently. The identification of variables in each data file and the display of data are dynamic, based on the content of the data file itself. It is expected that the database will be made accessible on the web with only a few modifications.

Assessment of the prototype database

Technical assistance provided by Palestinian experts and international consultants associated to Metagora allowed to improve the design of the database, its technical features and its structure. The prototype database was submitted to an external technical assessment conducted by Mrs. Marissa Mc Laughlin and Mr. Sufian Aba Harb. The technical assessment report pointed out the following:

- The use of XML to construct a framework for organising and presenting statistical data is one of the major strengths of the prototype database, which uses the most recent techniques and was developed in accordance with international standards.
- The three-level data structure (subjects, indicators and data sources/metadata) makes it easy for a computer to generate data, read data, and ensure that data relation is unambiguous.
- As long as a list of subjects – main categories – is maintained and organised according to predefined standards, the adopted design serves the purpose efficiently.
- The user can display the contents of the data file (the output) after each filtering operation. Functions in the filtering engine construct filtering expressions directly in the background without the need for users to know much about the syntax of the query language.
- An obvious advantage of the browsing interface is that the user has all the information he/she needs in one place. The user can directly go to any section – *e.g.* to a different subject, different indicator or different data source.
- The prototype relates one indicator to many data sources (data files) though it does not allow matching data from different sources or making comparisons. Although this is a structural challenge, it is worth tackling such an issue in future developments.
- Taking into consideration the importance of metadata for users, the prototype was designed to make these available; however, the feature could be made more user-friendly in the future.
- Future developments may investigate more dynamically generated graphical presentation.
- As a future development, the search engine should equip users with the tools to reach specific indicators or data sources directly, *i.e.* without having to go through the three-level structure.

The technical assessment report also notes that the tools of the prototype allow users to manipulate statistical data and perform data analysis in a dynamic and easy manner. It also highlights that "the initiatives taken by the PCBS project management to organise regular reviews of the different versions of the prototype were very important for ensuring stakeholders had an opportunity to participate in shaping the final product and defining the standards that they may wish to adopt."

Appendix 2

Questionnaire of the worldwide survey on initiatives

This worldwide survey on initiatives aimed at measuring democracy, human rights and governance was designed, prepared and supervised by a task team of the Metagora Partners Group, formed by Michelle Jouvenal (ISTAT – National Statistical Institute, Italy), Roberta D'Arcangelo (consultant), Hans-Otto Sano (Danish Institute for Human Rights, Denmark), Jan Robert Suesser (ADETEF, France) and Thomas Heimgartner (Metagora Co-ordination Team).

The collection, analysis and editing of the information was carried out by Ms. D'Arcangelo, under the supervision of Mrs. Jouvenal and Mr. Sano. Ms. D'Arcangelo was hosted by the National Statistical Institute of Italy, which provided working facilities and substantive support for the implementation of the project. Further work was later carried out by Ms. Quetzali Padilla Dulce.

Questionnaire for the Inventory of Initiatives on measuring democracy, human rights and governance

The present questionnaire intends to identify any relevant initiatives and related indicators which contribute directly or indirectly to the measurement of democracy, human rights and governance.

Your organisation may not call or define its initiative(s) and indicator(s) as proper measurement tools of democracy, human rights and/or governance. However, those initiatives may still collect information in a systematic way or document and measure some aspects or dimensions of democracy, human rights and/or governance. For instance, indicators commonly denominated as social and economic indicators may be considered as a useful source of information in situational analysis of social and economic rights (*e.g.* adult literacy rate, daily per capita supply of calories, % of infants with low birth weight). For this reason, we would also like these types of initiatives to be included in the inventory. As a consequence, a number of questions in the questionnaire may not always apply to the specific initiative you wish to refer to. Should this be the case, please feel free to leave them out.

The answers you provide will be used to categorise your initiative in a public database put online on the internet. By answering as many questions as accurately as possible, you will make it easier for future users of this inventory to learn about your particular initiative, locate it and, if required, get in touch with your organisation.

Please feel free to add any additional information that you think would be useful for the understanding of your initiative. This information may come in the form of publications, project outlines, questionnaires etc. Such material would of course be only for internal study and use, and will not be published without your prior consent.

If you know of any other organisation in your country that has recently collected, in a systematic way, data or information on democracy, human rights and governance, we would be grateful if you could send us their contact details (name of person in charge, e-mail, telephone or fax number) and forward our message or the address www.metagora.org/initiatives to them. All relevant documents can be downloaded from the link.

For any further questions, please do not hesitate to contact: initiatives@metagora.org (after the conclusion of Metagora, messages to this address will be forwarded to the UNDP Oslo Governance Centre).

A) Description of your organisation

1. Name of organisation	Indicate the name of the organisation(s) directly involved in the implementation of the initiative.
2. Contact address	Indicate your organisation's contact address: Street: ZIP/City: Telephone: e-mail:
3. Website of organisation	Indicate the organisation's website. http://www.
4. Country	Indicate the country your organisation is based in:
5. Type of organisation	Choose one or more of the following: O Academic (University) O NGO O Governmental Organisation O Intergovernmental Organisation O National Statistical Office O United Nations O National Human Rights Institution O Cultural Organisation O Research centre O Other _____
6. Other organisations involved in the implementation of the initiative	If the initiative is implemented in collaboration with other organisations, please give their name and contact address:
7. Organisation's main field of expertise	Indicate the field your organisation is specialised in: O Statistics O Democracy O Human Rights O Governance O Other:_____

B) Initiative contributing to the measurement of Democracy, Human Rights and Governance
(If your organisation is implementing or has implemented more than one such initiative, please fill in a form for each of them.)

a) General characteristics

8. Name of initiative	Indicate the specific name of the initiative.
9. Website of/on the initiative	Indicate the specific website for the initiative (if more specific than the website of organisation) in case your initiative does not have an own webpage, you may indicate a website where information about it can be found. http://www.
10. Contact address	Indicate contact address for the initiative (if more specific than the contact address of the organisation): Name (of person or department in charge within the organisation): Street: ZIP/City: Country: Telephone: e-mail:
11. Publications	Indicate where published results can be found, as well as the title and year of the publication.
12. Cost/Funding	Indicate the approximate total cost of implementation of the initiative and if possible the source of funding: Total cost (specify currency): Sources of funding:
13. Status of the initiative	Indicate the status of your initiative, choosing one of the following: O Ended (add if possible the time span from first design to final publication: from _____ until _____) O On-going (since _____ until _____) O In development (initiative is not operational yet, but in development)

14. Geographical location	Indicate the geographical location (continent/region/country/area) your initiative is/was implemented in.

b) Objectives of the initiative

15. Purpose	Give a brief description of your initiative (What are the general objectives? What was the need or demand that prompted the initiative? Are there links to specific laws, to human rights treaties or norms? Which is the target population? etc.)

16. Themes addressed	Check the circle(s) with the main theme(s) covered by the initiative on the left; if applicable, you may specify in the column on the right (Please select a maximum of 6 themes).	
	O Democracy	O Popular sovereignty O Legitimacy of rulers O Pluralism of political parties O Division of powers O Rule of law O Elections O Equality O Media freedom O other:_____
	O Human rights	O Political rights O Civil rights O Economic rights O Social rights O Cultural rights O Environmental rights O Right to development O Women's rights O Children's rights O Rights of indigenous peoples and minorities O other:_____
	O Governance	O Resource management O Accountability O Transparency O Corruption O Participation O Efficiency O Rule of law O Control/Monitoring/Supervision O Access to information O Ethics O other:_____

c) Source(s) and production of data / information

17. Source(s) of data	Indicate which source(s) of data are used, choosing one of the following: O Own source of data O Using other existing source(s) of data O Using a combination of own data and existing data O Initiative focusing on analysis not based on data
18. Type of data collection	Indicate type or method of data collection, choosing one or more of the following: O Census O Random sample population survey O Events registration O Secondary sources (literature, newspapers, etc.) O Administrative data (land records, etc.) O Focus groups O Panel of experts O In-depth interviews O Performance assessment / Desk studies O Aggregation of multiple indicators using various data sources O other:_____
19. Specifications of type of data collection	You may wish to provide specifications or technical details about the type of data collection, such as: population and sample size, nature of secondary sources or administrative data etc., level to which data can be disaggregated (country, village, household), etc.

20. Frequency of data collection / analysis	Indicate the frequency of data collection, choosing one of the following:
	O Continuous (as for instance for events registration)
	   Indicate time span: since_____ until _____
	O Repeated (Indicate frequency of repetition (annual, every 5 years, etc.) :
	   _____
	O Unique

21. Measurement methods / tools	Describe the (quantitative and qualitative[1]) measurement methods and/or measurement tools generated or used. Maximum length: 1500 characters
22. List of indicators	Indicate the list of main indicators and possibly their definitions/descriptions.

---

1. Information may be either qualitative, quantitative or a combination of the two. Quantitative information usually has units of measurement, such as total number of persons, % of population, % of children under 15, number of years. Qualitative information does not have measurement units. For quantifying qualitative information, a scale would generally be required (e.g. an evaluation using a scale as 1: "totally agree", 2: "partially agree", 3: "neither agree nor disagree", 4: "partially disagree", 5: "totally disagree").

d) Outcomes and users

23. Main outcomes (products)	Indicate which are the main outcomes/products generated by the initiative (e.g. reports, methods developed, database, etc.) Maximum length: 500 characters.
24. Main users	Indicate who are the main users of the information generated by the initiative, choosing one or more of the following: O Policy makers O Donor agencies O International agencies O Civil society O Researchers O Media O other:_____

Please return to: initiatives@metagora.org (after the conclusion of Metagora, messages to this address will be forwarded to the UNDP Oslo Governance Centre).

Reminder: If you happen to know of any other organisation in your country that is gathering data on democracy, human rights and governance, we would appreciate if you could send us their contact details, and forward to them the relevant documents or the following link from which relevant documents and the questionnaire can be downloaded:

http://www.metagora.org/html/activities/act_inventory.html

Appendix 3

Examples of initiatives documented in the Metagora Inventory

A project aimed at measuring torture in Georgia

Inventory of Initiatives

Initiative:	simple search I advanced search
Implemented by	• Anchor Consulting LLC • Georgian Center for Psychosocial and Medical Rehabilitation of Torture Victims (GCRT)
Name of initiative	Georgia - Focus on torture: Public Survey in Tbilisi
Website of initiative	gcrt.gol.ge
Contact Address	Nino Makhashvili 6, Shio Mghvimeli Street, Tblisi Georgia +995 (32) 232997 gcrt@gol.ge
Publications	Final Report available at http://gcrt.gol.ge/publications.htm
Cost	EUR 4,000
Funding	European Union
Status of the initiative	ended (from 2003-02-01 till 2003-12-31)
Geographical location	Tbilisi, Georgia
Region	• Europe and Russian Federation
Purpose	The Georgian Centre for Psychosocial and Medical Rehabilitation of Torture Victims (GCRT) is the not-for-profit non-governmental organisation providing psychosocial and medical assistance to torture victims in Georgia. The centre activities are assisted by the European Commission, UNVFTV, OHCHR, OSCE-ODIHR, and ICRC. It is perceived that reliable quantitative indicators reflecting relevant social trends are a precondition for the efficient planning of centre activities. To this end, the survey of torture incidence, and broadly of human rights awareness, in Tbilisi, Georgia was commissioned to Anchor Consulting. Anchor Consulting has carried out 800 face-to-face interviews with the citizens of Tbilisi, at their residences. The questionnaire is presented in the appendix (Part 8) of the report. Respondents were chosen according to district and demographical (gender and age) quotas. Quotas were determined according to the official statistical data. Field work was conducted in the second half of October 2003. The report presents the results of the survey. To evaluate the results of the survey correctly, one should bear in mind that it measured the attitudes of Tbilisi population just prior to the revolutionary events of November 2003. Thus, unintentionally, the important benchmark was created against which further HR developments may be measured in post-revolutionary Georgia. Primary purpose of this questionnaire survey was to explore the issue of torture – its incidence, public awareness of, attitudes to, and opinions regarding the surrounding topics and actors. The questionnaire was structured in accordance with the "funnel" principle, i.e. it started from relatively general and neutral questions and gradually approached more specific and sensitive topics. The report follows the questionnaire structure. This survey was conceived as the first survey of a series to be conducted regularly. Thus, it is expected that its public value will increase with time, as indicator trends are revealed. Hopefully, the report will catalyse public discussion and generate adequate critique. GCRT and Anchor Consulting are ready to answer all questions that may arise regarding the survey, and would gratefully accept any comments or suggestions.

Main themes adressed	• Human rights
Detailed themes adressed	• Rule of law • Equality • Political rights • Civil rights • Control/Monitoring/Supervision
Source of data	Own source of data
Type of data collection	• Random sample population survey • Administrative data
Specifications of type of data collection	800 respondents. Random sample. Tbilisi population Anchor Consulting has carried out 800 face-to-face interviews with the citizens of Tbilisi, at their residences. Respondents were chosen according to district and demographical (gender and age) quotas. Quotas were determined according to the official statistical data.
Frequency of data collection / analysis	Unique
Measurement methods / tools generated or used	Descriptive statistics, correlations, regressions. Sociological methods of research are difficult to apply in Georgia due to a number of specific problems – absence of population lists from which to sample, absence of reliable statistical data, constrained survey budgets to allow for adequate interview control, etc. All these problems usually decrease the reliability of snapshot survey results. The latter is an important argument for conducting repeated surveys, consistent in content and methodology. While there certainly may be some regular bias in the absolute figures reported by such surveys, the trends they capture are much more reliable and instructive.
List of indicators	Primary purpose of the questionnaire survey was to explore the issue of torture – its incidence, public awareness of, attitudes to, and opinions regarding the surrounding topics and actors. The extreme sensitivity of the issue under study made certain demands on the size and structure of the questionnaire. Namely, in order not to "scare" respondents from the beginning, and receive maximally adequate responses to the principal (i.e. torture-related) questions, the questionnaire began with general and neutral questions and gradually approached the principal topic of interest. The broader issues of general socio-economic problems facing Georgia, Human Rights, and aggression and violence in the society put the survey topic into the general context, what is particularly important for readers not well acquainted with Georgia. The questionnaire may be seen as consisting of four parts: - First part attempted to set the principal survey topic into broader socio-economic context of Georgia. The most urgent specific problems facing the country were rated in terms of their urgency and respective development trends. - In the second part, the notion of Human Rights was introduced. Public understanding of the notion was explored through recording the respondents' association with it and through connecting the notion with specific socio-economic problems discussed earlier. - In the third part, the incidence of severe abuse, both moral and physical, has been assessed. - In the fourth part, the principal topic of torture was explored: understanding of torture, its incidence, and public attitudes to it. Also the need for preventive/rehabilitative measures was determined.
Main outcomes (products)	Report
Main users	• Policy makers • Donor agencies • International agencies • Civil society • Researchers • Media

Development of a system of human rights indicators in Brazil

Inventory of Initiatives	
Initiative:	simple search | advanced search
Implemented by	• Escola Nacional de Ciências Estatísticas ENCE / IBGE
Name of initiative	Brazil - Construction of a system of human rights indicators
Website of initiative	www.ence.ibge.gov.br
Contact Address	Mr. Pedro Luis do Nascimento Silva, General Co-ordinator ENCE Rua André Cavalcanti, 106 Rio de Janeiro Brasil +55-21-21424548 pedrosilva@ibge.gov.br
Publications	
Cost	US$ 40,000
Funding	Ford Foundation
Status of the initiative	on-going (from 2002-09-01)
Geographical location	Brazil
Region	• Latin America and the Caribbean
Purpose	The purpose of the activities is to implement a system of human rights indicators based on public statistics, involving: • international and national experiences as well as the scope and evolution of human rights concepts. • a methodological instrument for the building of the system; human rights are considered in three lines: civil rights (access to justice and violence), economic, social and cultural rights (the ESCR) and sexual and reproductive rights; race and gender are cross cutting variables to account for discrimination. • the model contemplates distinct levels of disaggregation: national, state level, and municipal level; besides the systems is intended to be updated each year or at least each two years. • a case study on violence using homicide mortality among young males in Rio de Janeiro disaggregated to the smaller intra urban areas, ranked according the level of violence; this classification is linked to infrastructure, living conditions and income of the families, personnel and resources allocated in schooling and, defence, and so on. • The results are to be presented using geo-processing resources. All the results are to be distributed in several ways and are intended to serve as a guide for monitoring and evaluate public policies as well as in training and human rights education activities.

Main themes adressed	• Human rights
Detailed themes adressed	• Civil rights • Economic rights • Social rights • Cultural rights • Right to development • Women's rights • Children's rights
Source of data	Using other existing source(s) of data
Type of data collection	• Census • Random sample population survey • Events registration • Secondary sources • Panel of experts • Aggregation of multiple indicators using various data sources
Specifications of type of data collection	Other data utilised: Mortality statistics

Assessment of Human Rights in Malawi

Inventory of Initiatives

Initiative:	simple search | advanced search
Implemented by	• Malawi Human Rights Commission
Name of initiative	Malawi - Situation Analysis of Human Rights in Malawi
Website of initiative	http://www.malawihumanrightscommission.org/
Contact Address	Malawi Human Rights Commission HB House, along Chilambula Road Private Bag 378 Lilongwe 3 Malawi +265 1 750900/954/958 mhrc@sdnp.org.mw
Publications	
Cost	US$ 8,000 – 10,000
Funding	Government and donors
Status of the initiative	on-going (since 2001-01-01)
Geographical location	Malawi, Southern Africa
Region	• Sub-Saharan Africa
Purpose	- To ensure that the country monitors the actual situation on the ground with respect to each of the rights on a regular basis, and is thus aware of the extent to which those rights are, or are not, being enjoyed. - To show the problems encountered in the implementation of the bill of rights and other treaty obligations to which the country is a party. - To encourage and facilitate popular participation and public scrutiny of government policies and actions. - Facilitate exchange of information on enjoyment or non-enjoyment of human rights. - Linked to all human rights guaranteed in the Malawian Constitution, and including all international treaties to which Malawi is a party.

Main themes adressed	• Human rights
Detailed themes adressed	• Equality • Political rights • Civil rights • Economic rights • Social rights • Cultural rights • Women's rights
Source of data	Using a combination of own and existing data
Type of data collection	• Events registration • Secondary sources • Focus groups • In depth interviews • Performance assessment / Desk studies • Administrative data
Specifications of type of data collection	I. General statistical data. e.g. number of reported cases of domestic violence. II. Disaggregated number of school enrolment at country level. III. % of women in decision-making positions. IV. Health indicators such as maternal mortality rate. V. Qualitative data in terms of perceptions about improvement or otherwise. VI. Some of the secondary sources are yearly reports produced by reputable institutions.
Frequency of data collection / analysis	Repeated (Frequency: every two years)
Measurement methods / tools generated or used	Use of both closed and open-ended type of questions. For quantitative method: number of objects and % of the population are mostly used. For qualitative methods: improving, stable or worsening/declining have been guiding features.
List of indicators	- Total number of objects per given period, e.g. number of deaths of prisoners in a year vis-à-vis their respective causes. - % of population, e.g. % of women in decision- making positions. - Disaggregated data of children involved in child labour in sampled areas. - Number of cases of human rights violations reported, e.g. number of those denied the right to access to justice.
Main outcomes (products)	Human rights situation analysis report
Main users	• Policy makers • Donor agencies • International agencies • Civil society • Researchers • Media • Other

Appendix 4

List of illustrative human rights indicators developed by the OHCHR

List of illustrative indicators on the right to life (UDHR, Art. 3) (* MDG related indicators)

	Arbitrary Deprivation of life	Disappearances of Individuals	Health and Nutrition	Death Penalty
Structural	• International human rights treaties, relevant to the right to life, ratified by the State • Date of entry into force and coverage of the right to life in the Constitution or other forms of superior law • Date of entry into force and coverage of domestic laws for implementing the right to life • Date of entry into force and coverage of formal procedure governing inspection of police cells, detention centres and prisons by independent inspection agencies	• Date of entry into force and coverage of *habeas corpus* provision in the Constitution	• Time frame and coverage of national policy on health and nutrition	• Number of sub-national administrative entities that have abolished death penalty
	• Proportion of received complaints on the right to life investigated and adjudicated by the national human rights institution, human rights ombudsperson or other mechanisms and the proportion of these responded to effectively by the government • Type of accreditation of National Human Rights Institutions by the rules of procedure of the International Coordinating Committee of National Institutions			
Process	• Proportion of communications sent by the UN Special Rapporteur on Extrajudicial, Summary or Arbitrary Executions responded to effectively by the government in the reporting period • Proportion of law enforcement officials (including police, military and State security force) trained in rules of conduct concerning proportional use of force, arrest, detention, interrogation or punishment • Proportion of law enforcement officials formally investigated for physical or non-physical abuse or crime that caused death or threatened life in the reporting period • Proportion of formal investigations of law enforcement officials resulting in disciplinary actions or prosecution in the reporting period • Proportion of identified perpetrators of reported cases of arbitrary deprivation of life pursued, arrested, adjudicated, convicted or serving sentence in the reporting period	• Proportion of communications sent by the UN Working Group on Enforced or Involuntary Disappearances responded to effectively by the government in the reporting period • Proportion of cases where pre-trial detention (before being brought before a court) exceeded the legally stipulated time limit in the reporting period • Number of *habeas corpus* and similar petitions filed in courts in the reporting period • Proportion of identified perpetrators of reported cases of disappearances pursued, arrested, adjudicated, convicted or serving sentence in the reporting period	• Proportion of population using an improved drinking water source* • Proportion of births attended by skilled health personnel* • Proportion of population below minimum level of dietary energy consumption* • Proportion of targeted population covered under public nutrition supplement programmes • Proportion of population using an improved sanitation facility* • Proportion of one-year-old immunised against vaccine-preventable diseases (e.g. measles*) • Proportion of disease cases detected and cured (e.g. tuberculosis*)	• Number of convicted persons on death row in the reporting period • Average time spent by convicted persons on death row • Proportion of accused persons facing capital punishment provided with access to a counsellor or legal aid • Proportion of convicted persons facing capital punishment exercising the right to have their sentence reviewed by a higher court • Reported cases of expulsion or imminent expulsion of persons to a country where they may face death penalty
Outcome	• Number of homicides and life threatening crimes, per 100,000 population • Number of deaths in custody per 1,000 detained or imprisoned persons, by cause of death (e.g. illness, suicide, homicide) • Reported cases of arbitrary deprivation of life (e.g. as reported to the UN Special Rapporteur on Extrajudicial, summary or arbitrary executions)	• Reported cases of disappearances (e.g. as reported to the UN Working Group on Enforced or Involuntary Disappearances) • Proportion of cases of disappearance clarified, by status of person at the date of clarification (at liberty, in detention or dead).	• Infant and under-five mortality rates* • Life expectancy at birth or age 1 • Prevalence of and death rates associated with communicable and non-communicable diseases (e.g. HIV/AIDS, malaria* and tuberculosis*)	• Proportion of death penalty sentences commuted • Number of executions (under death penalty)

All indicators should be disaggregated by prohibited grounds of discrimination, as applicable and reflected in metasheets

24.4.08

List of illustrative indicators on the right to liberty and security of person (UDHR, Art. 3)

	Arrest and detention based on criminal charges	Administrative deprivation of liberty	Effective review by court	Security from crime and abuse by law enforcement officials
Structural	• International human rights treaties, relevant to the right to liberty and security of person, ratified by the State • Date of entry into force and coverage of the right to liberty and security of person in the Constitution or other forms of superior law • Date of entry into force and coverage of domestic laws for implementing the right to liberty and security of person • Time frame and coverage of policy and administrative framework against any arbitrary deprivations of liberty, whether based on criminal charges, sentences or decisions by a court or administrative grounds (e.g. immigration, mental illness, educational purposes, vagrancy) • Type of accreditation of National Human Rights Institutions by the rules of procedure of the International Coordinating Committee of National Institutions			• Legal time limits for an arrested or detained person before being informed of the reasons for the arrest or detention; before being brought to or having the case reviewed by an authority exercising judicial power; and for the trial duration of a person in detention • Time frame and coverage of policy and administrative framework on security, handling of criminality and abuses by law enforcement officials
	— • Proportion of received complaints on the right to liberty and security of person investigated and adjudicated by the national human rights institution, human rights ombudsperson or other mechanisms and the proportion of these responded to effectively by the government • Proportion of communications sent by the UN Working Group on Arbitrary Detention responded to effectively by the government • Proportion of law enforcement officials (including police, military and State security force) trained in rules of conduct concerning proportional use of force, arrest, detention, interrogation or punishment			
Process	• Number/proportion of arrests or entries into detention (pre- and pending trial) on the basis of a court order or due to action taken directly by executive authorities in the reporting period • Number/proportion of defendants released from pre- and trial detentions in exchange for bail or due to non-filing of charges in the reporting period	• Number/proportion of arrests or entries into detention under national administrative provisions (e.g. security, immigration control, mental illness and other medical grounds, educational purposes, drug addiction, financial obligations) in the reporting period • Number/proportion of releases from administrative detentions in the reporting period	• Proportion of cases where the time for arrested or detained persons before being informed of the reasons of arrest; before receiving notice of the charge (in a legal sense); or before being informed of the reasons of administrative detention exceeded the respective legally stipulated time limit • Number of *habeas corpus* and similar petitions filed in courts in the reporting period • Proportion of bail applications accepted by the court in the reporting period • Proportion of arrested or detained persons provided with access to a counsellor or legal aid • Proportion of cases subject to review by a higher court or appellate body • Reported cases where pre- and trial detentions exceeded the legally stipulated time limit in the reporting period	• Proportion of law enforcement officials formally investigated for physical and non-physical abuse or crime, including arbitrary arrest and detention (based on criminal or administrative grounds) in the reporting period • Proportion of formal investigations of law enforcement officials resulting in disciplinary actions or prosecution in the reporting period • Number of persons arrested, adjudicated, convicted or serving sentence for violent crime (including homicide, rape, assault) per 100,000 population in the reporting period • Proportion of law enforcement officials killed in line of duty in the reporting period • Firearms owners per 100,000 population / Number of firearms licences withdrawn in the reporting period • Proportion of violent crimes with the use of firearms • Proportion of violent crimes reported to the police (victimisation survey) in the reporting period
Outcome	• Number of detentions per 100,000 population, on the basis of a court order or due to action by executive authorities at the end of the reporting period • Reported cases of arbitrary detentions, including post-trial detentions (e.g. as reported to the UN Working Group on Arbitrary Detention) in the reporting period		• Proportion of arrests and detentions declared unlawful by national courts • Proportion of victims released and compensated after arrests or detentions declared unlawful by judicial authority	• Proportion of population feeling 'unsafe', (e.g. walking alone in area after dark or alone at home at night) • Incidence and prevalence of physical and non-physical abuse or crime, including by law enforcement officials in line of duty, per 100,000 population, in the reporting period

All indicators should be disaggregated by prohibited grounds of discrimination, as applicable and reflected in metasheets

24.04.08

List of illustrative indicators on the right to adequate food (UDHR, Art. 25) (* MDG related indicators)

	Nutrition	Food Safety and Consumer Protection	Food Availability	Food Accessibility
	• International human rights treaties, relevant to the right to adequate food, ratified by the State • Date of entry into force and coverage of the right to adequate food in the Constitution or other forms of superior law • Date of entry into force and coverage of domestic laws for implementing the right to adequate food • Number of registered and/or active non-governmental organizations (per 100,000 persons) involved in the promotion and protection of the right to adequate food			
Structural	• Time frame and coverage of national policy on nutrition and nutrition adequacy norms	• Time frame and coverage of national policy on food safety and consumer protection • Number of registered and/or active civil society organisations working in the area of food safety and consumer protection	• Time frame and coverage of national policy on agricultural production and food availability • Time frame and coverage of national policy on drought, crop failure and disaster management	
	• Proportion of received complaints on the right to adequate food investigated and adjudicated by the national human rights institution, human rights ombudsperson or other mechanisms and the proportion of these responded to effectively by the government • Net official development assistance (ODA) for food security received or provided as a proportion of public expenditure on food security or Gross National Income			
Process	• Proportion of targeted population that was brought above the minimum level of dietary energy consumption* in the reporting period • Proportion of targeted population covered under public nutrition supplement programmes • Coverage of targeted population under public programmes on nutrition education and awareness • Proportion of targeted population that was extended access to an improved drinking water source* in the reporting period	• Disposal rate or average time to adjudicate a case registered in a consumer court • Share of public social sector budget spent on food safety and consumer protection advocacy, education, research and implementation of law and regulations relevant to the right • Proportion of food producing and distributing establishments inspected for food quality standards and frequency of inspections • Proportion of cases adjudicated under food safety and consumer protection law in the reporting period	• Proportion of female headed households or targeted population with legal title to agricultural land • Arable irrigated land per person • Proportion of farmers availing extension services • Share of public budget spent on strengthening domestic agricultural production (e.g. agriculture-extension, irrigation, credit, marketing) • Proportion of per capita availability of major food items sourced through domestic production, import & food-aid • Cereal import dependency ratio in the reporting period	• Share of household consumption of major food items for targeted population group met through publicly assisted programmes • Unemployment rate or average wage rate of targeted segments of labour force • Proportion of targeted population that was brought above the poverty line in the reporting period • Work participation rates, by sex and target groups • Estimated access of women and girls to adequate food within household • Coverage of programmes to secure access to productive resources for target groups
Outcome	• Prevalence of underweight and stunting children under-five years of age* • Proportion of adults with body-mass index (BMI) <18.5	• Number of recorded deaths and incidence of food poisoning related to adulterated food	• Per capita availability of major food items of local consumption	• Proportion of population below minimum level of dietary energy consumption* / proportion of undernourished population • Average household expenditure on food for the bottom three deciles of population or targeted population
	• Death rates, including infant and under-five mortality rates, associated with and prevalence of malnutrition (including under-, overnutrition and inadequate intake of nutrients)			

All indicators should be disaggregated by prohibited grounds of discrimination, as applicable and reflected in metasheets

24.4.08

List of illustrative indicators on the right to enjoyment of the highest attainable standard of physical and mental health (UDHR, Art. 25) (* MDG related indicators)

The following structural indicators apply across all categories:
- International human rights treaties, relevant to the right to enjoyment of the highest attainable standard of physical and mental health (right to health), ratified by the State
- Date of entry into force and coverage of the right to health in the Constitution or other forms of superior law
- Date of entry into force and coverage of domestic laws for implementing the right to health, including a law prohibiting female genital mutilation
- Number of registered and/or active non-governmental organizations (per 100,000 persons) involved in the promotion and protection of the right to health
- Estimated proportions of births, deaths and marriages recorded through vital registration system

	Sexual and reproductive health	Child mortality and health care	Natural and occupational environment	Prevention, treatment and control of diseases	Accessibility to health facilities and essential medicines
Structural	• Time frame and coverage of national policy on sexual and reproductive health • Time frame and coverage of national policy on abortion and foetal sex-determination	• Time frame and coverage of national policy on child health and nutrition		• Time frame and coverage of national policy on physical and mental health, • Time frame and coverage of national policy for persons with disabilities • Time frame and coverage of national policy on medicines, including list of essential medicines, measures for generic substitution	
Process	• Proportion of births attended by skilled health personnel* • Antenatal care coverage (at least one visit and at least four visits)* • Increase in proportion of women of reproductive age using, or whose partner is using, contraception (CPR)* • Unmet need for family planning* • Medical terminations of pregnancy as a proportion of live births • Proportion of reported cases of genital mutilation, rape and other violence restricting women's sexual and reproductive freedom responded to effectively by the government	• Proportion of school-going children educated on health and nutrition issues* • Proportion of children covered under programme for regular medical check-ups in the reporting period • Proportion of infants exclusively breastfed during the first 6 months • Proportion of children covered under public nutrition supplement programmes • Proportion of children immunised against vaccine-preventable diseases (e.g. measles*)	• Proportion of targeted population that was extended access to an improved drinking water source* • Proportion of targeted population that was extended access to improved sanitation* • CO_2 emissions per capita * • Number of cases of deterioration of water sources brought to justice • Proportion of population or households living or working in or near hazardous conditions rehabilitated • Number of prosecutions under natural or domestic law on natural or workplace environment • Proportion of driving licences withdrawn for breaches of road rules	• Proportion of population covered under awareness raising programmes on transmission of diseases (e.g. HIV/AIDS*) • Proportion of population (above age 1) immunised against vaccine-preventable diseases • Proportion of population applying effective preventive measures against diseases (e.g. HIV/AIDS, malaria*) • Proportion of disease cases detected and cured (e.g. tuberculosis*) • Proportion of population abusing substances, such as drug, chemical and psychoactive substance, brought under specialised treatment • Proportion of mental health facilities inspected in the reporting period	• Per capita government expenditure on primary health care and medicines • (Improvement in) Density of medical and para-medical personnel, hospital beds and other primary health care facilities • Proportion of population that was extended access to affordable health care, including essential drugs*, on a sustainable basis • Proportion of people covered by health insurance in reporting period • Proportion of persons with disabilities accessing assistive device • Share of public expenditure on essential medicines met through international aid
Outcome	• Proportion of live births with low birth-weight • Perinatal mortality rate • Maternal mortality ratio*	• Infant and under-five mortality rates* • Proportion of underweight children under-five years of age*	• Prevalence of deaths, injuries, diseases and disabilities caused by unsafe natural and occupational environment		• Death rate associated with and prevalence of communicable and non-communicable diseases (e.g. HIV/AIDS*, malaria*, tuberculosis*) • Proportion of persons abusing harmful substances • Life expectancy at birth or age 1 and health-adjusted life expectancy • Suicide rates

Process indicators applicable across categories:
- Proportion of received complaints on the right to health investigated and adjudicated by the national human rights institution, human rights ombudsperson or other mechanisms and the proportion of these responded to effectively by the government
- Net official development assistance (ODA) for the promotion of health sector received or provided as a proportion of public expenditure on health or Gross National Income*

All indicators should be disaggregated by prohibited grounds of discrimination, as applicable and reflected in metasheets

24.04.08

List of illustrative indicators on the right not to be subjected to torture or to cruel, inhuman or degrading treatment or punishment (UDHR, Art. 5)

	Physical and mental integrity of detained or imprisoned persons	Conditions of detention	Use of force by law enforcement officials outside detention	Community and domestic violence
Structural	• International human rights treaties, relevant to the right not to be subjected to torture or to cruel, inhuman or degrading treatment or punishment (RtnT), ratified by the State • Date of entry into force and coverage of the RtnT in the Constitution or other forms of superior law • Date of entry into force and coverage of domestic laws for implementing the RtnT, including code of conduct on medical trials and scientific experimentation on human beings • Type of accreditation of National Human Rights Institution by the rules of procedure of the International Coordinating Committee of National Institutions	• Date of entry into force of code of conduct for law enforcement officials, including on rules of conduct for interrogation of arrested, detained and imprisoned persons • Date of entry into force and coverage of formal procedure governing inspection of police cells, detention centres and prisons by independent inspection institutions • Legal maxima for *incommunicado* detention • Time frame and coverage of health policy for detention centres and prisons		• Date of entry into force and coverage of specific legislations on community and domestic violence • Number of rehabilitation centres for victims of domestic violence including women, partners and children
(spanning indicators)	• Proportion of received complaints on the RtnT investigated and adjudicated by the national human rights institution, human rights ombudsperson or other mechanisms and the proportion of these responded to effectively by the government • Proportion of communications sent by the Special Rapporteur on torture and on violence against women responded to effectively by government in the reporting period • Proportion of law enforcement officials (including police, military, specialised investigation agencies and custodial staff) trained in rules of conduct concerning proportional use of force, arrest, detention, interrogation or punishment			
Process		• Proportion of detained or imprisoned persons in facilities inspected by an independent body in the reporting period • Proportion of custodial staff formally investigated for physical and non-physical abuse or crime on detained or imprisoned persons (including torture and disproportionate use of force) in the reporting period • Proportion of formal investigations of custodial staff resulting in disciplinary action or prosecution • Actual prisons occupancy as a proportion of prison capacity in accordance with relevant UN conventions on prison conditions • Proportion of detained and imprisoned persons in accommodation meeting legally stipulated requirements (e.g. drinking water, cubic content of air, minimum floor space, heating) • Number of custodial and other relevant staff per inmate • Proportion of detention centres and prisons with facilities to segregate persons in custody (by sex, age, accused, sentenced, criminal cases, mental health, immigration related or other cases)	• Proportion of law enforcement officials formally investigated for physical and non-physical abuse or crime (including torture and disproportionate use of force) in the reporting period • Proportion of formal investigations of law enforcement officials resulting in disciplinary action or prosecution • Proportion of arrests and other acts of apprehending persons where a firearm was discharged by law enforcement officials	• Proportion of public social expenditure on campaigns to sensitise people on violence against women & children (e.g. violence by intimate partners, genital mutilation, rape) • Proportion of healthcare and community welfare professionals trained in handling domestic violence issues • Proportion of teaching staff trained against the use of physical violence against children • Proportion of teaching staff subjected to disciplinary action, prosecuted for physical and non-physical abuse on children • Proportion of women reporting forms of violence (physical, sexual or psychological) against self or her children initiating legal action or seeking help from police or counselling centres • Number of persons arrested, adjudicated, convicted or serving sentence for violent crime (including homicide, rape, assault) per 100,000 population in the reporting period
Outcome		• Incidence and prevalence of death, physical injury and communicable and non-communicable diseases (HIV/AIDS, malaria/tuberculosis*, mental illness) in custody • Proportion of detained or imprisoned persons held *incommunicado* or in prolonged solitary confinement • Reported cases of inhuman methods of execution and treatment of persons sentenced to death /incarcerated in the reporting period • Proportion of detained or imprisoned persons with body mass index < 18.5	• Incidence of death and physical injury resulting from arrests or other acts of apprehending persons by law enforcement officials in the reporting period	• Proportion of children or pupils per 1000 enrolled and patients who experienced corporal punishment in teaching and medical institutions • Incidence and prevalence of deaths and crimes related to community and domestic violence (including homicide, rape, assault) in the reporting period
(spanning indicators)	• Reported cases of torture or cruel, inhuman or degrading treatment or punishment perpetrated by an agent of the State or any other person acting under government authority or with its complicity, tolerance, or acquiescence, but without any or due judicial process (e.g. as reported to the UN Special Rapporteur on Torture/ Violence against Women), in the reporting period • Proportion of victims of torture or cruel, inhuman or degrading treatment or punishment who received compensation and rehabilitation, in the reporting period			

All indicators should be disaggregated by prohibited grounds of discrimination, as applicable and reflected in metasheets

24.04.08

List of illustrative indicators on the right to participate in public affairs (UDHR, Art. 21) (* MDG related indicators)

	Exercise of legislative, executive and administrative powers	Universal and equal suffrage	Access to public service positions
Structural	• International human rights treaties, relevant to the right to participate in public affairs, ratified by the State • Date of entry into force and coverage of the right to participate in public affairs in the Constitution or other forms of superior law • Date of entry into force and coverage of domestic laws for implementing the right to participate in public affairs, including freedom of opinion, expression, information, media, association and assembly • Date of entry into force of universal suffrage, right to vote, right to stand for election, legal provisions defining citizenship and limitations (including age limits) on permanent residents with respect to the right to participate in public affairs at national and local level • Quota, time frame and coverage of temporary and special measures for targeted populations in legislative, executive, judicial and appointed bodies • Type of accreditation of National Human Rights Institutions by the rules of procedure of the International Coordinating Committee of National Institutions • Number of registered and/or active non-governmental organisations (per 100,000 persons) involved in the promotion and protection of the right to participate in public affairs • Periodicity of executive and legislative elections at national and local level • Date of entry into force and coverage of laws establishing an independent national electoral body		• Date of entry into force and coverage of legal provisions guaranteeing access to public service positions without discrimination • Date of entry into force and coverage of administrative tribunals or dedicated judicial redress mechanism for public service matters
Process	• Proportion of received complaints on the right to participate in public affairs investigated and adjudicated by the national human rights institution, human rights ombudsperson or other mechanisms and the proportion of these responded to effectively by the government • Number of suffrages (election, referendum and plebiscite) at national and local level held during the reporting period • Number of legislations adopted by national and sub-national legislatures during the reporting period • Proportion of elections and sessions of national and locally elected bodies held as per the schedule laid down by constitutional or statutory bodies • Proportion of election campaign expenditure at national and sub-national level met through public funding • Proportion of elected personnel whose term of service was interrupted, by cause of interruption • Proportion of women and target groups included in the membership of national political parties or presented as candidate for election	• Proportion of the voting-age population registered to vote • Reported irregularities (intimidation, corruption or arbitrary interference) with registration, maintenance and review of electoral rolls • Number of complaints per elected position recorded and addressed in the election process by national and sub-national electoral authorities • Share of public expenditure on national and sub-national elections spent on voter education and registration campaigns • Number of political parties registered or recognised at national level • Proportion of voting age population not affiliated to political parties	• Proportion of vacancies in (selected) public authorities at national and sub-national level filled through selection of women and candidates from target population groups • Proportion of cases filed in administrative tribunals and dedicated judicial redress mechanism for public service matters adjudicated and finally disposed during the reporting period • Proportion of positions in the public service reserved to nationals or citizen
Outcome	• Proportion of seats in parliament*, elected and appointed bodies at sub-national and local level held by women and target groups	• Average voter turnout in national and local elections, by sex and target groups • Proportion of invalid and blank votes in elections to national and sub-national legislatures	• Reported cases of denial of access to public service or position on account of discrimination • Proportion of public service positions held by women and members of target groups
24.04.08	*All indicators should be disaggregated by prohibited grounds of discrimination, as applicable and reflected in metasheets*		

List of illustrative indicators on the right to education (UDHR, Art. 26) (* MDG related indicators)

	Universal Primary Education	Accessibility to Secondary and Higher Education	Curricula and Educational Resources	Educational Opportunity and Freedom
Structural	• International human rights treaties, relevant to the right to education, ratified by the State • Date of entry into force and coverage of the right to education in the Constitution or other form of superior law • Date of entry into force and coverage of domestic laws for implementing the right to education, including prohibition of corporal punishment, discrimination in access to education, making educational institutions barrier free and inclusive education (e.g. children with disabilities, children in detention, migrant children, indigenous children) • Date of entry into force and coverage of domestic law on the freedom of individuals and groups (including minorities) to establish and direct educational institutions • Number of registered and/or active non-governmental organisations (per 100,000 persons) involved in the promotion and protection of the right to education	• Time frame and coverage of the *plan of action* adopted by State party to implement the principle of compulsory primary education free of charge for all • Stipulated duration of compulsory education and minimum age for admission into school	• Time frame and coverage of national policy on education for all, including provision for temporary and special measures for target groups (e.g. working and street children) • Time frame and coverage of national policy on vocational and technical education • Date of entry into force and coverage of regulatory framework including standardised curricula for education at all levels • Proportion of education institutions at all level teaching human rights / number of hours in curricula on human rights education • Proportion of education institutions with mechanisms (student council) for students to participate in matters affecting them	
	(spanning row) Proportion of received complaints on the right to education investigated and adjudicated by the national human rights institution, human rights ombudsperson or other mechanisms and the proportion of these responded to effectively by the government Public expenditure on primary, secondary and higher education as proportion of gross national income; Net official development assistance (ODA) for education received or provided as proportion of public expenditure on education *			
Process	• Net Primary Enrollment ratio* by target groups, including children with disabilities • Drop out rate for primary education by grades for target groups • Proportion of enrolled children in public primary education institutions • Proportion of students (by target groups) covered under publicly supported additional financial programmes or incentives for primary education • Proportion of public schools with user charges for services other than tuition fees • Proportion of primary education teachers fully qualified and trained • Proportion of children getting education in their mother tongue • Proportion of students in grade 1 who attended pre-school	• Transition rate to secondary education by target groups • Gross enrollment ratio for secondary and higher education by target groups • Drop out rate for secondary education by grades for target groups • Proportion of enrolled students in public secondary and higher education institutions • Share of annual household expenditure on education per child enrolled in public secondary or high school • Proportion of students (by target groups) receiving public support or grant for secondary education • Proportion of secondary or higher education teachers fully qualified and trained • Proportion of students enrolled in vocational education programmes at secondary and post secondary level	• Proportion of schools or institutions conforming to stipulated national requirements on academic and physical facilities • Periodicity of curricula revision at all levels • Number of educational institutions by level recognized or derecognised during the reporting period by relevant regulatory body • Average salary of school teachers as percentage of regulated minimum wages • Proportion of teachers at all levels completing mandatory in-service training during reporting period • Ratio of students to teaching staff, in primary, secondary, public and private education	• Proportion of education institutions engaged in "active learning" activities • Proportion of adult population covered under basic education programmes • Proportion of students, by level, enrolled under distance and continuing education programmes • Number of institutions of ethnic, linguistic minority and religious population groups recognized or extended public support • Proportion of labour force availing retraining or skill-enhancement at public or supported institutions • Proportion of higher learning institutions enjoying managerial and academic autonomy • Personal computers in use per 100 population*
Outcome	• Ratios of girls to boys in primary education* by grades for target groups • Proportion of students starting grade 1 who reach grade 5 (primary completion rate)* • Proportion of out of school children in primary education age group	• Ratio of girls to boys in secondary or higher education* by grades • Proportion of children completing secondary education (secondary completion rate) • Number of graduates (first level University degree) per 1000 population	• (Improvement in) Density of primary, secondary and higher education facilities in the reporting period	• Proportion of women and targeted population with professional or university qualification
	(spanning row) Youth (15-24 years)* and adult (15+) literacy rates (i.e. reading, writing, calculating, problem-solving and other life skills)			

All indicators should be disaggregated by prohibited grounds of discrimination, as applicable and reflected in metasheets

24.4.08

List of illustrative indicators on the right to adequate housing (UDHR, Art. 25) (* MDG related indicators)

	Habitability	Accessibility to Services	Housing Affordability	Security of Tenure
Structural	• International human rights treaties, relevant to the right to adequate housing, ratified by the State • Date of entry into force and coverage of the right to adequate housing in the Constitution or other forms of superior law • Date of entry into force and coverage of domestic laws for implementing the right to adequate housing • Type of accreditation of National Human Rights Institutions by the rules of procedure of the International Coordinating Committee of National Institutions. • Number of registered and/or active non-governmental organizations (per 100,000 persons) involved in the promotion and protection of the right to adequate housing • Time frame and coverage of national housing policy or strategy for the progressive implementation of measures, including special measures for target groups, for the right to adequate housing at different levels of government • Time frame and coverage of national policy on rehabilitation, resettlement and management of natural disaster			• Date of entry into force and coverage of legislation on security of tenure, equal inheritance and protection against forced eviction
	• Proportion of received complaints on the right to adequate housing investigated and adjudicated by the national human rights institution, human rights ombudsperson or other mechanisms and the proportion of these responded effectively by the government • Number of and total public expenditures on housing reconstruction and rehabilitation by evicted/displaced persons during the reporting period • Net official development assistance (ODA) for housing (including land and basic services) received or provided as proportion of public expenditure on housing or GNI*			
Process	• Proportion of habitations (cities, towns and villages) brought under the provisions of building codes and by laws in the reporting period • Share of public expenditure on social or community housing • Habitable area (sq. m) added through reclamation, including of hazardous sites and change in land use pattern in the reporting period • Habitable area (sq. m per capita) earmarked for social or community housing during the reporting period	• Share of public expenditure on provision and maintenance of sanitation, water supply, electricity and physical connectivity of habitations • Proportion of targeted population that was extended sustainable access to an improved water source*, access to improved sanitation*, electricity and garbage disposal in the reporting period	• Proportion of households that receive public housing assistance, including those living in subsidised rented housing and households subsidised for ownership • Proportion of targeted households living in squatter settlements rehabilitated in the reporting period • Proportion of homeless population that was extended the use of public and community based shelters in the reporting period	• Average time taken to settle disputes related to housing and land rights in courts and tribunals • Number/proportion of legal appeals aimed at preventing planned evictions or demolitions ordered by court in the reporting period • Number/proportion of legal procedures seeking compensation following evictions in the reporting period, by result after adjudication • Number and proportion of displaced or evicted persons rehabilitated or resettled in the reporting period
Outcome	• Proportion of population with sufficient living space (persons per rooms or rooms per household) or average number of persons per room among target households • Proportion of households living in permanent structure in compliance with building codes and by-laws • Proportion of households living in or near hazardous conditions	• Proportion of urban population living in slums* • Proportion of population using an improved drinking water (public / private) source, sanitation facility, electricity and garbage disposal • Proportion of household budget of target population groups spent on water supply, sanitation, electricity and garbage disposal	• Proportion of households spending more than 'X' percent of their monthly income or expenditure on housing or average rent of bottom three income deciles as a proportion of the top three • Annual average of homeless persons per 100,000 population ('X' being defined normatively for the country context)	• Reported cases of "forced evictions" (e.g. as reported to UN special procedures), in the reporting period • Proportion of households with legally enforceable, contractual, statutory or other protection providing security of tenure or proportion of households with access to secure tenure • Proportion of women with titles to land or property

24.4.08

All indicators should be disaggregated by prohibited grounds of discrimination, as applicable and reflected in metasheets

List of illustrative indicators on the right to social security (UDHR, Art. 22) (* MDG related indicators)

	Income security for workers	Affordable access to health care	Family, child and adult dependent support	Targeted social assistance schemes
Structural	• International human rights and ILO treaties relevant to the right to social security ratified by the State • Date of entry into force and coverage of the right to social security in the Constitution or other forms of superior law • Date of entry into force and coverage of domestic laws for implementing the right to social security, including in the event of sickness, old age, unemployment, employment related injury, maternity, paternity, disability or invalidity, survivors and orphans, health care (including reproductive health care), and family and child support • Time frame and coverage of policy for universal implementation of the right to social security			
	• Date of entry into force and coverage of insurance or tax-based social security scheme • Legally prescribed qualifying period, rate of contribution, duration (e.g. length of maternity / leave) and rate of benefits under different schemes • Date of entry into force and coverage of international agreements on export of social security benefits (including on double taxation) to country of origin for migrant workers and families	• Date of entry into force and coverage of regulation on mandatory health insurance • Time frame and coverage of national policy on health and access to health care, including for reproductive health and for persons with disabilities • Time frame and coverage of national policy on drugs, including on generic drugs	• Date of entry into force and coverage of public support for family, including single-parent family, children and dependent adults • Legally prescribed qualifying period, rate of contribution, duration and rate of allowances	• Timeframe and coverage of social assistance programmes and non-contributory schemes for persons in specific situation of needs (e.g. IDP, refugees, war victims, long-term unemployed, persons, homeless) • Time frame and coverage of national policy on unemployment
Process	• Proportion of received complaints on the right to social security investigated and adjudicated by the national human rights institution, human rights ombudsperson or other relevant mechanism and the proportion of these responded to effectively by the government • Proportion of targeted population appropriately informed on its entitlements and benefits (in cash or in kind) under the applicable social security schemes • Net official development assistance (ODA) for implementing this right, received or provided as a proportion of public expenditure on social security and Gross National Income			
	• Number of workers newly registered as participant in the social security scheme in the reporting period • Proportion of requests for benefits (e.g. unemployment, pension benefits) reviewed and met in the reporting period • Proportion of cases or complaints, concerning social security obligations of enterprises, effectively responded to by government or relevant social security agency • Proportion of enterprises covered under domestic social security regulations and proportion thereof subjected to administrative action or prosecution	• Per capita public expenditure on primary health facilities (including for reproductive health care) and essential medicines • Number of targeted individuals newly registered as participant in the health insurance system in the reporting period • Proportion of household expenditures on health goods and services covered by health insurance / public support • Proportion of births attended by skilled health personnel* • Proportion of target population within X hour of medical and para-medical personnel and relevant health care facilities	• Public expenditure on family, children and adult- dependent allowance or benefit schemes per beneficiary • Proportion of household expenditure (food, health, day care, education, housing) on children and adult- dependent covered by public support • (Improvement in) Density of nursery/child care centers and old age homes for the targeted population or regions in the reporting period	• Public expenditures for targeted social assistance schemes per beneficiary • (Improvement in)Density of administrative offices and personnel providing targeted social assistance • Proportion of requests for social assistance (e.g. income transfer, subsidized housing, calamity relief) reviewed and met
Outcome	• Proportion of labour force participating in social security scheme(s) • Proportion of workers covered under social security who availed and received stipulated social security benefits in the reporting period	• Proportion of population covered by health insurance (public or private) • Proportion of persons with affordable access to health care, including essential drugs*, on a sustainable basis	• Proportions of entitled families, children and dependents receiving public support	• Proportion of population in specific situations of needs receiving social assistance for food, housing, health care, education, emergency or relief services
	• Proportion of individuals in the formal or informal economy below national poverty line before and after social transfers*			
	All indicators should be disaggregated by prohibited grounds of discrimination, as applicable and reflected in metasheets			

24.4.08

List of illustrative indicators on the right to work (UDHR, Art. 23) (* MDG related indicators)

	Access to decent and productive work	Just and safe working conditions	Training, skill upgradation and professional development	Protection from forced labour and unemployment
Structural	• International human rights and ILO treaties relevant to the right to work ratified by the State • Date of entry into force and coverage of the right to work in the Constitution or other forms of superior law • Date of entry into force and coverage of domestic laws for implementing the right to work including regulations to ensure equal opportunities for all and eliminate employment-related discriminations and/or special measures for target groups (e.g. women, children, indigenous, migrants) • Number of registered and/or active non-governmental organisations (per 100,000 persons), including trade unions, involved in the promotion and protection of the right to work	• Time frame and coverage of a national policy for full and productive employment • Date of entry into force and coverage of regulations and procedures to ensure safe and healthy working conditions, including an environment free of sexual harassment, and establishing an independent monitoring body • Maximum number of working hours per week stipulated by law • Minimum age for employment by occupation type • Duration of maternity, paternity and parental leave and leave entitlements on medical grounds and proportion of wage paid in covered period	• Time frame and coverage of national policy on vocational education and skill upgradation • Proportion of administrative regions with specialised public agencies to assist individuals in finding employment	• Time frame and coverage of awareness raising programme on labour standards • Time frame and coverage of policy for the elimination of forced labour, including child labour, migrant worker and of domestic work
	• Proportion of complaints on the right to work, including just and safe working conditions, investigated and adjudicated by the national human rights institution, human rights ombudsperson or other mechanisms (e.g. ILO procedures, trade unions) and the proportion of these responded to effectively by the government			
Process	• Proportion of target population receiving effective support for their (re-) entry into the labour market • Annual employment growth (job creation rates), by education level • Average time spent on unpaid domestic family care work as well as in unpaid work of family business by women,, men and children • Proportion of requests by parent or guardian for certified child care arrangements reviewed and met in the reporting period • Proportion of workers who moved from precarious to stable contracts during the reporting period	• Proportion and frequency of enterprises inspected for conformity with labour standards and proportion of inspections resulting in administrative action or prosecution • Proportion of inspected enterprises conform with labour standards • Proportion of employed persons, including domestic workers, whose salary level is covered under legislation (e.g. minimum wage) and/or wage setting procedures involving social partners (unions)	• Proportion of labour force undergoing some training during their employment • Proportion of unemployed persons involved in skill upgradation and other training programmes, including publicly financed jobs • Improvement in secondary and tertiary enrolment ratios in the reporting period	• Proportion of informal sector workers shifted to formal sector employment in the reporting period • Proportion of economically active children • Estimated number of labour force in the informal sector receiving some public support • Proportion of targeted unemployed persons covered by unemployment / social security benefits
Outcome	• Employment-to-population ratios*, by sex, target group and education level • Proportion of voluntary part-time workers to total part-time employed population • Share of women in wage employment in the non-agricultural sector* • Proportion of workers in precarious employment (e.g. short, fixed term, casual, seasonal workers etc.)	• Incidence of accident at work and occupational diseases • Ratio of women to men wages, by sector and by other target groups • Proportion of identified positions (e.g. senior officials, managerial positions in public/private service)held by women and other target groups	• Proportion of workers employed after skill upgradation and other training programmes, including publicly finance jobs • Long-term unemployment rates (1 year or more of unemployment), by sex, target groups or regions • Distribution of labour force by level of education	• Unemployment rates, by sex, target groups and level of education (LFS/registered) • Incidence of forced labour, including worst forms of child labour and of domestic work • Reported cases of violations of the right to work, including forced labour, discrimination, worst forms of child labour and of domestic work and unlawful termination of employment and proportion of victims who received adequate compensation
	• Gini indices and ratio of lowest/highest income quintiles or consumption expenditures (before and after taxes)			
24.4.08	*All indicators should be disaggregated by prohibited grounds of discrimination, as applicable and reflected in metasheets*			

The right to freedom of opinion and expression (UDHR, Art. 19) (* MDG related indicators)

	Freedom of opinion and to impart information	Access to information	Special duties and responsibilities
Structural	• International human rights treaties, relevant to the right to freedom of opinion and expression (RFoE), ratified by the State • Date of entry into force and coverage of the RFoE in the Constitution or other forms of superior law • Date of entry into force and coverage of domestic laws for implementing the RFoE, including availability of judicial review of any decision taken by the State to restrict RFOE • Number of registered and/or active non-governmental organisations (per 100,000 persons) involved in the promotion and protection of the RFoE • Date of entry into force and coverage of code of conduct/ethics for journalists and other media persons • Date of entry into force and coverage of legislation for the protection of the freedom of the media, including decriminalization of libel, defamation and slander • Date of entry into force and coverage of domestic law for the protection and safety of journalists and any other media persons, including protection against disclosure of sources • Date of entry into force and coverage of domestic law for equal opportunity of access to radio concessions and TV broadcast frequencies • Time frame and coverage of national policy on education for all, including provisions for temporary special measures for target groups, human rights curricula and "active learning"	• Date of entry into force and coverage of legislation on access to information • Date of establishment of an independent monitoring mechanism (e.g. Information Commissioner) • Date of entry into force and coverage of statistical legislation to protect independence and quality of official statistics • Timeframe and coverage of national policy to promote access to information technology	• Date of entry into force and coverage of domestic law prohibiting propaganda for war • Date of entry into force and coverage of domestic law(s) prohibiting advocacy of national, racial, religious or sexist hatred constituting incitement of discrimination, hostility or violence
Process	• Proportion of received complaints on RFoE investigated and adjudicated by the national human rights institution, human rights ombudsperson or other mechanisms and the proportion of these responded to effectively by the government • Proportion of communications sent by the UN Special Rapporteurs (e.g. Special Rapporteur on the promotion and protection of RFoE), responded to effectively by the government • Number of newspapers, magazines, radio stations, TV broadcasts, internet sites by ownership (public or private) and audience figures • Number of mergers or buying by the media companies investigated, adjudicated and refused by an independent competition commission in the reporting period • Number of newspapers, articles, internet sites and other media broadcasts closed or censored by regulatory authorities • Proportion of complaints filled by journalists or any other media persons investigated, adjudicated and approved by court or other competent mechanisms • Number of media institutions of ethnic, linguistic minority and religious population groups recognized or extended public support • Proportion of requests for holding demonstrations accepted by administrative authorities • Proportion of schools engaged in "active learning" activities, giving children the opportunity to express themselves freely	• Proportion of information requests by the media responded to effectively by government • Subscriptions and average daily sales of national and main regional newspapers • Proportion of population with access to TV and radio broadcasts • Number of personal computers in use with internet access per 100 population* • Number of internet domains registered per 1000 population	• Proportion of judicial actions on alleged libel, defamation and slander investigated and resulting in conviction • Proportion of judicial actions against propaganda for war investigated and resulting in conviction • Proportion of (quasi-) judicial actions against advocacy of national, racial, religious or sexist hatred investigated and resulting in conviction
Outcome	• Number of journalists and any other media persons who reported sanctions, political or corporate pressure for the publication of information	• Reported cases of non-disclosure of documents, archives and administrative or corporate data of public interest (e.g. justice records, arms exports, environmental data, asylum seekers) • Proportion of linguistic population having access to media broadcasts in their own language	• Proportion of victims of libel, defamation and slander who received compensation and rehabilitation

• Reported cases of killing, disappearance, detention and torture against journalists, human rights defenders or any other persons who exercised her/his RFoE, perpetrated by an agent of the State or any other person acting under government authority or with its complicity, tolerance or acquiescence, but without any or due judicial process (e.g. reported to UN special procedures)

All indicators should be disaggregated by prohibited grounds of discrimination, as applicable and reflected in metasheets

24.4.08

List of illustrative indicators on the right to a fair trial (UDHR, Art. 10-11)

	Access to and equality before courts and tribunals	Public hearing by competent and independent courts	Presumption of innocence and guarantees in the determination of criminal charges	Special protection for children	Review by a higher court
Structural	• International human rights treaties, relevant to the right to a fair trial, ratified by the State • Date of entry into force and coverage of the right to a fair trial in the Constitution or other forms of superior law • Date of entry into force and coverage of domestic laws for implementing the right to a fair trial, including on procedures for appointment, remuneration, dismissal of persons exercising judicial functions • Number of registered and/or active non-governmental organisations (per 100,000 persons) involved in the promotion and protection of the right to a fair trial				
	• Date of entry into force and coverage of legislation guaranteeing non-discriminatory access to courts (e.g. for unaccompanied women, children and migrants) • Date of entry into force and periodicity of review of civil and criminal procedure codes	• Timeframe and coverage of national policy on judicial services, including on court strengths, against extortion, bribery or corruption • Date of entry into force and coverage of regulatory bodies for judicial and legal profession	• Identified/prescribed time limits to guide pre- and trial stages in the determination of charges against a person • Timeframe and coverage of national policy on the provision of legal aid to specific population groups	• Date of entry into force and coverage of juvenile court • Date of entry into force and coverage of rehabilitation systems for children involved in crime • Legal age of criminal responsibility	• Date of entry into force and coverage of the right to appeal in a higher court and full review of legal and material aspects of person's conviction and sentence
	• Proportion of received complaints concerning the right to a fair trial investigated and adjudicated by the national human rights institution, human rights ombudsperson or other mechanisms and proportion of these responded to effectively by the government • Number of communications sent by the Special Rapporteur on the independence of judges and lawyers and proportion responded to effectively by the government • Proportion of judges, prosecutors and lawyers trained on human rights and related standards for the administration of justice				
Process	• Proportion of population covered within X hour of a fully functioning court or number of persons with judicial functions per 100,000 population • Proportion of requests for legal assistance and free interpreters being met (criminal and civil proceedings) annually Number/proportion of cases referred to alternative dispute resolution (ADR) • Proportion of crimes (e.g. rape, physical assaults, domestic violence) reported to the police (victimisation survey) • Proportion of crime victims in cases sent to court by police who confirm charges or appear at proceedings with the court or prosecutors	• Proportion of persons with judicial functions (e.g. judges and prosecutors) formally investigated for breach of duty, irregularity, abuses (e.g. corruption) • Proportion of formal investigations of persons with judicial functions resulting in disciplinary action or prosecution • Number/proportion of civilians tried by military courts or special courts • Average number of cases assigned/completed by person with judicial functions at different levels of judiciary • Share of public expenditure on courts and prosecution system • Average salary of persons with judicial functions as percentage of regulated minimum wages	• Proportion of cases where the time for arrested persons before receiving notice of the charge (in a legal sense and in language they understand) exceeded statutory or mandated timeframe • Proportion of public attendees at court who rate services and court as highly accessible in their own language (court user survey) • Proportion of defendants with access to adequate facilities and counsellor for their defence • Proportion of pending cases and average duration of criminal trials • Proportion of cases where time between arrest and trial exceeded statutory or mandated timeframe • Reported cases of killing, assault, threat and arbitrary dismissal of persons with judicial functions	• Proportion of prosecutors and defence lawyers working on juvenile cases with specialized training in juvenile justice • Proportion of juvenile detainees provided with free legal assistance within 24 hours of the start of custody • Proportion of juveniles in custody receiving education/vocational training by trained teachers for same hours as student that age at liberty • Proportion of courts adapted to handling juvenile cases • Proportion of convicted juveniles sentenced to imprisonment • Proportion of juveniles accessing rehabilitation services after release	• Proportion of convictions for serious offences in which the person convicted received legal assistance to consider seeking review by higher court/tribunal • Proportion of cases appealed by defendants or by prosecutors • Proportion of cases where the right to appeal is excluded or restricted to specific issues of law
Outcome	• Conviction rates for indigent defendants provided with legal representation as a proportion of conviction rates for defendants with lawyer of their own choice • Proportion of crimes (e.g. rape, physical assaults) brought before judicial authorities	• Proportion of total hearings opened to general public • Proportion of adjudicated cases for which at least one irregularity in the pre-trial determination of charges was noted by the courts	• Proportion of convictions obtained in absentia (in whole or in part) • Reported cases of guilt presumption and prejudgment by a court or public authorities (e.g. adverse public statements)	• Number of children arrested/detained by 100,000 child population • Recidivism rates of juveniles	• Proportion of criminal convictions in which sentence was reduced or a criminal conviction vacated or returned for retrial or resentencing
	• Conviction rates by type of adjudicated crimes (e.g. rape, homicide, physical assaults) and characteristics of victims and perpetrators (e.g. sex, juvenile) • Reported cases of arbitrary detentions in the reporting period • Reported cases of miscarriage of justice and proportion of victims who received compensation within a reasonable time				
	*All indicators should be disaggregated by prohibited grounds of discrimination as reflected in metasheets*				

24.4.08

Appendix 5

Samples of meta-data sheets on identified human rights indicators by the OHCHR

Indicator 1	**International human rights treaties, relevant to the right to life, ratified by the state** (see structural indicators in the table on the right to life in *Appendix 4*).
Definition	Proportion of international and regional human rights treaties, with direct reference and/or relevance to the realisation of the right to life, that have been ratified by the state. 'International human rights treaties' is used as a generic term embracing all instruments binding under international human rights law, regardless of their formal designation (*e.g.* Covenant, Convention or Optional Protocol). The reference to the 'right to life' follows primarily the formulation used in article 3 of the *Universal Declaration of Human Rights*, article 6 of the *International Covenant on Civil and Political Rights* and its elaboration in *General Comment* No. 6 of the Human Rights Committee.
Rationale	Ratification of an international human rights treaty reflects a certain acceptance of concerned human rights standards by a state and gives an indication, notably at international level, of a state's commitment to undertake steps that help in the realisation of those rights. When the state has ratified a treaty it assumes a legal obligation to respect, protect and fulfil the human rights standards reflected in that treaty. The indicator is a *structural indicator* that captures the 'commitment' of a state to implement its human rights obligations.
Method of computation	The indicator is computed as a ratio of the actual number of treaties ratified by the state to the reference list of treaties. A reference list of core international human rights treaties, including optional protocols, adopted and opened for ratification by the General Assembly of the United Nations is available at: http://www2.ohchr.org/English/law/index.htm#instruments.
Data collection and source	The main source of data on the indicator is administrative records at the depository authority, namely the United Nations Office of Legal Affairs

(see http://untreaty.un.org/ola/). The OHCHR website also presents this information and updates it periodically.

Periodicity	The indicator database is reviewed periodically and information can be accessed on a continuous basis.
Disaggregation	Disaggregation of information is not applicable for this indicator.
Comments and limitations	The right to life finds its most general recognition in article 3 of the *Universal Declaration of Human Rights*. Article 6 of the *International Covenant on Civil and Political Rights* recognises the inherent right of every person to life, adding that this right "shall be protected by law" and that "no one shall be arbitrarily deprived of life". The right to life of persons under the age of 18 and the obligation of states to guarantee the enjoyment of this right to the maximum extent possible are both specifically recognised in article 6 of the *Convention on the Rights of the Child*. UDHR, article 3, ICESCR, article 12(2-a), CERD, article 5, ICRMW, article 9, CEDAW, article 12 and CRPD article 10 are other examples of provisions relevant to the right to life and this indicator.

The indicator provides information on acceptance by a state of international human rights standards and its intention or commitment to undertake steps to realise human rights in conformity with the provisions of the relevant instruments. It does not, however, capture the actual process of implementation or the results thereof.

Ratification constitutes an act whereby a state establishes its consent to be legally bound by the terms of a particular treaty. At the international level, it requires depositing a formal "instrument of ratification or accession" to the depository authority. At the national level, ratification may require a state to undertake certain steps, in accordance with its constitutional provisions, before it consents to be bound by the treaty provisions internationally. The process of ratifying a treaty is normally initiated with a state signing a treaty as a means of authentication and expression of its willingness to continue the treaty ratification process. The signature qualifies the signatory state to proceed to ratification. It also creates an obligation to refrain, in good faith, from acts that would defeat the object and the purpose of the treaty. Accession is the term used in situations where the state has not signed the treaty beforehand, but has directly expressed its consent to become a party to that treaty.

The indicator does not reflect possible "reservation" entered by a state on a treaty. A reservation is a declaration made by a state by which it purports to exclude or alter the legal effect of certain provisions of the treaty in their application to that state. A reservation enables a state to accept a multilateral treaty as a whole by providing it with the possibility of not applying certain provisions with which it does not want to comply. Reservations can be made by a state when the treaty is signed, ratified or acceded to and in conformity with the objective and purpose of the treaty itself and the *Vienna Convention of the Law of Treaties*, 1969.

Indicator 2	**Time frame and coverage of national policy on sexual and reproductive health** (see structural indicators in the table on the right to health in *Appendix 4*).
Definition	The indicator refers to the date of adoption or the period for which the national policy statement on sexual and reproductive health has been put into effect at the country level. The indicator also captures the population coverage or the spatial administrative scope of the policy statement, such as in countries where there is division of responsibilities between the national government and the sub-national/local governments.
Rationale	A national policy statement on a subject is an instrument that is expected to outline a government's objectives, policy framework, strategy and/or a concrete plan of action to address issues under that subject. While providing an indication on the commitment of the government to address the concerned subject, it may also provide relevant benchmarks for holding the government accountable for its acts of commission or omission concerning that subject. Moreover, a policy statement is a means to translate the human rights obligations of a state party into an implementable programme of action that helps in the realisation of the human rights. The indicator is a *structural indicator* that captures the 'commitment' of a state to implement its human rights obligations in respect of the 'sexual and reproductive health' attribute of the right to health.
Method of computation	The indicator is computed separately for time frame or period of application and the coverage or administrative scope of the policy. Time frame is the date of adoption (*e.g.* 1/1/2006) of the policy statement by a country or the time period for which the policy should be implemented (*e.g.* 1/1/2006 - 1/1/2010). Coverage is computed as a proportion of sub-national administrative units or population covered under the ambit of national policy.
Data collection and source	The main source of data is administrative records at the national and sub-national level.
Periodicity	The indicator database can be normally reviewed and accessed on a continuing basis.
Disaggregation	While disaggregation of information on the indicator is not conceptually feasible, a national policy may focus on specific areas, regions or population groups, in which case it may be desirable to highlight it.
Comments and limitations	The indicator provides information on a state's commitment to undertake steps, outlining its policy framework and programme of action, to realise human rights in conformity with the provisions of relevant human rights standards on sexual and reproductive health. It does not, however, capture the actual process of implementation or the results thereof.

For many countries, national policy on sexual and reproductive health may not be a separate policy document; rather it may well be a part of general policy statement on health or a human rights action plan. Accordingly, a judgment may have to be exercised on the extent to which sexual and reproductive health issues and the relevant human rights standards on reproductive health are reflected in the national policy on health or the human rights action plan.

In its *General Comment* No. 14 (ICESCR Art. 12) on the right to the highest attainable standard of health, the Committee on Economic, Social and Cultural Rights elaborates on the need to develop comprehensive national public health strategy and plan of action to address the health concerns of the population, including reproductive health. It underlines that such a strategy should inter alia be devised on the basis of a participatory and transparent process and include indicators and benchmarks relevant to monitor the right to health. The Committee points out that "Reproductive health means that women and men have the freedom to decide if and when to reproduce and the right to be informed and to have access to safe, effective, affordable, and acceptable methods of family planning of their choice as well as the right of access to appropriate health-care services that will, for example, enable women to go safely through pregnancy and childbirth." Similarly, CEDAW Committee *General Recommendation* 24 (1999) points out that access to health care, including reproductive health, is a basic right under the *Convention on the Elimination of All Forms of Discrimination against Women*.

UDHR, article 25, ICESCR, articles 10(2) and 12, ICERD, article 5(e-iv), ICRMW, articles 28 and 43(e), CEDAW, articles 12 and 14(2-b) and CRPD article 25 are examples of provisions relevant to the right to health.

Indicator 3	**Date of entry into force and coverage of the right to education in the Constitution or other form of superior law** (see structural indicators in the table on the right to education in *Appendix 4*).
Definition	The indicator refers to the date on which provisions of the Constitution or other superior laws relating to the right to education became enforceable. The indicator also captures the spatial or population coverage of the relevant provisions related to the right to education, such as in countries where there is division of legal competencies between the national government and the sub-national or local governments. 'Constitutional or other form of superior law' refers to the system of fundamental laws that prescribes the functions and limits of government action and against which other supportive legislation is assessed for its validity. The reference to the 'right to education' follows primarily the formulation used in article 26 of the *Universal Declaration of Human Rights*, article 13 of the *International Covenant on Economic, Social and Cultural Rights* and its elaboration in *General Comment* No. 13 of the Committee on Economic, Social and Cultural Rights. The right to education is also developed in other core international human rights treaties, such as in articles 23, 28 and 29 of the *Convention on the Rights of the Child*.

Rationale	Inclusion of the right to education in the Constitution or other form of superior law reflects a certain acceptance of this right by a state and gives an indication, notably at the national level, of a state's commitment to protect and implement this right. When the state has enshrined a right in its Constitution or other form of superior law, it also assumes a legal obligation to ensure that other legislation (national and sub-national legislation) is in conformity with and not contradictory to the right. The indicator is a *structural indicator* that captures the 'commitment' of a state to implement its human rights obligations in respect of the right to education.
Method of computation	The indicator is computed separately for the date of entry into force and the coverage or administrative scope of the law. The date of entry into force is the date on which the law or provision became enforceable. Coverage is computed as a proportion of sub-national administrative units or population covered under the law. Information on the date of entry into force should be provided with a direct and accurate link to the relevant provisions.
Data collection and source	The main source of data on the indicator is the legal records of the state.
Periodicity	The indicator data can be normally reviewed and accessed on a continuing basis.
Disaggregation	Disaggregation of information is not applicable for this indicator, however provisions under the Constitution or other superior law may have particular reference to the protection of the right to education for certain groups (*e.g.* minorities or girl child), in which case it may be desirable to highlight it.
Comments and limitations	This indicator provides information on the extent to which a state protects the right to education in its Constitution or superior laws, demonstrating its acceptance of international human rights standards and its intention or commitment to legally protect this right. It does not, however, capture the extent to which the legal protection of the right to education in the Constitution or superior laws is implemented and upheld at other levels of the legal system, nor how broadly or narrowly the right is applied, or the degree to which the right can be enforced and by whom. This indicator does not capture the actual process of implementation or the results thereof. This indicator could be difficult to assess if the right to education is not explicitly articulated in the Constitution or superior laws. Moreover, provision for the right to education in the Constitution does not necessarily mean that the right is being protected by law (for example, further judicial interpretations may have rendered the Constitutional protection meaningless). Likewise, a lack of Constitutional protection may lead one to believe that there is no recognition of the right when this may not be the case. For example, in some countries there are only a few rights written into the Constitution or superior laws, and it is left to the judiciary

to interpret the rights as being implied. In this instance, a mere reading of provisions may yield an inaccurate conclusion on the enforcement and coverage of the concerned right. A correct reading, in such cases, requires a detailed analysis of relevant jurisprudence/case law or administrative decisions.

UDHR, article 26, ICESCR, articles 13 and 14, ICERD, article 5 (e-v), ICRMW, articles 30 and 43 (a-c), CRC, articles 23, 28 and 29, CEDAW, articles 10 and 14(2-d), and CRPD, article 24 are examples of provisions relevant to the right to education and this indicator.

Indicator 4	**Proportion of births attended by skilled health personnel** (see process indicators in the table on the right to health in *Appendix 4*).
Definition	The indicator refers to proportion of deliveries attended by persons trained to give necessary supervision, care and counsel to women during pregnancy, labour and the post-partum period; to conduct deliveries on their own; and to care for newborns.
Rationale	Health and well-being of the woman and the child during and after delivery greatly depends on their access to birth delivery services, the quality of these services and the actual circumstances of delivery. All of these are influenced by the state health policies, public provisioning of health services and regulation of private health care. Indeed availability of professional and skilled health personnel to assist in child birth is essential for reducing mortality - maternal as well as of the child - during and after delivery. The indicator captures efforts being made by the state to promote and provide professional and skilled health personnel to attend to the medical needs of pregnancy and birth. It is a *process indicator* related to 'sexual and reproductive health' attribute of the right to health.
Method of computation	The indicator is computed as a ratio of births attended by skilled health personnel (doctors, nurses or midwives) to the total number of deliveries.
Data collection and source	The main sources of data are country level administrative records maintained by local authorities, registration system for population data, records of health ministries and household surveys, including Demographic and Health Surveys. The World Health Organisation (WHO) and the United Nations Population Fund (UNFPA) compile country data series based on these sources. The United Nations Children's Fund (UNICEF) also provides country data series through the implementation of its Multiple Indicator Cluster Surveys.
Periodicity	In general, the indicator based on administrative records is available annually and the indicator based on household survey every three to five years.

Disaggregation	Disaggregation of indicator by region or areas, for example between rural and urban areas, is useful in assessing disparities in the availability of health services. In addition, data should be disaggregated by the age of women (at least for women under the age of 18 years) and, as applicable, by relevant demographic groups (*e.g.* ethnic groups, minorities, indigenous and migrants) and socio-economic status (income or consumption expenditure quintiles).
Comments and limitations	Skilled health personnel include only those who are properly trained and who have appropriate equipment and drugs. Traditional birth attendants, even if they have received a short training course, are not included.
	CEDAW, in its *General Recommendation* No. 24 (1999), requests states to inform about the "supply of free services where necessary to ensure safe pregnancies, childbirth and post-partum periods for women. Many women are at risk of death or disability from pregnancy-related causes because they lack the funds to obtain or access the necessary services, which include antenatal, maternity and post-natal services. The Committee notes that it is the duty of states parties to ensure women's right to safe motherhood and emergency obstetric services and they should allocate to these services the maximum extent of available resources." The CESCR, in its *General Comment* No. 5 (1994) on Persons with disabilities, states that "Women with disabilities also have the right to protection and support in relation to motherhood and pregnancy."
	UDHR, article 25, ICESCR, articles 10(2) and 12, ICERD, article 5(e-iv), ICRMW, articles 28 and 43(e), CEDAW, articles 12 and 14(2-b) and CRPD article 25 are examples of provisions relevant to the right to health.
	This is a Millennium Development Goal indicator.
Indicator 5	**Proportion of received complaints on the *right not to be subjected to torture or to cruel, inhuman or degrading treatment or punishment* investigated or adjudicated by the national human rights institution, human rights ombudsperson and other mechanisms, and the proportion responded to effectively by the government in the reporting period** (see process indicators in the table on the right not to be subjected to torture or to cruel, inhuman or degrading treatment or punishment in *Appendix 4*).
Definition	The indicator refers to the proportion of received individual complaints on the right not to be subjected to torture or to cruel, inhuman or degrading treatment or punishment that were investigated or adjudicated by made to the national human rights institution, human rights ombudsperson and/or other officially recognised independent mechanisms during the reporting period. Where the mechanism transmits complaints to the government, or communicates in respect of the complaints, the indicator includes the proportion of such transmissions or communications that have received an effective response from the government. Useful guidance on what ought to be included in a complaint can be found on the OHCHR website, notably in

the model complaint form for communications to the Human Rights Committee, Committee Against Torture, Committee on the Elimination of Racial Discrimination and the Committee on the Elimination of Discrimination Against Women.

Rationale	The indicator captures to an extent the effort required of states to respect, protect and fulfil the right not to be subjected to torture or to cruel, inhuman or degrading treatment or punishment, in conformity with article 7 of the *International Covenant on Civil and Political Rights*, the provisions of the *Convention against Torture and Other Cruel, Inhuman or Degrading Treatment or Punishment* and the provisions of other international laws. States parties must ensure that individuals have access to effective remedies to vindicate their right. States Parties should make appropriate reparation, take provisional or interim measures as necessary, as well as measures to prevent a recurrence of violations of the right, and ensure that those responsible are brought to justice (Human Rights Committee *General Comment* 31, CCPR/C//Rev.1/Add.13). It is a *process indicator* that reflects the willingness of states to take steps towards the realisation of the right.
Method of computation	The number of complaints is calculated as the sum of individual complaints on the right not to be subjected to torture or to cruel, inhuman or degrading treatment or punishment received by all relevant independent bodies at national level. The proportion investigated or adjudicated is calculated as the ratio of the number of complaints received during the reporting period which were investigated or adjudicated to the total number of complaints received. The proportion effectively responded to by the government is calculated as the ratio of the number of complaints to which an effective response was made by the government to the total number of complaints communicated to the government during the reference period.
Data collection and source	The main sources of data are administrative records maintained by the national human rights institution, human rights ombudsperson and other mechanisms.
Periodicity	The information is normally compiled and published annually.
Disaggregation	To enable detection of the pattern of abuse against particular groups or in particular areas, the indicator should be disaggregated by region and the characteristics of the alleged victim (sex, age, ethnic/racial/national/ religious/political affiliation, disability, sexual orientation, profession, whether or not detained at the time of the alleged abuse). Similarly, the indicator should be disaggregated according to whether the abuse is alleged to have been committed by a state agent, with the complicity/tolerance/acquiescence of a state agent, or by a private individual or individuals.

To have an overall assessment of the effectiveness of investigation and adjudication procedures, data related to this indicator should be disaggregated by the end result of the procedure. |

Comments and limitations	Where there is a communication with a government, the indicator will require a judgement to be made on what constitutes an "effective" response. While an official denial without supporting evidence or investigation of the alleged facts will not meet the criterion of effectiveness, the precise application of the criterion may vary from case to case. An assessment of the effectiveness of the response is best carried out by the national human rights institution, human rights ombudsperson or other mechanism in a transparent manner and may involve considerations like timeliness and completeness of the response, its adequacy in responding to specific questions posed or suggestions for action, as well as the effectiveness of action initiated by the government, which may include investigation, release or changes in the treatment of a detained or imprisoned person, payment of compensation, amendment of legislation, etc.

The basic source of information for this indicator comes from *events-based data on human rights violations*. Such data may underestimate (or sometimes, though rarely, even overestimate) the incidence of torture or cruel, inhuman or degrading treatment or punishment, if used in a casual manner to draw generalised conclusions for the country as a whole. Moreover, in most instances, the number of cases reported to independent bodies depends on the awareness, access to information, motivation and perseverance of the alleged or potential victim, his or her family and friends, or civil society organisations in the country concerned.

The Human Rights Committee, in its *General Comment* No. 20 (1992) states, in its paragraph 14, that "the right to lodge complaints against maltreatment prohibited by article 7 must be recognised in the domestic law. Complaints must be investigated promptly and impartially by competent authorities so as to make the remedy effective. The reports of states parties should provide specific information on the remedies available to victims of maltreatment and the procedure that complainants must follow, and statistics on the number of complaints and how they have been dealt with."

UDHR, article 5, CAT, articles 1-16, ICERD, article 5(b), ICRMW, articles 10 and 11, CEDAW, articles 2 and 16, CRPD article 15 and CRC articles 37 and 39, are examples of provisions relevant to the right not to be subjected to torture or to cruel, inhuman or degrading treatment or punishment.

Model questionnaires for complaints are available on the OHCHR website at http://www2.ohchr.org/english/bodies/question.htm.

Indicator 6	**Ratio of students to teaching staff in primary and secondary, public and private, education institutions** (see process indicators in the table on the right to education in *Appendix 4*).
Definition	The ratio of students to teaching staff or the pupil-teacher ratio is the average number of pupils per teacher at the level of education specified in a given school-year, based on headcounts for both pupils and teachers. Teachers or teaching staff include the number of persons employed full

time or part time in an official capacity to guide and direct the learning experience of students, irrespective of their qualifications or the delivery mechanism, *i.e.* face-to-face and/or at a distance. This excludes educational personnel who have no active teaching duties (*e.g.* headmasters, headmistresses or principals who do not teach) and persons who work occasionally or in a voluntary capacity.

Rationale	The ratio of students to teaching staff is an important indicator of the resources that a country devotes to education. To a limited extent, the indicator can also be interpreted as reflecting a qualitative aspect of education infrastructure in a country. Teachers are the most important resource in an educational environment, particularly at the primary and secondary levels. The student-teacher ratio provides a measure of students' access to teachers, and thus reflects an important element of the provisioning that the state may have to make for meeting its obligations on the realisation of the right to education This indicator is a *process indicator* related to the 'curricula and educational resources' attribute of the right to education.
Method of computation	The indicator is computed by dividing the number of full-time equivalent students at a given level of education by the number of full-time equivalent "teachers" at that level and in similar types of institutions, in a given school year. Some data collection methods include counts of all teaching staff, and since all teaching staff includes staff with administrative duties and both full- and part-time teachers, comparability of these ratios may be affected as the proportion of part-time teachers may vary from one country to another.
Data collection and source	The main source of data at the country level is administrative records on school enrolments and staff strengths maintained by the relevant public agencies. The UNESCO Institute for Statistics (UIS) compiles and provides national level information on the pupil-teacher ratio for both primary and secondary education, based on data reported by national education ministries or national statistical agencies. The information is gathered through questionnaires sent annually to countries and is made available by UIS with a two years lag with respect to the reference year. While information on this indicator is not currently collated on a disaggregated basis for public and private schools at the international level, it should generally be available at the national level and could be useful to report in instances where there may be significant differences in the quality of public and private education at the primary and secondary levels.
Periodicity	For most countries the pupil-teacher ratio is available annually.
Disaggregation	Beyond the disaggregation referred to in the indicator itself (primary/secondary, public/private) further disaggregation may be necessary for this indicator, for instance, by region or areas. A break-up for

rural and urban areas, is useful in assessing possible disparities across different regions. In addition, it may be useful to disaggregate the data for teaching staff and students by sex and, as applicable, by relevant demographic groups (*e.g.* ethnic groups, minorities, indigenous, migrant children, children with disabilities).

Comments and limitations	Teachers are the most important resource in an educational environment, particularly at the primary and secondary levels. The student-teacher ratio provides a measure of students' access to teachers, and thus reflects an important element of the provisioning that the state may have to make for meeting its obligations on the realisation of the right to education.

Because of the difficulty of constructing direct measures of quality of education being imparted, this indicator is also used as a proxy for assessing the education quality, on the assumption that a smaller ratio of students to teaching staff means better access by students to teaching resources. A lower ratio would generally imply that a teacher can potentially pay more attention to individual students, which may, in the long run, result in a better performance of students. There may be situations where such a conclusion may not be true due to accountability issues and ineffective use of teaching resources. However, a very high ratio of students to teaching staff certainly suggests insufficient professional support for learning, particularly for students from disadvantaged home backgrounds.

"Teaching staff" refers to professional personnel directly involved in teaching students. The classification includes classroom teachers; special education teachers; and other teachers who work with students as a whole class in a classroom, in small groups in a resource room, or in one-to-one teaching inside or outside a regular classroom. Teaching staff also includes chairpersons of departments whose duties include some amount of teaching, but it does not include non-professional personnel who support teachers in providing instruction to students, such as teachers' aides and other para-professional personnel.

The concept of a ratio of students to teaching staff is different from that of class size. Although one country may have a lower ratio of students to teaching staff than another, this does not necessarily mean that classes are smaller in the first country or that students in the first country receive more teaching inputs. The relationship between the ratio of students to teaching staff and average class size is influenced by factors like differences between countries in the length of the school year, the annual number of hours for which a student attends class, the annual time teachers are expected to spend teaching, the grouping of students within classes, and the practices related to team learning.

This indicator does not take into account differences in teachers' qualifications, pedagogical training, experiences and status, teaching materials and variations in classroom conditions, factors which could affect the quality of teaching/learning.

UDHR, article 26, ICESCR, articles 13 and 14, ICERD, article 5 (e-v), ICRMW, articles 30 and 43 (a-c), CRC, articles 23, 28 and 29, and CEDAW, articles 10 and 14(2-d) are examples of provisions relevant to the right to education and this indicator.

Indicator 7	**Reported cases of forced evictions in the reporting period** (see outcome indicators in the table on the right to adequate housing in *Appendix* 4).
Definition	This indicator refers to the number of reported individual cases of forced eviction during the reference period. "Forced eviction" is defined as "the permanent or temporary removal against their will of individuals, families and/or communities from the homes and/or land which they occupy, without the provision of and access to appropriate forms of legal or other protection" (*General Comment* No. 7, ICESCR).
Rationale	The Committee on Economic, Social and Cultural Rights has observed that all persons should possess a degree of security of tenure which guarantees legal protection against forced eviction, harassment and other threats. It has argued that forced evictions are prima facie incompatible with the requirements of the ICESCR (*General Comment* No. 7). Moreover, given the interdependence of all human rights, forced evictions frequently violate other human rights. Thus, while manifestly breaching the rights enshrined in the ICESCR, the practice of forced evictions may also result in violations of civil and political rights, such as the right to life, the right to security of the person, the right to non-interference with privacy, family and home and the right to the peaceful enjoyment of possessions. It is an *outcome indicator* intended to analyse the degree to which states protect the security of tenure.
Method of computation	The indicator is computed as a head count of all reported cases of forced eviction in a specific period of time.
Data collection and source	The main data source for this indicator is records maintained by national human rights institutions, non-governmental organisations and in certain instances records of administrative agencies responsible for or monitoring rehabilitation.
Periodicity	Information on the indicator should be available on a periodic basis. It is often reported annually by organisations monitoring security of tenure.
Disaggregation	In order to be meaningful, the information on this indicator should be disaggregated by sex and age (at least for children or young people under the age of 18 years) and, as applicable, by relevant demographic groups (*e.g.* ethnic groups, minorities and migrants) and socio-economic status (income or consumption expenditure quintiles).
Comments and limitations	The indicator can be one good summary measure of the realisation of the right to adequate housing. Yet like all indicators that are based on *event-based data on human rights violations* and depend on multiple information sources, the indicator may suffer from reliability issues. It may underestimate (or sometimes, though rarely, even overestimate) the

incidence of forced evictions, if used in a casual manner to draw generalised conclusions for the country as a whole. Moreover, in most instances, the number of cases reported would depend on the awareness, access to information, motivation and perseverance of the civil society organisations agencies and the media in following the relevant events.

The term "forced evictions" is, in some respects, problematic. This expression seeks to convey a sense of arbitrariness and of illegality. For many observers, the reference to "forced evictions" is a tautology, while others have criticised the expression "illegal evictions" on the ground that it assumes that the relevant law provides adequate protection of the right to housing and conforms with the Covenant, which is by no means always the case. Similarly, it has been suggested that the term "unfair evictions" is even more subjective by virtue of its failure to refer to any legal framework at all. The international human rights community, especially in the context of the UN human rights system, has opted to use "forced evictions", primarily because all suggested alternatives also suffer from certain ambiguities. The prohibition on forced evictions does not, however, apply to evictions carried out by force in accordance with the law and in conformity with the provisions of the International Covenants on Human Rights.

Women, children, youth, older persons, indigenous people, ethnic and other minorities, and other vulnerable individuals and groups all suffer disproportionately from the practice of forced eviction. Women in all groups are especially vulnerable given the extent of statutory and other forms of discrimination which often apply in relation to property rights (including home ownership) or rights of access to property or accommodation, and their particular vulnerability to acts of violence and sexual abuse when they are rendered homeless. The non-discrimination provisions of articles 2.2 and 3 of ICESCR impose an additional obligation upon Governments to ensure that, where evictions do occur, appropriate measures are taken to ensure that no form of discrimination is involved.

UDHR article 25, ICESCR article 11, CERD article 5, CEDAW article 14, CRC article 27, CMW article 43 and CRPD article 28 have references of relevance to the indicator. The CESCR also recognises legal security of tenure under its *General Comment* No. 4 (1991) on the right to adequate housing: "Notwithstanding the type of tenure, all persons should possess a degree of security of tenure which guarantees legal protection against forced eviction, harassment and other threats".

Some institutions, such as the World Bank and the Organisation for Economic Co-operation and Development (OECD) have adopted guidelines on relocation and/or resettlement with a view to limiting the scale of and human suffering associated with forced evictions. Such practices often accompany large-scale development projects, such as dam-building and other major energy projects.

Indicator 8	**Conviction rates for indigent defendants provided with legal representation as a proportion of conviction rates for defendants with lawyers of their own choice** (see outcome indicators in the table on the right to fair trial in *Appendix 4*).
Definition	The indicator measures the ratio of conviction rate of defendants who were provided with free legal representation to that of defendants who had legal counsel of their own choice, in the reporting period. Though the indicator could be used separately for the two conviction rates, it is more useful when used as a ratio of the two.
Rationale	Article 14(3)(d) ICCPR provides that defendants should have legal assistance assigned to them, in any case where the interests of justice so requires, and without payment if they do not have sufficient means to pay for it. The Human Rights Committee, in its *General Comment 32*, states that "Counsel provided by the competent authorities on the basis of this provision must be effective in the representation of the accused". Furthermore, blatant incompetence by assigned counsel may entail the responsibility of the state. The indicator is an *outcome indicator* that relates to the access to and equality before the courts attribute of the right to a fair trial. As such, it measures the extent to which equality is achieved in practice.
Method of computation	The indicator is computed separately for defendants provided with legal representation and for defendants with a lawyer of their own choice before taking the ratio of the two. For each group, the indicator is calculated as the ratio of the number of defendants in that group who were convicted to the total number of defendants in that group who stood trial during the reporting period.
Data collection and source	The main sources of data are court records and reports of the office of the prosecutor at the national or sub-national level.
Periodicity	The data, if compiled, should be available on an annual basis.
Disaggregation	The indicator should be disaggregated by type of crimes (*e.g.* homicide, rape, assault, robbery, etc.), stage of proceedings (first hearing or appeal), and by region or administrative unit. It should also be disaggregated by characteristics of the defendant, in particular by sex, age (at least for children or young people under the age of 18 years), and, as applicable, by relevant demographic groups (*e.g.* ethnic groups, minorities, migrants, persons with disabilities, sexual orientation).
Comments and limitations	The indicator is a good measure of the relative level of competence of assigned lawyers, and thus of the effective implementation of the right to a fair trial regardless of economic status of the defendant. However, particularly in regions or states with a small number of cases, the indicator should not be over-analysed; each case must be assessed on its own merits. It may also be useful to use this indicator jointly with an indicator on the nature and average length of sentences for indigent defendants and defendants with lawyers of their own choice.

	UDHR articles 10-11, ICCPR articles 14-15, ICERD article 5(a), CEDAW article 2, CRC articles 12(2), 37(d) and 40, ICRMW articles 16(5-9) and 18, and CRPD article 13, are examples of references of relevance to the right to a fair trial.
Indicator 9	**Infant mortality rate** (see outcome indicators in the tables on the right to life, the right to adequate food and the right to health in *Appendix* 4).
Definition	The indicator refers to infants dying before reaching the age of one year per 1000 live births during the specified period.
Rationale	As a measure of child survival, the infant mortality rate is a key socio-economic statistic for many human rights, including the right to life, the right to health and the right to adequate food. The level of this indicator can be potentially influenced by a wide range of economic, social, political and environmental determinants. As a consequence, the indicator will be particularly important in the monitoring of the results of state parties' actions in fulfilling their obligations in creating favourable and necessary conditions in which infant mortality rates are minimised. In the tables of indicators, it has been identified as an *outcome indicator* for the right to life, the right to health and the right to adequate food.
Method of computation	The indicator is computed as number of deaths of infants under one-year of age per 1000 live births in that year. The number of deaths is divided by the number of births and the result is multiplied by 1000.
Data collection and source	The main sources of data at the country level are national administrative records, including the vital statistic registration system and records of statistical agency, sample surveys, population censuses and household surveys, including Demographic and Health Surveys. The World Health Organisation (WHO) compiles aggregate country data series based on administrative and survey data. The United Nations Children Fund (UNICEF) also provides country data series in its Multiple Indicator Cluster Surveys.
Periodicity	In general, the indicator based on administrative records is available annually, and the indicator based on household surveys every 3 to 5 years.
Disaggregation	Disaggregation of indicator by geographic or administrative regions, for example between rural and urban areas, is essential in assessing disparities in the infant mortality pattern across different regions. In addition, the indicator should be disaggregated by cause of death, by sex and, as applicable, by relevant demographic groups (*e.g.* ethnic groups, indigenous, minorities, migrants) and socio-economic status (income or consumption expenditure quintiles).
Comments and limitations	The indicator is widely used and can be a good summary measure of the realisation of the right to life, the right to highest attainable standard of physical and mental health and the right to adequate food. The infant mortality rate is considered to be a more robust estimate than the under-

five mortality rate if the information is drawn from vital statistics registration covering at least 90 per cent of vital events in the population. For household surveys, infant mortality estimates are obtained directly (Demographic and Health Surveys) or indirectly (Multiple Indicator Cluster Surveys). When estimated indirectly, the under-one mortality estimates must be consistent with the under-five mortality estimates.

Girls have a survival advantage over boys during the first year of life, largely based on biological differences. This is especially so during the first month of life when perinatal conditions are most likely to be the cause or a contributing cause of death. While infant mortality is generally higher for boys than for girls, in some countries girls' biological advantage is outweighed by gender-based discrimination. However, under-five mortality better captures the effect of gender discrimination than infant mortality, as nutrition and medical interventions are more important after age one.

In its *General Comment* No. 14 (ICESCR Art. 12) on the right to the highest attainable standard of health, the Committee on Economic, Social and Cultural Rights interprets that "the provision for the reduction of the stillbirth rate and of infant mortality and for the healthy development of the child" (Art. 12.2(a)) may be understood as requiring measures to improve child and maternal health, sexual and reproductive health services, including access to family planning, pre- and post-natal care, emergency obstetric services and access to information, as well as to resources necessary to act on that information.

In its *General Comment* No. 6 (ICCPR Art. 6) on the right to life, the Human Rights Committee noted that the right to life has been too often narrowly interpreted. The expression "inherent right to life" cannot properly be understood in a restrictive manner, and the protection of this right requires that states adopt positive measures. In this connection, the Committee considers that it would be desirable for states parties to take all possible measures to reduce infant mortality and to increase life expectancy, especially in adopting measures to eliminate malnutrition and epidemics.

Administrative and household survey data may underestimate infant mortality. It is also important that the main causes of mortality be carefully investigated to ascertain the extent to which it is caused by poor healthcare services, poor health conditions of infants and health problems of their mothers and/or due to some other extraneous reasons that are difficult to anticipate so that policy measures may be suitably formulated to address the problem.

UDHR articles 3 and 25, ICESCR articles 10-12, ICCPR articles 6, ICERD article 5, CEDAW article 2, 12 and 14, CRC articles 6, 27 and 24, ICRMW article 9, 28 and 43, and CRPD article 10, 28 and 25 are examples of references of relevance to the indicator.

This is a Millennium Development Goal indicator.

Appendix 6

Independent assessment report on the implementation and results of Metagora

Introduction

1. This document presents the conclusions and recommendations emerging from in-depth reviews and a general assessment of the implementation and results of the Metagora project. The assessment covers the period from February 2004 to July 2007.

2. Metagora is being implemented in the framework of the OECD-DCD/PARIS21. This project focuses on methods, tools and frameworks for measuring democracy, human rights and governance. Its strategic goal is to enhance evidence-based assessment and monitoring in these fields. Its main objective is to develop tools based on well-established statistical methods to obtain data and create indicators upon which national policies can be formulated and evaluated.

3. Metagora was initially launched for a two-year fixed term (February 2004 – February 2006); nevertheless, donors subsequently decided to finance supplementary work aimed at consolidating the achievements of the pilot phase (March 2006 – January 2007), and then agreed to support the implementation of a new phase of the project (Metagora II) to be implemented from February 2007 to December 2010.

4. Metagora is based on a North/South network of organisations and individual experts. Seven organisations, also called Partner Implementing Organisations, signed Partnership Agreements with the OECD for its implementation. The project therefore operates as a decentralised laboratory: it is an original international project on measuring human rights and democratic governance by undertaking several pilot experiences in different regions of the world simultaneously and in an interactive fashion.

This appendix presents the report adopted by the **Independent Panel of Experts** in Lisbon on 24 August 2007.

The Independent Panel of Experts (IPE) is composed of Mr. Jean-Louis Bodin (France, Chairman), Ms. Milva Ekonomi (Albania), Ms. Haishan Fu (ESCAP), Mr. Carlo Malaguerra (Switzerland), Mr. William Seltzer (USA), and Mr. Kwaku A. Twum-Baah (Ghana).

---

5. Metagora working structures include three distinct categories of bodies:

   i)   a steering body: the Steering Committee of Donors;

   ii) two implementing structures: the Partners Group that gathers together representatives of Partner Implementing Organisations and all experts involved in the project's operations, and a Co-ordination Team, based in the OECD/PARIS21 Secretariat;

   iii) an assessing body: the Independent Panel of Experts (IPE) that works on a strictly independent basis with regard to both the steering and implementing bodies.

6. The terms of reference of the IPE are:

   i)   to assess relevance, quality and reliability of methods and tools generated and used in each Metagora activity;

   iii) to review the Metagora Partners Group internal evaluation of the process and outcomes of the whole project;

   iii) to organise rigorous scientific peer-reviews of the project's results and products;

   iv) to provide advice and guidance for the validation of the final products; and

   v)   to formulate recommendations on the possible follow-up of the project.

7. The IPE is composed of Mr. Jean-Louis Bodin (France, Chairman), Ms. Milva Ekonomi (Albania), Ms. Haishan Fu (ESCAP), Mr. Carlo Malaguerra (Switzerland), Mr. William Seltzer (USA), and Mr. Kwaku A. Twum-Baah (Ghana).

Implementation of the IPE's work

8. The IPE was appointed in February 2005. It held its first meeting on 23 May 2005, and delivered a first Interim Report that was presented to the Metagora Committee of Donors on 26 May 2005. As a general intermediate assessment, the IPE considered that the project had made remarkable progress in a very short time and that a rich body of important and useful substantive results had been produced by several of the national pilot experiences. The IPE stressed that key factors of success were the synergy and networking between official and academic statisticians, human rights workers, researchers and other stakeholders. It identified some aspects of the project's implementation that had to be improved and it formulated a number of recommendations. These were presented by the IPE and discussed with the Metagora Partners Group at its fourth meeting (Paris, 28-30 November 2005).

9. The first Interim Report of the IPE identified the needs for:

   i)   simplifying the working structures,

   ii) having some representation of stakeholders on the Steering Committee;

   iii) strengthening further the links between Metagora and other relevant networks;

iv) sharing methodologies, results, findings and analytical work with countries that are not participating in Metagora;

v) translating key project outputs from English into at least French and Spanish;

vi) paying attention to data protection issues, as safeguards must be introduced into surveys dealing with sensitive personal data; and

vii) further development and testing of tools for the joint quantitative and qualitative analysis of data, as this is especially important for the understanding of data on human rights, democracy and governance.

10. Moreover, the intermediate report of the IPE considered that the achievements reached and the perspectives opened by Metagora merited further development. It therefore suggested the following orientations for future work:

i) enhancement of the involvement of official statistical agencies,

ii) continuation and deepening of comparative assessment of national governance indicators, and

iii) enhancement of the bottom up approach to complement and enrich the top down approach that underlies international indicators.

11. The first Interim Report of the IPE stressed that, at that stage (May 2005), the IPE had not organised rigorous scientific peer reviews of the project's results and products as envisioned in the IPE's terms of reference. On the occasion of its fifth meeting (18 October, 2005), however, the Metagora Steering Committee of Donors stressed the importance it attached to the evaluation of project results and requested that the IPE conduct an in-depth review of the project's pilot phase and that, on this basis, the IPE produce a substantial assessment report. Consequently, towards the end of 2005 (once most draft final reports of Metagora pilot activities were delivered), the Chair of the IPE requested Mr. William Seltzer, a member of the IPE, and an eminent independent researcher, Prof. Herbert Spirer (hereafter referred to as "the reviewers"), to conduct such a review. Their mandate was to produce an in-depth technical and scientific review of the pilot activities in the Philippines, Mexico and South-Africa, as well as on the regional surveys in Francophone Africa and the Andean Community. This review was conducted from December 2005 to April 2006 on the basis of documents available in October 2005 as well as on electronic exchanges with the persons in charge of the technical implementation of each pilot activity. The report of the independent reviewers (hereafter referred to as "the Seltzer/Spirer Review") was delivered to the IPE on 14th of April 2006.

12. The IPE held its second meeting in New York, on 20-21 April 2006. This meeting was aimed at: (i) discussing the content and conclusions of the Seltzer/Spirer Review; (ii) examining the results, lessons and conclusions of the pilot phase of the Metagora project presented in a draft synthesis report; and (iii) formulating conclusions and recommendations in particular with regard to the future of Metagora.

13. The IPE considered the Seltzer-Spirer review to be a sound technical and scientific base for its general assessment of the implementation and outcomes of the two first years of the Metagora pilot phase. While acknowledging the important achievements of the whole project, the reviewers identified some critical weaknesses and a number of technical shortcomings in the implementation of the pilot activities. They therefore formulated a set of strong recommendations that were broadly

endorsed by the IPE in its second Interim Report, which was discussed with the Partners Group on the occasion of its 5th meeting (Paris, 13-15 September 2006) and then presented to the Metagora Committee of Donors on 29 September 2006.

14. Despite the usefulness of the Seltzer-Spirer review, there was wide recognition by the reviewers themselves, the Metagora Partner Organisations, and the Co-ordination Team, that the assessment carried out by the reviewers was hampered by three critically important factors: (i) the evaluation was carried out retrospectively rather than prospectively, (ii) several of the country partners completed additional analytical and methodological outputs too late to be taken into account in the initial independent review, and (iii) insufficient time was allowed in the evaluation process to permit the Partner Organisations to comment on the assessment before it was finalised and thus correct possible misunderstandings. Adding to the impact of the second factor was that, in some cases, while the studies themselves had been completed, English translations of these works, on which the reviewers depended, were not available until a later date.

15. In order to overcome at least part of these limitations, the Chair of the IPE requested the Co-ordination Team to commission the two reviewers to carry out an "in-depth supplementary review of selected Metagora activities" beginning in late 2006. As in the initial review, these pilot experiences were examined in terms of the technical standards used and the quality of:

i)   sampling,

ii) data collection and processing,

iii) data analysis,

iv) data dissemination, including links to users, and

v)   protection of personal data and professional integrity.

16. To deal with the outputs, or translations of outputs, that did not become available to the reviewers in English language until after the cut-off date for the initial assessment, emphasis was placed on materials produced or made available by the Metagora Partners after October 2005 and thus not included in that assessment. At the request of the reviewers or the Partner Organisations, the Co-ordination Team facilitated the translation in English of the many materials that were considered relevant for the supplementary review. Also, to address the limitations arising from the fact that time for Metagora Partners' feedback was not provided in the initial assessment, the supplementary review included: (i) substantive exchanges between the Reviewers and the leadership and staff of the organisations responsible for the reviewed pilots, and (ii) a presentation and discussion of the main findings of the supplementary review at the joint IPE/Metagora Partners Group Methodological Workshop held in Paris on 29-31 January 2007.

17. This supplementary review was carried out in two phases. The first phase led to the presentation of a summary of intermediate tentative conclusions and recommendations at the joint IPE/Metagora Partners Group Methodological Workshop held on 29-31 January 2007. The second phase, the scope of which was restricted to the pilot experiences carried out in Mexico, Philippines and South Africa, led to the finalisation of a consolidated report that was delivered to the IPE members on 24 July 2007 and then reviewed at the third meeting of the IPE, held in Lisbon, back-to-back to the 56th Session of the International Statistical Institute, on 23 and 24 August 2007. Professor Spirer, who co-authored the initial in-depth review report and played an active role in the first phase of the supplementary review, had to withdraw from the review process for health reasons. Mr. Seltzer is therefore solely responsible

for the content of the new consolidated review report. The IPE would like to acknowledge Professor Spirer for his hard work and clear analysis in earlier stages of the review.

Conclusions and lessons from the Metagora pilot phase

18. As it has been stated in previous IPE interim reports, there is a total agreement among the IPE members and between the IPE and the Partners Group on the main conclusions and lessons from the Metagora pilot phase, formulated in the synthesis report "*Measuring Human Rights and Democratic Governance*". The IPE considers that Metagora made a major contribution in showing, through its various pilot experiences, that:

i) Measuring human rights and democratic governance is technically feasible and policy oriented; data on human rights, democracy and governance can be collected and indicators produced that are central for policy makers' decision.

ii) Quantitative and qualitative data can and should interrelate to properly inform assessment of democracy, human rights and governance.

iii) Official statistics can be efficiently involved in the measurement of democratic governance.

iv) Statistical analysis and quantitative indicators can substantially enhance the work of Human Rights Institutions as well as the research and advocacy of civil society's organisations in the fields of human rights and democracy.

v) The experiences, problems encountered and lessons learned in measuring human rights and democratic governance can and should be documented, structured and edited as training materials aimed at helping in replicating those experiences and properly applying the measuring methods in other countries.

vi) A North/South network of experts and institutions concerned with the measurement of human rights and democratic governance has been consolidated around Metagora and is continuously growing.

vii) The original multidisciplinary approach and the synergies among official and academic statisticians, human rights practitioners, social and political scientists and other stakeholders constitute a considerable value-added of the project.

viii) The implementation of the project by a community consisting of diverse types of institutions (National Statistical Offices, Human Rights Institutions, Research Centres and Civil Society Organisations) constitutes a major asset for ensuring the effective and sustainable appropriation and achievement of the project goals in each participating country.

19. In the course of the implementation of the project, the IPE identified a number of topics and issues that merited in-depth examination and were therefore discussed in the IPE meetings and in the joint IPE/Partners Group methodological workshop. These are, in particular:

i) the non-response issues, the quality control and the robustness/reliability of the information produced in the pilot phase of the project;

ii) data protection issues and the professional integrity of Metagora activities;

iii) issues related to linking quantitative and qualitative analysis, objective and subjective data, and building nationally-based indicators;

iv) the conditions and criteria for the involvement of official statistics in measuring democratic governance and/or human rights;

v) the structure and content of the Metagora Training Materials.

20. The consideration of these issues and topics evolved both within the IPE and within the Metagora Partners Group, in particular in the light of the findings and recommendations of the initial Seltzer-Spirer Review and the subsequent supplementary review. The reflection and broad dialogue on these issues matured considerably, thus allowing the IPE and the Partners Group to jointly formulate orientations and guidelines for future work. Indeed, one of the major outcomes of the project is the set of *Conclusions of the Joint IPE/Partners Group Methodological Workshop* that marked the end of the pilot phase and the transition towards the new phase of the project (Metagora II). Each paragraph of this document, was unanimously agreed by all members of the IPE and the Partners Group – and it therefore constitute a key reference document both for those who will be involved in the implementation of Metagora II, as well as for the donor institutions and the Metagora Steering Committee.

Recommendations emerging from the consolidated in-depth review

21. In the course of its third meeting the IPE discussed the main outcomes of the supplementary review, presented in the report of Mr. William Seltzer, *An Independent Review of Selected Metagora Surveys: A Consolidated Report*. The IPE noted that this Consolidated Report draws heavily on the earlier Seltzer-Spirer Report, as modified by the availability of an extensive documentation received by the reviewers in English after October 2005. The IPE also noted with satisfaction that, prior to its finalisation, a draft of this Consolidated Report was circulated to the Mexican, Philippine and South African pilots and to the Metagora Co-ordination Team for review and comment. As a result of this process, the author was able to correct a number of errors or omissions and to further clarify some points of emphasis.

22. Given the improved process that led to the finalisation of the Consolidated Report on the in-depth review of Metagora pilot experiences, the IPE focused its efforts on considering the implications of the reviews' findings and recommendations. Its first and more general conclusion (already agreed with the Partners Group in the joint Methodological workshop of January 2007) is that any future plans for Metagora must take into account both the achievements and the identified weaknesses of the pilot phase. The technical shortcomings identified by the independent review have to be duly addressed when planning, budgeting, designing and implementing all future activities. As stated in the second IPE Interim Report, stronger and more efficient working methods and qualified expertise (and therefore appropriate financial means) are required for properly addressing the complexity and magnitude of the scientific and technical issues at stake.

23. The IPE fully endorsed the recommendations formulated in the Consolidated Report, namely:

i) Continue Metagora Phase II drawing on the experience in Phase I.

ii) Strengthen the core staff of Metagora by adding high-level expertise in survey methods, including sampling, and, if possible, in analytical methods.

iii) Provide partners with appropriate training or training materials in such key areas as questionnaire construction, report preparation, and graphical presentation.

iv) Strengthen user-producer links at the national level using the experience from other countries.

v) Provide a full range of substantive and methodological outputs for each national effort.

vi) Produce estimates of sampling variability for all major survey estimates and analytical conclusions.

vii) Include clear statements concerning limitations of data in all outputs.

viii) Provide guidance to national and regional partners on respondent and field worker protections, as well as monitoring the implementation of such protection measures; if needed, be prepared to halt field work or destroy completed questionnaires.

ix) Establish ethics review bodies both at the national and global levels to review Metagora work, including direct or proxy representation for those at potential risk.

x) Both the Metagora Co-ordination Team and national partners should institute ongoing programmes of quality control of field work, data processing, analysis, and report preparation.

xi) Plan and carry out evaluation from the start.

24. The IPE also welcomed the delivery of the Metagora Training Materials which not only constitute a key successful outcome of the project, but are also a valuable tool for helping in implementing the above mentioned recommendations. The members of the IPE were provided information on the structure and content of these materials and were invited, together with a large number of senior international experts and practitioners, to contribute to a broad peer review of their contents. Two members of the IPE provided several comments and suggestions. Also, in order to duly inform the IPE on the result of the peer-review process and on the status of the finalisation of this flag product of the project, the Co-ordination Team provided the Panel with a note on the *Production and Contents of the Training Materials*. This document, together with the *Metagora Inventory of Initiatives Aimed at Enhancing Evidence-Based Assessment of Human Rights and Democratic Governance* (already available online in the Metagora website), attests to the impressive capacity gained by the project to generate tools that are informative, rigorous, innovative and useful. The IPE therefore strongly recommends that the highest priority be given (and appropriate resources allocated) for further continuous development and enrichment of the materials and the inventory in the course of the implementation of Metagora II.

Extending the pilot experiences and transmitting the results and lessons

25. In previous Interim Reports, the IPE has repeatedly recommended:

i) strengthening further the links between Metagora and other relevant international networks;

ii) sharing methodologies, results, findings and analytical work with countries that are not participating in Metagora;

iii) advocating for measuring human rights and democratic governance within the various instances, activities and events of the international statistical community;

iv) ensuring national appropriation and institutionalisation of the working methods and tools developed by the project, and

v) timely transmitting the results and lessons of the Metagora experience to the appropriate bodies and institutions of the international community.

The IPE emphasises that the two last recommendations are critical to ensure that at the end of the project, there will be a sustainable continuation of efforts for the proper measurement of human rights and democratic governance.

26. The IPE notes with satisfaction that the Co-ordination Team and the Metagora Partners are strongly committed in implementing these recommendations. Since the successful Metagora Forum organised in May 2005, the Metagora community has been increasingly extending and deepening its international network, integrating new partners and promoting, through many means, dialogue and exchanges among the various actors involved in measuring human rights and democratic governance over the world. A calendar of events organised or attended by Metagora in 2007, attests to an impressive activity of advocacy and dissemination of project methods and tools. Members of the IPE were associated with some of these advocacy events and, in particular, with the informal meeting of heads of National Statistical Offices (NSOs) organised back-to-back at the February 2007 Session of the UN Statistical Commission. As an immediate follow-up of this informal gathering, Metagora co-organised in Brazil one Latin-American workshop on measuring human rights (July 2007) and is co-organising a workshop on measuring democratic governance for the Arab States to be held in Amman in October 2007. The approach, results and lessons of Metagora were also presented within the Committee on Statistics of the OECD and the project was fully associated with the organisation and conduct of the OECD World Forum on Indicators of Progress of Societies held in Istanbul in June 2007. In addition, close links of collaboration established with the Office of the UN High Commissioner for Human Rights and with the UNDP – Oslo Governance Centre are now materialising in concrete forms of joint action and progressive transmission of experiences. As a result of this proactive position on the international scene, Metagora is today widely acknowledged as a key reference point and resource centre for developing improved measurement of human rights and democratic governance.

27. While such an impressive position gained by Metagora in the international scene appears as a tangible sign of effective success of the project in disseminating and transmitting its results and lessons, the IPE nevertheless calls attention to the other side of the coin: since the delivery and dissemination of results of the various pilot activities, there has not been any new field survey action launched by Metagora. As Mr. Seltzer stated in his oral presentation of the first IPE Interim Report to the donors in May 2005, "*the surveys implemented during the pilot phase are still too few for developing and duly documenting robust tools; thus further national survey work and additional country studies are needed to get more examples and lessons.*" This evidence led the Partners Group to formulate in December 2005 a *Strategy for Metagora II* that stresses, in its "rationale for future action", that "*robust measuring tools and analytical tools can be further developed and validated only by means of replication and extension of the experiences implemented in the pilot phase*".

28. In the opening session of the 3rd IPE meeting, the General Co-ordinator of Metagora recalled that the *Project Outline for Metagora II* (submitted to the donor institutions in September 2006) includes a working programme consisting of a wide-ranging study, based on the application of the methods and tools tested during the pilot phase to new, large and diversified sets of co-ordinated experiences

at national and regional (multi-country) levels. These planned new experiences consist of field surveys, statistical analysis and matching of quantitative and qualitative data. They will be designed, implemented and assessed with the view to documenting a comprehensive methodology. The Co-ordinator informed the IPE that costs of this working programme were estimated by the Co-ordination Team, taking into account the findings of the independent review as well as the recommendations of the IPE. The resulting budget was duly presented to the donor institutions. Although the Metagora donors decided to support the implementation of Metagora II, the IPE noted that the total amount of committed funds is far less than the total estimated costs and that during 2007 the project received very little of the committed funds. As a consequence, since the end of the pilot phase, the activities of the project have been limited to global advocacy and dissemination activities.

29. It is not the mandate of the IPE to assess or comment on funding issues. Nevertheless, it is obvious that recommendations for future work can be reasonably formulated only on the basis of the assumption that donor institutions seriously intend to provide the financial resources required to properly implement the planned working programme of Metagora II. The IPE therefore urges the community of donor institutions to consider the risk that, due to the absence of appropriate and timely funding, the current achievements and the promising dynamics of Metagora may be jeopardised by lack of continuity. As the Seltzer Consolidated Report states in its conclusion, it is clear that many of the recommendations endorsed by the IPE will cost money to implement properly. *"In these circumstances, donors will have to weigh expected costs against expected benefits. In thinking about the trade-offs involved and likely benefits to be achieved one may note that most of these recommendations involve the implementation of well-tested and widely-recognized principles, that most them are interrelated in nature, and that they were developed in light of specific problems identified during Metagora Phase I. Finally, if implemented, they will together help make Metagora a more useful, cost-effective, and responsible endeavour."*

Conclusion

30. Reiterating its positive assessment formulated already in its first Interim Report of 2005, the IPE:

i) appreciated the remarkable progress accomplished by Metagora in a very short time, including the rich body of important and useful substantive results produced by several of the national pilot projects;

ii) noted the real enthusiasm and commitment within both the Metagora staff and the Partners of the project, that has permitted such remarkable progress; and

iii) noted that key factors of success are the synergy and networking between official and academic statisticians, human rights workers, researchers and other stakeholders.

31. The IPE reiterates that Metagora II must give particular attention to how its activities can be associated over time with appropriate existing institutions at the international, regional and country level. The forthcoming activities should lead to a progressive and well structured final institutional shape of the various Metagora activities.

32. Finally, based on the recommendations emerging from the independent review and its own assessment of the work and results of Metagora over the 2004-2007 period, the IPE:

i) strongly recommends to the community of donors to support the continuation and enhancement of the Metagora project in its second phase so that it can complete its work;

ii) encourages the Metagora Partners and the Co-ordination Team to continue their efforts to address the weaknesses, technical shortcomings and problems identified by the reviewers and jointly discussed with the IPE; and

iii) expresses its readiness to continue to evaluate the implementation of Metagora and provide advice and guidance to both the donors and the Partners of the project.

Bibliography

NB: All the hyperlinks quoted in this bibliography were controlled, and the related web sites last accessed on 28 and 29 July 2008.

AAAS (AMERICAN ASSOCIATION FOR THE ADVANCEMENT OF SCIENCE) and HURIDOCS (HUMAN RIGHTS INFORMATION AND DOCUMENTATION SYSTEMS) (2000), *Promoting and Defending Economic, Social and Cultural Rights: A Handbook*, Versoix and Washington D.C. [authored by A. McCHESNEY], at: http://shr.aaas.org/escr/handbook/ and http://www.huridocs.org/tools/ESCRHandbook/escrenfr.PDF

AAAS and HURIDOCS (2002), *Thesaurus of Economic, Social and Cultural Rights*, Versoix and Washington [authored by S. HANSEN, web redesigned version, available in English and Spanish], at: http://shr.aaas.org/thesaurus/

ÅBO HUMAN RIGHTS INSTITUTE (2005), *Report of the Turku Expert Meeting on Indicators* (10-13 March), Åbo Akademi University, Turku, at: http://web.abo.fi/instut/imr/research/seminars/indicators/Report.doc

ABOUBACAR DJIMRAO, A. (2005) [see INSTITUT NATIONAL DE LA STATISTIQUE, Niger, 2005].

ABU-LIBDEH, H. (2007), "Statistical Data on Palestinian Refugees: What We Know and What We Don't", in R. Brynen and R. El-Rifai (eds.), *Palestinian Refugees: Challenges of Repatriation and Development*, International Development Research Centre, Ottawa, at: http://www.idrc.ca/fr/ev-107711-201-1-DO_TOPIC.html#begining

ACEMOGLU, D. (2005), "Constitutions, Politics and Economics: A Review Essay on Persson and Tabellini's 'The Economic Effects of Constitutions'", *Journal of Economic Literature*, Vol. 43, pp. 1025-1048, at: http://papers.nber.org/papers/w11235 and http://econ-www.mit.edu/files/298

ACEMOGLU, D., S. JOHNSON and J. ROBINSON (2001), "The Colonial Origins of Comparative Development: An Empirical Investigation", *American Economic Review*, Vol. 91(5), pp. 1369-1404, at: http://www.jstor.org/sici?sici=0002-8282(200112)91%3A5%3C1369%3ATCOOCD%3E2.0.CO%3B2-9

ACHARYA, A.K. (2004), "Toward Establishing a Universal Basic Health Norm", *Ethics & International Affairs*, Vol. 18, No.3, pp. 65-78, Cambridge University Press.

ACUÑA-ALFARO, J. (2005), "Measuring Democracy in Latin America (1972-2002)", Committee on Concepts and Methods of the International Political Science Association, Political Concepts, Working Paper No. 5, Centro de Investigación y Docencia Económicas (CIDE), Mexico City, at: http://www.concepts-methods.org/papers_list.php?id_categoria=1&titulo=Political%20Concepts and http://oxford.academia.edu/JairoAcuna/attachment/23/full/Measuring-Democracy-in-Latin-America—1972-2002-

ADCOCK, R. and D. COLLIER (2001), "Measurement Validity: A Shared Standard for Qualitative and Quantitative Research", *American Political Science Review*, Vol. 95, No. 3, pp. 529-546.

ADES, A. and R. DI TELLA (1996), "The Causes and Consequences of Corruption: A Review of Recent Empirical Contributions," in B. HARRIS-WHITE and B. WHITE (eds.), *Liberalisation and the New Corruption*, Brighton, Institute of Development Studies Bulletin, Vol. 27, No. 2, pp. 6-12.

ADES, A. and R. DI TELLA (1997), "National Champions and Corruption: Some Unpleasant Interventionist Arithmetic," *The Economic Journal*, No. 107, pp. 1023-1042.

AFRISTAT (OBSERVATOIRE ÉCONOMIQUE ET STATISTIQUE D'AFRIQUE SUBSAHARIENNE) (1998), *État du système statistique dans les États membres d'AFRISTAT: Rapport de synthèse de l'enquête réalisée en 1996*, Série Études No.1, AFRISTAT, Bamako, at:
http://www.afristat.org/contenu/ressources/etude01.html

AFRISTAT (1999), *État des réflexions sur les principes fondamentaux de la statistique publique*, Série Études No. 2, AFRISTAT, Bamako, at:
http://www.afristat.org/contenu/ressources/etude02.html

AFRISTAT (2004), *État des lieux sur l'architecture des systèmes d'information de suivi des Documents de stratégie de réduction de la pauvreté et des Objectifs du millénaire pour le développement dans les pays francophones d'Afrique au Sud du Sahara*, AFRISTAT and UNDP, Bamako, at:
http://www.afristat.org/contenu/pdf/rsc/etatlieux_sirp.pdf

AFRISTAT (2006), *CRESMIC : Cadre de référence et support méthodologique minimum commun pour la conception d'un système d'information pour le suivi des Documents de stratégie de réduction de la pauvreté (DSRP) et des Objectifs du millénaire pour le développement (OMD) [Reference framework and common methodological guidelines for designing a PSRP and MDG information tracking system]*, AFRISTAT and UNDP, Bamako, at:
http://www.afristat.org/contenu/ressources/CRESMIC/index.html (French)
http://www.afristat.org/contenu/ressources/CRESMIC/en/index.html (English)

AFROBAROMETER (2008), Surveys, at:
http://www.afrobarometer.org/surveys.html

AFROBAROMETER (2008), Working Papers, at:
http://www.afrobarometer.org/abseries.html

AGENCE FRANÇAISE DE DÉVELOPPEMENT *et al.* (2005), *Pro-Poor Growth in the 1990s: Lessons and Insights from 14 Countries*, at:
http://siteresources.worldbank.org/INTPGI/Resources/342674-1119450037681/Pro-poor_growth_in_the_1990s.pdf

AGNÉ, H. (2006), "Measuring Democratic Deliberation", Committee on Concepts and Methods of the International Political Science Association, Political Concepts, Working Paper Series, No. 11, Centro de Investigación y Docencia Económicas (CIDE), Mexico City, at:
http://www.concepts-methods.org/papers_list.php?id_categoria=1&titulo=Political%20Concepts

AHADO, D. AND B. CAMPBELL (2006), "La gouvernance: entre l'État et le marché, qui gouverne l'ordre social?", Les Cahiers de la Chaire C.-A. Poissant, Collection recherché, No. 2006-01, Université du Québec a Montréal, at
http://www.er.uqam.ca/nobel/ieim/IMG/pdf/Cahier_2006-01_Campbell_et_Ahado_-_Gouvernance_dec06.pdf

ALIBER, M. (2001), *Study of the Incidence and Nature of Chronic Poverty and Development Policy in South Africa: An Overview*, Programme for Land and Agrarian Studies, University of the Western Cape, Chronic Poverty and Development Policy Series, No. 1, Cape Town.

ALIBER, M and R. MOKOENA (2002), "The interaction between the land redistribution programme and the land market in South Africa: A perspective on the willing-buyer/willing-seller approach", Programme for Land and Agrarian Studies, University of the Western Cape, Land Reform and Agrarian Change in Southern Africa Occasional Paper, No. 21, Cape Town.

ALIBER, M., M. REITZES and M. ROEFS (2006), *Assessing the Alignment of South Africa's Land Reform Policy to People's Aspirations and Expectations: A Policy-Oriented Report Based on a Survey in Three Provinces,* results of the Metagora pilot experience in South Africa, Human Science Research Council, Pretoria, at: http://www.metagora.org

ALSTON, P. (1987), "Out of the abyss: the challenges confronting the new UN Committee on Economic, Social and Cultural Rights", in: *Human Rights Quarterly*, Vol. 9, pp. 332-81.

ALSTON, P. (1997), "Making Economic and Social Rights Count: A Strategy for the Future", *The Political Quarterly*, Vol. 68, No. 2, pp. 188-195, at: http://www.blackwell-synergy.com/action/ showPdf?submitPDF=Full+Text+PDF+%2891+KB%29&doi=10.1111%2F1467-923X.00083

ALSTON, P. (2005), "Ships Passing in the Night: The Current State of the Human Rights and Development Debate Seen Through the Lens of the Millennium Development Goals", *Human Rights Quarterly*, Vol. 27, No. 3, pp. 755-829.

ALSTON, P. and G. QUINN (1987), "The Nature and Scope of States Parties: Obligations under the International Convenant on Economic, Social and Cultural Rights", *Human Rights Quarterly*, Vol. 9, No. 2, pp. 156-229.

ALSTON P. and M. ROBINSON (2005), *Human Rights and Development: Towards Mutual Reinforcement*, Oxford University Press, Oxford.

ALSTON, P. and H.J. STEINER (1996), *International Human Rights in Context: Law, Politics, Morals*, Clarendon Press, Oxford.

ALSTON, P. and C. SCOTT (2000), "Adjudicating Constitutional Priorities in a Transnational Context: A Comment on Soobramoney's Legacy and Grootboom's Promise", *South African Journal on Human Rights*, Vol. 16.

ALTMAN, D. and A. PÉREZ-LIÑÁN (2002), "Assessing the Quality of Democracy: Freedom, Competitiveness and Participation in Eighteen Latin American Countries", *Democratization*, Vol. 9, No. 2, pp. 85-100.

ALVAREZ, M. et al., "Classifying Political Regimes", *Studies in Comparative International Development*, Vol. 31, No. 2, pp. 3-36.

AMANI, M. (2005) [see INSTITUT NATIONAL DE LA STATISTIQUE, Côte d'Ivoire, 2005].

AMES, R. et al. (2000), *Democracy Report for Peru*, IDEA International, Stockholm.

AMNESTY INTERNATIONAL (2008a), *Report 2008, report 2007, Facts and Figures* and *Browser by Country and region*, at: http://thereport.amnesty.org/

AMNESTY INTERNATIONAL (2008b), News and Updates, at: http://www.amnesty.org/

AMOWITZ, L. et al. (2004), "Letter from Iraq: a Population-Based Assessment of Health and Human Rights in Southern Iraq", in *JAMA, Journal of the American Medical Association*, 291, pp. 1471-1479.

ANDERSON, J.E. and E.A. SUNGUR (1999), "Community Service Statistics Projects", *The American Statistician*, vol. 53, pp. 132-136.

ANDERSON, M. and W. SELTZER (2000), "After Pearl Harbor: The Proper Use of Population Data in Time of War," paper presented at the Annual Meeting of the Population Association of America, Los Angeles, at: http://www.uwm.edu/%7Emargo/govstat/paapaper.htm and http://www.amstat.org/about/statisticians/index.cfm?fuseaction=paperinfo&PaperID=1

ANDERSON, M. and W. SELTZER (2001), "The Dark Side of Numbers: The Role of Population Data Systems in Human Rights Abuses", *Social Research*, Vol. 68, No 2, pp. 481-513, at: http://www.uwm.edu/%7Emargo/govstat/socres.htm

ANDERSON, M. and W. SELTZER (2002), "NCES and the Patriot Act", Paper presented at the Joint Statistical Meetings, New York, at: http://www.uwm.edu/%7Emargo/govstat/jsm.pdf

ANDERSON, M. and W. SELTZER (2003), "Government Statistics and Individual Safety: Revisiting the Historical Record of Disclosure, Harm, and Risk", Paper prepared for a workshop on "Access to Research Data: Assessing Risks and Opportunities," organised by the Panel on Confidential Data Access for Research Purposes, Committee on National Statistics (CNSTAT), Washington, DC, October 16-17, at: http://www.uwm.edu/%7Emargo/govstat/WS-MAcnstat.pdf

ANDERSON, M. and W. SELTZER (2004), "The Challenges of 'Taxation, Investigation, and Regulation': Statistical Confidentiality and U.S. Federal Statistics, 1910-1965," Paper prepared for Census Bureau Symposium, Woodrow Wilson International Center for Scholars, March 4-5, at: http://www.uwm.edu/%7Emargo/govstat/Challenges.pdf and http://www.uwm.edu/%7Emargo/govstat/incidenttable2.pdf

ANDERSON, M. and W. SELTZER (2005), *Official Statistics and Statistical Confidentiality: Recent Writings and Essential Documents* [Internet site providing relevant literature, documents and links], at: http://www.uwm.edu/~margo/govstat/integrity.htm

ANDERSON, M. and W. SELTZER (2008), "Using Population Data Systems to Target Vulnerable Population Subgroups and Individuals: Issues and Incidents", in ASHER, BANKS and SCHEUREN (2008), pp. 273-328.

ANDREASEN, B.A. and H.O. SANO (2004), "What's the Goal? What's the Purpose? Observations on Human Rights Impact Assessment," Norwegian Centre for Human Rights, Research Notes 02/2004, University of Oslo, at: http://www.humanrights.uio.no/forskning/publ/rn/2004/0204.pdf#search='what%27s%20the%20goal%20what%27s%20the%20purpose%20human%20rights%20impact%20assessment'

ANDREASEN, B.A. and H.O. SANO (2006), *Human Rights Indicators at Program and Project Level: Guidelines for Defining Indicators, Monitoring and Evaluation*, The Danish Institute for Human Rights, Copenhagen, at: http://www.humanrights.dk/files/pdf/indikatorMANUALwebPDF.pdf

APODACA, C. (1998), "Measuring Women's Economic and Social Rights Achievement", *Human Rights Quarterly*, Vol.20, No. 1, pp. 139-72.

APODACA, C. (2007), "Measuring the Progressive Realization of Economic and Social Rights", in S. Hertel and A. Minkler (2007), pp. 165-181.

ARAT, Z.F. (1991), *Democracy and Human Rights in Developing Countries*, Lynne Riener, Boulner, CO, reprint by Backinprint.com, 2003, at: http://books.google.ch/books?id=zIW1XzybUJ4C&dq=Democracy+and+Human+Rights+in+Developing+Countries&pg=PP1&ots=Z_ukF1IcG7&sig=9HumBuY2hNDE_uJBWsEikti9zaU&hl=fr&sa=X&oi=book_result&resnum=1&ct=result#PPP1,M1

ARNDT, C. and C. OMAN (2006), *Uses and Abuses of Governance Indicators,* Development Centre Studies, OECD, Paris, at:
http://www.oecd.org/dataoecd/21/16/40037762.pdf

ARON, J. (2000), "Growth and Institutions: A Review of the Evidence", *World Bank Research Observer,* Vol. 15, No. 1, pp. 99-135.
http://www.worldbank.org/research/journals/wbro/obsfeb00/Article_6.pdf

ASATASHVILI, A., M.C. FIX FIERRO and M.E. LOZANO (eds.) (2003), *International Seminar on Indicators and Diagnosis on Human Rights: the Case of Torture in Mexico,* National Commission for Human Rights, Mexico City [available also in Spanish: *Seminario Internacional sobre indicadores y diagnosis de los derechos humanos: el caso de la tortura en México,* Comisión Nacional de Derechos Humanos, México].

ASHAGRIE, K. (1998), "Statistics on Working Children and Hazardous Child Labour in Brief", International Labour Organization, Geneva.

ASHAGRIE, K. (2000), "Current Progress in Implementing new Methods and Conducting Innovative Surveys for Measuring Exploitation of Children", in IAOS (2000), at:
http://www.portal-stat.admin.ch/iaos2000/ashagrie_final_final_paper.doc
and in *Statistical Journal of the United Nations Economic Commission for Europe,* Vol. 18 (2001), pp.187-203.

ASHER, J. (2007) [see METAGORA, 2007a].

ASHER, J. and P. BALL (2001), "Understanding Human Rights Violations Data Through the Analysis of Circuits", *Proceedings of the Section on Government Statistics and Section on Social Statistics,* American Statistical association [reprinted in N.D. BIVINGS (2002), pp. 8-14].

ASHER, J. and P. BALL (2002), "Statistics and Slobodan: Using Data Analysis and Statistics in the War Crimes Trial of Former President Milosevic", *Chance,* Vol. 15, No. 4, pp. 17-24, at:
http://www.amstat.org/publications/chance/pdfs/154.ball.asher.pdf

ASHER, J., D. BANKS and F.J. SCHEUREN (eds.) (2008), *Statistical Methods for Human Rights,* Springer, New York.

AWARTANI, F. and M. KASSIS (2000), "Measuring Transition to Democracy in Palestine: A Statistical Approach", in IAOS (2000), at:
http://www.portal-stat.admin.ch/iaos2000/awartani_final_paper.doc

BALL, P. et al. (1994), *A Definition of Database Design Standards for Human Rights Agencies,* American Association for the Advancement of Science (AAAS), Washington D.C., at:
http://shr.aaas.org/DBStandards/cover.html

BALL, P. (1996a), *Who did What to Whom?: Planning and Implementing a Large Scale Human Rights Data Project,* American Association for the Advancement of Science (AAAS), Washington D.C., at:
http://shr.aaas.org/www/cover.htm

BALL, P. (1996b), "Types of Human Rights Organizations and Their Information Needs", paper presented at the Annual Meeting of the American Association for the Advancement of Science, Baltimore.

BALL, P. et al. (1999), "Multiple or N-System Estimates of the Number of Political killings in Guatemala", Proceedings of the Section of Government Statistics and Section of Social Statistics, American Statistical Association, Alexandria, pp. 156-160.

BALL, P. (2000a), "Making the case: The role of statistics in human rights reporting", in IAOS (2000), at:
http://www.portal-stat.admin.ch/iaos2000/ball_final_paper.doc
and *Statistical Journal of the United Nations Economic Commission for Europe,* Vol. 18 (2001), No. 2-3, pp. 163-173.

BALL, P. (2000b), *Policy or Panic?: the Flight of Ethnic Albanians from Kosovo, March-May 1999*, American Association for the Advancement of Science (AAAS) and American Bar Association Central and East European Law Initiative, Washington D.C., at:
http://shr.aaas.org/kosovo/policyorpanic/

BALL, P. (2001a), *Political Killings in Kosova/Kosovo, March-June 1999*, A cooperative report by the Central and East European Law Initiative of the American Bar Association and the Science and Human Rights Program of the American Association for the Advancement of Science (AAAS), Washington D.C, at:
http://shr.aaas.org/kosovo/pk/politicalkillings.pdf

BALL, P. (2001b), "On the Quantification of Horror: Field Notes on Statistical Analysis of Human Rights Violations", paper presented at the conference on *Mobilization and Repression: What We Know and Where We Should Go From Here?*, University of Maryland, June 21-24.

BALL, P. *et al.* (2002a), *Killings and Refugee Flow in Kosovo, March-June 1999: A Report to the International Criminal Tribune for the Former Yugoslavia*, American Association for the Advancement of Science (AAAS), Washington D.C., at:
http://shr.aaas.org/kosovo/icty_report.pdf

BALL, P. *et al.*, "Addendum to Expert Report of Patrick Ball", American Association for the Advancement of Science (AAAS), Washington D.C., at:
http://hague.bard.edu/reports/hr_ball-6mar2002.pdf

BALL, P. *et al.* (2003), *How many Peruvians Have Died? An Estimate of the Total Number of Victims Killed or Disappeared in the Armed Internal Conflict Between 1980 and 2000*, American Association for the Advancement of Science (AAAS), Washington D.C., at:
http://www.smallarmssurvey.org/files/portal/issueareas/victims/Victims_pdf/2003_Ball_et_al.pdf

BALL, P., A.R. CHAPMAN and M. GIROUARD (1997) "Information Technology, Information Management, and Human Rights: A Response to Metzl", *Human Rights Quarterly*, Vol. 19, No. 4, pp. 836-859.

BALL, P. and A.R. CHAPMAN, (2001), "The Truth of Truth Commissions: Comparative Lessons from Haiti, South Africa, and Guatemala", in: *Human Rights Quarterly*, Vol. 23, pp. 1-43, at:
http://www.restorativejustice.org/articlesdb/articles/4901

BALL, P., P. KOBRAK and H.F. SPIRER (1999), *State violence in Guatemala, 1960-1996 : A Quantitative Reflection*, American Association for the Advancement of Science (AAAS), Washington D.C. [also available in Spanish: *Violencia institucional en Guatemala,1960 a 1996: una reflexión cuantitativa*], at:
http://shr.aaas.org/guatemala/ciidh/qr/english/qrtitle.html (English)
http://shr.aaas.org/guatemala/ciidh/qr/spanish/ (Spanish)

BALL, P., H.F. SPIRER and L. SPIRER (eds.) (2000), *Making the Case: Investigating Large Scale Human Rights Violations Using Information Systems and Data Analysis*, American Association for the Advancement of Science (AAAS), Washington D.C., at:
http://shr.aaas.org/mtc/.

BALL P. and R. SILVA (2006a), *The Profile of Human Rights Violations in Timor-Leste, 1974-1999*. Report to the Commission on Reception, Truth and Reconciliation, Human Rights Data Analysis Group, Benetech Initiative, Palo Alto, at:
http://www.hrdag.org/timor.

BALL P. and R. SILVA (2006b), "The Demography of Large-Scale Human Rights Atrocities: Integrating Demographic and Statistical Analysis into Post-conflict Historical Clarification in Timor-Leste", Human Rights Data Analysis Group, Benetech, Palo Alto, at:
http://paa2006.princeton.edu/download.aspx?submissionId=60827

BANKS, D.L. (1986), "The Analysis of Human Rights Data Over Time", *Human Rights Quarterly*, Vol. 8, No. 4, pp. 654-680.

BANKS, D.L. (1989), "Patterns of Oppression: An Exploratory Analysis of Human-Rights Data", *Journal of the American Statistical Association*, Vol. 84, No. 407, pp. 674-681;

BANKS, D.L. (1991), "Measuring Human Rights", in I. BRECHER (ed.), *Human Rights, Development and Foreign Policy*, Institute for Research on Public Policy, Halifax, Nova Scotia, pp. 539-562.

BANKS, D.L. (1999), "The Collision of Government, Ethics, and Statistics: Case Studies and Comments"', *Proceedings of the Social Statistics Section of the American Statistical Association*, pp. 167-172.

BANKS, D.L. and Y.H. SAID (2008), "New Issues in Human Rights Statistics", in ASHER, BANKS and SCHEUREN (2008), pp. 241-269.

BANKS, D.L. and H. SPIRER (1989), "New Human Rights Patterns", *Proceedings of the Social Statistics Section of the American Statistical Association*, pp. 320-325 [reprinted in N.D. BIVINGS (2002), pp. 20-25].

BARDHAN, P, (2002), "Decentralization of Governance and Development", in *Journal of Economic Perspectives*, pp.185-205.

BARDHAN, P. and D. MOOKHERJEE (2002), *Relative Capture of Local and Central Governments. An Essay in the Political Economy of Decentralization*, Center for International and Development Economics Research, University of California, Berkeley.

BARRAGUES, A. and M.A. ADAUTA DE SOUSA, (2000), "Vers le développement d'indicateurs pour mesurer le niveau de conscientisation concernant la connaissance, la pratique et la défense des droits de l'homme en Angola / Towards the Development of Indicators to Measure Levels of Awareness on Knowledge, Exercise and Defence of Human Rights in Angola" (in Portuguese), in IAOS (2000), at: http://www.portal-stat.admin.ch/iaos2000/barragues_final_paper_portuguais.doc

BARRERA, A. (2007), "Economic Rights in the Knowledge Economy: An Instrumental Justification", in HERTEL and MINKLER (2007), pp. 76-93.

BARRIOS, A. (1999), "Indicadores de medición: aspectos metodológicos y estratégicos de exigibilidad" (Measurement Indicators: Methodological and Strategic Aspects Related to the Exigency [of Rights] / Indicateurs de mesure: aspects méthodologiques et stratégiques relatifs à l'exigibilité [des droits]), in CEDAL (1999), pp. 94-102.

BARSH, R.L. (1991), "The Right to Development as a Human Right: Results of the Global Consultation", in *Human Rights Quarterly*, Vol. 13, No. 3, pp. 322-38, at: http://www.ciesin.org/docs/010-152/010-152.html

BARSH, R. L. (1993), "Measuring Human Rights: Problems of Methodology and Purpose", *Human Rights Quarterly*, Vol. 15, No. 1, pp. 87-121.

BARTELSON, J. (2006), "Making Sense of Global Civil Society", *European Journal of International Relations*, Vol. 12, No.3, pp. 371-395.

BASU, K. (2007), "Human Rights as Instruments of Emancipation and Economic Development ", in HERTEL and MINKLER (2007), pp. 345-362.

BAYEFSKY.COM (2008), *The United Nations Human Rights Treaties Database*, at: http://www.bayefsky.com/

BECK, T. *et al.* (2000), "New Tools and New Tests in Comparative Political Economy: The Database of Political Institutions", World Bank Policy Research Working Paper No. 2283, Washington D.C., at: http://www.worldbank.org/wbi/governance/pdf/wps2283.pdf

BEETHAM, D. (ed.) (1994a), *Defining and Measuring Democracy*, Sage, London.

BEETHAM, D. (1994b), "Conditions for Democratic Consolidation", in *Review of African Political Economy*, Vol. 21, No. 60, pp.157-172.

BEETHAM, D. (ed.) (1995a), *Politics and Human Rights,* Blackwell Publishers, Cambridge and Oxford.

BEETHAM, D. (1995b), "What Future for Economic and Social Rights", *Political Studies*, Vol. 43, pp. 41-60.

BEETHAM, D. (1999), *Democracy and Human Rights*, Polity Press and Blackwell Publishers, Cambridge, Oxford and Malden MA.

BEETHAM, D. (2002) [see INTERNATIONAL IDEA, 2002].

BEETHAM, D. (2003a), "Human Rights and Democracy", in R. AXTMANN, (ed.), *Understanding Democratic Politics*, Sage Publications, London.

BEETHAM, D. (2003b), "Democratic Quality: Freedom and Rights", paper presented at the workshop on *Quality of Democracy*, held at Stanford University on 10-11 October, Center on Democracy, Development and the Rule of Law, Freeman Spogli Institute for International studies, Stanford University, Stanford [text modified in 2004], at: http://iis-db.stanford.edu/pubs/20433/Freedom_and_Rights.pdf

BEETHAM, D. (2005), "The State of Democracy Project", in INTERNATIONAL IDEA, *Ten Years of Supporting Democracy Worldwide*, Stockholm, pp.145-155.

BEETHAM, D. (2008) [see INTERNATIONAL IDEA (2008)].

BEETHAM, D. *et al.* (2002), *Democracy under Blair: A Democratic Audit of the United Kingdom*, Methuen and Politico's , London [2nd edition (2003)].

BELLVER, A. and D. KAUFMANN (2005), "Transparenting Transparency: Initial Empirics and Policy Applications", discussion paper presented at the IMF conference on *Transparency and Integrity*, held on 6-7 July, at: http://www.worldbank.org/wbi/governance/pubs/TransparencyIMF.html

BEMELMANS-VIDEC, M.L., R.C. RIST and E. VEDUNG (eds.) (1998), *Carrots, Sticks and Sermons: Policy Instruments and Their Evaluation*, Transaction Publishers, New Brunswick and London.

BENKO, E. [see CARR CENTER FOR HUMAN RIGHTS POLICY, 2005].

BERG-SCHLOSSER, D. (2004a), "Indicators of Democracy and Good Governance as Measures of the Quality of Democracy in Africa: A Critical Appraisal", *Acta Politica*, Vol. 39, No. 3, pp. 248-278.

BERG-SCHLOSSER, D. (2004b), "The Quality of Democracies in Europe as Measured by Current Indicators of Democratization and Good Governance", *Journal of Communist Studies and Transition Politics*, Vol. 20, No. 1, pp. 28-55.

BERRY, A. and F. STEWART (2000), "The real causes of inequality", *Challenge*, Vol. 43, No. 1, pp. 44-93.

BERRY, J.W. and W.J. LONNER (1986), *Field Methods in Cross Cultural Research*, Sage, London.

BERTELSMANN FOUNDATION (2005), *Bertelsmann Transformation Index 2003*, Bertelsmann Stiftung, Gütersloh, at: http://bti2003.bertelsmann-transformation-index.de/

BERTELSMANN FOUNDATION (2008a), *Bertelsmann Transformation Atlas 2006:*, Bertelsmann Foundation, Gütersloh, at: http://bti2006.bertelsmann-transformation-index.de/

BERTELSMANN FOUNDATION (2008b), *Status Index: Trend 2005-2007*, Bertelsmann Stiftung, Gütersloh, at: http://www.bertelsmann-transformation-index.de/37.0.html?&L=1

BERTHELIER, P., A. DESDOIGTS and J. OULD AOUDIA (2004a), "Profils institutionnels: une base de données sur les caractéristiques institutionnelles de pays en développement, en transition et développés", *Revue Française d'Économie*, Vol. 19, pp. 121-196.

BERTHELIER, P., A. DESDOIGTS and J. OULD AOUDIA (2004b), "Institutional Profiles: Presentation and Analysis of an Original Database of the Institutional Characteristics of Developing, in Transition and Developed Countries ", LEG - Documents de Travail – Économie, No. 2004-01, Laboratoire d'Économie et de Gestion, Université de Bourgogne, at: http://econpapers.repec.org/paper/latlegeco/2004-01.htm

BESANÇON, M. (2003), "Good Governance Rankings: The Art of Measurement", *World Peace Foundation Reports*, No. 36, Cambridge MA, at: http://belfercenter.ksg.harvard.edu/files/wpf36governance.pdf

BEWSHER, J., E. CARVALHO and T. LANDMAN (2007), "Preliminary Survey on Donor Use of Governance Assessments", paper presented at the CMI/UNDP Seminar on *Governance Assessments and the Paris Declaration: Towards Inclusive Participation and National Ownership* (Bergen, 23-25 September), Chr. Michelsen Institute and UNDP Oslo Governance Centre, at: http://www.undp.org/oslocentre/docs07/bergen_2007/Survey%20of%20Donor%20Use%20of%20Governance%20Assessments.pdf

BIAOU, A. (2005) [see INSTITUT NATIONAL DE LA STATISTIQUE ET DE L'ANALYSE ÉCONOMIQUE, Bénin]

BING-PAPPOE, A. (2007), "The Ghana APRM Process: A Case Study", paper presented at the CMI/UNDP Seminar on *Governance assessments and the Paris Declaration: Towards Inclusive Participation and National Ownership* (Bergen, 23-25 September), Chr. Michelsen Institute and UNDP Oslo Governance Centre, at: http://www.undp.org/oslocentre/docs07/bergen_2007/Governance%20Assessments%20Ghana%20Case%20Study.pdf

BIVINGS, N.D. (ed.) (2002), *Human Rights Papers: Social Statistics Proceedings and Joint Statistical Meetings, 1984 to 2001*, Social Statistics Section of the American Statistical Association (ASA), University of Chicago, Chicago, at: http://www.amstat.org/sections/ssoc/SSS_Human_Rights_Papers.pdf

BLACKWOOD, D. and R. LYNCH (1994), "The Measurement of Inequality and Poverty: A Policy Maker's Guide to the Literature", in *World Development*, Vol. 22, No. 4, pp. 567-578.

BLONDIAUX, L. (1998), *La fabrique de l'opinion: une histoire sociale des sondages*, Seuil, Paris.

BLUME, L. et al. (2007), "The Economic Effects of Constitutions: Replicating and Extending Persson and Tabellini", CESifo Working Paper Series No. 2017, Category 2: Public Choice, at: http://www.cesifo-group.de/pls/guestci/download/CESifo%20Working%20Papers%202007/CESifo%20Working%20Papers%20June%202007/cesifo1_wp2017.pdf

BLYTH, S. (1995), "The Dead of the Gulag: An Experiment in Statistical Investigation", *Applied Statistics*, Vol. 44, pp. 307-321.

BOIX, C. and S. ROSATO (2001), *A Complete Data Set of Political Regimes, 1800-1999*, University of Chicago, Department of Political Science, Chicago [a dataset extending PRZEWORSKI *et al.* (2000)].

BOIX, C. (2003), *Democracy and Redistribution*, Cambridge Studies in Comparative Politics, Cambridge University Press, Cambridge, at:
http://books.google.ch/books?id=2_nYWobBKlQC&dq=Democracy+and+Redistribution&pg=PP1&ots=BHPHkJq3eW&sig=xiHmDO0ttG6rss62Op4nnMkkYx0&hl=fr&sa=X&oi=book_result&resnum=1&ct=result#PPR7,M1

BOLLEN, K.A. (1979), "Political Democracy and the Timing of Development", *American Sociological Review*, Vol. 44, pp. 572-87, at:
http://www.odum.unc.edu/odum/content/pdf/Bollen_1979_ASR.pdf

BOLLEN, K.A. (1980), "Issues in the Comparative Measurement of Political Democracy", *American Sociological Review*, Vol. 45, pp. 370-90, at:
http://www.odum.unc.edu/odum/content/pdf/Bollen_1980_ASR.pdf

BOLLEN, K.A (1983), "World System Position, Dependency and Political Democracy: the Cross-National Evidence", *American Sociological Review*, Vol. 48, pp. 468-79, at:
http://www.odum.unc.edu/odum/content/pdf/Bollen_1983_ASR.pdf

BOLLEN, K.A. (1986), "Political Rights and Political Liberties in Nations: An Evaluation of Human Rights Measures, 1950 to 1984", *Human Rights Quarterly*, Vol. 8, No. 4, pp. 567-91 [and in CLAUDE and JABINE (1992), pp. 188-215].

BOLLEN, K.A. (1990), "Political Democracy: Conceptual and Measurement Traps", *Studies in Comparative International Development*, Vol. 25, No. 1, pp. 7-24 [reprinted in INKELES (1991), pp. 3-20], at:
http://www.odum.unc.edu/odum/content/pdf/Bollen%20(1990%20SCID).pdf

BOLLEN, K.A. (1993), "Liberal Democracy: Validity and Method Factors in Cross-National Measures", *American Journal of Political Science*, Vol. 37, No. 4, pp. 1207-1230, at:
http://www.odum.unc.edu/odum/content/pdf/Bollen_1993_AJPS.pdf

BOLLEN, K.A. (1995), "Democracy, Measures of", in M.L. SEYMOUR (ed.), *The Encyclopedia of Democracy*, Congressional Quarterly, Washington, D.C., pp. 817-21.

BOLLEN, K. A. (2001), "Indicator: Methodology", in N.J. SMELSER and P.B. BALTES (eds.), *International Encyclopedia of the Social and Behavioral Sciences*. U.K. Elsevier Science, Oxford, pp. 7282-87.

BOLLEN, K.A. and B. GRANDJEAN (1981), "The Dimension(s) of Democracy: Further Issues in the Measurement and Effects of Political Democracy", *American Sociological Review*, Vol. 46, pp. 651-659, at:
http://www.odum.unc.edu/odum/content/pdf/Bollen_Grandjean_1981ASR.pdf

BOLLEN, K.A. and R. HOYLE (1990), "Perceived Cohesion: A Conceptual and Empirical Examination", *Social Forces*, Vol. 69, No. 2, pp. 479-504, at:
http://www.odum.unc.edu/odum/content/pdf/Bollen_Hoyle_SF1990.pdf

BOLLEN, K.A. and R.W. JACKMANN (1985), "Political Democracy and the Size Distribution of Income", *American Sociological Review*, Vol. 50, pp. 438-57, at:
http://www.odum.unc.edu/odum/content/pdf/Bollen%20Jackman%20(1985%20ASR).pdf

BOLLEN, K.A. and R.W. JACKMANN (1989), "Democracy, Stability, and Dichotomies", *American Sociological Review*, Vol. 54, No. 4, pp. 612-621.

BOLLEN, K.A. and P. PAXTON (1997), "Democracy Before Athens", in M. MIDLARSKY (ed.) *Inequality and Democracy*, Cambridge University Press, New York, pp. 13-44.
http://www.odum.unc.edu/odum/content/pdf/Bollen%20Paxton%20(1997%20IDED).pdf

BOLLEN, K.A. and P. PAXTON (1998), "Detection and Determinants of Bias in Subjective Measures", *American Sociological Review*, Vol. 63, pp. 465-478.

BOLLEN, K.A. and P. PAXTON (2000) "Subjective Measures of Liberal Democracy", *Comparative Political Studies*, Vol. 33, No. 1, pp.58-86, at:
http://www.unc.edu/~bollen/bollen_paxton_2000.pdf

BOLLEN, K.A. *et al.* (2003), "A Half Century of Suffrage: New Data and a Comparative Analysis", *Studies in Comparative International Development*, Vol. 38, pp. 93-122, at:
http://www.odum.unc.edu/odum/content/pdf/Bollen%20Kim%20Lee%20Paxton%20(2003%20SCID).pdf

BOLLEN, K.A., P.M. PAXTON, and R. MORISHIMA (2005) "Assessing International Evaluations: An Example from USAID's Democracy and Governance Programs", *American Journal of Evaluation*, Vol. 26, pp. 189-203., at:

http://www.odum.unc.edu/odum/content/pdf/Bollen%20Paxton%20Morishima%202005%20AJE.pdf

BOLLEN, K.A. *et al.*, (2005), "What Are We Measuring? An Evaluation of the CES-D across Race, Ethnicity, and Immigrant Generation", *Social Forces*, Vol. 83, pp. 1567-1602, at:
http://www.odum.unc.edu/odum/content/pdf/Perreira%20Deeb-Sossa%20Harris%20Bollen%20(2005,%20SF,%20CES-D).pdf

BOLYARD, M., A. IPPOLITO and J. SMITH (1999), "Human Rights and the Global Economy: A Response to Meyer", *Human Rights Quarterly*, Vol. 21, pp. 207-219.

BOOZER, M.A. *et al.* (2003), "Paths to Success: The Relationship between Human Development and Economic Growth", Yale University Economic Growth Center, Discussion Paper No. 874, at:
http://ssrn.com/abstract=487469

BOURDIEU, P. (1980), "L'opinion publique n'existe pas", in *Questions de sociologie*, Editions de Minuit, Paris, pp. 222-235.

BOURGUIGNON, F., F.H.G. FERREIRA and M. MENÉNDEZ (2003), "Inequality of Outcomes and Inequality of Opportunities in Brazil", William Davidson Institute Working Paper, No. 630, and Texto para Discussão 478, Departamento de Economia, PUC, Rio de Janeiro, at:
http://www.cgdev.org/doc/event%20docs/MADS/BFM.pdf and
http://www.econ.puc-rio.br/pdf/td478.pdf

BOWMAN, K., F. LEHOUCQ and J. MAHONEY (2005), "Measuring Political Democracy: Case Expertise, Data Adequacy, and Central America", *Comparative Political Studies*, Vol. 38, No. 8, pp. 939-970.

BRACKING, S. (2002) [see INTERNATIONAL IDEA, 2002].

BRAND D. and S. RUSSELL (eds.) (2002) *Exploring the Core Content of Socio-Economic Rights: South African and International Perspectives*, Protea Press, Menlo Park, South Africa

BRATTON, M., MATTES, R. and E. GYIMAH-BOADI (2005), *Public Opinion, Democracy, and Market Reform in Africa*, Cambridge University Press, Cambridge.

BRIGNARDELLO, J.H. (2000) [see CEDAL, 2000].

BRUNBORG, H. (2000), "Contribution of statistical analysis to the investigations of the International Criminal Tribunals", in IAOS (2000), at:
http://www.portal-stat.admin.ch/iaos2000/brunborg_final_paper.doc
and in *Statistical Journal of the United Nations Economic Commission for Europe*, Vol. 18 (2001), pp.227-238.

BRUNBORG, H. (2002), "Report on the Size and Ethnic Composition of the Population of Kosovo", Case of Slodovan Milosevic (IT-02-54), ICTY, The Hague.

BRUNBORG, H (2003), "Needs for Demographic and Statistical Expertise at the International Criminal Court", contribution to an expert consultation process on general issues relevant to the International Criminal Court Office of the Prosecutor (ICC-OTP), at:
http://www.icc-cpi.int/library/organs/otp/brunborg.pdf

BRUNBORG, H. (2004) [see PCBS (2004)].

BRUNBORG H. and B.A. LACINA (2004), *Report on the Seminar on the Demography of Conflict and Violence, Organized by the IUSSP Working Group* (Oslo 8-11 November 2003) International Union for the Scientific Study of Population (IUSSP), at:
http://www.iussp.org/Activities/wgc-con/con-report04.php

BRUNBORG, H., T.H. LYNGSTAD and H. URDAL (2003), "Accounting for Genocide: How Many Were Killed in Srebrenica?", *European Journal of Population / Revue européenne de démographie*, Vol. 19, no. 3, pp. 229-248.

BRUNBORG H. and E. TABEAU (2005), "The Demography of Conflict and Violence", in *European Journal of Population / Revue européenne de démographie*, Vol. 21, No. 2-3, pp. 131-144.

BRUNBORG, H. and H. URDAL (eds.) (2005), *Demography and Conflict*, special issue of the *Journal of Peace Research*, Vol. 42, Nr. 4, at:
http://dbh.nsd.uib.no/nfi/litteratur/?key=465883&language=no

BRUNBORG, H., E. TABEAU and H. URDAL (eds.) (2006), *The Demography of Armed Conflicts*, International Studies in Population, Springer, Dordrecht.

BRYSK, A. (1994), "The Politics of Measurement: The Contested Count of the Disappeared in Argentina", *Human Rights Quarterly*, Vol. 16, No. 4, pp. 676-692.

BUCHANAN, A.E. (1984), "The Right to a Decent Minimum of Health Care", *Philosophy and public affairs*, Princeton N.J., Vol. 13, No. 1, pp. 55-78.

BURCHARDT, T. (2006), "Foundations for Measuring Equality: A Discussion Paper for the Equalities Review", Centre for Analysis of Social Exclusion, CASE Paper No. 111, London School of Economics, London, at:
http://sticerd.lse.ac.uk/dps/case/cp/CASEpaper111.pdf

BURKHARDT, R.E. and M. LEWIS-BECK (1994), "Comparative Democracy: The Economic Development Thesis", *American Political Science Review*, Vol. 88, No. 4, pp.903-10.

BURR, M. (1993), "Quantifying Genocide in the Southern Sudan, 1983-1993", U.S.Committee for Refugees, Washington, D.C.

BUTLER, E.W., G.L. JONES and J.B. PICK (1989), "Socioeconomic Inequality in the U.S.-Mexico Borderlands", *Proceedings of the Social Statistics Section of the American Statistical Association*, pp. 326-332.

CACCIA, I. (2008) [SEE HURIDOCS, 2008].

CÁCERES, E. (1999), "La Necesidad de Instrumentos Cualitativos" (The Need for Qualitative Instruments / Le besoin d'outils qualitatifs), in CEDAL (1999), pp. 82-84.

CAMPBELL, B. (1997), "Quelques enjeux conceptuels, idéologiques et politiques autor de la notion de gouvernance", in Bonne gouvernance et développement: Actes du symosium international, Institut africain pour la démocratie, Dakar, pp 65-94.

CAMPBELL, B. (1999), "La Banque mondiale prône l'État efficace : pour quoi faire?", Revue québécoise de droit international, Vol. 10, pp.189-199.

CAMPBELL, B. (2001), "La bonne gouvernance: une notion éminemment politique", in Les non-dits de la bonne gouvernance, Haut conseil de la coopération internationale, Karthala, Paris, pp. 119-149.

CAMPBELL, B. (ed.) (2005), Qu'allons-nous faire des pauvres? Réformes institutionnelles et espaces politiques ou les pièges de la gouvernance pour les pauvres, L'Harmattan, Paris.

CAMPBELL, P.R. (1987), "South Africa 1960 to 1986: A Statistical View of Racial Differences", Proceedings of the Social Statistics Section of the American Statistical Association, pp. 270-275.

CARDIA, N. (2000), "Monitoring Human Rights in Latin America with the Assistance of Statistical Information", in IAOS (2000), at: http://www.portal-stat.admin.ch/iaos2000/cardia_final_paper.doc

CARDINAL, L. and C. ANDREW (2001), La démocratie à l'épreuve de la gouvernance, Presses de l'Université d'Ottawa, Ottawa.

CAREY, S.C., S.C. POE and T.C. VAZQUEZ (2001), "How are These Pictures Different? A Quantitative Comparison of the US State Department and Amnesty International Human Rights Reports, 1976-1995", Human Rights Quarterly, Vol. 23, No. 3, pp. 650-677.

CARLSON, B.A. (2000), "Women in Statistics: Where are We?" in IAOS (2000), at: http://www.statistik.admin.ch/about/international/carlson_final_paper.doc

CARR CENTER FOR HUMAN RIGHTS POLICY (2005), Measurement & Human Rights: Tracking Progress, Assessing Impact, A Carr Center for Human Rights Policy Project Report, John F. Kennedy School of Government, Harvard University, Cambridge [edited by K. DESORMEAU, A. HINES, M. IGNATIEFF and F. RAINE] background papers and report on the Carr Center Conference on Measuring Impact in Human Rights: How Far We Come, and How Far to Go?, held in Harvard on 5-7 May.

CARRIQUIRIBORDE, A. and A. SANDOVAL TERÁN (2007) "Indicadores en materia de derechos económicos, sociales, culturales y ambientales (DESCA): Identificación y propuesta de indicadores para el monitoreo de algunas dimensiones del derecho a la salud, el derecho a la alimentación adecuada, et derecho al trabajo y el derecho a la vivienda adecuada (segunda versión)" (proposal of indicators for monitoring some dimensions of the rights to health, to food, to work and to housing / proposition d'indicateurs pour le suivi de certaines dimensions des droits à la santé, à l'alimentation, au travail et au logement), INCIDE Social, Mexico City, at: http://incidesocial.org/observatorio/images/PDF/Biblioteca/matriz%20indicadores%20salud-version2.pdf

CARTER CENTER (1992), "Quality of Democracy Indicators", Atlanta [Mimeo].

CARVALHO, E. (2008) [see INTERNATIONAL IDEA, 2008a].

CASPER, G. and C. TUFIS (2003), "Correlation Versus Interchangeability: The Limited Robustness of Empirical Findings on Democracy Using Highly Correlated Data Sets", *Political Analysis*, Vol. 11, No. 2, pp. 196-203; abstract at:
http://pan.oxfordjournals.org/cgi/content/abstract/11/2/196

CASTAÑÓN ÁLVAREZ, F. (2000), "Statisticians as human rights defenders: The lessons of an innovative experience in Guatemala", in IAOS (2000), at:
http://www.portal-stat.admin.ch/iaos2000/castanon_final_paper.doc

CAYROL, R. (2000), *Sondages: mode d'emploi*, Presses de Sciences Po, Paris.

CEDAL (CENTRO DE ASESORÍA LABORAL DEL PERÚ) (1998), *Indicadores para la vigilancia social de los derechos económicos, sociales y culturales,* (Indicators for social monitoring of economic, social and cultural rights / Indicateurs pour la surveillance sociale des droits économiques, sociaux et culturels), Lima.

CEDAL (1998b), *Declaración de Quito acerca de la exigibilidad y realización de los derechos económicos, sociales y culturales en América Latina y el Caribe,* (Quito Declaration on the exigency and realisation of the economic, social and cultural rights in Latin America and the Caribbean / Déclaration de Quito sur l'exigibilité et la réalisation des droits économiques, sociaux et culturels), CEDAL, Lima.

CEDAL (1998c), *Los derechos económicos sociales y culturales: Enfrentando un mar de pobreza y exclusión social* (Report on the status of economic, social and cultural rights in Peru: facing massive poverty and social exclusion / Rapport sur la situation des droits économiques, sociaux et cultures au Pérou: face à une immense pauvreté et à l'exclusion social), CEDAL, Lima.

CEDAL (2000), *Derechos económicos, sociales y culturales: Balance en siete países latinoamericanos,* Vigilancia social en Argentina, Brasil, Chile, Colombia, México, Perú y Venezuela (Economic, social and cultural rights: their status in seven Latin American countries / Droits économiques, sociaux et culturels: bilan dans sept pays d'Amérique Latine), Lima [authored by J.H. BRIGNARDELLO].

CEDAL (2001), *Pueblos indígenas y derechos humanos: El Convenio 169 de la OIT, vigilancia y exigibilidad* (Indigenous peoples and human rights: the ILO Convenant 169 / Les peuples indigènes et les droits de l'homme: la convention 169 de l'OIT), Lima [authored by P. GARCÍA HIERRO], at:
http://www.cedal.org.pe/libros/2001/convenio169.pdf

CEDAL and FIDH (FEDERACIÓN INTERNACIONAL DE DERECHOS HUMANOS) (2001), *Guía de indicadores para la vigilancia social de los derechos humanos en la empresa* (Gide on indicators for social monitoring of human rights in the enterprises / Gide sur les indicateurs pour la surveillance des droits de l'homme dans les entreprises), Lima, Peru.

CHAMPAGNE, P. (1990), *Faire l'opinion: Le nouveau jeu politique*, Editions de Minuit, Paris.

CHAPMAN, A.R. (1995), "Monitoring Women's Right to Health Under the International Covenant on Economic, Social and Cultural Rights", *American University Law Review*, vol. 44, pp. 1157-75.

CHAPMAN, A.R. (1996), "A 'Violations Approach' for Monitoring the International Covenant on Economic, Social and Cultural Rights", *Human Rights Quarterly*, vol. 18, no. 1, pp.29-36.

CHAPMAN, A.R. (1999). "How Truth Commission Processes Shape their Truth-Finding", paper presented at TRC Commissioning the Past, Witz University, 11-14 June.

CHAPMAN, A.R. (2005a), "Developing Indicators for Monitoring the Right to Education", paper presented at the first Metagora Forum held in Paris on 24-25 May.

CHAPMAN, A.R. (2005b), "Working with National Human Rights Commissions in Africa", working paper submitted to the Metagora Partners' Group, American Association for the Advancement of Science (AAAS), Washinton D.C.

Chapman, A.R. (2007), "The Status of Efforts to Monitor Economic, Social, and Cultural Rights", in Hertel and Minkler (2007), pp. 143-164.

CHAPMAN, A.R. and S. RUSSELL (eds.) (2002), *Core Obligations: Building a Framework for Economic, Social and Cultural Rights*, Intersentia, Antwerp, Oxford and New York; preview at:
http://books.google.co.uk/books?hl=en&id=_JcIXuYJWyEC&dq=core+obligations&printsec=frontcover&source=web&ots=52MsUo2eHa&sig=9IFfs94-IVN8n2NRYRGAyM7LT6g#PPP1,M1

CHAUHAN, A. (2005) "Measuring Indigenous Peoples' Rights in the Philippines: Quantitative and Qualitative Outcomes", paper presented at the first Metagora Forum, held in Paris on 24-25 May.

CHEN, X. and H.I. WEISBERG (1992), "Can Statistics Reveal When a Death Sentence is Disproportionate?", *Proceedings of the Social Statistics Section of the American Statistical Association*, pp. 280-285.

CHILDWATCH (1996), "Indicators for Children's Rights: Sources of Information for Country Case Studies", a project outline, at:
http://www.childwatch.uio.no/cwi/projects/indicators/sourcesE.html

CHILDWATCH (1999), "Monitoring Children's Rights Indicators for Children's Rights Project", at:
http://child.cornell.edu/childhouse/childwatch/cwi/projects/indicators/index.html

CINGRANELLI, D. L. and D. L. RICHARDS (2001), *Coding Government Respect For Human Rights, Manual Version One*, State University of New York, Binghamton University, New York.

CINGRANELLI, D.L. and D.L. RICHARDS (2004), *The Cingranelli-Richards (CIRI) Human Rights Database Coder Manual*, at:
ciri.binghamton.edu/documentation/web_version_7_31_04_ciri_coding_guide.pdf

CINGRANELLI, D.L. and D.L. RICHARDS (2007), "Measuring Government Efforts to Respect Economic and Social Human Rights: A Peer Benchmark", in Hertel and Minkler (2007), pp. 214-232.

CINGRANELLI, D.L. and D.L. RICHARDS (2008a), "The CIRI Human Rights Data Project", at:
http://ciri.binghamton.edu/index.asp

CINGRANELLI, D.L. and D.L. RICHARDS (2008b), "CIRI Variable Short Descriptions", at:
http://ciri.binghamton.edu/documentation/ciri_variables_short_descriptions.pdf

CINGRANELLI, D.L. and D.L. RICHARDS (2008c), *Revised CIRI Human Rights Data Project Coding Manual*, at:
http://ciri.binghamton.edu/documentation/ciri_coding_guide.pdf

CIVICUS (2005), *CIVICUS Civil Society Index: Summary of Conceptual framework and Research Methodology*, at:
http://www.civicus.org/

CIVICUS (2007), *Global Survey of the State of Civil Society*, Kumarian Press, Bloomfield [authored by V.F. HEINRICH].

CLAUDE, R.P. and T.B. JABINE (eds.) (1986), *Symposium: Statistical Issues in the Field of Human Rights*, special issue of *Human Rights Quarterly*, Vol. 8, pp. 551-699.

CLAUDE, R.P. and T.B. JABINE (eds.) (1992), *Human Rights and Statistics: Getting the Record Straight*, University of Pennsylvania Press, Philadelphia, at:
http://books.google.ch/books?id=yMABbuKyN9wC&pg%20%20lCVvs9b4Qs0NENJRaEQ

CLING J.-P., M. RAZAFINDRAKOTO and F. ROUBAUD (eds.) (2002), *Les nouvelles stratégies internationales de lutte contre la pauvreté*, Economica/IRD, Paris [*New International Poverty Reduction Strategies*, Routledge, London and New York, 2003].

COCKROFT, L. (1998), "Corruption and Human Rights: A Crucial Link", Transparency International Working Paper.

COLLIER, D., F.D. HIDALGO and A.O. MACIUCEANU (2007), "Essentially Contested Concepts: Debates and Applications", Committee on Concepts and Methods of the International Political Science Association, Political Concepts, Working Paper Series, No. 12, Centro de Investigación y Docencia Económicas (CIDE), Mexico City, at:
http://www.concepts-methods.org/papers_list.php?id_categoria=1&titulo=Political%20Concepts

CONIBERE, R. *et al.* (2004), *Statistical Appendix to the Report of the Truth and Reconciliation Commission of Sierra Leone*, report by the Benetech Human Rights Data Analysis Group and the American Bar Association to the Truth and Reconciliation Commission, at:
http://hrdag.org/resources/publications/SL-TRC-statistics-chapter-final.pdf

COPPEDGE, M. (2005), "Defining and Measuring Democracy", Committee on Concepts and Methods of the International Political Science Association, Political Concepts, Working Paper Series, No. 2, Centro de Investigación y Docencia Económicas (CIDE), Mexico City, at:
http://www.concepts-methods.org/papers_list.php?id_categoria=1&titulo=Political%20Concepts

COPPEDGE, M. (2008, forthcoming), *Approaching Democracy*, Cambridge University Press, Cambridge.

COPPEDGE, M. and W. REINICKE (1990), "Measuring Polyarchy," *Studies in Comparative International Development*, Vol. 25, No. 1, pp. 51-72 [reprinted in INKELES (1991), pp. 47-68].

CÓRDOVA, P. and M. SELIGSON (2004), *Auditoría de la Democracia, Ecuador 2004*, Vanderbilt University, CEDATOS, Quito.

CORNER, L. (2005), "Gender Sensitive and Pro-Poor Indicators of Good Governance", paper prepared as a background document for the UNDP-ICSSR technical workshop on *Governance Indicators for Pro-poor and Gender-sensitive Policy Reform* held in New Delhi, 20-22 April, at:
http://www.undp.org/oslocentre/docs05/cross/2/Gender-sensitive%20and%20pro-poor%20indicators%20for%20Democratic%20Governance.pdf

CORSTANGE, D. (2007), "Ethnic Politics and Surveys: How Do We Measure What We Want to Measure?", Committee on Concepts and Methods of the International Political Science Association, Political Concepts, Working Paper Series, No. 13, Centro de Investigación y Docencia Económicas (CIDE), Mexico City, at:
http://www.concepts-methods.org/papers_list.php?id_categoria=1&titulo=Political%20Concepts

COULIBALY, M. and A. DIARRA (2004), "Gouvernance, démocratie et lutte contre la pauvreté au Mali: Éclairage méthodologique et analytique à partir des résultats Afrobaromètre", in METAGORA, DIAL and IRD (2004), pp. 65-101.

COURBAGE, Y. (2000), "Utilisation et abus dans l'analyse démographique des minorités / Uses and Abuses in Demographic Analysis of Minorities", in IAOS (2000), at:
http://www.portal-stat.admin.ch/iaos2000/courbage_final_paper.doc

COURT J., G. HYDEN and K. MEASE (2002a), "Governance and Development: Sorting Out the Basics", World Governance Survey Discussion Paper 1, United Nations University, Tokyo
http://www.odi.org.uk/WGA_governance/Docs/WGS-discussionPaper1.pdf

COURT, J., G. HYDEN and K. MEASE (2002b), "Assessing Governance: Methodological Challenges", World Governance Survey Discussion Paper 2, United Nations University, Tokyo.

COURT, J., G. HYDEN and K. MEASE (2003a), "Governance Performance: the Aggregate Picture", World Governance Survey Discussion Paper 3, United Nations University, Tokyo, at
http://www.odi.org.uk/wga_governance/Docs/WGS-discussionPaper3.pdf

COURT, J., G. HYDEN and K. MEASE (2003b), "Making Sense of Governance: The Need for Involving Local Stakeholders", Development Dialog, ODI, London, at:
http://www.odi.org.uk/WGA_governance/Docs/Making_sense_Goverance_stakeholders.pdf

COURT, J., G. HYDEN and K. MEASE (2004), *Making Sense of Governance: Empirical Evidence from Sixteen Developing Countries*, Lynne Rienner Publishers, Boulder CO.

COYLE, A. (2000), "How Does Statistical Information Aid the Development of Appropriate Policies in Prisons?", in IAOS (2000), at:
http://www.portal-stat.admin.ch/iaos2000/coyle_final_paper.doc

CRACKNELL, B. (2000), *Evaluating Development Aid: Issues, Problems and Solutions*, Sage, London.

CRAWFORD, G. and KEARTON, I. (2002), *Evaluating Democracy and Governance Assistance*, Centre for Development Studies, University of Leeds.

DAKOLIAS, M. (2006), "Are We There Yet?: Measuring Success of Constitutional Reform", *Vanderbilt Journal of Transnational Law*, Vol. 39, No. 4, pp. 1117-1231.

DALTON, R.J., W. JUY and D.C. SHIN (2007) "Popular Conceptions of Democracy", Committee on Concepts and Methods of the International Political Science Association, Political Concepts, Working Paper Series, No. 15, Centro de Investigación y Docencia Económicas (CIDE), Mexico City, at:
http://www.concepts-methods.org/papers_list.php?id_categoria=1&titulo=Political%20Concepts

DANKWA, V., C. FLINTERMAN, and S. LECKIE (1998), "Commentary to the Maastricht Guidelines on the Violations of Economic, Social and Cultural Rights," in: *Human Rights Quarterly*, Vol. 20, No. 3, 706-707. Available also as a SIM Special at:
http://www.uu.nl/uupublish/content/20-02.pdf

DAPONTE, B.O. (1993), "A Case Study in Estimating Casualties from War and Its Aftermath: The 1991 Persian Gulf War", PSR *Quarterly* (Physicians for Social Responsibility Quarterly), No. 3, pp. 57-66.

DAPONTE, B.O. (1995), "How Many People Live in Soweto? Results from the 1995 Soweto Population Survey," Report to the Greater Johannesburg Transitional Metropolitan Council, Human Rights Institute of South Africa, Johannesburg.

DAPONTE, B.O. (2008), "Why Estimate Direct and Indirect Casualties from War? The Rule of Proportionality and Casualty Estimates", in ASHER, BANKS and SCHEUREN (2008), pp. 51-63.

DAPONTE, B.O., J.B. KADANE and L. WOLFSON (1997), "Bayesian Demography: Projecting the Iraqi Kurdish Population, 1977-1990," *Journal of the American Statistical Association*, Vol. 92, pp. 1256-1267.

D'ARCANGELO, R. (2006) [see METAGORA, 2006].

DAVENPORT, C. (2003), *Minorities at Risk Dataset Users Manual 030703* [see also MAR, 2008], at:
http://www.cidcm.umd.edu/mar/margene/mar-codebook_040903.pdf

DAVENPORT, C. and D.A. ARMSTRONG (2004), *American Journal of Political Science*, Vol. 48, No. 3, pp. 538-554; draft at:
http://www.ajps.org/articles/48.3.Davenport.ms30211.pdf

DELAMONICA, E.E., M. KOMARECKI and A. MINUJIN (eds.) (2006), *Human Rights and Social Policy for Children and Women: The Multiple Indicator Cluster Survey (MICS) in Practice*, Graduate Program in International Affairs, The New School, New York.

DELAMONICA, E.E. and A. MINUJIN (2007), "Incidence, Depth and Severity of Children in Poverty", in *Social Indicators Research*, Vol. 82, No. 2, pp. 361-374.

DELL, S. (1979), "Basic Needs or Comprehensive Development: Should the UNDP Have a Development Strategy?", *World Development*, Vol. 7, No. 3, pp. 291-308.

DEMOCRATIC AUDIT (2008), Organisation and web site attached to the Human Rights Centre of the University of Essex, at:
http://www.democraticaudit.com/auditing_democracy/index.php

DENEULIN, S. and F. STEWART (2002), "Amartya Sen's Contribution to Development Thinking", *Studies in Comparative International Development*, Vol. 37, No. 2, *pp.* 61-70.

DESORMEAU, K. (2005) [see CARR CENTER FOR HUMAN RIGHTS POLICY (2005)].

DEUTCH KARLEKAR, K. (2008) [see FREEDOM HOUSE, 2008a].

DFID (DEPARTMENT FOR INTERNATIONAL DEVELOPMENT OF THE UNITED KINGDOM) (2000) *Justice and Poverty Reduction*, London.

DFID (2004), *Drivers of Change*, Public Information Note, London, at:
http://139.184.194.47/docs/open/DOC59.pdf

DFID (2007), *How to Note on Country Governance Analysis,*DFID, London, at:
http://www.dfid.gov.uk/pubs/files/how-to-cga.pdf

DIAL (2006), *Module Gouvernance*, at:
http://www.dial.prd.fr/dial_enquetes/dial_enquetes_modulegouvernance.htm

DIAL (2007), *Enquêtes 1-2-3*, at:
http://www.dial.prd.fr/dial_enquetes/dial_enquetes_enquete123.htm

DIAS, C. and D. GILLIES (1993), *Human Rights, Democracy and Development*, Documents of the International Centre for Human Rights and Democratic Development, Montreal.

DICKLITCH, S. and R.E. HOWARD-HASSMANN (2007), "Public Policy and Economic Rights in Ghana and Uganda", in HERTEL and MINKLER (2007), pp. 325-344.

DIJSTRA, A.G. and L.C. HANMER (2000), "Measuring Socio-economic Gender Inequality: Towards an Alternative to UNDP Gender-related Development Index", *Feminist Economics*, vol. 6, No. 2, pp. 41-75.

DIRECTION GÉNÉRALE DE LA STATISTIQUE ET DE LA COMPTABILITÉ NATIONALE, Togo (2005), *Gouvernance, démocratie et lutte contre la pauvreté au Togo : Le point de vue de la population de la capitale (Enquêtes 1-2-3)*, Ministère du développement et de l'aménagement du territoire, DIAL-Metagora and AFRISTAT, Lomé [authored

by A.K. EGUIDA, M. RAZAFINDRAKOTO and F. ROUBAUD], at:
http://www.dial.prd.fr/dial_enquetes/PDF/togo.pdf

DIRECTION NATIONALE DE LA STATISTIQUE ET DE L'INFORMATIQUE, Mali (2005), *Démocratie et lutte contre la pauvreté : Le point de vue de la population de l'agglomération de Bamako (enquêtes 1-2-3, premiers résultats)*, DNSI, AFRISTAT et DIAL, Bamako [authored by M.A. SAKO, M. RAZAFINDRAKOTO and F. ROUBAUD], at:
http://www.dial.prd.fr/dial_enquetes/PDF/mali.pdf

DOLLAR, D. and V. LEVIN (2004), "The Increasing Selectivity of Foreign Aid (1984-2002)", World Bank Policy Research Working Paper No. 3299, World Bank, Washington, D.C.

DONNELLY, J. (1989), *Universal Human Rights in Theory and Practice*, Cornell University Press, Ithaca

DONNELLY, J. (2007), "The West and Economic Rights", in HERTEL and MINKLER (2007), pp. 37-55.

DONNELLY, J. AND D.J. WHELAN (2007), "The West, Economic and Social Rights, and the Global Human Rights Regime: Setting the Record Straight", *Human Rights Quarterly*, Vol. 29, No. 4, pp. 908-949.

DORMAN, P. (2007), "Worker Rights and Economic Development: The Cases of Occupational Safety and Health and Child Labor", in HERTEL and MINKLER (2007), pp. 363-378.

DOYAL, L. and I. GOUGH (1991), *A Theory of Human Need*, Macmillan, London.

DRÈZE, J. (2005), "Democracy and the Right to Food", in ALSTON and ROBINSON (2005), pp. 45-64.

DUECK, J. (2001) [see HURIDOCS, 2001a, 2001b].

DUNCAN, G.T., TH.B. JABINE and V.A. DE WOLF (eds.) (1993) *Private Lives and Public Policies: Confidentiality and Access of Government Statistics*, Panel on Confidentiality and Data Access, Committee on National Statistics, National Research Council and the Social Science Research Council, National Academy Press, Washington, D.C.

DUNNELLY, J. and H. RHODA (1986), "Assessing National Human Rights Performance: A Theoretical Framework", *Human Rights Quarterly*, Vol. 8, pp. 681-699.

DYBLE, M. (2000), "Developing Statistics on Human Rights and Government in Developing Countries", in IAOS (2000), at:
http://www.portal-stat.admin.ch/iaos2000/dyble_final_paper.doc

EASTERLIN, R. A. (1974), "Does Economic Growth Improve the Human Lot? Some Empirical Evidence", in P.A. DAVID and M.W. REDER (eds.), *Nations and Households in Economic Growth*, Academic Press, New York, pp. 89-125.

EGUIDA, A.K. (2005) [see DIRECTION GÉNÉRALE DE LA STATISTIQUE ET DE LA COMPTABILITÉ NATIONALE, Togo, 2005].

EIDE, A. (1989), "Realization of Social and Economic Rights and the Minimum Threshold Approach", *Human Rights Law Journal*, Vol. 10, p.35.

ELKINS, Z. (2000), "Gradations of Democracy? Empirical Tests of Alternative Conceptualizations", *American Journal of Political Science*, Vol. 44, No. 2, pp. 287-294.

ELKINS, Z. and J. SIDES (2007) "Evaluating Equivalence in Cross-National Survey Data", Committee on Concepts and Methods of the International Political Science Association, Political Concepts, Working Paper Series, No. 17, Centro de Investigación y Docencia Económicas (CIDE), Mexico City, at:
http://www.concepts-methods.org/papers_list.php?id_categoria=1&titulo=Political%20Concepts

ELSON, D. (2006), *Budgeting for Women's Rights: Monitoring Government Budgets for Compliance with CEDAW*, UN Publications, New York.

ENOH, M. (2005) [see INSTITUT NATIONAL DE LA STATISTIQUE, Côte d'Ivoire, 2005].

ENGEL, E. and A. VENETOULIAS (1992), "The Chilean Plebiscite: Projections Without Historic Data", *Journal of the American Statistical Association*, Vol. 87, pp. 933-941.

ERSSON, S. and J.E. LANE (1996), "Democracy and Development: A Statistical Exploration", in A. LEFTWICH (ed.), *Democracy and Development*, Polity, Cambridge, pp. 45–73.

ESDS INTERNATIONAL (ECONOMIC AND SOCIAL DATA SERVICE) (2008a), Access to aggregate and survey international datasets for further and higher education, at:
http://www.esds.ac.uk/International/

ESDS INTERNATIONAL (2008b), *Countries and Citizens: Linking international macro and micro data*, an interactive training resource, at:
http://www.esds.ac.uk/international/elearning/limmd/index.html

EUROBAROMETER (2008): *Public Opinion in the European Union*, Standard Eurobarometer, at:
http://ec.europa.eu/public_opinion/archives/eb/eb67/eb_67_first_en.pdf

EUROPEAN COMMISSION (2003), *Governance and Development*, Communication from the Commission to the Council, the European Parliament, the European Economic and Social Council and the Committee of Regions, 20 October, Brussels [EU document COM(2003) 615 final], at:
http://eur-lex.europa.eu/LexUriServ/LexUriServ.do?uri=COM:2003:0615:FIN:EN:PDF

EUROPEAN COMMISSION (2005), *Proposal for a Joint Declaration by the Council, the European Parliament and the Commission on the European Union Development Policy: "The European Consensus"*, Communication from the Commission to the Council, the European Parliament, the European Economic and Social Council and the Committee of Regions, 30 August, Brussels, 13 July, Brussels, [EU document COM(2005) 311 final], at:
http://ec.europa.eu/commission_barroso/michel/Policy/key_documents/docs/COMM_PDF_COM_2005_0311_F_EN_ACTE.pdf

EUROPEAN COMMISSION (2006), *Governance in the European Consensus on Development: Towards a harmonised approach within the European Union*, Communication from the Commission to the Council, the European Parliament, the European Economic and Social Council and the Committee of Regions, 30 August, Brussels, [EU document COM(2006) 421 final], at:
http://ec.europa.eu/development/icenter/repository/COM_2006_421_EN.pdf

EUROSTAT (STATISTICAL OFFICE OF THE EUROPEAN COMMUNITIES) (2002), *Statistics and Human Rights*, Report of the international seminar held in Brussels, 27-29 November 2002 [commissioned to InWent, Munich], at:
http://www.paris21.org/documents/998.pdf

EUROSTAT and UNDP (UNITED NATIONS DEVELOPMENT PROGRAM) (2004), *Governance Indicators: A Users' Guide,* Eurostat and UNDP-Oslo Governance Centre, Luxembourg, New York and Oslo. [authored by J. Nahem and M. Sudders], at:
http://www.undp.org/oslocentre/docs04/UserGuide.pdf

EVANS, P. and J. RAUCH (1999), "Bureaucracy and Growth: A Cross-National Analysis of the Effects of 'Weberian' State Structures on Economic Growth", *American Sociological Review,* Vol. 64, pp. 748-765.

FAIR, M.E., P. LALONDE and H.B. NEWCOMBE (1992), "The Use of Names for Linking Personal Records", *Journal of the American Statistical Association*, Vol. 87, pp. 1193-1204.

FASEL, N. and R. MALHOTRA (2005), "Quantitative Human Rights Indicators: A Survey of Major Initiatives", paper presented at the Åbo Human Rights Institute's *Expert Meeting on Indicators*, held at the Åbo Akademi, Turku, Finland, on 10-13 March, as well as at the first Metagora Forum held in Paris on 24-25 May, at:
http://www.jus.uio.no/forskning/grupper/humrdev/Project-Indicators/Workshop06/Background/Malhotra&Fasel.pdf.

FELDMAN, E. and R. MARTIN (1998), *Access to Information in Developing Countries*, Transparency International, Berlin, at:
http://ww2.unhabitat.org/cdrom/TRANSPARENCY/html/yellowp/y004.html

FENG, Y. (2003), *Democracy, Governance, and Economic Performance: Theory and Evidence*, The MIT Press, Cambridge and London.

FERREIRA, F.H.G. and J. GIGNOUX (2008), "The Measurement of Inequality of Opportunity: Theory and an Application to Latin America", Development Research Group Poverty Team, World Bank Policy Research Working Paper No. 4659, Washington D.C., at:
http://www-wds.worldbank.org/external/default/WDSContentServer/WDSP/IB/2008/07/02/000158349_20080702133145/Rendered/PDF/WPS4659.pdf

FIENBERG, S.E. (1997), "Ethics, Objectivity and Politics: Statistics in a Public Policy Perspective", in Spencer, B.D. (1997), pp. 62-84

FILMER-WILSON, E. (2005), "Practical Guidance to Implementing Rights Based Approaches, Human Rights Analyses for Poverty Reduction and Human Rights Benchmarks", report prepared for the Department for International Development, United Kingdom (DFID), London, at:
http://www.gsdrc.org/go/display/document/legacyid/1554

FILMER-WILSON, E. (2006) [see UNDP, 2006b].

FORRESTER D. AND J. HARWIN (2000), "Monitoring Children's Rights Globally: Can Child Abuse be Measured Internationally?", *Child Abuse Review*, Vol. 9, No. 6, pp. 427-38.

FORSS, K. (2002), *Finding Out Results from Projects and Programmes Concerning Democratic Governance and Human Rights*, Swedish International Development Cooperation Agency (SIDA), Stockholm, in:
http://www.sida.se/sida/jsp/sida.jsp?d=118&a=2603&language=en_US

FORSYTHE, D.P. (2000), *Human Rights in International Relations*, Themes in International Relations, Cambridge University Press, New York.

FORSYTHE, D.P. (2007), "The United States and International Economic Rights: Law, Social Reality, and Political Choice", in HERTEL and MINKLER (2007), pp. 310-324.

FOWERAKER, J. and T. LANDMAN (1997), *Citizenship Rights and Social Movements: A Comparative and Statistical Analysis*, Oxford University Press

FOWERAKER, J. and R. KRZNARIC (2000), "Measuring Liberal Democratic Performance: An Empirical and Conceptual Critique", *Political Studies*, Vol. 48, No. 4, pp. 759-787.

FRANK, H.G. (1988), "Review of 'Statistical Issues in the Field of Human Rights'", *Journal of Official Statistics*, Vol. 4, pp. 271-272.

FREEDEN, M. (1991), *Rights*, Open University Press, Buckingham.

FREEDOM HOUSE (2007a), "Methodology", in *Freedom in the World 2007: Annual Survey of Political Rights and Civil Liberties*, Freedom House and Rowman &Littlefield Publishers, at: http://www.freedomhouse.org/template.cfm?page=351&ana_page=333&year=2007

FREEDOM HOUSE (2007b), *Countries at the Crossroads*, at: http://www.freedomhouse.org/template.cfm?page=139&edition=8

FREEDOM HOUSE (2008a), "Freedom of the Press 2007: A Year of Global Decline" [authored by K. DEUTCH KARLEKAR], at: http://www.freedomhouse.org/uploads/fop08/OverviewEssay2008.pdf

FREEDOM HOUSE (2008b), *Freedom of the Press 2008*, at: http://www.freedomhouse.org/template.cfm?page=362

FREEDOM HOUSE (2008c), *Nations in Transit 2008: Democratization from Central Europe to Eurasia*, Freedom House and Rowman &Littlefield Publishers, at: http://www.freedomhouse.hu/index.php?option=com_content&task=view&id=196

FREEDOM HOUSE (2008d), *The Worst of the Worst: The World's most Repressive Societies*, in: http://www.freedomhouse.org/uploads/special_report/62.pdf

FUKUDA-PARR, S. (2000), "Indicators of Human Development and Human Rights: Overlaps, Differences... and what about the Human Development Index?", in IAOS (2000), at:. http://www.portal-stat.admin.ch/iaos2000/fukuda_parr_final_paper.doc and in *Statistical Journal of the United Nations Economic Commission for Europe*, Vol. 18 (2001), No. 2-3, pp. 239-248.

FUKUDA-PARR, S. (2007), "International Obligations for Economic and Social Rights: The Case of the Millenium Development Goal Eight", in HERTEL and MINKLER (2007), pp. 284-309.

FUNDAR, CENTRE FOR ANALYSIS AND RESEARCH (2003), *Latin-American Index of Budget Transparency. A comparison of 10 Countries / Índice Latinoamericano de Transparencia Presupuestaria: Una comparación de 10 países*, México [authored by B. LAVIELLE, M. PERÉZ and H. HOFBAUER], at: http://www.fundar.org.mx/secciones/publicaciones/pdf/Latin_american_index.pdf and http://www.fundar.org.mx/secciones/publicaciones/pdf/indice_latinoamericano.pdf

FUNDAR (2005), *Latin American Index of Budget Transparency: A comparison of 8 countries / Índice Latinoamericano de Transparencia Presupuestaria: Una comparación de 8 países*, México [authored by M. PERÉZ], at: http://www.fundar.org.mx/indice2005/docs/Regional%20Transparency%20Report%202005.pdf and http://www.fundar.org.mx/indice2005/docs/IndiceLat.pdf_sid=QgBAO9AN984&mbox=INBOX&charset=escaped_unicode&uid=13&number=2&filename=IndiceLat.pdf

FUNDAR (2007a), *Índice Latinoamericano de Transparencia Presupuestaria: Estudio regional*, México [authored by M. PERÉZ], at : http://www.fundar.org.mx/pdf/INDICE%20REGIONAL%2020071%20(2).pdf

FUNDAR (2007b), *Índice Latinoamericano de Transparencia Presupuestaria: Estudio sobre México*, México [authored by B. LAVIELLE], at: http://www.fundar.org.mx/pdf/DocumentoMEXICO-Final%20_2_.pdf

FUNDAR, INTERNATIONAL BUDGET PROJECT and INTERNATIONAL HUMAN RIGHTS INTERNSHIP PROGRAM (2004), *Las cuentas de la dignidad: una guía para utilizar el análisis de presupuestos en la promoción de derechos humanos / Dignity Counts: A Guide to Using Budget Analysis to Advance Human Rights*, Mexico City and Washington D.C., at: http://www.iie.org/IHRIP/Dignity_Counts.pdf#search=%22Dignity%20Counts%22 (English) http://www.fundar.org.mx/secciones/publicaciones/pdf/cuentas_de_dignidad.pdf (Spanish)

GALTUNG, F. (2005), "Measuring the Immeasurable: Boundaries and Functions of (Macro) Corruption Indices", in *Measuring Corruption*, Ashgate.

GALTUNG, J. (1994), *Human Rights in Another Key*, Polity Press, Cambridge and Oxford.

GAMERO, J. et al. (2004), *Vigilancia social: teoría y práctica en el Perú* (Social monitoring: theory and practice in Peru / La surveillance sociale: théorie et pratique au Pérou), Consorcio de Investigación Económica y Social, Investigaciones Breves No. 20, Lima.

GARCÍA HIERRO, P. (2001) [see CEDAL, 2001].

GARONNA, P. and C. MALAGUERRA (eds.) (2001), *Measurement of Human Development and Human Rights*, special issue of the *Statistical Journal of the United Nations Economic Commission for Europe*, Vol. 18., No. 2-3, pp. 125-283 [containing selected contributions to the IAOS 2000 Montreux Conference on *Statistics, Development and Human Rights*].

GASIOROWSKI, M.J. (1996), "An Overview of the Political Regime Change Dataset", *Comparative Political Studies*, Vol. 29, No. 4, pp. 469-483.

GAURI, V. (2004), "Social Rights and Economics: Claims to Health Care and Education in Developing Countries", *World Development*, Vol. 32, No. 3, pp. 465-477 [and in ALSTON and ROBINSON (2005), pp. 65-84].

GBORIE, A.V. (2000), "Administrative Records as Basis for Statistics on Human Rights Violations in the Civil War in Sierra Leone: Problems and Prospects", in IAOS (2000), at: http://www.portal-stat.admin.ch/iaos2000/gborie_final_paper.doc

GELB, A., B. NGO and X. YE (2004), *Implementing Performance-Based Aid in Africa: The Country Policy and Institutional Assessment*, World Bank Africa Region Working Paper Series, No. 77, Washington, D.C., at: http://www-wds.worldbank.org/external/default/WDSContentServer/WDSP/IB/2004/12/27/000090341_20041227100706/Rendered/PDF/310070PAPER0AFR0wp77.pdf

GERRING, J. (2008), "Outline for a Disaggregated Meso-Level Democracy Index", in NATIONAL RESEARCH COUNCIL OF THE NATIONAL ACADEMIES (2008), pp. 268-284.

GIBNEY M. and S.I. SKOGLY (2007), "Economic Rights and Extraterritorial Obligations", in HERTEL and MINKLER (2007), pp. 267-283.

GILLIES, D. (1995), *Human Rights and Democratic Governance: A Framework for Analysis and Donor Action*, International Centre for Human Rights and Democratic Development, Montreal.

GIOVANNINI, E. (2005) [see OECD, 2005b].

GIRVAN, N. (2002), "Problems with UNDP Governance Indicators: The Greater Caribbean This Week", at: www.acs-aec.org/column/index45.htm

GLAESER, E. et al. (2004), "Do Institutions Cause Growth?", NBER Working Paper Series, National Bureau of Economic Research, Cambridge, MA, at: http://www.nber.org/papers/w10568

GLEDITSCH, K.S. and M.D. WARD (1997), "Double Take: A Re-examination of Democracy and Autocracy in Modern Polities", *Journal of Conflict Resolution*, Vol. 41, No. 3, pp. 361-383.

GLOBAL INTEGRITY (2006a) "2006 Global Integrity Country Assessments and Global Integrity Index: Methodology White Paper", at:
http://www.globalintegrity.org/documents/2006methodology.pdf

GLOBAL INTEGRITY (2006b), *Assessment and Data*, at:
http://www.globalintegrity.org/data/2006index.cfm

GLOBAL INTEGRITY (2007), *Global Integrity Report*, at:
http://report.globalintegrity.org/

GOLDMANN, G. (2000), "Defining and Observing Minorities: An Objective Assessment", in IAOS (2000), at:
http://www.portal-stat.admin.ch/iaos2000/goldmann_final_paper.doc

GOLDSMITH, L.J. and P. SIMMONS (2001), "Sample Size and the Nuremberg Code", *Proceedings of the Annual Meeting of the American Statistical Association,* JSM, Atlanta, at:
http://www.amstat.org/meetings/jsm/2001/index.cfm?fuseaction=abstract_details&abstractid=30101 3 (abstract).

GOLDSTEIN, R.J. (1992), "The Limitations of Using Quantitative Data in Studying Human Rights Abuses", in R.P. Claude and T.B. Jabine (1992), pp. 35-61.

GOLDSTON, J.A. (2000), "Statistics in the Combat of Racial Discrimination: A Necessary Tool", in IAOS (2000), at:
http://www.portal-stat.admin.ch/iaos2000/goldston_final_paper.doc

GOMEZ, M. (1995), "Social Economic Rights and Human Rights Commissions", in: *Human Rights Quarterly*, Vol.17, No. 1, pp. 155-169.

GOODHART, M. (2007), "'None So Poor That He Is Compelled to Sell Himself': Democracy, Subsistence, and Basic Income", in HERTEL and MINKLER (2007), pp. 94-114.

GORDON, D. and P. TOWNSEND (eds.) (2002), *World Poverty: New Policies to Defeat an Old Enemy,* The Policy Press, Bristol.

GORDON, D. et al. (2003), *The Distribution of Child Poverty in the Developing World,* Studies in Poverty, Inequality and Social Exclusion, Bristol University, Policy Press, Bristol.

GREEN, M. (2001), "What We Talk About When We Talk About Indicators: Current Approaches to Human Rights Measurement", *Human Rights Quarterly*, Vol. 23, No. 2, pp. 1062-1097.

GRUSKIN, S. et al. (eds.) (2005), *Perspectives on Health and Human Rights*, Routledge, New York and London.

GUPTA, D., A. JONGMAN and A. SCHMID (1994), "Creating a Composite Index for Assessing Country Performance in the Field of Human Rights: Proposal for a New Methodology", *Human Rights Quarterly*, Vol. 16, No. 1, pp. 131-162.

GURRÍA, A., (2008) "Measuring the Progress of Societies: Does it Make a Difference for Policy Making and Democracy?", in OECD (2008c).

GUZMAN, M.M. (2000), "The Investigation and Documentation of Events as a Methodology in Monitoring Human Rights Violations", in IAOS (2000), at:
http://www.portal-stat.admin.ch/iaos2000/guzman_final_paper.doc

GUZMAN, M.M. [see HURIDOCS, 2001a, 2001b, 2003a, 2003b].

HABBARD, A.C. (2006), "Human Rights, Governance and Economic Development: Building Human Rights Indicators for IDA", World Bank, Washington D.C.

HADENIUS, A. (1992), *Democracy and Development*, Cambridge University Press, Cambridge.

HADENIUS, A. and J. TEORELL (2005), "Assessing Alternative Indices of Democracy", Committee on Concepts and Methods of the International Political Science Association, Political Concepts, Working Paper Series, No. 6, Centro de Investigación y Docencia Económicas (CIDE), Mexico City, at:
http://www.concepts-methods.org/papers_list.php?id_categoria=1&titulo=Political%20Concepts

HAMMARBERG, T. (2000), "Searching the truth: The need to monitor human rights with relevant and reliable means", in IAOS (2000), at:
http://www.portal-stat.admin.ch/iaos2000/hammarberg_final_paper.doc

HANCIOGLU, A. and D. VADNAIS (2008), "The Strategic Intent of Data Collection and Analysis. The Case of Multiple Indicator Cluster Surveys (MICS)", in *Bridging the Gap. The Role of Monitoring and Evaluation in Evidence-based Policy Making*, UNICEF in partnership with DevInfo, IDEAS, MICS and The World Bank, UNICEF regional office of CEE/CIS, Geneva, at:
http://www.unicef.org/ceecis/evidence_based_policy_making.pdf

HANSEN, S. (2002) [see AAAS and HURIDOCS, 2002].

HARRINGTON, J., C. PORTER and S. REDDY (2001), "Financing Basic Social Services," in A. GRINSPUN, (ed.), *Choices for the Poor: Lessons from National Poverty Strategies*, UNDP, New York.

HART, S.N., Z. PAVLOVIC and M. ZEIDNER (2001), "The ISPA Cross-National Children's Rights Research Project", in *School Psychology International*, Vol. 22, No. 2, pp. 99-129.

HARVEY, P. (2002), "Human Rights and Economic Policy Discourse: Taking Economic and Social Rights Seriously", *Columbia Human Rights Law Review*, vol. 33, no. 2, pp. 363-471.

HARVEY, P. (2007), "Benchmarking the Right to Work", in HERTEL and MINKLER (2007), pp. 115-142.

HÄUSERMANN, J. (2000), "Measuring the Impact of a Human Rights Approach to Development: Challenges and Opportunities" (abstract), in IAOS (2000), at:
http://www.portal-stat.admin.ch/iaos2000/hausermann_final_abstract.doc

HAYDEN, P. (2003), *Scoping Study for Developing Indicators for Safety, Security and Access to Justice (SSAJ) Programmes*, Performance Assessment Resource Centre, Birmingham.

HAYNER, P.B. (1994), "Fifteen Truth Commissions, 1974 to 1994: A Comparative Study", *Human Rights Quarterly*, Vol. 16, No. 4, pp. 597-655, at:
http://www.accessmylibrary.com/coms2/summary_0286-9296310_ITM

HAYNER, P.B. (2001), *Unspeakable Truths: Confronting State Terror and Atrocity*, Routledge, New York.

HEALEY, J. and M. ROBINSON (1992), *Democracy, Governance and Economic Policy*, ODI, London.

HEIMGARTNER, T. (2006) [see METAGORA, 2006].

HEINRICH, V.F (2007) [see CIVICUS, 2007].

HERMAN, B. (2004), *How well Do Measurement of an Enabling Domestic Environment for Development Stand Up?*, UNCTAD, Geneva, at:
www.g24.org/003gva04.pdf

HERRERA, J. and F. ROUBAUD (2005), "Gobernabilidad, democracia, participación política y lucha contra la pobreza en los países andinos a través de encuestas a hogares" (Gouvernance, démocratie, participation politique et lutte contre la pauvreté dans les pays Andins à la lumière d'enquêtes auprès des ménages / Governance, Democracy, Political Participation and Fight against Poverty in the Andean countries on the Lens of Household Surveys), Document de travail DIAL No. 2005-18, Paris.

HERRERA J., M. RAZAFINDRAKOTO and F. ROUBAUD (2006), "Gouvernance, démocratie et lutte contre la pauvreté : Enseignements tirés des enquêtes auprès des ménages en Afrique sub-saharienne et en Amérique latine / Governance, Democracy and Poverty Reduction : Lessons Drawn from Household Surveys in Sub-Saharan Africa and Latin America", Série Études, Ministère des affaires étrangères, Paris [report commissioned by the French Ministry of Foreign Affairs and the French Development Agency], at: http://www.diplomatie.gouv.fr/fr/IMG/pdf/Gouvernance_int_FR.pdf (French) http://www.diplomatie.gouv.fr/en/IMG/pdf/Gouvernance_int_ANG.pdf (English)

HERTEL, S. (2006), "Why Bother? Measuring Economic Rights: The Research Agenda", in: International Studies Perspectives, Vol. 7, No. 3, pp. 215-230, at: http://www.blackwell-synergy.com/doi/abs/10.1111/j.1528-3585.2006.00247.x

HERTEL, S. and A. MINKLER (eds.) (2007), Economic Rights: Conceptual, Measurement, and Policy Issues, Cambridge University Press, New York [papers contributed to the conference that, under the same title, was convened by the Human Rights Institute of the University of Connecticut, and held on 27-29 October 2005].

HEWITT DE ALCANTARA, C. (1998), "Uses and Abuses of the Concept of Governance", International Social Science Journal, Vol. 11, No. 155, pp. 105-113.

HILLENBRAND, O. and P. THIERY (2005), "The Bertelsmann Transformation Index 2006: On the Way to Democracy and Market Economy", Strategic Insights, Vol. 4, No. 12, at: http://www.ccc.nps.navy.mil/si/2005/Dec/hillenbrandDec05.asp

HINES, A. (2005) [see CARR CENTER FOR HUMAN RIGHTS POLICY, 2005].

HO, K., S.C. POE and D. WENDEL-BLUNT (1997), "Global Patterns in the Achievement of Women's Human Rights to Equality", Human Rights Quarterly, Vol. 19, pp. 813-835.

HODESS, R.B. [see TRANSPARENCY INTERNATIONAL, 2001, 2003a, 2004a, 2005 and 2006].

HOFBAUER, E. (2003) [see FUNDAR, 2003].

HOFFMAN, A. (2005) [see OECD, 2005b].

HOVY, B. (2000), "Fifty Years of Data Collection: The UNHCR Experience", in IAOS (2000), at: http://www.portal-stat.admin.ch/iaos2000/hovy_final_paper.doc

HRAC (HUMAN RIGHTS ACCOUNTABILITY COALITION OF SRI LANKA) (2006), Data Collection & Data Coding Reference Manual, Version 4.0.1, Colombo.

HRIRC (HUMAN RIGHTS IMPACT RESOURCE CENTRE) (2008), A website offering centralised access to a broad range of information and expertise on human rights impact assessment (HRIA), at: http://www.humanrightsimpact.org

HULAN, H., (2007), "Assessing Democratic Governance in Mongolia", paper presented at the CMI/UNDP Seminar on Governance Assessments and the Paris Declaration: Towards Inclusive Participation and National Ownership (Bergen, 23-25 September), Chr. Michelsen Institute and UNDP Oslo Governance Centre, at: http://www.undp.org/oslocentre/docs07/bergen_2007/Governance%20Assessments%20Mongolia%20Case%20Study.pdf

HUMAN RIGHTS WATCH (2001), *Under Orders : War Crimes in Kosovo*, Human Rights Watch, New York [Chapter 15 presents the statistical analysis of the violations], at: http://www.hrw.org/reports/2001/kosovo..

HUMAN RIGHTS WATCH (2006) *World Report 2007*, Human Rights Watch, New York, at http://hrw.org/wr2k7/

HUNT, P. (1996), *Reclaiming Social Rights: International and Comparative Perspectives*, Dartmouth Pub. Co., Aldershot.

HUNT, P. (1998), "State Obligations, Indicators, Benchmarks, and the Right to Education", background paper submitted to the UN Committee on Economic, Social and Cultural Rights at its Nineteenth session held in Geneva, on 16 November-4 December, OHCHR document E/C.12/1998/11, at: http://www.unhchr.ch/tbs/doc.nsf/(Symbol)/3e83f2a145015575802566ab0051ce4e?Opendocument

HUNT, P. (2003), [see UN-HRI, 2003b].

HUNT, P., M. NOWAK and S. OSMANI (2002), *Draft Guidelines on a Human Rights Approach to Poverty Reduction Strategies*, Office of the High Commissioner for Human Rights, Geneva [see also OHCHR, 2004].

HUNT, P. and G. MACNAUGHTON (2006), *Impact Assessments, Poverty and Human Rights: A Case Study Using The Right to the Highest Attainable Standard of Health*, UNESCO, Paris, at: http://www.humanrightsimpact.org/fileadmin/hria_resources/unesco_hria_paper.pdf

HUNTINGTON, S. and J. NELSON (1976), *No Easy Choice: Political Participation in Developing Countries*, Harvard University Press, Cambridge, MA.

HURIDOCS (HUMAN RIGHTS INFORMATION AND DOCUMENTATION SYSTEMS, INTERNATIONAL) (1993) *Standard Formats for the Recording and Exchange of Bibliographic Information Concerning Human Rights*, second, revised edition, Versoix [also known as "Bibliographic Standard Formats". The first edition was authored in 1985 by B. STORMORKEN, the second was edited by a team led by A.M. NOVAL; available in English, French and Arabic], at: http://www.huridocs.org/tools/overview

HURIDOCS (2001a) *Events Standard Formats: A Tool for Documenting Human Rights Violations*, revised, second edition, Versoix. [the fist edition was edited in 1993 by a team led by J. DUECK, the second was edited by J. DUECK, M. GUZMAN and B. VERSTAPPEN; available in English, French and Spanish], at: http://www.huridocs.org/tools/tools/esfen.pdf

HURIDOCS (2001b) *Micro-Thesauri: A Tool for Documenting Human Rights Violations*, Versoix. [edited by J. DUECK, M. GUZMAN and B. VERSTAPPEN; a compilation of 48 human rights thesauri derived or adapted from various sources, available in English, French, Russian and Spanish], at: http://www.huridocs.org/tools/tools/mictheen.pdf

HURIDOCS (2003a), *What is Monitoring*, Human Rights Monitoring and Documentation Series, No. 1, Versoix [authored by M. GUZMAN and B. VERSTAPPEN]. http://www.huridocs.org/tools/tools/monitoring.pdf/index_html

HURIDOCS (2003b), *What is Documentation*, Human Rights Monitoring and Documentation Series, No. 2, Versoix [authored by M. GUZMAN and B. VERSTAPPEN]. http://www.huridocs.org/tools/tools/basdocen.pdf

HURIDOCS (2007), *HuriSearch*, Multi-lingual (77 languages) web search engine providing access to over 2 million pages on 3000 human rights websites, developed by HURIDOCS, and hosted by Fast Search and

Transfer ASA, Norway; at:
http://www.hurisearch.org/

HURIDOCS (2008), *Classification Scheme for Human Rights Documentation / Système de classification pour la documentation sur les droits de l'homme*, authored by I. Caccia, Ottawa, at: http://www.huridocs.org/tools/tools/classeng.pdf (English) and http://www.huridocs.org/tools/tools/classfra.pdf (French).

Hyden, G. (2007), "The Challenges of Making Governance Assessments Nationally Owned", paper presented at the CMI/UNDP Seminar on *Governance Assessments and the Paris Declaration: Towards Inclusive Participation and National Ownership* (Bergen, 23-25 September), Chr. Michelsen Institute and UNDP Oslo Governance Centre, at: http://www.undp.org/oslocentre/docs07/bergen_2007/Key%20Note%20speech%20Goran%20Hyden.pdf

Hyden, G. *et al.* (2008), "Governance Assessments for Local Stakeholders: What the World Governance Assessment Offers", Overseas Development Institute, Working Paper No. 287, London, at: http://www.odi.org.uk/publications/working_papers/WP287.pdf

IAOS (International Association for Official Statistics) (2000), Conference on *Statistics, Development and Human Rights*, held in Montreux, Switzerland, on 4-8 September. Numerous contributed papers to this conference can be accessed online through the "Detailed Scientific Program" entry, at: http://www.portal-stat.admin.ch/iaos2000/index2.htm

ICHRP (International Council on Human Rights Policy) (2002), Local Rule: Decentralisation and Human Rights, Versoix, at: http://www.ichrp.org/files/reports/13/116_-_Local_Government_and_Human_Rights.pdf

ICHRP (2005), Assessing the Effectiveness of National Human Rights Institutions, Versoix, at: http://www.ichrp.org/files/reports/18/125_report.pdf

ICHRP (2008a) Corruption and Human Rights: Conceptual Paper, Draft Report [authored by Magdalena Sepúlveda Carmona], Versoix, at: http://www.ichrp.org/files/drafts/4/131a_draft.pdf

ICHRP (2008) Reports, working papers and documents of ICHRP by themes at: http://www.ichrp.org/en/themes

ICNRD (International Conference of New or Restored Democracies) (2003) *Ulaanbaatar Declaration* and *Plan of Action,* both adopted at the Fifth ICNRD Conference (Ulaanbaatar, Mongolia, 10-12 September), at: http://huachen.org/english/law/compilation_democracy/planofaction.htm

Ignatieff, M. (2005) [see Carr Center for Human Rights Policy, 2005].

Inkeles, A. and L. Sirowy (1990), "The effects of Democracy on Economic Growth and Inequality: A Review", *Studies in Comparative International Development*, Vol. 25, pp. 126-57.

Inkeles, A. (ed.) (1991), *On Measuring Democracy: its Consequences and Concomitants*, Transaction Books, New Brunswick and Jersey.

Inglehart, R. (1997), *Modernization and Postmodernization: Cultural, Economic and Political Change in 43 Societies*, Princeton University Press, Princeton.

Inglehart R. and C. Welzel (2005), *Modernization, Cultural Change and Democracy: The Human Development Sequence*, Cambridge University Press, New York and Cambridge.

INSTITUT NATIONAL DE LA STATISTIQUE, Côte d'Ivoire (2005), *Gouvernance, démocratie et lutte contre la pauvreté en Côte d'Ivoire : Le point de vue de la population de l'agglomération d'Abidjan (enquêtes 1-2-3, premiers résultats)*, INS, AFRISTAT and DIAL, Abidjan [authored by M. AMANI, M. ENOH, M. RAZAFINDRAKOTO and F. ROUBAUD], at: http://www.dial.prd.fr/dial_enquetes/PDF/cotedivoire.pdf

INSTITUT NATIONAL DE LA STATISTIQUE, Madagascar (2003), *Gouvernance, démocratie et lutte contre la pauvreté à Madagascar: Le point de vue de la population de la capitale (enquêtes 1-2-3, premiers résultats)*, Ministère de l'économie, des finances et du budget, INSTAT et DIAL, Antananarivo [authored by F. RAKOTOMANANA, M. RAZAFINDRAKOTO and F. ROUBAUD], at: HTTP://WWW.DIAL.PRD.FR/DIAL_ENQUETES/PDF/MADAGASCAR.PDF

INSTITUT NATIONAL DE LA STATISTIQUE, Madagascar (2004), *Perceptions des citoyens sur le DSRP, la gestion des affaires publiques et la gestion du budget de l'État*, Antananarivo.

INSTITUT NATIONAL DE LA STATISTIQUE, Niger (2005), *Gouvernance, démocratie et lutte contre la pauvreté au Niger: Le point de vue de la population de la capitale (enquêtes 1-2-3)*, Secrétariat permanent de la Stratégie de réduction de la pauvreté, AFRISTAT, DIAL-Metagora and UNDP, Niamey [authored by A. ABOUBACAR DJIMRAO, A. MADAÏ BOUKAR, M. RAZAFINDRAKOTO and F. ROUBAUD], at : http://www.dial.prd.fr/dial_enquetes/PDF/niger.pdf

INSTITUT NATIONAL DE LA STATISTIQUE ET DE L'ANALYSE ÉCONOMIQUE, Bénin (2005), *Gouvernance, démocratie et lutte contre la pauvreté au Bénin: Le point de vue de la population de l'agglomération de Cotonou (enquêtes 1-2-3, premiers résultats)*, DIAL-Metagora et AFRISTAT, Cotonou [authored by A. BIAOU, D. MOUSTAPHA, M. RAZAFINDRAKOTO and F. ROUBAUD], at: http://www.dial.prd.fr/dial_enquetes/PDF/benin.pdf

INSTITUT NATIONAL DE LA STATISTIQUE ET DE LA DÉMOGRAPHIE, Burkina Faso (2005), Gouvernance, démocratie et lutte contre la pauvreté à Ouagadougou »Le point de vue de la population de la capitale (enquêtes 1-2-3, premiers résultats), DIAL et AFRISTAT, Ouagadougou, at : http://www.dial.prd.fr/dial_enquetes/PDF/burkina.pdf

INTER-AMERICAN DEVELOPMENT BANK (2007), *Governance Indicators Database (DataGob)*, at: http://www.iadb.org/datagob/index.html

INTERNATIONAL BUDGET PROJECT (2008), a web site devoted to budget analysis and economic and social rights: http://www.internationalbudget.org/themes/ESC/index.htm.

INTERNATIONAL CRISIS GROUP (2008), Databases and Resources, at: http://www.crisisgroup.org/home/index.cfm?id=2937&l=1

INTERNATIONAL COMMISSION OF JURIST (1997), *Economic, Social and Cultural Rights: a Compilation of Essential Documents*, Geneva.

INTERNATIONAL IDEA (2002), *Handbook on Democracy Assessment*, IDEA and Kluwer Law International, Stockholm [authored by D. BEETHAM, S. BRACKING, I. KEARTON, and S. WEIR].

INTERNATIONAL IDEA (2003), *The State of Democracy: Democracy Assessments in Eight Nations Around the World*, IDEA and Kluwer Law International, Stockholm.

INTERNATIONAL IDEA (2008a), *Assessing the Quality of Democracy: An Overview of the International IDEA Framework* [edited by T. LANDMAN; contributors: D. BEETHAM, E. CARVALHO and S. WEIR], IDEA, Stockholm, at: http://www.idea.int/publications/aqd/index.cfm

INTERNATIONAL IDEA (2008b), *Reforma política y electoral en América Latina, 1978-2007*, edited by D. ZOVATTO and J.J. OROZCO HENRÍQUEZ [available also in English: *Political and Electoral Reform in Latin America 1978-2007*],

IDEA, Stockholm, at:
http://www.idea.int/publications/perla/index.cfm

ISAAC, J. and I. ABEDRABBO (2000), "Political Use of Land and Water Distribution: An Analysis Through Statistical Data, Demography and Remote Sensing", in IAOS (2000), at:
http://www.portal-stat.admin.ch/iaos2000/isaac_final_paper.doc

ISCI (INTERNATIONAL SOCIETY OF CHILD INDICATORS) (2007), 1st International Society of Child Indicators Conference, contributed papers at:
http://www.childindicators.org/conference.html

ISI (INTERNATIONAL STATISTICAL INSTITUTE) (1985), Declaration on Professional Ethics, at:
http://isi.cbs.nl/ethics.htm

JABINE, T.B. (1985), "What can Statisticians Contribute to the Protection and Advancement of Human Rights?", Proceedings of the 45th Session of the International Statistical Institute, Book 1, pp. 85-86.

JABINE, T.B. (1989), "Statistics and Human Rights: Some Recent Developments", in: Proceedings of the 47th Session of the International Statistical Institute, Book 1, pp. 463-464, Presser.

JABINE, T.B. (1996), "Comment on 'Developing Samplers for Developing Countries'", International Statistical Review, Vol. 64, pp. 153-156.

JABINE, T.B. (1997), "The Emerging Field of Human Rights Statistics", in SPENCER (1997), pp. 33-51.

JABINE, T.B. (2000), "Thesaurus of Economic, Social & Cultural Rights: Terminology and Potential Violations (Book Review)", Human Rights Quarterly, Vol. 22, pp. 1108-1110.

JABINE, T.B., J.P. LYNCH and H.F. SPIRER (1995), "Statistics in an International Human Rights Treaty Report", Proceedings of the Section on Government Statistics of the American Statistical Association, pp. 77-86.

JABINE, T.B. and D.A. SAMUELSON (2008), "Human Rights of Statisticians and Statistics of Human Rights: Early History of the American Statistical Association's Committee on Scientific Freedom and Human Rights", in ASHER, BANKS and SCHEUREN (2008), pp. 195-226.

JACKSON, E.T. and Y. KASSAM (eds.) (1998), Knowledge Shared: Participatory Evaluation in Development Cooperation, Kumarian Press and IDRC, Connecticut and Ottawa.

JANNUZZI, P.M. (2001), Indicadores sociais no Brasil: conceitos, fonte de dados e aplicaçoes (Social Indicators in Brazil: Concepts, Data Sources and Applications / Indicateurs sociaux au Brésil: concepts, sources de données et applications), Alínea, Campinas.

JANNUZZI, P.M. (2003), "Considerações sobre o uso, mau uso e abuso dos indicadores sociais na formulaçao de políticas públicas municipais" (Considerations on the Use, Misuse and Abuse of Social Indicators in the Design of Municipal Public Policies / Considérations sur l'usage, le mauvais usage et l'abus d'indicateurs sociaux dans la formulation des politiques publiques municipales), Revista de Administração Pública, Rio de Janeiro, Vol. 36, No.1, pp. 51-72.

JANNUZZI, P.M. and N.L. PATARRA (2006), Manual para capacitação em indicadores sociais nas políticas públicas e em direitos humanos: textos básicos e guia de uso e referência do material multimídia (Training Manual on Social Indicators Within Public Policies and on Human Rights Indicators / Manuel de formation en indicateurs sociaux pour les politiques publiques et en indicateurs des droits de l'homme) [a book complemented by a set of CD-Roms and DVDs], Ford Foundation, ENCE, SCIENCE, Oficina Editorial, Rio de Janeiro and Sao Paulo.

JENNINGS, P.J. *et al.* (1998), "Violence Against Women During the Liberian Civil Conflict", *JAMA, Journal of the American Medical Association*, Vol. 279, No. 8, pp. 625-629.

JENNINGS, P.J. and S. SWISS (2000), "Statistical Information on the Violence Against Women during the Civil War in Liberia", in IAOS (2000), at:
http://www.portal-stat.admin.ch/iaos2000/jennings_final_paper.doc

JOSEPH, J. (1999), "Métodos alternativos en la construcción de indicadores" (Alternative methods for building indicators / Méthodes alternatives pour la construction d'indicateurs), in CEDAL (1999), pp. 22-24.

JUSTINO, P. (2005), "Empirical Applications of Multidimensional Inequality Analysis", PRUS Working Paper, No. 23.

JUSTINO, P., J. LICHTFIELD and Y. NIIMI (2004), "Multidimensional Inequality: An Empirical Application to Brazil", PRUS Working Paper, no. 24.

JUTTING, J. P. *et al.* (2006), "Measuring Gender (In)Equality: Introducing the Gender, Institutions and Development Data Base (GID)", OECD Development Centre, Working Paper No. 247, Paris, at:
http://www.oecd.org/dataoecd/17/49/36228820.pdf

KAUFMANN, D. (1997), "Corruption: The Facts", *Foreign Policy*, No. 107, Carnegie Endowment for International Peace, Washington, D.C., at:
http://www.worldbank.org/wbi/governance/pubs/corrfacts.html

KAUFMANN D. (ed.) (1999), *Collective Action to Improve Governance and Control Corruption in Seven African Countries*, prepared as background paper for the 9th Annual International Conference Against Corruption, Durban, South Africa, 10–15 October, World Bank Institute, Washington, D.C., at:
http://www.worldbank.org/wbi/governance/pdf/durban_pdfs/durban1.pdf

KAUFMANN D. (2003b), "Rethinking Governance: Empirical Lessons Challenge Orthodoxy", Chapter 3.6 of *Global Competitiveness Report 2002-03*, World Economic Forum, at:
http://www.worldbank.org/wbi/governance/pubs/rethink_gov.html.

KAUFMANN D. (2004), "Human Rights and Governance: The Empirical Challenge", paper presented at a conference co-sponsored by the Ethical Globalization Initiative and the New York University Center for Human Rights and Global Justice, New York University School of Law, New York, March 1, 2004, at:
http://www.worldbank.org/wbi/governance/pdf/humanrights.pdf

KAUFMANN, D. (2005), Bibliography, at:
http://www.worldbank.org/wbi/governance/pdf/DKaufmann_Bibliography.pdf

KAUFMANN D. and A. KRAAY (2002a) "Growth without Governance", in: *Economia*, Vol. 3, No. 1, pp. 169-215 [Also Policy Research Working Paper No. 2928, The World Bank: Washington, D.C.], at:
http://www.worldbank.org/wbi/governance/pubs/growthgov.html

KAUFMANN, D., A. KRAAY and P. ZOIDO-LOBATON (1999a), *Aggregating Governance Indicators*, World Bank Policy Research Working Paper No. 2195, Washington, D.C., at:
http://www.worldbank.org/wbi/governance/pubs/aggindicators.html

KAUFMANN, D., A. KRAAY and P. ZOIDO-LOBATON (1999b), *Governance Matters*, World Bank Policy Research Working Paper No. 2196, Washington, D.C., at:
http://www.worldbank.org/wbi/governance/pubs/govmatters.html [Also *Local Government Brief*, January 2001.]

KAUFMANN D., A. KRAAY and P. ZOIDO-LOBATON (2002), *Governance Matters II: Updated Indicators from 2000-01*, World Bank Policy Research Working Paper No. 2772, Washington, D.C., at: http://www.worldbank.org/wbi/governance/pubs/govmatters2001.html

KAUFMANN D., A. KRAAY and M. MASTRUZZI (2004), *Governance Matters III: Governance Indicators for 1996, 1998, 2000 and 2002*, World Bank Policy Research Working Paper No. 3106, Washington, D.C. [and *World Bank Economic Review*, Vol. 18, No. 4, pp. 253-287] at: http://papers.ssrn.com/sol3/papers.cfm?abstract_id=405841

KAUFMANN D., A. KRAAY and M. MASTRUZZI (2005), *Governance Matters IV: Governance Indicators for 1996-2004*, World Bank Policy Research Working Paper No. 3630, Washington, D.C., at: http://www.worldbank.org/wbi/governance/pubs/govmatters4.html

KAUFMANN D., A. KRAAY and M. MASTRUZZI (2006a), *Governance Matters V: Governance Indicators for 1996-2005*, World Bank Policy Research Working Paper No. 4012, Washington, D.C., at: www.worldbank.org/wbi/governance/govmatters5

KAUFMANN D., A. KRAAY and M. MASTRUZZI (2006b), "Measuring Governance Using Cross-Country Perceptions Data", in S. ROSE-ACKERMAN (ed.), *International Handbook on the Economics of Corruption*, Edward Elgar Publishing, Chapter 2, pp. 52-104, at: http://siteresources.worldbank.org/DEC/Resources/MeasuringGovernancewithperceptionsdataFinalforPublisher.pdf

KAUFMANN D., A. KRAAY and M. MASTRUZZI (2006c), "Measuring Corruption: Myths vs. Realities", *Development Outreach* (September), World Bank, Washington D.C.

KAUFMANN D., A. KRAAY and M. MASTRUZZI (2007a), *Governance Matters VI: Governance Indicators for 1996-2006*, Policy Research Working Paper No. 4280, World Bank: Washington, D.C., at: http://papers.ssrn.com/sol3/papers.cfm?abstract_id=999979

KAUFMANN D., A. KRAAY and M. MASTRUZZI (2007b), "The Worldwide Governance Indicators Project: Answering the Critics", World Bank Policy Research Working Paper No. 4149, Washington, D.C., at: http://www-wds.worldbank.org/external/default/WDSContentServer/WDSP/IB/2007/02/23/000016406_20070223093027/Rendered/PDF/wps4149.pdf

KAUFMANN D., G. MEHREZ and T. GURGUR (2002), *Voice or Public Sector Management? An Empirical Investigation of Determinants of Public Sector Performance Based on a Survey of Public Officials*, World Bank Research Working Paper, World Bank, Washington D.C., at: http://papers.ssrn.com/sol3/papers.cfm?abstract_id=316865

KAUFMANN, D. and L. PRITCHETT (1998), "Civil Liberties, Democracy and the Performance of Government Projects", in *Finance and Development*, March 1998, pp.26-29, at: http://www.imf.org/external/pubs/ft/fandd/1998/03/pdf/pritchet.pdf

KAUFMANN, D. and M. SCHLOSS (eds.) (1998), *New Perspectives on Combating Corruption*, The World Bank and Transparency International, Washington D.C., at: http://www.worldbank.org/wbi/governance/pubs/challenges.html

KEARTON, I. (2002) [see INTERNATIONAL IDEA (2002)]

KECK, M. and K. SIKKINK (1998), *Activists Beyond Borders: Advocacy Networks in International Politics*, Cornell University Press, Ithaca.

KEKIC, L. (2007), *The Economist Intelligence Unit's Index of Democracy*, at:
http://www.economist.com/media/pdf/DEMOCRACY_INDEX_2007_v3.pdf

KIMENYI, M.S. (2007), "Economic Rights, Human Development Effort, and Institutions", in HERTEL and MINKLER (2007), pp. 182-213.

KING, E. and A. MASON (2001), *Engendering Development Through Gender Equality in Rights, Resources, and Voice*, Vol. 1, A World Bank policy research report, World Bank and Oxford University Press.

KISH, L. (1996), "Developing Samplers for Developing Countries", *International Statistical Review*, Vol. 64, pp. 143-152.

KLUG, F. (1993), *Human Rights as Indicators of Democracy*, Human Rights Centre, University of Essex.

KNACK, S. (2000), Aid Dependence and the Quality of Governance: A Cross-Country Empirical Analysis World Bank Policy Research Working Paper No. 2396, Washington D.C., at
http://www.worldbank.org/wbi/governance/pdf/wps2396.pdf

KNACK, S. (2002), "Governance and Growth: Measurement and Evidence", Forum Series on the Role of Institutions in Promoting Economic Growth, USAID, Washington, D.C. [and The IRIS Discussion Papers on Institutions and Development, Paper No. 02/05, Center for Institutional Reform and the Informal Sector at the University of Maryland], at:
http://www.iris.umd.edu/Reader.aspx?TYPE=FORMAL_PUBLICATION&ID=16b9661e-0d22-4a67-8dae-ad2f14afb73f

KNACK, S. (2006), "Measuring Corruption in Eastern Europe and Central Asia: A Critique of the Cross-Country Indicators", World Bank Policy Research Department Working Paper No. 3968, Washington D.C., at:
http://econ.worldbank.org/external/default/main?pagePK=64165259&piPK=64165421&theSitePK=4693
72&menuPK=64166093&entityID=000016406_20060713140304

KNACK, S. and N. MANNING (2000), "Towards Consensus on Governance Indicators: Selecting Public Management and Broader Governance Indicators", World Bank, Washington D.C., at:
http://www1.worldbank.org/publicsector/dac13.doc

KNACK, S. and M. KUGLER (2002), *Constructing an Index of Objective Indicators of Good Governance*, PREM Public Sector Group, World Bank, Washington, D.C.
www.worldbank.org/publicsector/anticorrupt/FlagshipCourse2003/SecondGenerationIndicators.pdf

KNACK, S., M. KUGLER and N. MANNING (2003), "Second-Generation Governance Indicators", *International Review of Administrative Sciences*, Vol. 69, No. 3, pp. 345-364.

KOMINSKI, R. (1989), "How Good Is 'How Well'? An Examination of the Census English-Speaking Ability Question", *Proceedings of the Social Statistics Section of the American Statistical Association*, pp. 333-338.

KOOIMAN, J. (2002), *Governing as Governance*, Sage, London.

KOTHARI, M. (1993), "The Human Right to Adequate Housing: Towards Ideal Indicators and Realistic World Views", Background paper presented at the United Nations Expert Seminar on Indicators and Economic, Social and Cultural Rights, Geneva, 25-29 January, UN document HR/Geneva/1993/Sem./BP.16.

KOTHARI, M. (2003) [see UN-HRI, 2003b].

KOTHARI, M. (2007) [see UN-HRI, 2007].

KUBHEKA, T. (2000), "The South African Truth and Reconciliation Commission: Data Processing", in BALL, SIPRER AND SPIRER (2000).

KUCERA, D. (2000), "Measuring Fundamental Rights at Work, in IAOS (2000), at:
http://www.portal-stat.admin.ch/iaos2000/kucera_final_paper.doc

KURTZ, M.J. and A. SCHRANK (2007), "Growth and Governance: Models, Measures, and Mechanisms", *Journal of Politics*, Vol. 69, No. 2, pp. 538-554, at:
http://papers.ssrn.com/sol3/papers.cfm?abstract_id=1065965

KVALE, S. (1996), *Interviews: An Introduction to Qualitative Research Interviewing*, Sage, London.

LAGOS, M. (2005) [SEE LATINOBARÓMETRO, 2005].

LAGOUTTE, S., H.O. SANO and P. SCHARFF Smith (eds.) (2006), *Human Rights in Turmoil: Facing Threats, Consolidating Achievements*, Martinus Nijhoff Publishers, Den Haag.

LAMBSDORFF, J.G. (1998), "An Empirical Investigation of Bribery in International Trade", *European Journal for Development Research*, Vol. 10, pp. 40-59 [reprinted in: M. ROBINSON (ed.), *Corruption and Development*, Frank Cass Publishers, London].

LAMBSDORFF, J.G. (2004), "Framework Document to the 2004 Corruption Perceptions Index", Transparency International Background Paper, at:
http://www.icgg.org/downloads/FD_CPI_2004.pdf

LAMBSDORFF, J.G. (2005), "Between Two Evils - Investors Prefer Grand Corruption!", University of Passau Discussion Paper V-31-05, January.

LAMBSDORFF, J.G. (2005), "Consequences and Causes of Corruption: What do We Know From a Cross-Section of Countries?", Diskussionsbeitrag Nr. V-34-05, Witschaftswissenschaftliche Fakultät, Passau University, at:
http://www.icgg.org/downloads/Causes%20and%20Consequences%20of%20Corruption%20-%20Cross-Section.pdf

LANCELOT, A. (1984), "*Sondage et démocratie* ", in SOFRES, *Opinion publique*, Gallimard, Paris.

LANDMAN, T. (2004) "Measuring Human Rights: Principles, Practice, and Policy", in *Human Rights Quarterly*, Vol. 26, pp. 906-931.

LANDMAN, T. (2006a), *Studying Human Rights*, Routage, New York.

LANDMAN, T. (2006b) [see UNDP, 2006b].

LANDMAN, T. (2008a) [see INTERNATIONAL IDEA, 2008].

LANDMAN, T. and J. HÄUSERMANN (2003), *Map-Making and Analysis of the Main International Initiatives on Developing Indicators on Democracy and Good Governance*, final report of a study commissioned by Eurostat, Human Rights Centre, University of Essex, at:
www.oecd.org/dataoecd/0/28/20755719.pdf

LANDMAN, T., M. LARIZZA and C. McEVOY (2006), *State of Democracy in Mongolia: A Desk Study*, conducted by the Human Rights Centre of Essex University in collaboration with International IDEA, published by the Government of Mongolia and UNDP/Mongolia, Ulaanbaatar, at:
http://www.idea.int/democracy/upload/sodMongolia05.pdf

LANDMAN, T. *et al.* (2006), *State of Democracy in Central Asia: A Comparative Study*, conducted by the Human Rights Centre of Essex University in collaboration with International IDEA, published by the Government of Mongolia and UNDP/Mongolia, Ulaanbaatar.

LARIK, N.M. (2000), "Conducting Surveys on Children Issues and Reporting on Poverty and Childhood: The Experience of Pakistan", in IAOS (2000), at:
http://www.portal-stat.admin.ch/iaos2000/larik_final_paper.doc

LATINOBARÓMETRO (OPINIÓN PÚBLICA LATINOAMERICANA) (2005), "Historia de Latinobarómetro, 1995-2005: De un estudio a una institución", Santiago de Chile [authored by M. LAGOS], at:
http://www.latinobarometro.org/ (press "publicaciones")

LATINOBARÓMETRO (2007), *Data Bank, Online Analysis, Time Series, Documents on Methods and Annual Reports* at:
http://www.latinobarometro.org/

LAVIELLE, B. (2003) [see FUNDAR, 2003].

LEBLANG, D., W.T. MILNER and S.C. POE (1999), "Security Rights, Subsistence Rights, and Liberties: A Theoretical Survey of the Empirical Landscape", *Human Rights Quarterly*, Vol. 21, pp. 403-443.

LECKIE, S. (1998), "Another Step Towards Indivisibility: Identifying the Key Features of Violations of Economic, Social and Cultural Rights", in: *Human Rights Quarterly*, vol.20, no.1, p.81.

LECKIE, S. (2000), "Keeping People Housed: Using Statistics and Digital Technology in Support of Housing Rights", in IAOS (2000), at:
http://www.portal-stat.admin.ch/iaos2000/leckie_final_paper.doc

LECOURS, A. (2002), "L'approche néo-institutionnaliste en science politique: Unité ou diversité?", *Politique et Sociétés*, Vol. 21, No. 3, pp.3-19.

LEDUC, L., R.G. NIEMI and P. NORRIS (eds.) (1996), *Comparing Democracies*, Sage, London.

LEDUC, L., R.G. NIEMI and P. NORRIS (eds.) (2002), *Comparing Democracies*, revised and updated second edition, Sage, London.

LEHOHLA, P. (2008), "Fragile States and Statistics", Keynote Address to the Second Metagora Forum held in Paris on 9-10 July, Metagora/OECD.

LIE, R. (2004), "Health, human rights and mobilization of resources for health", *BMC International Health and Human Rights*, 4, at:
http://www.biomedcentral.com/1472-698X/4/4

LINDHOLT, L. and H.O. SANO (2000), *Human Rights Indicators: Country Data and Methodology*, Danish Institute for Human Rights, Copenhagen; at:
http://www.jus.uio.no/forskning/grupper/humrdev/Project-Indicators/Workshop06/Background/Sano&Lindholt.pdf

LOKSHIN, M., S. PATERNOSTRO and N. UMAPATHI (2004), *Robustness of Subjective Welfare Analysis in a Poor Developing Country*, World Bank Policy Research Working Paper No. 3191, Washington D.C.

LOPEZ, G.A. and M. STOHL (1992), "Problems of Concept and Measurement in the Study of Human Rights", in CLAUDE and JABINE (1992), pp. 216-234.

LOUIS, G. (2007) "De l'opacité à la transparence: les limites de l'indice de perceptions de la corruption de Transparency International", *Déviance et Société*, Vol. 31, No. 1, pp. 41-64.

MACDONALD, A.L. (2000), "Reconstructing the Demographic and Economic Impact of Slavery on the Basis of Colonial Reports: The Case of Surinam", in IAOS (2000), at: http://www.portal-stat.admin.ch/iaos2000/macdonald_final_paper.doc

MADAÏ BOUKAR, A. (2005) [see INSTITUT NATIONAL DE LA STATISTIQUE, Niger, 2005].

MADDISON, A. (2001), *The World Economy: A Millennial Perspective*, Development Centre Studies, OECD, Paris.

MADDISON, A. (2003), *The World Economy: Historical Statistics*, Development Centre Studies, OECD, Paris.

MALAGUERRA, C. (2000), "Summary of the Conclusions of the Conference on Statistics, Development and Human Rights", in IAOS (2000), at: http://www.portal-stat.admin.ch/iaos2000/03iaos_det11.htm

MALIK, A. (2002), "State of the Art in Governance Indicators", UNDP Office of the Human Development Report, Occasional Paper No. 2002/7 [background paper for the HDR 2002], New York, at: http://hdr.undp.org/en/reports/global/hdr2002/papers/malik_2002.pdf

MAR (MINORITIES AT RISK) (2008), *Qualitative and Quantitative Data*, tracking 284 politically-active ethnic groups throughout the world from 1945 to the present, Center for International Development and Conflict Management (CIDCM), University of Maryland [see also C. DAVENPORT, 2003], at: http://www.cidcm.umd.edu/mar/data.asp

MARKS, S. (2004), "The Human Right to Development: Between Rhetoric and Reality", *Harvard Human Rights Journal*, Vol. 17, pp. 137-168, at: http://www.law.harvard.edu/students/orgs/hrj/iss17/marks.pdf and http://www.law.harvard.edu/students/orgs/hrj/iss17/marks.shtml

MARSHALL, M.G. and K. JAGGERS (2002), "Polity IV Project: Political Regime Characteristics and Transitions, 1800-2002: Dataset Users Manual", Center for International Development and Conflict Management, University of Maryland http://www.cidcm.umd.edu/inscr/polity/

MARSHALL, M.G., K. JAGGERS and T.R. GURR (2005), "Polity IV Project", at: http://www.cidcm.umd.edu/inscr/polity/index.htm

MARTIN-GUZMÁN, P. (2000), "Producing Information for the Open Society: The Lessons of the Spanish Transition to Democracy (abstract)", in IAOS (2000), at: http://www.portal-stat.admin.ch/iaos2000/martinguzman_final_abstract.doc

MATOVU, G. and D. CONYERS (2001), *Service Delivery Surveys: A Means of Increasing Accountability, Transparency and Integrity in Local Government*, Municipal Development Programme (MDP), Harare, at: http://ww2.unhabitat.org/cdrom/TRANSPARENCY/html/yellowp/Y023.html

MAYERHÖFFER, E. (2006) [see TRANSPARENCY INTERNATIONAL and UNDP, 2006].

MAZARIEGOS, O. (2000a), "The Recovery of Historical Memory Project of the Human Rights Office of the Archbishop of Guatemala: Data Processing, Database Representation", in BALL, SPIRER and SPIRER (2000).

MAZARIEGOS, O. (2000b), "The International Center for Human Rights Investigations: Generating Analytical Reports", in BALL, SPIRER and SPIRER (2000).

McCHESNEY, A. (2000) [see AAAS and HURIDOCS, 2000].

McCormick, J.M. and N.J. Mitchell (1997), "Research Note: Human Rights Violations, Umbrella Concepts, and Empirical Analysis", *World Politics*, Vol. 49, pp. 510-525.

McHenry, D.E. (2000), "Quantitative Measures of Democracy in Africa: An Assessment", *Democratization*, Vol. 7, No. 2, pp. 168-185.

McKay, A. and P. Vizard (2005), "Rights and Economic Growth: Inevitable Conflict or 'Common Ground'?", Rights in Action and ODI, March, at:
http://www.odi.org.uk/rights/Meeting%20Series/Growth&Rights.pdf

Meisel, N. (2004), *Governance Culture and Development: A Different Perspective on Corporate Governance*, Development Centre Studies, OECD, Paris.

Metagora (2005), *Metagora Forum*, collection of draft contributed papers and powerpoint presentations, OECD, Paris.

Metagora (2006), *Inventory of Initiatives Aimed at Enhancing Evidence-based Assessment of Human Rights and Democratic Governance*, online database [authored by R. D'Arcangelo, T. Heimgartner and Q. Padilla Dulche], at:
http://www.metagora.org/html/aboutus/about_inventory.html

Metagora (2007a), *Training Materials on Measuring Human Rights and Democratic Governance*, an online resource [authored by J. Asher and C. Naval], at:
http://www.metagora.org/training/

Metagora (2007b), "Reference Note for the Metagora High Level Meeting of Human Rights Institutions", held in Paris on 25-26 January, OECD, Paris, at:
www.metagora.org

Metagora (2008), *Relevant Literature on Measuring Human Rights and Democratic Governance*, at:
www.metagora.org

Metagora, DIAL and IRD (2004), *Gouvernance, démocratie et lutte contre la pauvreté: Éclairage méthodologique et analytique à partir des résultats de trois projets régionaux*, Direction Nationale de la Statistique et de l'Informatique du Mali, Bamako [report of the International Seminar held in Bamako on 11-12 June, and studies comparing the methods and results of three survey approaches for measuring governance and democracy issues in the context of fighting against poverty, with special focus on the case of Mali: the UNECA surveys, the Afrobarometer and the 1-2-3 method developed by DIAL].

Metzl, J.F. (1996), "Information Technology and Human Rights", *Human Rights Quarterly*, Vol. 18, No. 4, pp. 705-746.

Meunier, N. and T. Solloquob (2005), *Économie du risque pays*, La Découverte, Paris.

Meyer, W.H. (1996), "Human Rights and MNCs: Theory Versus Quantitative Analysis", *Human Rights Quarterly*, Vol. 18, No. 2, pp. 368-397.

Meynaud, H. and D. Duclos (1996), *Les sondages d'opinion*, Repère, La Découverte, No. 38, Paris.

Mezquita, R. (2000), "The Guatemalan Commission for Historical Clarification: Data Processing", in Ball, Spirer and Spirer (2000).

Miller, D.C. and N.J. Salkind (2002), *Handbook of Research Design and Social Measurement* (6th edition), Sage, London.

MINUJIN, A. (2000), "Making Child Poverty Visible", in IAOS (2000), at:
http://www.portal-stat.admin.ch/iaos2000/minujin_final_paper.doc

MOKHIBER, C.G. (2000), "Towards a Measure of Dignity: Indicators for Rights-Based Development", in IAOS (2000), at:
http://www.portal-stat.admin.ch/iaos2000/mokhiber_final_paper.doc
also in *Statistical Journal of the United Nations Economic Commission for Europe,* Vol. 18 (2001), No. 2-, 155-162, and in S. GRUSKIN *et al.* (2005), pp. 383-392.

MOON, B.E. *et al.* (2006), "Voting Counts: Participation in the Measurement of Democracy", *Studies in Comparative International Development,* Vol. 41, No. 2, pp. 3-32.

MOORE, M., J. LEAVY and H. WHITE (2003), "How governance affects poverty?", in P.P. HOUTZAGER and M. MOORE (eds.), *Changing Paths - International Development and the New Politics of Inclusion,* University of Michigan Press, Ann Arbor.

MORLINO, L. (2004), "'Good' and 'Bad' Democracies: How to Conduct Research into the Quality of Democracy", *Journal of Communist Studies and Transition Politics,* Vol. 20, No. 1, pp. 5-27.

MOTTET, C. (2003) [see SWISS FEDERAL STATISTICAL OFFICE, 2003].

MOUSTAPHA, D. (2005) [see INSTITUT NATIONAL DE LA STATISTIQUE ET DE L'ANALYSE ÉCONOMIQUE, Bénin]

MUNK, G.L. (2005), "How to Craft Intermediate Categories of Political Regimes", Committee on Concepts and Methods of the International Political Science Association, Political Concepts, Working Paper Series, No. 4, Centro de Investigación y Docencia Económicas (CIDE), Mexico City, at:
http://www.concepts-methods.org/papers_list.php?id_categoria=1&titulo=Political%20Concepts

MUNCK, G.L. and J. VERKUILEN (2002), "Conceptualizing and Measuring Democracy: Evaluating Alternative Indices", *Comparative Political Studies,* Vol. 35, No. 1, pp. 5-34. Previous 2000 version at:
http://rboyd.web.wesleyan.edu/wescourses/2001f/govt366/01/Course%20Documents/Munck_Verkuilen.pdf

MURAKAMI, Y. (2000), *La Democracia según C y D. Un estudio de la conciencia y el comportamiento político de los sectores populares de Lima,* IEP, JCAS, Lima.

NAHEM, J. (2004) [see EUROSTAT and UNDP, 2004].

NAHEM, J. (2005), "UNDP National Human development Reports and the Use of Governance Indicators", a UNDP Oslo Governance Centre background paper for the UNDP-ICSSR technical workshop on *Governance Indicators for Pro-poor and Gender-Sensitive Policy Reform* held in New Delhi on 20-22 April, at:
http://www.undp.org/oslocentre/docs05/cross/2/UNDP%20National%20Human%20Development%20Reports%20and%20the%20Use%20of%20Governance%20Indicators.pdf

NANDA V.P., J.R. SCARRITT and G.W. SHEPHERD Jr. (eds.) (1981), *Global Human Rights: Public Policies, Comparative Measures, and NGO Strategies,* Westview, Boulder CO.

NARANG, S. (2005) "Disaggregating Governance Indicators: Why Local Governance is Important and how It can be Measured", a UN-HABITAT Urban Governance section's background paper for the UNDP-ICSSR technical workshop on *Governance Indicators for Pro-poor and Gender-Sensitive Policy Reform* held in New Delhi on 20-22 April, at:
http://www.undp.org/oslocentre/docs05/cross/2/Disaggregating%20Governance%20Indicators%20-%20Why%20local%20governance%20is%20important%20and%20how%20it%20can%20be%20measured.pdf

NARAYAN, D. *et al.* (2000a), *Can Anyone Hear Us? Voices from 47 countries* (Voices of the Poor, Vol.1), World Bank, Oxford University Press.

NARAYAN, D. *et al.* (2000b), *Crying out for Change* (Voices of the Poor, Vol. 2), World Bank, Oxford University Press.

NARDO, M. (2005) [see OECD, 2005b].

NATIONAL RESEARCH COUNCIL OF THE NATIONAL ACADEMIES (2008), *Improving Democracy Assistance: Building Knowledge Through Evaluation and Research*, Report of the Committee on Evaluation of the USAID Democracy Assistance Programs, the National Academies Press, Washington D.C. [Chapter 3: "Measuring Democracy", pp. 71-98, and Appendix C, pp. 259-284], at:
http://books.nap.edu/openbook.php?record_id=12164&page=71

NAVAL, C. (2007) [see METAGORA, 2007a].

NAVAL, C. and J. SALGADO (2006), *Irregularities, Abuses of Power, and Ill-treatment in the Federal District: The Relations between Police Officers and Ministerio Público Agents, and the Population / Irregularidades, abusos de poder y maltratos en el Distrito Federal: La relación de los agents policiales y del Ministerio Público con la Población*, policy-oriented report based on the Metagora experience in Mexico, Fundar, Centre for Analysis and Research, Mexico City, at:
http://www.fundar.org.mx/PDF/metagora_eng_long.pdf (English)
http://www.fundar.org.mx/PDF/Metagora%20Grande.pdf (Spanish)

NEPAD (THE NEW PARTNERSHIP FOR AFRICA'S DEVELOPMENT) (2001), *The New Partnership for Africa's Development: Framework Document*, Abuja, Nigeria, at:
http://www.nepad.org/2005/files/documents/inbrief.pdf

NEPAD (2002), *Durban Declaration on Democracy, Political, Economic and Corporate Governance*, NEPAD document AHG/235 (XXXVIII) Annex I, at:
http://www.nepad.org/2005/files/documents/2.pdf

NEPAD (2003) *Objectives, Standards, Criteria and Indicators for the African Peer Review Mechanism*, APRM, NEPAD document HSGIC-03-2003/APRM/Guideline/OSCI, at:
http://www.nepad.org/2005/files/documents/110.pdf

NEWMAN, J.S. (1983), "Some Indicators of Women's Economic Roles in Sub-Saharan Africa", *Proceedings of the Social Statistics Section of the American Statistical Association*, pp. 78-87.

NICKEL, J.W. (1987), *Making Sense of Human Rights: Philosophical Reflections on the Universal Declaration of Human Rights*, University of California Press, Berkley:

NOBEL, J. (2000), "The experience of Dutch Official Statistics During the Second World War (abstract)", in IAOS (2000), at:
http://www.portal-stat.admin.ch/iaos2000/nobel_final_abstract.doc

NORAD (NORWEGIAN AGENCY FOR DEVELOPMENT CO-OPERATION) (2001), *Handbook in Human Rights Assessment: Sate Obligations, Awareness & Empowerment*, Oslo, at:
www.norad.no/items/968/38/9556558330/Handbook%20in%20human%20rights%20assessment.pdf

NOVAL, A.M. (1993) [see HURIDOCS, 1993]

NSCB (NATIONAL STATISTICAL COORDINATION BOARD OF PHILIPPINES) (2003), *Governance Statistics Project: Development of Indicators and Design of a Database and Information Network*, NSCB, Makati City.

NURAINI, A. (2000), "The Measurement of Gross Human Rights Violations in Indonesia", in IAOS (2000), at: http://www.statistik.admin.ch/about/international/nuraini_final_paper.doc

NUSSBAUM, M. (1997), "Capabilities and Human Rights", 66 *Fordham L. Review*, No. 273.

ODI (OVERSEAS DEVELOPMENT INSTITUTE) (2008), *World Governance Assessment* (WGA Project), at: http://www.odi.org.uk/wga_governance/Index.html

OECD (1995), *DAC Orientations on Participatory Development and Good Governance / Orientations du CAD sur le développement particiatif et la bonne gestion des affaires publiques*, Development Aid Committee (DAC), Development Cooperation Guidelines Series, OECD, Paris, at : http://www.acdi-cida.gc.ca/INET/IMAGES.NSF/vLUImages/HRDG/$file/Dac-e.pdf

OECD (1996), *Shaping the 21st Century: The Contribution of Development Co-operation*, report adopted at the thirty-fourth High Level Meeting of the OECD Development Assistance Committee, held on 6-7 May, at: http://www.oecd.org/dataoecd/23/35/2508761.pdf

OECD (1997a), *Final Report of the ad hoc Working Group on Participatory Development and Good Governance*, Development Assistance Committee, OECD, Paris, at: http://www.oecd.org/dataoecd/44/11/1894634.pdf

OECD (1997b), *Final Report of the ad hoc Working Group on Participatory Development and Good Governance, Part 2: Lessons from Experiences in Selected Areas of Support for Participatory Development and Good Governance*, Development Assistance Committee, OECD, Paris, at: http://www.oecd.org/dataoecd/44/11/1894634.pdf

OECD (1997c), *Evaluation of Programs Promoting Participatory Development and Good Governance: Synthesis Report*, Development Assistance Committee, OECD, Paris, at: http://www.oecd.org/dataoecd/39/44/35019452.pdf

OECD (2003), *Metagora*, OECD Council document C(2003)224-final, Paris.

OECD (2005a), *Paris Declaration on Aid Effectiveness: Ownership, Harmonisation, Alignement, Results and Mutual Accountability*, adopted at the High Level Forum held in Paris from 28 February to 2 March, at: http://www.oecd.org/dataoecd/11/41/34428351.pdf

OECD (2005b), *Handbook on Constructing Composite Indicators: Methodology and User Guide*, OECD Statistics Directorate, Paris [authored by M. NARDO, M. SAISANA, A. SALTELLI, S. TARANTOLA, A. HOFFMAN and E. GIOVANNINI], at: http://www.olis.oecd.org/olis/2005doc.nsf/LinkTo/std-doc(2005)3

OECD (2005c), *Management in Government: Comparative Country Data*, OECD, Paris, at: http://www.oecd.org/gov/indicators

OECD (2005), *Statistics, Knowledge and Policy: Key Indicators to Inform Decision Making*, OECD, Paris [proceedings of the first OECD World Forum on Key Indicators, held in Palermo on10-13 November, edited by E. GIOVANNINI].

OECD (2006), *Statistics, Knowledge and Policy: Key Indicators to Inform Decision Making*, Proceedings of the first World Forum on Key Indicators, OECD, Paris.

OECD (2007a), *Action-oriented Policy Paper on Human Rights and Development*, adopted by the Development Assistance Committee on 15 February, document DCD/DAC(2007)15/FINAL, at: http://www.oecd.org/dataoecd/52/61/38764442.pdf

OECD (2007b), *Integrating Human Rights into Development: Donor Approaches, Experiences and Challenges*, The Development Dimension, OECD, Paris, at: http://www.sourceoecd.org/development/9264022090

OECD (2007c), "Towards Better Measurement of Government", OECD Working Papers on Public Governance, No. 1, OECD, Paris, at: http://www.oecd.org/dataoecd/11/61/38134037.pdf

OECD (2008a), "Towards Government at a Glance", OECD Working Papers on Public Governance, No. 2, OECD, Paris, at: http://caliban.sourceoecd.org/vl=11722526/cl=16/nw=1/rpsv/workingpapers/19934351/wp_5kzr8qxrj76k.htm

OECD (2008b), *Donor Approaches to Governance Assessments and Aid Effectiveness*, Report of the Conference held in London on 20-21 February, Governance Network of the OECD Development Assistance Committee (GOVNET), OECD, Paris, at: http://www.oecd.org/dataoecd/16/27/40266891.pdf

OECD (2008c, forthcoming), Statistics, Knowledge and Policy 2007: Measuring and Fostering the Progress of Societies [proceedings of the 2007 OECD World Forum held in Istanbul, edited by E. GIOVANNINI].

OHCHR (OFFICE OF THE HIGH COMMISSIONER FOR HUMAN RIGHTS) (2004), *Human Rights and Poverty Reduction: A Conceptual Framework*, OHCHR, United Nations HR/PUB/04/1, New York and Geneva [based on the discussion paper by HUNT, NOWAK and OSMANI (2002)], at: http://www2.ohchr.org/english/issues/poverty/docs/povertyE.pdf

OHCHR (2005), "Conclusions and Recommendations of the Expert Consultation on Indicators for Monitoring Compliance with International Human Rights Instruments", OHCHR, Geneva.

OLKEN, B. (2006), "Corruption Perceptions vs. Corruption Reality", *Working Paper*, Harvard University and NBER, at: http://papers.nber.org/papers/w12428

OLSON, M. (1965), *The Logic of Collective Action: Public Goods and the Theory of Groups*, Harvard University Press, Cambridge.

OLSON, M. (1982), *The Rise and Decline of Nations: Economic Growth, Stagflation and Social Rigidities*, Yale University Press, New Haven.

OLSON, M. (2000), *Power and Prosperity: Outgrowing Communist and Capitalist Dictatorships*, Basic Books, New York.

OMAN, C. AND G. WIGNARAJA (1991), *The Postwar Evolution of Development Thinking*, Palgrave MacMillan Ltd., London, in association with the OECD Development Centre Studies, Paris.

OKIN, S.M. (1981), "Liberty and Welfare: Some Issues in Human Rights Theory", in J.W. CHAPMAN and J.R. PENNOCK (eds.), *Human Rights*, New York University Press, New York.

OMAR, E. (1998), "Statistics and Human Rights", Paper prepared for the HURIDOCS international conference on *Human Rights Information, Impunity and Challenges of the Post-Conflict Healing Process*, held in Gammarth (Tunisia) on 22-25 March.

OMAR, E. (2000), "Development and Human Rights: The Growing Demand for Statistics from the International Community", in IAOS (2000), at: http://www.portal-stat.admin.ch/iaos2000/omar_final_paper.doc

O'NEIL, T. and L.H. PIRON (2003), "Rights-Based Approaches to Tackling Discrimination and Horizontal Inequality", ODI Background Paper, London.

O'NEILL, W.G. (2003), "An Introduction to the Concept of Rights-Based Approach to Development: A Paper for InterAction", InterAction, Washington D.C., at:
http://www.interaction.org/files.cgi/2495_RBA_1-5-04.pdf

ORKIN, M. (2000a), "From Apartheid to Democracy: Global Lessons from a National Experience", in IAOS (2000), at:
http://www.portal-stat.admin.ch/iaos2000/orkin_final_paper.doc

ORKIN, M. (2000b), "Conference on Statistics, Development and Human Rights: Concluding Address", in IAOS (2000), at:
http://www.portal-stat.admin.ch/iaos2000/03iaos_det11.htm

O'SULLIVAN, G. (2000), "The South African Truth and Reconciliation Commission: Database Representation", in Ball, P., H. Siprer and L. Spirer (2000).

O'SULLIVAN, M. and F. STEWART (1999), "Democracy, Conflict and Development: Three Cases", in G. RANIS, S.-C. HU and Y.-P. CHU (eds.), *The Political Economy of Comparative Development into the 21st Century: Essays in Memory of John C.H.Fei*, Edward Elgar, Cheltenham.

OULD AOUDIA, J. (2007), "Profils institutionnels: une base de données originale sur les caractéristiques institutionnelles des pays en développement et développés", paper presented at the workshop on *Measuring Law*, held in Paris on 15-16 December, at :
http://www.cepii.fr/institutions/02_2007.pdf

PADILLA DULCHE, Q. (2006) [see METAGORA, 2006].

PALMLUND, TH. (2006) [see UNDP, 2006b].

PARIS21 (PARTNERSHIP IN STATISTICS FOR DEVELOPMENT IN THE 21ST CENTURY) (2004), *Why Statistics? Making the Case for Official Statistics*, Paris, at:
http://www.paris21.org/documents/1099.pdf

PARIS21 (2005), *Measuring up to the Measurement Problem: the Role of the Statistics in Evidence Based Policy Making / Prendre la mesure du problème de la mesure: Rôle des statistiques dans la prise de décision fondée sur l'observation des faits*, PARIS21, Paris [advocacy paper based on CHR. SCOTT, 2005], at:
http://www.paris21.org/documents/2086.pdf (English)
http://www.paris21.org/documents/2087.pdf (French)

PARIS21 (2008a), *National Strategy for the Development of Statistics: Knowledge Base,* at:
http://www.oecd.org/document/22/0,3343,en_21571361_38288834_38296214_1_1_1_1,00&&en-USS_01DBC.html

PARIS21 (2008b), Web site, at:
http://www.paris21.org/

PATEL, N. (2007), "Governance Assessments and the Paris Declaration: Opportunities and Challenges for Inclusive Participation and National Ownership. The Malawi Scenario", paper presented by R. HAJAT at the CMI/UNDP seminar on *Governance Assessments and the Paris Declaration: Towards Inclusive Participation and National Ownership* (Bergen, 23-25 September), Chr. Michelsen Institute and UNDP Oslo Governance Centre, in:
http://www.undp.org/oslocentre/docs07/bergen_2007/Governance%20Assessments%20Malawi%20Case%20Study.pdf

PATTON, M.Q. (2002), *Qualitative Research and Evaluation Methods*, Sage, London.

PAVLOVIC, Z. and T. RUTAR (2007), "Children's Rights International Study Project: A Shift from the Children's Rights Focus to the Quality of Life Instrument", in ISCI (2007).

PCBS (Palestinian Central Bureau of Statistics) (2004), *Demographic and Social Consequences of the Separation Barrier on the West Bank*, Ramallah [authored by H. BRUNBORG].

PECCOUD, D. (2000), "Nouveaux défis pour le suivi des droits de l'homme; Commentaire: un théorème et ses corollaires / Emerging challenges in Human Rights Monitoring; Comment: a theorem and its corollaries", in IAOS (2000), at:
http://www.portal-stat.admin.ch/iaos2000/peccoud_final_comment.doc

PEDERSEN, J. (2000), "Palestinian Refugees in Jordan and Lebanon", in IAOS (2000), at:
http://www.portal-stat.admin.ch/iaos2000/Pedersen_final_paper.doc (abstract)

PEPINSKY, T.B. (2007), "How to Code", Committee on Concepts and Methods of the International Political Science Association, Political Concepts, Working Paper Series, No. 18, Centro de Investigación y Docencia Económicas (CIDE), Mexico City, at:
http://www.concepts-methods.org/papers_list.php?id_categoria=1&titulo=Political%20Concepts

PERÉZ, M. [see FUNDAR, 2003, 2005, 2007a].

PERSSON, T. and G. TABELLINI (2003), *The Economic Effects of Constitutions*, Munich Lectures in Economics, MIT Press, Cambridge MA, at:
http://books.google.fr/books?id=NjCw9eSvNPMC

Peterson, M.J (1995), "Community and Individual Stakes in the Collection, Analysis, and

Availability of Data", *PS: Political Science and Politics*, Vol. 28, No. 3, pp. 462-64.

PHYSICIANS FOR HUMAN RIGHTS (1999), *War Crimes in Kosovo: A Population-Based Assessment of Human Rights Violations Against Kosovar Albanians*, Physicians for Human Rights, Boston.

PINHEIRO, P.S. (1999), "Human Rights Indicators in New Democracies", Center for the Study of Violence, Sao Paulo University, Paper presented at the OHCHR consultative Workshop on *Indicators on Civil and Political Rights* held in Geneva.

PINTAT, C. (2000), "Les statistiques s'agissant du processus démocratique et des droits civils et politiques: expérience et réflexion de l'Union Interparlementaire / The Democratic Process and Civil and Political Rights Under the Lens of Statistics: An Insight Into the Experience of the Inter-parliamentary Union", in IAOS (2000), at:
http://www.portal-stat.admin.ch/iaos2000/pintat_final_paper.doc

PITF (POLITICAL INSTABILITY TASK FORCE) (2007), *Internal Wars and State Failure Problem Datasets, 1955-2006*, at:
http://globalpolicy.gmu.edu/pitf/ and
http://www.systemicpeace.org/inscr/inscr.htm

POGGE, T. (2002), *World Poverty and Human Rights: Cosmopolitan Responsibilities and Reforms*, Blackwell/Polity, Malden.

POGGE, T. (2003), "Severe Poverty as a Human Rights Violation", UNESCO, at:
http://portal.unesco.org/shs/fr/ev.php-URL_ID=4363&URL_DO=DO_TOPIC&URL_SECTION=201.html

POLITY IV PROJECT (2007), *Political Regimes Characteristics and Transitions Datasets*, at:
http://www.systemicpeace.org/inscr/inscr.htm

POPE, J. (2000) [see TRANSPARENCY INTERNATIONAL, 2000].

PRESSER, S. (1989), "Review of Human Rights Quarterly (November 1986)", *Journal of the American Statistical Association*, Vol. 84, pp. 633-634.

PRZEWORSKI, A. et al. (2000), *Democracy and Development: Political Institutions and Material Well-Being in the World*, 1950-1990, Cambridge University Press, Cambridge; related datasets available at:
http://www.ssc.upenn.edu/~cheibub/data/Default.htm and
http://politics.as.nyu.edu/object/przeworskilinks.html

QUIROGA, J. et al. (1987), "Surveillance and Monitoring of Human Rights Violations", *Proceedings of the Section on Survey Research Methods of the American Statistical Association*, pp. 8-16.

QUIROGA, J., R. REITER and M.V. ZUNZUNEGUI (1986), "Guidelines for Field Reporting of Basic Human Rights Violations", *Human Rights Quarterly*, Vol. 8, pp. 628-653.

QUISUMBING, A. and J.A. MALUCCIO (1999), *Intra-household Allocation and Gender Relations: New Empirical Evidence*, The World Bank Development Research Group.

RADSTAAKE, M. (1999), "Human Rights Assessments and Indicators Equally Needed to Enhance Human Rights Policies", Humanist Committee on Human Rights (HOM), paper presented at the OHCHR workshop on *Indicators on Civil and Political Rights* held in Geneva.

RADSTAAKE, M. (2002), "Human Rights Impact Assessment: Steps and Tools", Humanist Committee on Human Rights (HOM), Utrecht.

RADSTAAKE, M. and D. BRONKHORST (2002), *Matching Practice with Principles, Human Rights Impact Assessment: EU Opportunities*, Report on the HRIA Conference held in Brussels in November 2001, Humanist Committee on Human Rights (HOM), Utrecht, at:
http://www.aimforhumanrights.nl/fileadmin/user_upload/pdf/Matching_Practice_with_Principles_in_cl_cover.pdf

RAINE, F. (2005) [see CARR CENTER FOR HUMAN RIGHTS POLICY, 2005]

RAINE, F. (2006), "The Measurement Challenge in Human Rights", *SUR, International Journal on Human Rights*, No. 4, pp. 7-29, at:
http://www.surjournal.org/eng/index4.php

RAKNER, L. and V. WANG (2007), "Governance Assessments and the Paris Declaration", paper presented at the CMI/UNDP seminar on *Governance Assessments and the Paris Declaration: Towards Inclusive Participation and National Ownership* (Bergen, 23-25 September), Chr. Michelsen Institute and UNDP Oslo Governance Centre, at:
http://www.undp.org/oslocentre/docs07/CMI%20paper.pdf

RAKOTOMANANA, F. (2003) [see INSTITUT NATIONAL DE LA STATISTIQUE, Madagascar, 2003].

RAMIREZ, A., G. RANIS and F. STEWART (2000), "Economic Growth and Human Development", *World Development*, Vol. 28, No. 2, pp. 197-219.

RANIS G, E. SAMMAN and F. STEWART (2006), "Human Development: Beyond the Human Development Index", Journal of Human Development, Vol. 6, No. 3, pp. 323-358.

RANIS G. and F. STEWART (1999), "Growth and Human Development: Comparative Latin American Experience", in YCIAS Working Paper Series, *Institutional Reforms, Growth and Human Development in Latin America*, pp. 239-284, New Haven, Yale.

RANIS G. and F. STEWART (2000), "Strategies for Success in Human Development", Economic Growth Center Discussion Paper No. 808, Yale University, at: http://www.econ.yale.edu/growth_pdf/cdp808.pdf

RANIS G. and F. STEWART (2002), "Crecimiento económico y desarrollo humano en American Latina", *Revista de la Cepal*, No. 78, pp. 7-24.

RANIS, G. and F. STEWART (2003), "Paths to Success: The Relationship Between Human Development and Economic Growth", Economic Growth Center Discussion Paper No. 874, Yale University, at: http://papers.ssrn.com/sol3/papers.cfm?abstract_id=487469

RANIS G. and F. STEWART (2004), "Economic Growth and Human Development in Latin America", in G. INDART (ed.), *Economic Reforms, Growth and Inequality in Latin America: Essays in Honour of Albert Berry*, Ashgate, Burlington, pp 63-89.

RANIS, G. and F. STEWART (2005), "The Priority of Human Development", in E. HERSHBERG and C. THORNTON (eds.), *The Development Imperative*, Social Science Research Council, New York, 2005, at: http://www.ssrc.org/programs/ifd/publications/DevImperative/RanisStewart.pdf

RAWORTH, K. (2005), "Measuring Human Rights", in GRUSKIN *et al.* (2005), pp. 393-412.

RAZAFINDRAKOTO M. (2000), "La statistique au service du débat démocratique en Afrique: l'exemple du projet MADIO à Madagascar", in IAOS (2000), at: http://www.portal-stat.admin.ch/iaos2000/razafindrakoto_final_paper.doc

RAZAFINDRAKOTO M. and F. ROUBAUD (1996), "Ce qu'attendent les Tananariviens de la réforme de l'Etat et de l'économie", *Politique africaine*, No. 61, pp.54-72.

RAZAFINDRAKOTO M. and F. ROUBAUD (2001), "Les multiples facettes de la pauvreté dans un pays en développement : le cas de la capitale malgache", Document de travail DIAL N°2001-07, *Économie et Statistique*, No. 383-384-385, pp. 131-155.

RAZAFINDRAKOTO M. and F. ROUBAUD (2003a), "Statistics at the Service of the Democratic Debate in Africa: The Example of the MADIO Project in Madagascar", *InterStat* No. 26, pp. 33-50.

RAZAFINDRAKOTO M. and F. ROUBAUD (2003b), "Wage and Corruption: the Case of Madagascar", in TRANSPARENCY INTERNATIONAL (2003), pp. 292-294 [French edition: pp. 381-383].

RAZAFINDRAKOTO M. and F. ROUBAUD (2003c), "Pensent-ils différemment ? La voix des pauvres à travers les enquêtes statistiques", in CLING, RAZAFINDRAKOTO and ROUBAUD (2003), pp. 141-165.

RAZAFINDRAKOTO M. and F. ROUBAUD (2004a), "Daily Corruption in French Speaking Africa", in Transparency International, *Global Corruption Report 2004*, pp.346-348.

RAZAFINDRAKOTO M. and F. ROUBAUD (2004b), "Les pauvres, la démocratie et le rôle de l'Etat. Le point de vue de la population en Afrique de l'Ouest et à Madagascar", paper presented at the IAOS – IASS- Joint Conference on *Poverty, Social Exclusion and Development: a Statistical Perspective*, Amman, Jordan, 29 November - 1st December, at: http://www.dial.prd.fr/dial_evenements/conf_scientifique/pdf/amman/razafin_roubaud.pdf

RAZAFINDRAKOTO M. and F. ROUBAUD (2005a), "Les pauvres, la démocratie et le marché à Madagascar: une analyse à partir de trois séries d'enquêtes auprès de la population malgache", *Revue d'économie du développement*, No. 1, pp.56-89.

RAZAFINDRAKOTO M. and F. ROUBAUD (2005b), "Gouvernance, démocratie et lutte contre la pauvreté: enseignements tirés des *enquêtes 1-2-3 en Afrique francophone*", *STATÉCO* No. 99, pp. 117-141.

RAZAFINDRAKOTO M. and F. ROUBAUD (2005c), "Gouvernance, démocratie et lutte contre la pauvreté en Afrique : Le point de vue de la population de huit métropoles : Enquêtes 1-2-3, Premiers résultats", Document de Travail DIAL No. 2005-17, Paris.

RAZAFINDRAKOTO M. and F. ROUBAUD (2005d), "How Far Can We Trust the Experts' Opinion on Corruption? An Experiment Based on Surveys in Francophone Africa", in: TRANSPARENCY INTERNATIONAL (2005), pp. 292-295.

RAZAFINDRAKOTO, M. and F. ROUBAUD, (2006a) "Are International Databases on Corruption Reliable? A Comparison of Expert Opinion Surveys and Household Surveys in Sub-Saharan Africa", Document de Travail DIAL No. 2006/17, Paris, at:
http://www.dial.prd.fr/dial_publications/PDF/Doc_travail/2006-17.pdf.

RAZAFINDRAKOTO, M. and F. ROUBAUD (2006b), "Les déterminants du bien-être individuel en Afrique francophone: le poids des institutions", *Afrique Contemporaine* No. 220. pp.191-223.

RAZAFINDRAKOTO, M. and F. ROUBAUD (2007), "Corruption, Institutional Discredit, and Exclusion of the Poor: A Poverty Trap," Afrobarometer Working Papers No. 86, at:
http://www.afrobarometer.org/papers/AfropaperNo86.pdf

RAZAFINDRAKOTO M., F. ROUBAUD and L. WANTCHEKON (eds.) (2007), "Gouvernance, démocratie et opinion publique en Afrique", *Afrique Contemporaine*, No. 220.

RED INTERAMERICANA PARA LA DEMOCRACIA (2005), *Índice de participación ciudadana 2005: Informe 7 (México)*, Buenos aires, at:
http://www.redinter.org/UserFiles/File/ipc/Informe7_Mex.pdf

REICH, G. (2002), "Categorizing Political Regimes: New Data for Old Problems", *Democratization*, Vol. 9, No. 4, pp. 1-24.

RESNICK D. and R. BIRNER (2006), "Does Good Governance Contribute to Pro-Poor Growth? A Review of the Evidence from Cross-Country Studies", International Food Policy Research Institute, Development Strategy and Governance Division, Discussion Paper 30, Washington D.C.

RIGOBON, R. and D. RODRIK (2005), "Rule of Law, Democracy, Openness, and Income: Estimating the Interrelationships", NBER Working Paper No. 10750, National Bureau of Economic Research, Cambridge MA, at:
http://www.nber.org/papers/W10750
and *Economics of Transition*, Vol. 13 (2005) No. 3, pp. 533-564.

ROBERTSON, G. (1999), *Crimes Against Humanity*, The New Press, New York.

ROBERTSON, R.E. (1994), "Measuring State Compliance with the Obligaion to Devote the 'Maximum Available Resources' to Realizing Economic, Social and Cultural Rights", in *Human Rights Quarterly*, Vol. 16, pp. 693-714.

ROBINSON, M. (2005), "What Rights can Add to Good Development Practice", in ALSTON and ROBINSON (2005), pp. 25-42.

ROEMER, J. (1998), "Equalizing Opportunities for Human Development (in One Country)", Discussion Paper, Inter-American Development Bank, Washington D.C.

ROMEU, J.L. (2008), "Statistical Thinking and Data Analysis: Enhancing Human Rights Work", in ASHER, BANKS and SCHEUREN (2008), pp. 65-85.

ROUBAUD, F. (ed.) (2000), *Le Projet MADIO à Madagascar: l'information statistique au service du débat démocratique sur la politique économique*, special issue of STATÉCO, No. 95-96-97, INSEE, Paris.

ROUBAUD, F. (2000), "Enquête auprès des ménages et élections politiques dans les pays en développement: l'exemple de Madagascar", in IAOS (2000), at:
http://www.portal-stat.admin.ch/iaos2000/roubaud_final_paper.doc

ROUBAUD, F. (2003a), "Measuring Democracy and Governance: The Contribution of Household Surveys", *InterStat*, No. 26, pp. 5-32.

ROUBAUD, F. (2003b), "Household Surveys and Political Elections in Developing Countries: The Example of Madagascar", *InterStat*, No. 26, pp. 51-62.

ROUBAUD, F. (2003c), "The MADIO Project in Madagascar: Objective, Approach, Results", *InterStat* No27, pp.5-34.

ROUBAUD, F. (2003d), "La crise vue d'en bas à Abidjan : ethnicité, gouvernance et démocratie", *Afrique contemporaine*, No, 206, pp. 57-86.

ROUBAUD, F. *et al.* (2005), "La conception et la mise en œuvre des enquêtes 1-2-3 en UEMOA, les enseignements méthodologiques", *Statéco*, No. 99.

RUBENSTEIN, L. (2004), "Economic, Social, and Cultural Rights: A Response to Kenneth Roth" *Human Rights Quarterly*, Vol. 26, No. 4, pp. 845-864.

SADIK, N. (2000), "Statistics, Human Rights and Population Issues", in IAOS (2000), at:
http://www.statistik.admin.ch/about/international/sadik_final_address.doc

SAISANA, M. (2005) [see OECD, 2005b].

SAKO, M.A. (2004), "Gouvernance, démocratie et lute contre la pauvreté au Mali : Résultats de l'enquête 1-2-3/Secteur informel", in in METAGORA, DIAL and IRD (2004), pp. 43-64.

SAKO, M.A. (2005) [see DIRECTION NATIONALE DE LA STATISTIQUE ET DE L'INFORMATIQUE, Mali].

SALDOMANDO, A. (2002), *Gobernabilidad: Entre democracia y mercado* (Governance: between democracy and market / Gouvernance: entre démocratie et marché), Managua.

SALDOMANDO, A. (2003), *Mesurer la gouvernance: Instrument de travail ou chimère?*, Institut de Gouvernance de Catalogne, Barcelona.

SALDOMANDO, A. (2005a), *Nicaragua, la gobernabilidad al servicio de las reformas: Premier informe independiente* (Nicaragua: Governance at the service of the reforms, First independent report / Nicaragua: la gouvernance au service des réformes, Premier rapport indépendant), Centro de Investigaciones de la Comunicación (CINCO), Managua.

SALDOMANDO, A. (2005b), "L'impossible gouvernance pro-pauvres au Nicaragua", in B. Campbell (2005), pp.45-112.

SALTELLI, A. (2005) [see OECD, 2005b).

SAMUELSON, D.A. and Spirer, H.F. (1992), "Use of Incomplete and Distorted Data in Inference About Human Rights Violations", in CLAUDE and JABINE (1992), pp. 62-77.

SANDOZ, Y. (2000), "Importance of Statistics for Emergency Humanitarian Action: The Perspective of the ICRC", in IAOS (2000), at:
http://www.statistik.admin.ch/about/international/sandoz_final_paper.doc

SANDOZ, Y. and G. HOLLEUFER (2000), "The ICRC 'People on War' Project", in IAOS (2000), at:
http://www.portal-stat.admin.ch/iaos2000/sandoz_holleufer_final_paper.doc

SANO, H.O. and L. LINDHOLT (2000), Human Rights Indicators: Country Data and Methodology, Danish Institute for Human Rights, Copenhagen.

SARSFIELD, R. and A SCHEDLER (2005), "Democrats with Adjectives: Linking Direct and Indirect Measures of Democratic Supports", Committee on Concepts and Methods of the International Political Science Association, Political Concepts, Working Paper Series, No. 3, Centro de Investigación y Docencia Económicas (CIDE), Mexico City, at:
http://www.concepts-methods.org/papers_list.php?id_categoria=1&titulo=Political%20Concepts

SAVAGE, R.I. (1985), "Hard-soft Problems", in Journal of the American Statistical Association, Vol. 80, pp. 1-7.

SAVANÉ, M.A. (2007), "The African Peer Review Mechanism: a Challenge for Good Governance", paper presented at the CMI/UNDP Seminar on Governance Assessments and the Paris Declaration: Towards Inclusive Participation and National Ownership (Bergen, 23-25 September), Chr. Michelsen Institute and UNDP Oslo Governance Centre, in:
http://www.undp.org/oslocentre/docs07/bergen_2007/Key%20note%20speech%20Marie-Angelique%20Savane.pdf

SCHAFFER, F.C. (1998), Democracy in Translation: Understanding Politics in an Unfamiliar Culture, Cornell University Press, Ithaca N.Y.

SCHAKIROVA, R. (2008), "Measuring Democracy: Statistical Analysis (Spearman vs. Pearson Coefficients)", in NATIONAL RESEARCH COUNCIL OF THE NATIONAL ACADEMIES (2008), pp. 259-265.

SCHEIBREITHNER, E. (2000), "The Guatemalan Commission for Historical Clarification: Generating Analytical Reports", in Ball, Spirer and Spirer (2000).

SCHEUREN, F. (1997), "Linking Health Records: Human Rights Concerns", in Record Linkage: Proceedings of an International Workshop and Exposition, pp. 404-426.

SCHMID, A.P., and A.J. JONGMAN (1992), Monitoring Human Rights Violations, Center for the Study of Social Conflicts, Leiden.

SCHOKKENBROEK, J. (2000), "What Kind of Information do We Need for Monitoring the Implementation of Fundamental Rights of Minorities?: A Council of Europe Experience", in IAOS (2000), at:
http://www.portal-stat.admin.ch/iaos2000/schokkenbroek_final_paper.doc

SCOBLE, H.M. and L.S. WISEBERG (1981), "Problems of Comparative Research on Human Rights", in NANDA, SCARRITT and SHEPHERD (1981), pp. 147-171.

SCOTT, CHR. (2005), Measuring up to the Measurement Problem: the Role of the Statistics in Evidence Based Policy Making, PARIS21 / OECD, Paris, at:
http://www.paris21.org/documents/1509.pdf

SCOTT, CHR. (2006) [see UNDP, 2006a].

SCOTT, I.G. (2000), "Reception and Analysis of Statistical Information and Indicators on Human Rights by the Media: Human Rights and UK Statistics / Réception et analyse d'informations et d'indicateurs statistiques sur les droits de l'homme par les medias: les droits de l'homme et les statistiques au Royaume-Uni, in IAOS (2000), at:
http://www.portal-stat.admin.ch/iaos2000/scott_final_paper.doc

SELTZER, W. (1994), "Politics and Statistics: Independence, Dependence or Interaction?", UN Department for Economic and Social Information and Policy Analysis, Working Paper Series, No. 6, New York.

SELTZER, W. (1998), "Population Statistics, the Holocaust, and the Nuremberg Trials", *Population and Development Review*, Vol. 24, No. 3, pp. 511-552, at:
http://www.uwm.edu/%7Emargo/govstat/pdr.htm

SELTZER, W. (1999), "Excluding Indians Not Taxed: Federal Censuses and Native-Americans in the 19th Century", Paper presented at the Joint Statistical Meetings, Baltimore, MD, at:
http://www.uwm.edu/%7Emargo/govstat/ind.pdf

SELTZER, W. (2000), "Population data systems: A review of human rights abuses and potential abuses", in IAOS (2000), at:
http://www.portal-stat.admin.ch/iaos2000/seltzer_final_paper.doc

SELTZER, W. (2001), "U.S. Federal Statistics and Statistical Ethics: The Role of the American Statistical Association's Ethical Guidelines for Statistical Practice", Paper based on a presentation at the Washington Statistical Society, at:
http://www.uwm.edu/%7Emargo/govstat/wss.pdf

SELTZER, W. (2005a) "Official Statistics and Statistical Ethics: Selected Issues," paper prepared for the International Statistical Institute, 55th Session, at:
http://www.uwm.edu/%7Emargo/govstat/WS2005ISIpaper.pdf

SELTZER, W. (2005b), "On the Use of Population Data Systems to Target Vulnerable Population Subgroups for Human Rights Abuses," *Coyuntura Social*, No. 30, at:
http://www.uwm.edu/%7Emargo/govstat/CoyunturaSocialpaper2005.pdf

SEN, A. (1987), *The Standard of Living,* Cambridge University Press, New York.

SEN, A. (1999), *Development as Freedom*, Oxford University Press, Oxford.

SEN, A. (2000a), "Human Rights and Human development", in UNDP (2000), chapter 1.

SEN, A. (2000b). "A Decade of Human Development", *Journal of Human Development*, Vol. 1, No. 1, pp. 17-23, at:
http://hdr.undp.org/docs/training/oxford/readings/Sen_HD.pdf

SEN, A. (2004), "Elements of a Theory of Human Rights", *Philosophy and Public Affairs,* Vol. 32, No.4, pp. 315-356, at:
http://www.mit.edu/~shaslang/mprg/asenETHR.pdf

SEQUEIRA, H. (2000), "The Guatemalan Commission for Historical Clarification: Database Representation", in BALL, SPIRER and SPIRER (2000).

SHABANA, L. (2000), "The Role of Official Statistics in Measuring and Implementing the Economic and Social Human Rights", in IAOS (2000), at:
http://www.portal-stat.admin.ch/iaos2000/shabana_final_paper.doc

SHIRLEY, M. (2002), "On Stephen Knack's 'Governance and Growth: Measurement and Evidence'", Forum Series on the Role of Institutions in Promoting Economic Growth, USAID and the IRIS Center, Washington, D.C., at:
http://www.usaid.gov/our_work/economic_growth_and_trade/eg/forum_series/f2-shirley-on-knack.pdf

SHUE, H. (1980), *Basic Rights: Subsistence, Affluence, and U.S. Foreign Policy,* Princeton University Press, Princeton, NJ [2nd edition: 1996].

SIDA (SWEDISH INTERNATIONAL DEVELOPMENT COOPERATION AGENCY) (2001), *A Democracy and Human Rights Based Approach to Development Cooperation,* Ministry of Foreign Affairs and SIDA, Stockholm, at:
http://www.sida.se/sida/jsp/sida.jsp?d=118&a=3060&language=en_US

SIDA (2005), *Education, Democracy and Human Rights,* Position Paper, SIDA, Stockholm, at:
http://www.sida.se/sida/jsp/sida.jsp?d=118&a=3481&language=en_US

SIDIBÉ, K. (2004), "Gouvernance, démocratie et lutte contre la pauvreté au Mali: Résultats de l'étude commandité par la Commission économique pour l'Afrique", in METAGORA, DIAL and IRD (2004), pp. 19-42.

SILVA, R. (2000), "Moral Mathematics vs. Momentous Miscalculations: In Search of a Coherent Measure of Human Well-Being", in IAOS (2000), at:
http://www.statistik.admin.ch/about/international/silva_final_paper.doc

SILVA, R. (2002) "On the Maintenance and Measurement of Inter-Rater Reliability when Documenting Large-Scale Human Rights Violations", in Proceedings of the Joint Statistical Meetings of the American Statistical Association, the International Biometric Society (ENAR and WNAR), the Institute of Mathematical Statistics, and the Statistical Society of Canada, New York.

Silva, R. (2005), "Quantitative Data Analysis and Large-Scale Human Rights Violations: An Example of Applied Statistics at the Grassroots", *Gazette of the Australian Mathematical Society,* Vol. 32, No. 2, pp. 90-94, at:
http://www.austms.org.au/Publ/Gazette/2005/May05/careersilva.pdf

SILVA, R., B. FERNANDO and V. NESIAH. 2007. "Clarifying the Past and Commemorating Sri Lanka's Disappeared: a Descriptive Analysis of Enforced Disappearances Documented by Families of the Disappeared", Benetech, Families of the Disappeared and International Center for Transitional Justice, Colombo, at:
http://www.hrdag.org/resources/publications/FoD-HRDAG-ICTJ-2007-10-27-report.pdf

SIWAKOTI, G.K. (2000), "Statistics of Refugees Influx in South Asia: Developing a More Global Regime ", in IAOS (2000), at:
http://www.statistik.admin.ch/about/international/siwakoti_final_paper.doc

SKAANING, S.E. (2006), "Measuring Civil Liberty", Committee on Concepts and Methods of the International Political Science Association, Political Concepts, Working Paper Series, No. 8, Centro de Investigación y Docencia Económicas (CIDE), Mexico City, at:
http://www.concepts-methods.org/papers_list.php?id_categoria=1&titulo=Political%20Concepts

SONG, L. (1999), "In Search of Gender Bias in Household Resource Allocation in Rural China", University of Oxford, IES Applied Economics Discussion Paper series No. 212.

SPENCER, B.D. (ed.) (1997), *Statistics and Public Policy*, Oxford University Press, Oxford .

SPIRER, H.F. (1990), "Violations of Human Rights: How Many?", *American Journal of Economics and Sociology*, Vol. 49, pp. 199-210.

SPIRER, H.F. (2000), Meeting the Statistical Needs of NGOs for Training and Education", in IAOS (2000), at: http://www.portal-stat.admin.ch/iaos2000/spirer_final_paper.doc and http://www.statistik.admin.ch/about/international/spirer_final_paper.doc

SPIRER, H.F. and W. SELTZER (1999), "Obtaining Evidence for International Criminal Tribunals Using Data and Quantitative Analysis", Columbia University School of International and Public Affairs (SIPA) Research Center Working Paper 99-8.

SPIRER, H.F. and L. SPIRER (1991), "Death and numbers: Semmelweis the Statistician", *Physicians for Social Responsibility Quarterly*, Vol. 1, pp. 43-52.

SPIRER, H.F, and L. SPIRER (1993), *Data Analysis for Monitoring Human Rights*, AAAS American Association for the Advancement of Science and HURIDOCS, Washington D.C., at: http://shr.aaas.org/pubs/detail.php?p_id=18

SPIRER, H., and L. SPIRER (1997), *L'Analyse des données pour le contrôle des droits de l'homme*, AAAS et HURIDOCS, Washington D.C. and Versoix, at: http://erc.hrea.org/Library/monitoring/analyse.zip

SPIRER, H. and L. SPIRER (2001), *Intermediate Data Analysis for Human Rights: A Handbook*, Columbia University, New York, at: http://www.columbia.edu/itc/sipa/U8165/>, Spirer & Spirer, Intermediate Data Analysis for Human Rights — Full Text for Download and https://courseworks.columbia.edu/cms/outview/courseenter.cfm?no=INAFU8165_001_2002_3

SPIRER, H. and L. SPIRER (2002), *Accounting for Human Rights Violations by Non-State Actors*, Columbia University, New York.

SRINIVASAN, T.N. (2001), "Croissance et allègement de la pauvreté: les leçons tirées de l'expérience du développement", *Revue d'économie du développement*, No. 1-2, pp.115-168.

STANKOVIC, V., M. ZIZIC and S. KAPURAN (2000), "Census Documentation In Studying Migration Processes in Yugoslavia", in   IAOS (2000), at: http://www.portal-stat.admin.ch/iaos2000/stankovic_final_paper.doc

STEINER, H.J., P. ALSTON, and R. GOODMAN (2008), *International Human Rights in Context: Law, Politics and Morals*, Third Edition, Oxford University Press, Oxford

STEWART, F. et al., (1981), *First Things First: Meeting Basic Human Needs in Developing Countries*, Oxford University Press.

STEWART, F. (1985), *Planning to Meet Basic Needs*, Macmillan, London.

STEWART, F. (1989), "Basic Needs Strategies, Human Rights and the Right to Development", *Human Rights Quarterly*, Vol. 11, No. 3, pp. 347-74.

STEWART, F. (2001), "Horizontal Inequalities: a Neglected Dimension of Development", WIDER Annual Lectures 5, WIDER, Helsinki [reprinted in *WIDER Perspectives on Development*, Palgrave, London, 2005].

STEWART, F. (2002), "Horizontal Inequalities as a Source of Conflict", in F.O HAMPSON and D.M. MALONE, (eds.) *From Reaction to Conflict Prevention, Opportunities for the UN System*, Rienner, Boulder.

STEWART, F. (2003), "Conflict and the Millennium Development Goals", *Journal of Human Development*, Vol. 4, No. 3, pp. 325-352.

STEWART, F. (2004), "Evaluating Evaluation in a World of Multiple Goals, Interests and Models", in G.K. PITMAN, O.N. FEINSTEIN and G.K. INGRAM (eds.), *Evaluating Development Effectiveness*, World Bank Series on Evaluation and Development, Vol. 7, Transaction Publishers, New Brunswick, 2004.

STEWART, F. (2005), "Groups and Capabilities", *Journal of Human Development*, Vol. 6, No. 2, pp. 185-204.

STEWART, F. (2006), "The evolution of Economic Ideas: from Import Substitution to Human Development", in V. FITZ GERALD and R. THORP (eds.), *Economic Doctrines in Latin America*, Palgrave, London

STEWART, F., G. BROWN and L. MANCINI (2005), "Why Horizontal Inequalities Matter: Some Implications for Measurement", Centre for Research on Inequality, Human Security and Ethnicity (CRISE), Working Paper No. 19, Queen Elizabeth House, University of Oxford, at: http://www.crise.ox.ac.uk/pubs/workingpaper19.pdf

STEWART, F. and M. WANG (2005) "Poverty Reduction Strategy Papers within the Human Rights Perspective", in ALSTON and ROBINSON (2005), pp 447-474.

STORMORKEN, B. (1993) [see HURIDOCS, 1993].

STOUDMANN, G. (2000), "The use of statistics on OSCE/ODIHR election observation missions", in IAOS (2000), at: http://www.portal-stat.admin.ch/iaos2000/stoudmann_final_paper.doc

STREETEN, P. et al. (1982), *First Things First: Meeting Basic Human Needs in Developing Countries*, a World Bank Research Publication, Washington D.C.

STREETEN, P. (1984), "Basic Needs: Some Unsettled Questions", *World Development*, Vol. 12, No. 9, pp. 973-978; at: http://www.sciencedirect.com/science/article/B6VC6-45DHV8F-9H/2/831b59e8ae7977f8a2019875932d7562

SUAREZ DE MIGUEL, R. and J.R. SUESSER, "Metagora: An Experiment in the Measurement of Democratic Governance", in ASHER, BANKS and SCHEUREN (2008), pp. 157-178.

SUDDERS, M. [see EUROSTAT and UNDP, 2004].

SUESSER, J.R. (2000), "Droits de l'homme et coopération statistique dans les pays en transition: les mille chemins d'une question implicite / Human Rights and Statistical Co-operation in the Transition Countries: A Thousand Variations on the Theme of an Unstated Question", in IAOS (2000), at: http://www.portal-stat.admin.ch/iaos2000/suesser_final_paper.doc

SWEENEY, S.E. (2007), "Government Respect for Women's Economic Rights: A Cross-National Analysis, 1981-2003", in HERTEL and MINKLER (2007), pp. 233-266.

SWISS FEDERAL STATISTICAL OFFICE (2003), "Statistics and Indicators in the Fields of Human Rights and Governance: The 2000-2003 Follow-up to the Montreux Conference on *Statistics, Development and Human Rights*", Background document submitted by Switzerland to the UN Statistical Commission at its thirty-fourth Session, held in New York on 4-7 March [authored by C. MOTTET and R. SUAREZ DE MIGUEL], at: http://unstats.un.org/unsd/statcom/doc03/montreux.pdf

TALBI, S. (2000), "The role of Statistics in Evaluating the Political Rights of Women in Arabic-Islamic Countries," in IAOS (2000), at:
http://www.portal-stat.admin.ch/iaos2000/talbi_final_paper.doc

TARANTOLA, S. (2005) [see OECD, 2005b].

TAYLOR, CH.L. and D. JODICE (1983), *World Handbook of Political and Social Indicators III,* Yale University Press, New Haven.

TAYLOR, L. (1996), "Sustainable Development: an Introduction", *World Development,* vol. 24, pp. 215-225.

TELLES, V.S. (1999), *Direitos sociais: afinal do que se trata?* (Social rights : at the end, what are they about? / Droit sociaux: en fin de compte, de quoi s'agit-il?), Editora da UFMG, Belo Horizonte; at:
http://www.fflch.usp.br/sociologia/veratelles/artigos/1996%20Direitos%20Sociais.pdf

TETLOCK, P. (2005), *Expert Political Judgement: How Good Is It? How Can We Know?* Princeton University Press, Princeton N.J.

THEDE, N. *et al.* (1996), *The Democratic Development Exercise: Terms of Reference and Analytical Framework,* Documents of Rights & Democracy, International Centre for Human Rights and Democratic Development, Ottawa, at:
www.dd-rd.ca/site/publications/index.php?lang=en&subsection=catalogue&id=1273&page=5#(1)

THEDE, N. (2000a), *Droits humains et statistique : quelques réflexions sur le fossé séparant concepts et indicateurs / Human Rights and Statistics : Some Reflections on the No-Man's-Land Between Concept and Indicator,* Droits et démocratie / Rights and Democracy, Ottawa, at :
http://www.dd-rd.ca/site/publications/index.php?id=1317&lang=fr&subsection=catalogue
http://www.dd-rd.ca/site/publications/index.php?id=1317&subsection=catalogue

THEDE, N. (2000b), "Human Rights and Statistics: Some Reflections on the No-Man's-Land Between Concept and Indicator" [a short version of the 2000a study], in IAOS (2000), at:
http://www.portal-stat.admin.ch/iaos2000/thede_final_paper.doc

THEDE, N. (2002), *Le développement démocratique de 1990 à 2000 : une vue d'ensemble / Democratic Development 1990-2000: An Overview,* Centre international des droits de la personne et du développement démocratique, Montréal, at :
http://www.ichrdd.ca/francais/commdoc/publications/devDemo/ddSurvol10Ans.html

THOMAS, A., J. CHATAWAY and M. WUYTS (1998), *Finding out Fast: Investigative Skills for Policy and Development,* Sage, London.

THOMAS, M. (2007), "What Do the Worldwide Governance Indicators Measure?", Johns Hopkins University, Paul H. Nitze School of Advanced International Studies (SAIS), at SSRN:
http://papers.ssrn.com/sol3/papers.cfm?abstract_id=1007527

THOOLEN, H. AND B. VERSTAPPEN (1986), *Human Rights Missions: A study of the Fact-finding Practice of Non-governmental Organizations,* Netherlands Institute of Human Rights (SIM), Martinus Nijhoff Publishers, Dordrecht.

TOMAŠEVSKI, K. (2002) [see UN-HRI, 2002b].

TOWNSEND, P. (1993), *The International Analysis of Poverty,* Harvester Wheatsheaf.

TRANSPARENCY INTERNATIONAL (2000), *The TI Source Book 2000,* Berlin [authored by J. POPE].

TRANSPARENCY INTERNATIONAL (2001), *Global Corruption Report 2001*, Berlin [edited by R.B. HODESS], at:
http://www.transparency.org/publications/gcr/download_gcr/download_gcr_2001

TRANSPARENCY INTERNATIONAL (2003), *Global Corruption Report 2003. Special Focus: Access to Information*, Pluto Press, London – Ann Arbor - Berlin [edited by R.B. HODESS], at:
http://www.transparency.org/publications/gcr/download_gcr/download_gcr_2003#download

TRANSPARENCY INTERNATIONAL (2004a), *Global Corruption Report 2004. Special Focus: Political Corruption*, Pluto Press, London – Ann Arbor - Berlin [edited by R.B. HODESS]. Also available in French: *Rapport Mondial sur la Corruption 2004. Thème spécial: l'accès à l'information*, Karthala, Paris], at:
http://www.transparency.org/publications/gcr/download_gcr/download_gcr_2004#download

TRANSPARENCY INTERNATIONAL (2004b), *Frequently Asked Questions About the TI Corruption Perceptions Index (CPI)*, at:
www.transparency.org/cpi/2004/cpi2004_faq.en.html#five

TRANSPARENCY INTERNATIONAL (2005), *Global Corruption Report 2005. Special Focus: Corruption in Construction and Post-conflict Reconstruction*, Pluto Press, London – Ann Arbor MI - Berlin [edited by R.B. HODESS], at:
http://www.transparency.org/publications/gcr/download_gcr/download_gcr_2005

TRANSPARENCY INTERNATIONAL (2006a), *Global Corruption Report 2006. Special Focus: Access to Information*, Pluto Press, London – Ann Arbor - Berlin [edited by R.B. HODESS], at:
http://www.transparency.org/publications/gcr/download_gcr

TRANSPARENCY INTERNATIONAL (2006b), *Bribe Payers Index*, at
http://www.transparency.org/policy_research/surveys_indices/bpi

TRANSPARENCY INTERNATIONAL (2007a), *Corruption Perception Index*, at:
http://www.transparency.org/policy_research/surveys_indices/cpi

TRANSPARENCY INTERNATIONAL (2007b), *Global Corruption Barometer*, at:
http://www.transparency.org/policy_research/surveys_indices/cpi

TRANSPARENCY INTERNATIONAL and UNDP (2006), *Corruption and Governance Measurement Tools in Latin American Countries*, Berlin and Oslo [edided by E. MAYERHÖFFER, A. WILDE and M. WOLKERS; also available in Spanish: *Herramientas para medir la corrupción en América Latina*], at:
http://www.undp.org/oslocentre/docs06/Corruption%20and%20Governance%20Measurement%20Tools%20in%20Latin%20American%20Countries%20-%20June.pdf

TROCHIM, W.M.K. (2006). "Construct Validity", Research Methods Knowledge Base, at:
http://www.socialresearchmethods.net/kb/constval.htm

UNDP (UNITED NATIONS DEVELOPMENT PROGRAM) (1992), *Human Development Report*, Oxford University Press, 1992, New York and Oxford.

UNDP (1997), *Human Development Report 1997: Human Development to Eradicate Poverty*, UNDP and Oxford University Press, New York and Oxford, at:
http://hdr.undp.org/en/reports/global/hdr1997/chapters/

UNDP (2000) *Human development report 2000: Human Rights and Human Development*, UNDP and Oxford University Press, New York and Oxford, at:
http://hdr.undp.org/reports/global/2000/en/ and
http://hdr.undp.org/en/media/hdr_2000_en.pdf

UNDP (2001) "CONTACT (Country Assessment in Accountability and Transparency)", at: http://www.undp.org/governance/docs/AC_Guides_CONTACT2001.pdf

UNDP (2002), *Human Development Report: Deepening Democracy in a Fragmented World*, UNDP Human Development Report Office and Oxford University Press, New York and Oxford, at: http://hdr.undp.org/en/media/hdr_2002_en_complete.pdf

UNDP (2003a), "Poverty Reduction and Human Rights: A Practice Note", at: *http://www.undp.org/governance/docs/HRPN_(poverty)En.pdf*

UNDP (2003b), **"Human Rights-Based Reviews of UNDP Programmes: Working Guidelines"**, at: http://hdr.undp.org/en/media/hrba_guidelines.pdf

UNDP (2004a), *Democracy in Latin America: Towards a Citizens' Democracy / La Democracia en América Latina: Hacia una democracia de ciudadanos y ciudadanas,* Report and Annexes [with extensive set of statistical data], Aguilar, Altea, Taurus, Alfaguarra, Buenos Aires, at: http://democracia.undp.org/Informe/Default.asp?Menu=15&Idioma=2

UNDP (2004b), *La democracia en América Latina: contribuciones para el debate*, Aguilar, Altea, Taurus, Alfaguarra, Buenos Aires, at: http://democracia.undp.org/Informe/Default.asp?Menu=15&Idioma=2

UNDP (2004c), *La democracia en América Latina: El debate conceptual sobre la democracia* [a brief version available in English: *Brief Contributions for the Debate*], Aguilar, Altea, Taurus, Alfaguarra, Buenos Aires, at: http://democracia.undp.org/Informe/Default.asp?Menu=15&Idioma=2

UNDP (2005a), *Framework for Piloting Pro-poor and Gender Sensitive Governance Indicators for Policy Reform,* UNDP-Oslo Governance Centre, Oslo, at: http://www.undp.org/oslocentre/docs05/cross/Framework%20for%20piloting.pdf

UNDP (2005b), "Governance Indicators for Pro-Poor and Gender-Sensitive Policy Reform", background paper for the UNDP-ICSSR technical workshop on *Governance Indicators for Pro-poor and Gender-Sensitive Policy Reform* held in New Delhi on 20-22 April, UNDP-Oslo Governance Centre, Oslo, at: http://www.undp.org/oslocentre/docs05/cross/2/Workshop%20background%20Paper.pdf

UNDP (2005c), "Empowering and Engendering Governance Indicators", Report of the UNDP-ICSSR technical workshop on *Governance Indicators for Pro-poor and Gender-Sensitive Policy Reform* held in New Delhi on 20-22 April, UNDP-Oslo Governance Centre, Oslo, at: http://www.undp.org/oslocentre/docs05/cross/Workshop%20report.pdf

UNDP (2006a), *Measuring Democratic Governance. A Framework for Selecting Pro-Poor and Gender Sensitive Indicators,* UNDP-Oslo Governance Centre, Oslo [authored by CHR. SCOTT and A. WIDE], at: http://www.undp.org/oslocentre/docs06/Framework%20paper%20-%20entire%20paper.pdf

UNDP (2006b), *Indicators for Human Rights Based Approaches to Development in UNDP Programming: A Users' Guide,* UNDP-Oslo Governance Centre, Oslo [authored by T. LANDMANN, TH. PALMLUND, A. WIDE and E. FILMER-WILSON], at: www.undp.org/oslocentre/docs06/HRBA%20indicators%20guide.pdf

UNDP (2007), Governance and democracy indicators literature and online resources at: www.undp.org/oslocentre/docs06/Bibliography_of_governance_and_democracy_indicators_resources_.pdf

UNDP and CMI (2004), "Governance in Post-Conflict Situations", background paper for the UNDP/CMI Bergen Seminar (5-7 May), Bergen and Oslo, Chr. Michelsen Institute and UNDP Oslo Governance

Centre, at:
http://www.undp.org/oslocentre/docs04/Complete%20UNDP%20Background%20Document.pdf

UNDP and CMI (2007), *Governance Assessment and the Paris Declaration: Opportunities for Inclusive Participation and National Ownership*, report of the Bergen Seminar (23-25 September), Chr. Michelsen Institute and UNDP Oslo Governance Centre, Bergen and Oslo, at:
http://www.undp.org/oslocentre/docs07/BergenSeminar.pdf

UNDP and InWent (2007), Measuring and Assessing Democratic Governance, Report of the workshop held in Oslo on 28-29 August, Oslo, at:
http://www.undp.org/oslocentre/docs07/oslo_workshop_report.pdf

UNECA (UNITED NATIONS ECONOMIC COMMISSION FOR AFRICA) (2005), *Striving for Good Governance in Africa*, Addis Abeba.

UN-ECOSOC (UNITED NATIONS ECONOMIC AND SOCIAL COUNCIL) (1994), *Fundamental Principles of Official Statistics*, adopted by The United Nations Statistical Commission, at its Special Session of 11-15 April [on the basis of a declaration earlier set out in the Economic Commission for Europe's Decision C (47)], New York, at:
http://unstats.un.org/unsd/dnss/gp/fundprinciples.aspx

UN-ECOSOC (2002), *Report of the Friends of the Chair of the Statistical Commission on an Assessment of the Statistical Indicators Derived from United Nations Summit Meetings,* UN document E/CN.3/2002/26 submitted to the United Nations Statistical Commission at its Thirty-third session (5-8 March), New York, at:
http://www.paris21.org/documents/1120.pdf (English)

UN-HRI (UNITED NATIONS HUMAN RIGHTS INSTRUMENTS) (1989), *General Comment 1 of the Committee on Economic, Social and Cultural Rights on Reporting by State Parties,* third session of the Committee, UN document E/1989/22, at:
http://www.unhchr.ch/tbs/doc.nsf/(Symbol)/38e23a6ddd6c0f4dc12563ed0051cde7?Opendocument

UN-HRI (1990a), *General Comment 2 of the Committee on Economic, Social and Cultural Rights on International Technical assistance Measures (Art. 2 of the Covenant),* fourth session of the Committee, OHCHR document E/1990/23, at:
http://www.unhchr.ch/tbs/doc.nsf/(Symbol)/3659aaf3d47b9f35c12563ed005263b9?Opendocument

UN-HRI (1990b), *General Comment 3 of the Committee on Economic, Social and Cultural Rights on the Nature of State Parties Obligations (Art. 2, par. 1 of the Covenant),* fifth session of the Committee, OHCHR document E/1991/23, at:
http://www.unhchr.ch/tbs/doc.nsf/(Symbol)/94bdbaf59b43a424c12563ed0052b664?Opendocument

UN-HRI (1991), *General Comment 4 of the Committee on Economic, Social and Cultural Rights on the Right to Adequate Housing (Art. 11 (1) of the Covenant),* sixth session of the Committee, OHCHR document E/1992/23, at:
http://www.unhchr.ch/tbs/doc.nsf/(Symbol)/469f4d91a9378221c12563ed0053547e?Opendocument

UN-HRI (1994), *General Comment 5 of the Committee on Economic, Social and Cultural Rights on Persons with Disabilities,* eleventh session of the Committee, OHCHR document E/1995/22, at:
http://www.unhchr.ch/tbs/doc.nsf/(Symbol)/4b0c449a9ab4ff72c12563ed0054f17d?Opendocument

UN-HRI (1995), *General Comment 6 of the Committee on Economic, Social and Cultural Rights on the Economic, Social and Cultural Rights of the Older Persons,* thirteenth session of the Committee, OHCHR document E/1996/22, at:
http://www.unhchr.ch/tbs/doc.nsf/(Symbol)/482a0aced8049067c12563ed005acf9e?Opendocument

UN-HRI (1997a), *General Comment 7 of the Committee on Economic, Social and Cultural Rights on the Right to Adequate Housing (Art. 11.1): Forced Evictions*, sixteenth session of the Committee, OHCHR document E/1998/22, at:
http://www.unhchr.ch/tbs/doc.nsf/(Symbol)/959f71e476284596802564c3005d8d50?Opendocument

UN-HRI (1997b), *General Comment 8 of the Committee on Economic, Social and Cultural Rights on the Relationship Between Economic Sanctions and Respect for Economic, Social and Cultural Rights*, seventeenth session of the Committee, OHCHR document E/1998/22, at:
http://www.unhchr.ch/tbs/doc.nsf/(Symbol)/974080d2db3ec66d802565c5003b2f57?Opendocument

UN-HRI (1998a), *General Comment 9 of the Committee on Economic, Social and Cultural Rights on the Domestic Application of the Covenant*, nineteenth session of the Committee, document E/C.12/1998/24, CESCR, at:
http://www.unhchr.ch/tbs/doc.nsf/099b725fe87555ec8025670c004fc803/4ceb75c5492497d9802566d500516036?OpenDocument#Notes

UN-HRI (1998b), *General Comment 10 of the Committee on Economic, Social and Cultural Rights on the Role of National Human Rights Institutions in the Protection of Economic, Social and Cultural Rights*, nineteenth session of the Committee, document E/C.12/1998/25, CESCR, at:
http://www.unhchr.ch/tbs/doc.nsf/(Symbol)/af81bf2fed39cec1802566d50052f53b?Opendocument

UN-HRI (1999a), *General Comment 11 of the Committee on Economic, Social and Cultural Rights on the Plans of Action for Primary Education (Art. 14 of the Covenant)*, twentieth session of the Committee, OHCHR document E/C.12/1999/4, at:
http://www.unhchr.ch/tbs/doc.nsf/099b725fe87555ec8025670c004fc803/59c6f685a5a919b8802567a50049d460?OpenDocument#Notes

UN-HRI (1999b), *General Comment 12 of the Committee on Economic, Social and Cultural Rights on the Right to Adequate Food (Art. 11 of the Covenant)*, twentieth session of the Committee, OHCHR document E/C.12/1999/5, at:
http://www.unhchr.ch/tbs/doc.nsf/099b725fe87555ec8025670c004fc803/3d02758c707031d58025677f003b73b9?OpenDocument#Notes

UN-HRI (1999c), *General Comment 13 of the Committee on Economic, Social and Cultural Rights on the Right to Education (Art. 13 of the Covenant)*, twenty-first session of the Committee, OHCHR document E/C.12/1999/10 at:
http://www.unhchr.ch/tbs/doc.nsf/(symbol)/E.C.12.1999.10.En?OpenDocument

UN-HRI (2000), *General Comment 14 of the Committee on Economic, Social and Cultural Rights on the Right to the Highest Attainable Standard of Health (Art. 12 of the Covenant)*, twenty-second session of the Committee, OHCHR document E/C.12/2000/4 at:
http://www.unhchr.ch/tbs/doc.nsf/(Symbol)/40d009901358b0e2c1256915005090be?Opendocument

UN-HRI (2002a), *General Comment 15 of the Committee on Economic, Social and Cultural Rights on the Right to Water (Art. 11 and 12 of the Covenant)*, twenty-ninth session of the Committee, OHCHR document E/C.12/2002/11, at:
http://www.unhchr.ch/tbs/doc.nsf/(Symbol)/a5458d1d1bbd713fc1256cc400389e94?Opendocument

UN-HRI (2002b), *Annual Report of the Special Rapporteur on the Right to Education, Katarina Tomaševski, Submitted Pursuant to Commission on Human Rights Resolution 2001/29*, fifty-eighth session of the Commission for Human Rights, 7 January, UN document E/CN.4/2002/60, at:
http://www.unhchr.ch/Huridocda/Huridoca.nsf/0/ff9709c1d502132ec1256b810058ca6d/$FILE/G0210012.pdf

UN-HRI (2003a), *The Right of Everyone to Enjoy the Highest Attainable Standard of Physical and Mental Health: Interim report of Mr. PAUL HUNT, Special Rapporteur of the Commission on Human Rights on the right to health*,

fifty-ninth session of the Commission for Human Rights, UN document A/58/427, at:
http://www.unhchr.ch/Huridocda/Huridoca.nsf/0/306eaaf7b4938ba9c1256dd70051435d/$FILE/N0356469.pdf

UN-HRI (2003b), *Report of Mr. MILOON KOTHARI, the Special Rapporteur on adequate housing as a component of the right to an adequate standard of living, and on the right to non-discrimination, submitted in accordance with Commission resolution 2002/21*, fifty-ninth session of the Commission for Human Rights, 3 March, UN document E/CN.4/2003/5, at,
http://www2.ohchr.org/english/issues/housing/annual.htm

UN-HRI (2004), *Compilation of Guidelines on the Form and Content of Reports to be Submitted by States Parties to the International Human Rights Treaties*, Report of the Secretary-General, UN document HRI/GEN/2/Rev.2, at:
http://daccessdds.un.org/doc/UNDOC/GEN/G04/420/20/PDF/G0442020.pdf?OpenElement

UN-HRI (2005a), *General Comment 16 of the Committee on Economic, Social and Cultural Rights on the Equal Right of Men and Women to the Enjoyment of All Economic, Social and Cultural Rights (Art. 3 of the Covenant)*, thirty-fourth session of the Committee, OHCHR document, E/C.12/2005/3, at:
http://www2.ohchr.org/english/bodies/cescr/docs/CESCR-GC16-2005.pdf

UN-HRI (2005b), *General Comment 17 of the Committee on Economic, Social and Cultural Rights on the Right of Everyone to Benefit from the Protection of the Moral and Material Interests Resulting from any Scientific, Literary or Artistic Production of Which He or She is the Author (Art. 15, para 1 (c), of the Covenant)*, thirty-fifth session of the Committee, document E/C.12/GC/17, at:
http://www.unhchr.ch/tbs/doc.nsf/(Symbol)/E.C.12.GC.17.En?OpenDocument

UN-HRI (2005b), *General Comment 18 of the Committee on Economic, Social and Cultural Rights on the Right to Work (Art. 6 of the Covenant)*, thirty-fifth session of the Committee, document E/C.12/GC/18, at:
http://www.unhchr.ch/tbs/doc.nsf/(Symbol)/E.C.12.GC.18.En?OpenDocument

UN-HRI (2006a), *Harmonized Guidelines on Reporting under the International Human Rights Treaties, Including Guidelines on a Common Core Document and Treaty-Specific Documents*, Report of the Inter-Committee Technical Working Group, UN document HRI/MC/2006/3, at:
http://www2.ohchr.org/english/bodies/icm-mc/docs/HRI.MC.2008.3EN.pdf

UN-HRI (2006b), *Report on Indicators for Monitoring Compliance with International Human Rights Instruments*, submitted by the OHCHR at the fifth inter-committee meeting of the human rights treaty bodies (Geneva, 19-21 June) and at the eighteenth meeting of chairpersons of the human rights treaty bodies (Geneva, 22-23 June), UN document HRI/MC/2006/7, at:
http://daccessdds.un.org/doc/UNDOC/GEN/G06/419/60/PDF/G0641960.pdf?OpenElement

UN-HRI (2007), *Report of Mr. MILOON KOTHARI, the Special Rapporteur on Adequate Housing as a Component of the Right to an Adequate Standard of Living*, fourth session of the Human Rights Council, 5 February, UN document A/HRC/4/18, at:
http://www2.ohchr.org/english/issues/housing/annual.htm

UN-HRI (2008a), *Report on Indicators for Promoting and Monitoring the Implementation of Human Rights*, submitted by the OHCHR at the seventh inter-committee meeting of the human rights treaty bodies and at the twentieth meeting of chairpersons of the human rights treaty bodies, held in Geneva, respectively on 23-25 and 2627 June 2008, Geneva, at:
http://www2.ohchr.org/english/bodies/icm-mc/docs/HRI.MC.2008.3EN.pdf

UN-HRI (2008b), *General Comment 19 of the Committee on Economic, Social and Cultural Rights on the Right to Social Security*, forthcoming at:
http://www2.ohchr.org/english/bodies/cescr/comments.htm

UNICEF (UNITED NATIONS CHILDREN'S FUND) (1996), *Basic Services for All?*, Innocenti Research Centre, Florence.

UNICEF (1998), *Indicators for Global Monitoring of Childs Rights*, Summary report and background papers of the international meeting sponsored by UNICEF (Geneva, 9-12 February), New York.

UNICEF (2000), *The State of World's Children 2000*, New York and Geneva.

UNICEF (2002), *UN Special Session on Children: End-decade Review process*, at: http://www.unicef.org/specialsession/about/end-decade-process.htm.

UNICEF (2004), *Executive Directive on Mid-decade Assessment: Assessing the Need for Multiple Indicator Cluster Surveys*, UNICEF document CF/EXD/2004-20, at: http://www.childinfo.org/files/MICS_exddir_r6.doc

UNICEF (2007), *The State of the World's Children 2008: Child Survival*, New York, at: http://www.unicef.org/sowc08/report/report.php

UNICEF (2008), *Multiple Indicator Cluster Surveys 3*, at: www.childinfo.org/mic/mics3/

UNITED NATIONS (2004) "Common Country Assessment and United Nations Development Assistance Framework: Guidance for UN Country Teams Preparing a CCA and UNDAF in 2004", at: http://www.undp.or.id/mdg/documents/Guidance%20for%20CCA%20and%20UNDAF.pdf

URRA, F.J. (2007), "Assessing Corruption: An Analytical Review of Corruption Measurement and its Problems: Perception, Error and Futility", Edmund A. Walsh School of Foreign Service, Georgetown University, at: http://governance.developmentgateway.org/uploads/media/governance/Assesing%20Corruption.%20Francisco%20Javier%20Urra.pdf

USAID (U.S. AGENCY FOR INTERNATIONAL DEVELOPMENT) (1998), *Handbook of Democracy and Governance Program Indicators*, Center for Democracy and Governance, Washington D.C.

VAN DER AUWERAERT, P. (2002), *Social, Economic and Cultural rights: An Appraisal of Current European and International Developments*, R. Bayliss, Antwerp.

VANHANEN, T. (1990), *The Process of Democratization*, Crane Russak, New York.

VANHANEN, T. (2000), "A New Dataset for Measuring Democracy, 1810-1998", *Journal of Peace Research*, Vol. 37, No. 2, pp. 251-265.

VERA INSTITUTE OF JUSTICE (2005), *Justice Indicators*, background paper for the UNDP-ICSSR technical workshop on *Governance Indicators for Pro-poor and Gender-sensitive Policy Reform* held in New Delhi, 20-22 April 2005 http://www.undp.org/oslocentre/docs05/cross/Justice%20Indicators%20Background%20Paper.pdf

VERMA, V. (1996), "Comment on 'Developing Samplers for Developing Countries'", *International Statistical Review*, Vol. 64, pp. 156-162.

VERMILLON, J. (2006), "Problems in the Measurement of Democracy", *Democracy at Large*, Vol. 3, No. 1, pp. 26-30.

VERSTAPPEN, B. (ed.) (1987), *Human Rights Reports: An Annotated Bibliography of Fact-Finding Missions*, Netherlands Institute of Human Rights (SIM), Dordrecht.

VERSTAPPEN, B. [see HURIDOCS, 2001a, 2001b, 2003a, 2003b].

VERSTEGEN, S., L. VAN DE GOOR, and J. DE ZEEUW (2005), *The Stability Assessment Framework: Designing Integrated Responses for Security, Governance and Development,* The Netherlands Ministry of Foreign Affairs and Netherlands Institute of International Relations 'Clingendael', The Hague.

VIROLA, R.A., M.D. SALUTAN and R.Z. CABRALES (2001), *Measuring the quality of products and services of the Philippine Statistical system,* Paper presented at the 8th National Convention of Statistics, Manila.

VIROLA, R. A. et al. (2004), *Philippines in 2003 and What Happened to their Leaders in the 2004 Elections,* Paper presented at the 9th National Convention on Statistics, Manila (abstract), at:
http://www.nscb.gov.ph/ncs/abstracts/sessions/0201.pdf

VIZARD, P. (2005), "The Contributions of Professor Amartya Sen in the Field of Human Rights", Centre for Analysis of Social Exclusion, CASE Papers No. 91, London School of Economics, London, at:
http://sticerd.lse.ac.uk/dps/case/cp/CASEpaper91.pdf

WALKER, D. (2008), "How Key National Indicators can Improve Policymaking and Strengthen Democracy", in OECD (2008c).

WARD, K. (2000), "The United Nations Mission for the Verification of Human Rights in Guatemala: Database Representation", in Ball, Spirer and Spirer (2000).

WARD, M. (2000), "Monitoring the Delivery of Government Services", in IAOS (2000), at:
http://www.portal-stat.admin.ch/iaos2000/ward_final_paper.doc

WELCH, C.E. Jr. (ed.) (2000), *NGOs and Human Rights: Promise and Performance,* Pennsylvania Studies in Human Rights, University of Pennsylvania Press, Philadelphia.

WELCH, C.E. Jr. (2001), *Protecting Human Rights in Africa: Roles and Strategies of Nongovernmental Organizations,* Pennsylvania Studies in Human Rights, University of Pennsylvania Press, Philadelphia.

WEIR, S. [see INTERNATIONAL IDEA, 2002, 2008a].

WHO (WORLD HEALTH ORGANISATION), UNICEF and UNFPA (1997), "Methodological Issues in Measuring Maternal Mortality", *Guidelines for Monitoring the Availability and Use of Obstetric Services,* at:
http://www.who.int/reproductive-health/publications/unicef/monitoring_obstetric_services.pdf

WIEGANDT, M.H. (1996), "The Pitfalls of International Human Rights Monitoring: Some Critical Remarks on the 1995 Human Rights Watch/Helsinki Report on Xenophobia in Germany", *Human Rights Quarterly,* Vol. 18, No. 4, pp. 833-842.

WILDE, A. [see UNDP, 2006a, 2006b; TRANSPARENCY INTERNATIONAL and UNDP, 2006].

WILSON, R.A. (ed.) (1999), *Human Rights, Culture & Context: Anthropological Perspectives,* Pluto Press, London.

WILLIAMSON, P. et al. (2000), "Statistical Review by Research Ethics Committees", *Journal of the Royal Statistical Society. Series A (Statistics in Society),* Vol. 163, No. 1, pp. 5-13.

WOLKERS, M. [see TRANSPARENCY INTERNATIONAL and UNDP, 2006].

WOODS, J.M., H. LEWIS, and I. GASSAMA (eds.) (2004), *Economic, Social and Cultural Rights: International and Comparative Perspectives,* Transnational Publishers, Ardsley.

WORLD BANK (1992), *Governance and Development,* World Bank, Washington D.C.

WORLD BANK (1997). *Helping Countries Combat Corruption: The Role of The World Bank*. Poverty Reduction and Economic Management, New York: Oxford University Press.

WORLD BANK (1988), *Development and Human Rights: The Role of the World Bank / Développement et droits de l'homme: Le rôle de la Banque Mondiale*, Washington D.C., at:
http://www.worldbank.org/html/extdr/rights/hrtext.pdf (English)
http://www.worldbank.org/html/extdr/rights/hrtextfr.pdf (French)

WORLD BANK (2000a), *World Development Report 2000/2001: Attacking Poverty*, World Bank by Oxford University Press, Washington D.C.

WORLD BANK (2000b), *The Quality of Growth*, New York: Oxford University Press.

WORLD BANK (2002), *A Sourcebook for Poverty Reduction Strategies*, Volumes 1 and 2, Washington D.C.: The World Bank.

WORLD BANK (2005), *World Development Report 2006: Equity and Development*, New York: Oxford University Press

WORLD VALUES SURVEY (2006), "Surveys Data Files", "Online Data Analysis" and technical information at:
http://www.worldvaluessurvey.org/

WÜRTH, A. and F.L. SEIDENSTICKER (2005): *Indices, Benchmarks, and Indicators: Planning and Evaluating Human Rights Dialogues*, Berlin: German Institute for Human Rights, at:
files.institut-fuer-menschenrechte.de/488/d44_v1_file_438eb21f40c35_FLS_AW_HRDialogues_Nov_2005_A4.pdf

ZAMBRANO, S. (2000), "The Guatemalan Commission for Historical Clarification: Database Representation and Data Processing", in Ball, Spirer and Spirer (2000).

OECD PUBLICATIONS, 2, rue André-Pascal, 75775 PARIS CEDEX 16
PRINTED IN FRANCE
(43 2008 02 1 P) ISBN 978-92-64-04943-7 – No. 56331 2008